STUDIES IN
TERTULLIAN AND AUGUSTINE

BY

BENJAMIN BRECKINRIDGE WARFIELD

Professor of Didactic and Polemic Theology
in the Theological Seminary of Princeton
New Jersey, 1887–1921

GREENWOOD PRESS, PUBLISHERS
WESTPORT, CONNECTICUT

Originally published in 1930 by Oxford University Press,
New York

Reprinted in 1970 by Greenwood Press,
a division of Congressional Information Service, Inc.
88 Post Road West, Westport, Connecticut 06881

Library of Congress catalog card number 73-109980
ISBN 0-8371-4490-6

Printed in the United States of America

10 9 8 7 6 5 4 3 2

PREFATORY NOTE

Rev. Benjamin Breckinridge Warfield, D.D., LL.D., Professor of Didactic and Polemic Theology in the Theological Seminary of the Presbyterian Church at Princeton, New Jersey, provided in his will for the collection and publication of the numerous articles on theological subjects which he contributed to encyclopaedias, reviews and other periodicals, and appointed a committee to edit and publish these papers. In pursuance of his instructions, this, the fourth volume, containing his articles on Tertullian and Augustine, has been prepared under the editorial direction of this committee.

The generous permission to publish articles contained in this volume is gratefully acknowledged as follows: Charles Scribner's Sons, for the article entitled " Augustine " taken from " Encyclopaedia of Religion and Ethics," ed. by James Hastings, and for the article entitled " Augustine and the Pelagian Controversy " taken from " A Select Library of the Nicene and Post-Nicene Fathers of the Christian Church," First Series, volume v.

The clerical preparation of this volume has been done by Mr. Johannes G. Vos, to whom the thanks of the committee are hereby expressed.

Ethelbert D. Warfield
William Park Armstrong
Caspar Wistar Hodge
Committee.

CONTENTS

I

TERTULLIAN AND THE BEGINNINGS OF THE DOCTRINE OF THE TRINITY

TERTULLIAN AND THE BEGINNINGS OF THE DOCTRINE OF THE TRINITY [1]

First Article

It is exceedingly impressive to see Christian Latin literature Athena-like spring at once into being, fully armed, in the person of an eminently representative man, in whom seem summed up the promise and potency of all that it was yet to be. This is what occured in Tertullian, whose advent and career provide a remarkable illustration of the providential provision of the right man for the right place. Seldom has one been called to a great work who was better fitted for it by disposition and talents as well as by long and strenuous preparation. Ardent in temperament, endowed with an intelligence as subtle and original as it was aggressive and audacious, he added to his natural gifts a profound erudition, which far from impeding only gave weight to the movements of his alert and robust mind. A jurist of note, he had joined to the study of law not only that of letters, but also that of medicine; born and brought up in the camp he had imbibed from infancy no little knowledge of the military art; and his insatiable curiosity had carried him into the depths of every form of learning accessible to his time and circumstances, not even excepting the occult literature of the day. When he gave himself in his mature manhood to the service of Christianity, he brought in his hands all the spoils of antique culture, smelted into a molten mass by an almost incredible passion.

The moment when he appeared on the scene was one well calculated to call out all his powers. It was shortly after the beginning of the last decade of the second century. Commodus

[1] From *The Princeton Theological Review*, iii. 1905, pp. 529–557; iv. 1906, pp. 1–36, 145–167.

3

had died and left a trail of civil war behind him, in the midst of which persecution had broken out afresh in Africa. Harassed from without, the African Church was also torn from within by an accumulation of evils; apostasies, heresies, and schisms abounded. Up through the confusion were thrust Tertullian's mighty shoulders, casting off the enemies of the Gospel upon every side. He was not formed for defensive warfare. Even against the persecuting heathenism he took the offensive. Not content with repelling its calumnies and ridiculing the popular hatred of Christianity, he undertook to demonstrate, as a jurist, the illegality of the persecuting edicts, and, as a moralist, the absurdity of the heathen superstitions. He broke out a short and easy way for the refutation of heretics, by which he put them out of court at the start, and then followed them remorselessly into every corner of their reasoning. Within the Church itself he pursued with mordant irony the crowding abuses which had grown up in the Christian life. Of course he had the defects of his qualities. This terrible adversary of others was a terrible adversary also of his own peace. The extremity of his temper made him a prey to the fanatical claims of the Montanists and ultimately drove him beyond even them. He died the head of a new sect of his own.

Meanwhile he had rendered a service to the Church which it is no exaggeration to call inestimable. There is certainly discoverable in the writings of his immediate successors little open recognition of the immensity of the debt which Christianity owed to him. Throughout the whole of the remainder of the third century — a period of some eighty years — his name is not once mentioned. In the Greek Church, indeed, no one but the historian Eusebius seems ever to have heard of him. Even in his own West, Lactantius (305–306) is the first to allude to him, and he does so with obvious depreciation. Jerome, it is true, gives free vent to his admiration for the learning and acuteness, the vehemence and elegance of this " torrent of eloquence," and not only places him formally among the " illustrious men " of the Church, but calls him fondly " our Tertullian." With Hilary and Augustine, however, he has already taken his place definitely in the catalogue of heretics, and thenceforward he found hardly any who were prepared to do him reverence.[2] All this appearance of neglect passing into reprobation, however, is appearance only. Men might carefully avoid speaking of Tertullian; they could not escape his influence. Cyprian, for example, never breathes his name; yet the works of Cyprian are filled with the silent witnesses of the diligence with which he studied his brilliant predecessor; and his secretary told Jerome he never passed a day without reading him, and was accustomed to ask for him in the significant formula, "Hand me the Master." This is not far from a typical instance. "The man was too great a scholar, thinker, writer," remarks Harnack,[3] "and he had done the Western Church too distinguished service during a long series of years for his memory to become effaced."

In modern times the vigor of Tertullian's mind and the brilliancy of his literary gifts have perhaps generally been fully recognized. It is questionable, however, whether the greatness of his initiative in the development of Christian doctrine is even yet estimated at its true value. That many of the streams of doctrinal thought that have flowed down through the Western Church take their rise in him is indeed universally understood. But perhaps it comes to us with a little surprise when Harnack claims for him, for example, that it was he who broke out the road for the formulation of the Christian doctrine of the Trinity. "When the Nicene formulary is praised," says Harnack,[4] "it is always of Athanasius that we think; when the Chalcedonian decree is cited, it is the name of Leo the Great that is magnified. But that Tertullian is in reality the father of the orthodox doctrines of the Trinity and of the Person of Christ, and that in the whole patristic literature there is no treatise that can be compared in importance and

---

[2] The generous but qualified praise of Vincent, "Commonitorium," xviii. [24] stands almost alone by the side of Jerome's.

[3] *Sitzungsberichte der königlich preussischen Akademie der Wissenschaften zu Berlin*, June, 1895, p. 545: "Tertullian in der Litteratur der alten Kirche."

[4] *Loc. cit.*

influence with his tract " Against Praxeas," it has necessarily been left to the . . . investigation of our own day to exhibit." If such a statement as this can be substantiated it is enough to mark Tertullian out not merely as a man of exceptional gifts and worthy performance, but as one of the greatest forces which have wrought in history.

It is proposed to subject this statement to such testing as is involved in going to the tract " Against Praxeas " and seeking to form a judgment of its value and of the place in the development of the Christian doctrine of the Trinity which it vindicates for its author.

The tract " Against Praxeas," it must be borne in mind from the outset, is not an extended treatise. It is a brief document filling but some fifty pages. Nor is it a calm constructive work in which the author sets himself to develop in its completeness a doctrinal elaboration. It is a vigorous and lively polemic designed to meet an immediate crisis. In other words, it is distinctly an occasional writing, devoted to the refutation of a heresy which was at the moment troubling the churches. Any doctrinal construction which may be found in it is accordingly purely incidental, and rather betrays the underlying conceptions of the writer's mind than forms the calculated burden of the document. If this constructive element, thus emerging, is nevertheless epoch-making for the history of thought, it will redound with peculiar force to the honor of the author. That it so emerges, however, renders it necessary that, for the proper estimate of the tract, we should begin by obtaining a somewhat exact understanding of the circumstances which gave birth to it.

We must not be misled by its title or by the reversion of the discourse now and then to the form of direct address into supposing the tract a personal assault upon Praxeas himself. It is quite clear that Praxeas was a figure resurrected by Tertullian from a comparatively remote past, and given prominence in the discussion, perhaps, as a sort of controversial device. Tertullian, apparently, would represent the teachings he is opposing as a mere recrudescence of an exploded notion, discredited in its vacillating and weak propounder a generation ago.[5] Of Praxeas himself we know nothing except what Tertullian tells us: there is no independent mention of his name in the entirety of Christian literature. He is represented as an Asian confessor who was the first to import into Rome the type of doctrine which Tertullian calls Monarchianism or Patripassianism.[6] Evidently he had made himself felt for a time in Rome, and among other things had succeeded in reversing the favorable policy of the Roman bishops with respect to the Montanists. By this achievement he naturally earned from Tertullian a twofold scorn. Tertullian bitingly remarks that thus Praxeas had doubly done the devil's business in Rome — "he had expelled prophecy and brought in heresy, had exiled the Paraclete and crucified the Father." [7] His heresy passed over into Africa — while the people, says Tertullian, slept in doctrinal simplicity. But God raised up a defender of the truth: and the heresy was exposed and seemingly destroyed; Praxeas

[5] Even were this motive not operative it would not follow from the use of Praxeas' name that he and the book were contemporaneous. Josephus controverted Apion and Origen Celsus only after a considerable interval of years. The same seems to be true of the use of Fronto's name in the "Octavius" of Minucius Felix. (See Harnack, "Chronologie," ii. p. 326, and note; and compare what is said by Hagemann, "Die Römische Kirche," pp. 235–236.)

[6] Hagemann's attempt ("Die Römische Kirche," pp. 234, *sq.*) to identify Praxeas with Callistus is only a part of his general attempt so to manipulate the facts as to make Callistus the real protagonist for fundamental Christian truth and Tertullian the real errorist. In the prosecution of this endeavor he gives to Callistus all that belongs rightfully to Tertullian (and more). He speaks of him (p. 128) as setting forth "the doctrine of the unity of nature of the Father and Son and the doctrine of the hypostatic union of the two natures in Christ, with a completeness of formal development such as they received later through the instrumentality of the General Councils only after long and bitter controversies," and as thus more than a hundred years in advance of the Church at large refuting Arianism and establishing for Rome a triune creed (see especially pp. 101 and 128). On the other hand, he represents Tertullian as, under the influence of Hippolytus, so misunderstanding Callistus that, under the nick-name of Praxeas, he treats his epoch-making orthodox definitions as if they were Monarchian.

[7] "Against Praxeas," i. *Ita duo negotia diaboli Praxeas Romæ procuravit: prophetiam expulit et hæresim intulit, paracletum fugavit et patrem crucifixit.*

himself submitted to correction and returned to the old faith. Apparently this was the end of it all: *exinde silentium,* says Tertullian, with terse significance. But it is the curse of noxious growths that they are apt to leave seeds behind them. So it happened in this case also. The tares had been rooted up and burned. But lo, after so long a time, the new crop appeared, and the last state was unspeakably worse than the first. The tares had everywhere, says Tertullian, shaken out their seed, and now, after having lain hid so long, their vitality had become only too manifest. It is not then an individual that Tertullian is facing; it is a widespread condition. This tract is not an attempt to silence a heretic menacing the peace of the Church; it is an effort to correct a rampant evil already widely spread in the community, by which the very existence of the truth is endangered.

The tones in which Tertullian speaks of the rise of the heresy in the person of Praxeas and of its prevalence at the time of his writing are noticeably different. Then it was an exotic vagary seeking footing in the West and finding none: now it is a native growth, springing up everywhere. The tares had cast their seed, he says, " everywhere " (*ubique*). Nor can he look with comfort on the task of rooting them up. Though he is not the man to lose courage, and reminds himself of the past success, he yet finds his deepest consolation in the assurance that all tares shall be burnt up at the last day. When a man looks forward to the Judgment Day for the vindication of his cause, he is not far from despairing of success here and now. It looks very much as if Tertullian felt himself in a hopeless minority in his defense of what he calls the pristine faith (*pristinum*). He does not conceal the difficulty he experienced in obtaining even a fair hearing for his doctrine. Christians at large were impatient of everything that seemed to their uninstructed minds to imperil their hard-won monotheism. The majority of believers he tells us are ever of the simple, not to say the unwise and untaught (*simplices, ne dixerim imprudentes et idiotæ*); and they were nothing less than terrified (*expavescunt*) by the mention of an " economy " within the being of God by virtue of which the one only God may be supposed to present distinctions within His unity. They continuously cast in the teeth of those who inculcated such doctrines the charge of preaching two or three gods, while they arrogated to themselves alone the worship of the one only true God.

If we are to take this literally, it will mean that Christians at large in Tertullian's day — that is, at the time when he wrote this tract — were suspicious of the doctrine of the Trinity and looked upon it almost as a refined polytheism; that they were inclined rather strongly to some form of Monarchianism as alone comporting with a real monotheism. There are not lacking other indications that something like this may have been the case. Hippolytus, in approaching in the course of his great work " On Heresies " the treatment of the Monarchianism of his day, betrays an even more poignant sense of isolation than Tertullian. He speaks of the promoters of the Monarchian views as bringing great confusion upon believers throughout the whole world.[8] In Rome at least, he tells us, they met with wide consent;[9] and he represents himself as almost single-handed in his opposition to their heresy. In effect it seems to be quite true that through no less than four episcopates — those of Eleutherus, Victor, Zephyrinus and Callistus — the Modalistic theology was dominant and occupied the place indeed of the official faith at Rome. We may neglect here hints in Origen[10] that something of the same state of affairs may have obtained in the Eastern churches also. Enough that it is clear that at the time when Tertullian's tract was written — say during the second decade of the third century[11] — the common sentiment of the West was not untouched by Modalistic tendencies.

It must not be supposed that the mass of the Christian

---

[8] " Philosophumena," ix. 1: μέγιστον τάραχον κατὰ πάντα τὸν κόσμον ἐν πᾶσι τοῖς πιστοῖς ἐμβάλλοντες.

[9] Do., ix. 6.

[10] See Harnack, " History of Dogma," iii. p. 53, note 2; Dorner, " Doctrine of the Person of Christ," Div. I. vol. ii. p. 3.

[11] Harnack (" Chronologie," ii. pp. 285–286, 296) sets the date of the book at c. 213–218.

population, in the West at least — for it is with the West that we have particularly to do — held to a Modalistic theory as a definitely conceived theological formula. What is rather to be said is that the Modalistic formula when warily presented roused in the minds of most men of the time no very keen sense of opposition, while the Trinitarian formula was apt to offend their monotheistic consciousness. This is by no means surprising; and it is partially paralleled by the situation in the East after the promulgation of the Nicene creed. The difficulty in obtaining assent to that symbol did not turn on the prevalence of definitely Arian sentiments so much as upon the indefiniteness of the conceptions current among the people at large and the consequent difficulty experienced by so definite a formula in making its way among them. Men were startled by these sharp definitions and felt more or less unprepared to make them the expression of their simple and somewhat undefined faith. So here, a century before the Nicene decision, the people in the West found similar difficulty with the Trinitarian distinctions. The naïve faith of the average Christian crystallized around the two foci of the unity of God and the Deity of Christ: and the Modalistic formulas might easily be made to appear to the untrained mind to provide simply and easily for both items of belief, and so to strike out a safe middle pathway between the Dynamistic Monarchianism of the Theodotuses and Artemodites, on the one hand, and the subtle constructions of Hippolytus and Tertullian on the other. The one extreme was unacceptable because it did not allow for the true deity of the Redeemer: the other seemed suspicious as endangering the true unity of God.

It is not at all strange, therefore, that the unsophisticated Christian should tremble on the verge of accepting Modalistic Monarchianism, especially when presented, in a guarded form, as a simple and safe solution of a vexing problem. It was thus that it was quick to commend itself; and it was on this ground that it was in its most prudent formulation exploited at Rome as the official faith. When it was brought to Rome, we must remember, it was set over against, not developed Trinitarianism, but rather, on the one side, the crude humanitarianism of the Dynamistic school of Monarchianism which was at the moment troubling the Church there, and, on the other, the almost equally crude emanationism of the Logos speculation, which had held the minds of thinking men for a generation. It was therefore naturally treated as a deliverance from opposite heresies, along whose safe middle way men might walk in the light of the twin truths of the deity of Christ and the unity of God. When Hippolytus assailed it, therefore, he obtained no hearing and was treated as merely another disturber of the Church's peace. His assault did not, indeed, fail of all effect: he rendered it impossible for Modalism to be adopted in its crudest form, and forced modifications in it by which it was given the appearance of more nearly covering the main facts of the revelation of God in the Gospel. But he could by no means turn the thoughts of men into a different channel; neither, indeed, was he capable of digging a channel into which their thoughts might justly flow. The outcome, therefore, was only that Callistus excommunicated both Sabellius and Hippolytus and set forth as the Christian faith a new doctrine which was intended to declare the central truths of the Gospel as understood by men of moderation and balanced judgment. Hippolytus looked on this new doctrine as itself essentially Modalism, with a tendency downward. And Hippolytus was right. But it commended itself powerfully to the age, and that not merely in Rome, but in Africa. It is this refined Modalism of the Roman compromise, which seemed to be threatening to become the Christianity of the West, that Tertullian attacks in his tract " Against Praxeas."

It is not necessary for our present purpose to trace the gradual modifications which the Monarchian teaching underwent from its earliest form as taught at Rome by Noëtus and possibly by Praxeas to its fullest development and most advanced adjustment in the hands of Callistus to the fundamental Church doctrines of God and Christ. Suffice it to say that the modifications by which Callistus sought to " catholicize " Monarchian Modalism, proceeded by according some sort of recognition to the Logos doctrine on the one hand, and on the other by softening the crass assertion that it was the Father who suffered on the cross. Of course no personal distinction between Father and Son, or God and Logos, was admitted. But a nominal distinction was accorded, and this distinction was given quasi-validity by a further distinction of times. "Callistus says," explains Hippolytus,[12] " that the same Logos is at once Son and Father, distinguished in name, but really one individual Spirit, . . . and that the Spirit incarnated in the virgin is not different from the Father but one and the same. . . . For that which is seen, which is of course the man — it is that which is the Son; but the Spirit which is contained in the Son is the Father, since there are not two Gods, Father and Son, but one. Now, the Father being in him " — i.e., the Son, which is the "man " or the " flesh " — " seeing that he had assumed the flesh, deified it by uniting it with Himself, and made it one, so that the Father and Son are called one God, while this person being one cannot be two, and so the Father suffered along with the Son." Hippolytus adds that Callistus worked out this form of statement because he did not " wish to say the Father suffered." The point here, therefore, is that the Son differs from the Father not as the incarnate differs from the unincarnate God, but rather as the incarnating man differs from the incarnated Spirit. As then the flesh is properly designated by the " Son " and it is the flesh that suffers, the Father, who is properly the Spirit incarnated in the " Son," may more exactly be said to have suffered along with the flesh, i.e., the " Son," than Himself to have endured the suffering. The suffering was, in other words, in the " flesh ": the informing " Spirit " only partook in the suffering of the " flesh " because joined in personal union with it. The artificiality of this construction is manifest on the face of it; as also is its instability. Hippolytus himself pointed out its evident tendency to fall back into the lower Dynamistic Monarchianism; since in proportion as the Father as the Spirit and the Son as the flesh were separated in thought, the reality of the incarnation was likely to give way in favor of a more or less clearly conceived inhabitation. Thus Jesus would become again only a man in whom God dwelt. The formula of "the Father suffering with the Son" was really, therefore, a mediation toward humanitarianism rather than toward full recognition of the deity of the Son; and it is interesting to observe in the later Arians the reëmergence of the mode of expression thus struck out by Callistus. With them of course it was not a question of the Father but of that "Middle Being" which they called the Son of God; but what they affirm of it is that having taken "man" from the Virgin Mary, it "shared in" the sufferings of this "man" on the cross.[13] The obvious meaning of the Arians will throw light back upon the idea which Callistus meant to convey. This was clearly that the incarnation of the Spirit which was God in the man which was Christ, brought that Spirit into definite relations to the sufferings endured by this man properly in his flesh.

What it concerns us to note here particularly, however, is that it is just this Callistan formula which underlies the Monarchianism which Tertullian is opposing in his tract.[14] The evidence of this is pervasive. It will doubtless be enough to adduce the manifest agreement of his opponents with the Callistan formula in the two chief points to which we have adverted. Tertullian's opponents, it appears, while allowing to the Word a sort of existence, would not admit Him to be a really *substantiva res*, "so that He could be regarded as a *res et persona*" and, being constituted as a second to God the Father, make with the Father "two, Father and Son, God and the Word."[15] They "sought to interpret the distinction be-

[13] At the Synod of Sirmium, A.D. 357. See Hahn, "Bibliothek der Symbole und Glaubensregeln der alten Kirche,"[3] § 161. The idea is that the "man" alone "suffers" (*patitur*): the Logos incarnate in the "man" only co-suffers (*compatitur*) with it. The Spirit, say the Arians at Sardica, A.D. 343, "did not suffer, but the man (ἄνθρωπος) which it put on suffered"; because, as it is immediately explained, this is "capable of suffering." Cf. Hahn, "Bibliothek der Symbole und Glaubensregeln der alten Kirche,"[3] p. 189.

[14] Cf. Rolffs in the "Texte und Untersuchungen zur Geschichte der altchristlichen Literatur," XII. iv. pp. 94 *sq.*

[15] "Against Praxeas," chap. vii.

tween Father and Son conformably to their own notion, so as
to distinguish between them within a single person, saying that
the Son is the flesh, that is, the man, that is Jesus, but the
Father the Spirit, that is God, that is Christ." [16] Similarly Tertullian's opponents seeking to avoid the charge that they
blasphemed the Father by making him suffer, granted that the
Father and Son were so far two that it was the Son that suffered while the Father only suffered with Him.[17]

The special interest of this for us at the moment lies in a
corollary which flows from it. Tertullian was not breaking out
a new path in his controversy with the Monarchians. He was
entering at the eleventh hour into an old controversy, which
had dragged along for a generation, and was now only become
more acute and more charged with danger to the Church. This,
to be sure, is already implied in his reference to an earlier refutation of Praxeas, and in his representation of the error at
present occupying him as merely a repristination of that old
heretic's teaching. Accordingly, not only is the controversy old,
but it is old to Tertullian. The general fact is evident on every
page of his tract. It is quite clear that Tertullian is not here
forging new weapons to meet novel attacks. On both sides
much acuteness had already been expended in assault and defense [18] and the lines of reasoning had already long been laid
down and even the proofs *pro* and *con* repeatedly urged. The
very exegetical arguments bear on them the stamp of long use
and betray the existence on both sides of a kind of exegetical
tradition already formed. The emergence of this fact throws us
into doubt as to how much even of what seems new and original
in the tract may not likewise be part of the hereditary property
of the controversy. Even the technical terms which Tertullian
employs with such predilection and which are often thought of
as contributions of his own to the discussion, such as οἰκονομία,

---

[16] Chap. xxvii.

[17] Chap. xxix. " Filius quidem patitur, pater vero compatitur." " Compas-
sus est pater filio."

[18] We are here drawing upon Lipsius' admirable article, " On Tertullian's
Tract Against Praxeas," published in the *Jahrbücher für deutsche Theologie*,
xiii. (1868), pp. 701-724. For the present matter see especially p. 710.

trinitas,[19] for example, need not be new, but may owe it only to accident that they come here for the first time strikingly before us. Indeed, Tertullian does not use them as if they were novelties. On the contrary, he introduces them as well-known terms, which he could freely employ as such. He speaks [20] of " that dispensation which we call the οἰκονομία," that is to say, apparently, " which is commonly so called." And in the same connection he joins the " distribution of the Unity into a Trinity " [21] with the οἰκονομία in such a manner as inevitably to suggest to the reader that this mode of explaining the οἰκονομία belonged to its tradition. Assuredly no reader would derive from the tract the impression that such terms were new coinages struck out to meet the occasion.

Additional point is given to this impression by the circumstance that Tertullian not only puts forward no claim to originality, but actually asserts that his teaching is the traditional teaching of the Church. As over against the novel character of the new-fangled teaching of Praxeas, which falls as such under the prescription which Tertullian was wont to bring against all heresies as innovations and therefore no part of the original deposit of the faith, he sets his doctrine as a doctrine which had always been believed and now much more, under the better instruction of the Paraclete. " We, however, as always, so now especially, since better instructed by the Paraclete, who is the leader into all truth, believe that there is one God indeed, but yet under the following dispensation, which we call the οἰκονομία." [22] An attempt has been made, it is true, to read in this statement a hint that the doctrine of the Trinity was a peculiarity of the Montanists; [23] and to make out that Tertul-

---

[19] Lipsius, as above, p. 721, instances these two terms as " expressions which meet us here for the first time." Both terms appear in Hippolytus' " Contra Noëtum," and if that tract antedates Tertullian's this would be an earlier appearance; and each appears once in earlier literature.

[20] Chap. ii.

[21] Chap. ii. Cf. chap. iii.

[22] Chap. ii.

[23] That Tertullian owed his Trinitarianism to Montanism was already suggested by the younger Christopher Sand in the seventeenth century —

lian means to say only that " we Montanists " have always so believed. The language, however, will not lend itself to this interpretation. Tertullian does say that since he became a Montanist his belief has been strengthened, and elsewhere (chap. xiii.) he intimates that the Montanists were especially clear as to the " economy," as he calls the distinction within the unity of the Godhead. Perhaps he means that special prophetic deliverances expounding the Trinity in unity had among the Montanists been added to the traditionary faith. Perhaps he means only that the emphasis laid by the Montanistic movement, in distinction from the Father and Son, on the activity and personality of the Paraclete as the introducer of a new dispensation, had conduced to clearer views of the distinctions included in the unity of the Godhead. But the very adduction of this clearer or fuller view as consequent upon his defection to Montanism, only throws into prominence the fact that the doctrine itself belonged to his pre-Montanistic period also. " We as always, so now especially," contrasts two periods and can only mean that this doctrine dated in his consciousness from a day earlier than his Montanism. We must understand Tertullian then as affirming that the doctrine of the Trinity in unity which he is teaching belongs to the traditionary lore of the Church. His testimony, in this case, is express that what he teaches in this tract is nothing new, but only a part of his original faith.

This testimony is supported by the occurrence in earlier

---

whose " Nucleus Historiæ Ecclesiasticæ " was one of the works which Bull's " Defensio " was intended to meet. See Bull, " Defensio Fidei Nicaenæ," II. vii. 7 (E. T. 1851, i. p. 203). It was revived vigorously by the Tübingen School (Baur, " Die christliche Lehre von der Dreieinigkeit und Menschwerdung Gottes," i. p. 177, and especially Schwegler, e.g., " Nachapostolischer Zeitalter," ii. p. 341). Lipsius, as quoted, p. 719, opposes the notion, but argues that nevertheless in Africa, at least, there was a connection between Montanism and Trinitarianism. Besides his own paper in the *Zeitschrift für wissenschaftliche Theologie*, 1866, p. 194, Lipsius refers for information to Ritschl, " Altkatholische Kirche," 2d ed. pp. 487 f, and Volckmar, " Hippolyt.," p. 115. Stier argues the question in his " Die Gottes- und Logos-Lehre Tertullians," p. 93, note; cf. Dorner, " Doctrine of the Person of Christ," Div. I. ii. p. 20, and especially p. 448–449.

treatises by Tertullian — notably in his great " Apology " [24] —
of passages in which essential elements of his doctrine are given
expression in his characteristic forms. And it is still further
supported by the preservation of such a treatise by the hand of
another, as Hippolytus' fragment against Noëtus,[25] in which
something similar to the same doctrine is enunciated. It has
been contended, indeed, that Tertullian borrowed from Hippolytus, or that Hippolytus borrowed from Tertullian. And
there may be little decisive to urge against either hypothesis if
otherwise commended. But in the absence of such further commendation it seems much more probable that the two treatises
independently embody a point of view already traditional in
the Church.[26] In any case Hippolytus must be believed to be
stating in essence no other doctrine than that which he had
striven for a generation to impress upon the Roman Church;
and he makes the same impression that Tertullian does of
handling well-worn weapons. Indeed we need bear in mind
nothing more than the most obvious New Testament data
culminating in the baptismal formula, the ritual use of which
kept its contents clearly before the mind of every Christian,
and the prevalence attained throughout the Christian world
by the Logos speculation of the Apologists, to be assured à
priori that it was not left either to Hippolytus or to Tertullian
to work out the essential elements of the doctrine of the Trinity in unity. But this compels us to recognize that something
more entered into the naïve faith of the average Christian
man as essential constituents of his Christian confession than
the two doctrines of the unity of God and the deity of the Redeemer. Even the simple Christian could not avoid forming
some conception of the relation of his divine Redeemer to the
Father, and in doing so could not content himself with an absolute identification of the two. Nor could he help extending his
speculation to embrace some doctrine of the Spirit whom he

[24] Chap. 21. It seems to have been written about the end of A.D. 197.
[25] " Contra Noëtum." Cf. " Philosophumena," ix.
[26] On Tertullian's relations to the anti-Modalistic writings of Hippolytus,
see Harnack in the *Zeitschrift für die historische Theologie*, 1874, pp. 203 *sq.*

was bound to recognize as God, and yet as in some way neither the Father nor the Son, along with whom He was named in the formula of baptism. In proportion as the believer was aware of the course of the debate that had gone on in the Church, and was affected by the movements which had agitated it from the beginning — all of which touched more or less directly on these points — he would have been driven along a pathway which, in attempting to avoid the heresies that were tearing the Church, could emerge in nothing else than some doctrine of Trinity in unity. The presence of a Trinitarian tradition in the Church is thus so far from surprising that its absence would be inexplicable. There is no reason, therefore, why we should discredit Tertullian's testimony that Christians had always believed in essence what he teaches in his tract " Against Praxeas."

If it is very easy to exaggerate the originality of Tertullian's doctrine as set forth in this tract, however, it is equally easy to underestimate it. Let us allow that Trinitarianism is inherent in the elements of the Gospel, and that, under the influence of the Logos Christology and in opposition to Gnostic emanationism, a certain crude Trinitarianism must have formed a part of the common faith of naïve Christendom. It remains none the less true that men were very slow in explicating this inherent doctrine of Christianity, at least with any clearness or concinnity; and meanwhile they were a prey to numerous more or less attractive substitutes for it, among which the Logos Christology long held the field, and its contradictory, Modalistic Monarchianism, as we have seen, at one time bade fair to establish itself as the common doctrine of the churches. And it remains true, moreover, that no one earlier than Tertullian and few besides Tertullian, prior to the outbreak of the Arian controversy, seem to have succeeded in giving anything like a tenable expression to this potential Trinitarianism. If Tertullian may not be accredited with the invention of the doctrine of the Trinity, it may yet be that it was through him that the elements of this doctrine first obtained something like a scientific adjustment, and that he may not unfairly, therefore, be accounted its originator, in a sense somewhat similar to that in which Augustine may be accounted the originator of the doctrines of original sin and sovereign grace, Anselm of the doctrine of satisfaction, and Luther of that of justification by faith. Whether he may be so accounted, and how far, can be determined only by a careful examination of what he has actually set down in his writings.

When now we come to scrutinize with the requisite closeness the doctrine which underlies Tertullian's enunciations in his tract, " Against Praxeas," we perceive that it is, in point of fact, fundamentally little else than the simple Biblical teaching as to the Father, Son, and Holy Spirit elaborated under the categories of the Logos Christology.

This Logos Christology had been simply taken over by Tertullian from the Apologists, who had wrought it fully out and made it dominant in the Christian thought of the time. Its roots were planted alike in Jewish religion and in Gentile speculation. Its point of origin lay in a conception of the transcendence of God which rendered it necessary to mediate his activity *ad extra* by the assumption of the interposition of intermediate beings. In their highest form, the speculations thus induced gave birth to the idea of the Logos. Under the influence of passages like the eighth chapter of Proverbs and the first chapter of John, the historical Jesus was identified with this Logos, and thus the Logos Christology was, in principle, completed. It will be observed that the Logos Christology was in its very essence cosmological in intention: its reason for existence was to render it possible to conceive the divine works of creation and government consistently with the divine transcendence: it was therefore bound up necessarily with the course of temporal development and involved a process in God. The Logos was in principle God conceived in relation to things of time and space: God, therefore, not as absolute, but as relative. In its very essence, therefore, the Logos conception likewise involved the strongest subordinationism. Its very reason for existence was to provide a divine being who does the will of God in the regions of time and space, into which it were inconceivable that the Invisible God should be able to intrude in His own person. The Logos was therefore necessarily conceived as reduced divinity — divinity, so to speak, at the periphery rather than at the center of its conception. This means, further, that the Logos was inevitably conceived as a protrusion of God, or to speak more explicitly, under the category of emanation. The affinity of the Logos speculation with the emanation theories of the Gnostics is, therefore, close. The distinction between the two does not lie, however, merely in the number of emanations presumed to have proceeded from the fountain-deity, nor merely in the functions ascribed to these emanations, bizarre as the developments of Gnosticism were in this matter. The distinction lies much more in the fundamental conception entertained of the nature of the fountain-deity itself, and more directly in the conception developed of the nature of the emanation process and the relation of the resulting emanations to the primal-deity. The Gnostic systems tended ever to look upon the source-deity as a featureless abyss of being, to conceive the process of emanation from it as a blind and necessary evolution, and to attribute to the emanations resulting from this process a high degree of independence of the primal-deity. In direct contradiction to the Gnostic construction, the Logos speculation conceived God as personal, the procession of the Logos as a voluntary act on the part of God, and the Logos itself as, so to say, a function of the eternal God Himself, never escaping from the control of His will, or, as it might be more just to say, from participation in His fullness. The effect of the Gnostic speculation was to create a hierarchy of lesser divinities, stretching from the primal abyss of being downward in ever-widening circles and diminishing potencies to the verge of the material world itself. The value of the Logos speculation to the first age of Christianity was that it enabled Christian thinkers to preserve the unity of God while yet guarding His transcendence; and to look upon the historical Jesus, identified with the Logos, as very God, the Creator and Governor of the world, while yet recognizing His subordination to the will of God and His engagement with the course of development of things in time and space. It is probable that it was only by the help of the Logos speculation that Christianity was able to preserve its fundamental confession in the sharp conflict through which it was called to pass in the second century. By the aid of that speculation, at all events, it emerged from this conflict with a firm and clear hold upon both of the fundamental principles of the unity of the Indivisible God and the deity of the historical Jesus, who was, as John had taught in words, the Logos of God; that is to say, as the leaders of the day interpreted the significance of the term, the pretemporal protrusion of the deity for the purpose of creating the world of time and space and the mediating instrument of the deity in all His dealings with the world of time and space.

Tertullian, now, was the heir of this whole Logos construction, and he took it over from the Apologists in its entirety, with his accustomed clearness and even intensity of perception.[27] There was no element in it which he did not grasp with the most penetrating intuition of its significance and of the possibilities of its development at the call of fresh doctrinal needs. The demand for a new application of it came to him in the rise of the Monarchian controversy, and he opposed the Logos doctrine to the new construction with a confidence and a skill in adaptation which are nothing less than astonishing. This seems the precise account to give of the scope of the tract, " Against Praxeas." It is in essence an attempt to adapt the old Logos speculation, which Tertullian had taken over in its entirety from the Apologists, to the new conditions induced by the rise and remarkable success of the Monarchian movement.

[27] The general dependence of Tertullian on the Apologists is very marked. Loofs says justly: " Tertullian's general conception of Christianity is determined by the apologetical tradition " (Herzog, " Realencyklopädie für protestantische Theologie und Kirche,"[3] xii. p. 264, line 46); and again: " Novatian and Tertullian were much more strongly influenced than Irenæus by the Apologists: their general conception of Christianity received its color from this influence " (*Sitzungsberichte der königlich preussichen Akademie der Wissenschaften zu Berlin,* June, 1902, p. 781).

Whatever contributions, then, to the development of the doctrine of the Trinity Tertullian was able to make were made because of the emergence of need for such new adjustments of the old Logos speculation, and because he met this need with talents of the first order.

We must not underestimate the significance of the rise and rapid spread of the Monarchian Christology; or imagine that it could have filled the place in the history of the late second and early third centuries which it did, if it had found no justification for itself in the condition of Christian thought at the time, or had brought no contribution for the Christian thought of the future. The truth is, the Logos speculation left much to be desired in the formulation of the Christian doctrines of God and the Mediator between God and man; and the Monarchian speculation came bearing these very desiderata in its hands. The Logos Christology put itself forward as the guardian alike of the unity of God and of the deity of Jesus. But the unity it ascribed to God was, after all, apt to be but a broken unity, and the deity it ascribed to Jesus was at best but a derived deity. According to it, Jesus was not the God over all that Paul called Him, but the Logos; and the Logos was not one with the Father, as John taught, and indeed as Jesus (who was the Logos) asserted, but an efflux from the Father — by so much lower than the Father as the possibility of entrance into and commerce with the world of space and time implied. Men might very well ask if this construction did justice either to the unity of God or to the deity of Jesus which it essayed to protect; whether every attempt to do justice on its basis to the unity of God would not mean disparagement of the perfect deity of Jesus, and every attempt to do justice to the deity of Jesus would not mean the erection of the Logos, with whom Jesus was identified rather than with God, to a place alongside of God, which would involve the confession of two Gods. By the rise of Monarchianism, in other words, the traditional Logos construction was put sharply on its trial. It was demanded of it that it show itself capable of doing justice to the deity of Jesus, while yet retaining in integrity the unity of God, or else give place to a better scheme which by identifying Jesus directly with the One God, certainly provided fully for these two focal conceptions.

The difficulty of the situation into which the assault of Monarchianism brought the Logos Christology, by its insistence that Jesus should be recognized as all that God is, becomes manifest when we reflect that every attempt to elevate the deity that was in Jesus to absolute equality with the God over all seemed to involve in one way or another the abandonment of the entire Logos speculation. The simple identification of Jesus with God would be, of course, the formal abolishment of the Logos speculation altogether. But the attempt to retain the distinction beween God and the Logos, while Jesus as the Logos was made all that God is, seemed only a roundabout way to the same goal. Since the postulation of a Logos turned precisely on the assumption that God in Himself is too transcendent to enter into commerce with the world of space and time, the obliteration of the difference between the Logos and God appeared to reduce the whole Logos hypothesis to an absurdity. Either the primal-deity would need no Logos, or the Logos Himself would require another Logos. The task Tertullian found facing him when he undertook the defense of the Logos Christology over against the Monarchian assault was thus one of no little delicacy and difficulty. It was a task of great delicacy. For the Monarchians did not come forward as innovators in doctrine, but as protestants in the interest of the fundamental Christian doctrines of the divine unity and of the Godhead of the Redeemer against destructive speculations which were endangering the purity of the Christian confession. They embodied the protest of the simple believer against philosophic evaporations of the faith. Above all they were giving at last, so they said, his just due to Christ. It means everything when we hear Hippolytus quoting Noëtus as exclaiming: "How can I be doing wrong in glorifying Christ?" [28] — a cry, we may be sure, which found an echo in

[28] τί οὖν κακὸν ποιῶ, δοξάζων τὸν Χριστόν;

every Christian heart. And it was a task of great difficulty. For what Tertullian had to do was to establish the true and complete deity of Jesus, and at the same time the reality of His distinctness as the Logos from the fontal-deity, without creating two Gods. This is, on the face of it, precisely the problem of the Trinity. And so far as Tertullian succeeded in it, he must be recognized as the father of the Church doctrine of the Trinity.

Of course Tertullian was not completely successful in so great a task. On his postulates, indeed, complete success was difficult to the verge of impossibility. The Logos Christology was, to speak shortly, in its fundamental assumptions incompatible with a developed doctrine of immanent Trinity. Its primary object was to provide a mediating being through which the essentially " Invisible " God could become " visible " — the absolute God enter into relations — the transcendent God come into connection with a world of time and space. To it Jesus must by the very necessity of its fundamental postulates be something less than the God over all. So soon as He was allowed to be Himself all that God is, the very reason for existence of the Logos speculation was removed. Nor was it easy on the assumptions of the Logos Christology to allow a real distinctness of person for the Logos. On its postulates the Logos must be itself God — God prolate — God in reduction — God, as we have said, on the periphery of His Being: but God Himself nevertheless. On every attempt to sharpen the distinction by conceiving it as truly personal rather than gradual, the whole speculation begins to evaporate. The distinction inherent in the Logos speculation may be a distinction of transcendent and immanent, of absolute and relative, of more or less: a distinction between person and person is outside the demands of its purpose. How can a distinct person be the absolute God become relative? And these difficulties reach their climax when we suppose this distinction to be eternal. What function can be conceived for a relative God in the depths of eternity, when nothing existed except God Himself? A meaningless God is just no God at all. Tertullian, in a word, as a convinced adherent of the Logos Christology, was committed to conceptions which were not capable of holding a doctrine of immanent Trinity. The most that could be expected from him would be that he should approach as closely to a doctrine of Trinity as was possible on his presuppositions — that he should fill the conceptions of the Logos Christology, the highest as yet developed in the Church, so full that they should be nigh to bursting: We shall see that he did more than this. But in proportion as he did more than this has he transcended what could legitimately have been expected of him; and we shall be forced to allow that, in his effort to do justice to elements of faith brought into prominence in this controversy, he filled the conceptions of the Logos speculation so full that they actually burst in his hands. The Logos Christology, in other words, was stretched by him beyond its tether and was already passing upward in his construction to something better.

A great deal has been said of Tertullian's failure in perfect consistency: a great deal of his indebtedness to the Monarchians themselves for many of his ideas: a great deal of elements of compromise with his opponents discoverable in his construction. These things are not, however, proofs of weakness, but indications of strength in him. They mean that with all his clearness of grasp upon the Logos Christology, and with all his acuteness in adapting it to meet the problem he was facing, he yet saw the truth of some things for which, for all his acumen, it could not be made to provide — and stretched it to make it cover them also. They mean that he was not misled into the denial of positive elements of truth, always confessed by the Church, by zeal against the body of errorists that had taken them under their especial charge. For it is not quite exact to speak of these elements of truth as accepted by Tertullian at the hands of the Monarchians. They were rather elements of truth embodied in the general Christian confession, hitherto more or less neglected by the theologians, but now thrown into prominence by the presently raging controversy. It is the nemesis of incomplete theories that neglected elements of truth rise up after awhile to vex them. So it happened with the Logos Christology. But Tertullian sought to stretch the Logos Christology to cover these truths, not because they were urged with so much insistence by his opponents — he was not quite the man to meet insistence by yielding: but because they were parts of the Rule of Faith and were universally accepted by Christians as imposed on their belief by the divine Oracles, and he, for his part, was determined to be loyal to the Rule of Faith and to the teaching of Scripture.

There was one thing, in other words, which was more fundamental to Tertullian's thinking than even the Logos Christology. That was the Rule of Faith — the immemorial belief of Christians, grounded in the teaching of the Word of God.[29] The insistence on certain truths by his opponent may have been the occasion of Tertullian's notice of them: his attempt to incorporate them into his construction was grounded in recognition of them as elements in the universal Christian faith. This Rule of Faith had come down to him from " the

[29] This is, briefly, what appears to be the meaning of the Rule of Faith, or the Rule of Truth, in the writings of Tertullian as of the other early Fathers. There has been much discussion among scholars as to the exact relation of the conception to Scripture, on the one hand, and to the Baptismal Creed — what we know as " The Apostles' Creed " — on the other. Kunze, in his " Glaubensregel, Heilige Schrift und Taufbekenntnis," seems greatly to have advanced the matter. It seems clear that the Rule of Faith means the common fundamental faith of the Church, as derived from Scripture and expressed especially in the Baptismal Creed. That is to say, it is (1) the authoritative teaching of Scripture as a whole; (2) but this teaching conceived as the common faith of the whole Church; (3) most commodiously set out in brief in the Apostles' Creed. This may be sharply expressed by saying that the Rule of Faith was supposed to be the Scriptures, and the Creed was supposed to be the Rule of Faith. In the East the consciousness that the Rule of Faith was merely the teaching of the Scriptures as drawn from them and confessed by the Church, in the West the consciousness that the Apostles' Creed was a summary setting forth of the Rule of Faith, tended to rule the usage of the term. Accordingly the tendency was in the East to see most pointedly the Scriptures *through* the Rule of Faith, or, if you will, the Rule of Faith *in* the Scriptures; in the West to see the Apostolicum *in* the Rule of Faith, or, if you will, the Rule of Faith *through* the Apostolicum. On Tertullian's conception of the relation of the Rule of Faith to Scripture see especially Kunze, p. 178.

beginning of the Gospel," as he phrased it; [30] and he recognized it as his first duty to preserve it whole and entire. The Logos Christology had not been able to take up all the items of belief which Christians held essential to their good profession: perhaps it was due to the Monarchian controversy that Christians were enabled to see that clearly. It is to the credit of Tertullian, that seeing it, he sought rather to stretch his inherited Christology to include the facts thus brought sharply to his notice, than to deny the facts in the interest of what must have seemed to him the solidly worked out philosophy of revealed truth. By his sympathetic recognition of these elements of truth he built a wider foundation, on which a greater structure could afterward be raised. To his own consciousness the principle of his doctrine remained ever the data of Scripture embodied in the Rule of Faith and interpreted under the categories of the Logos Christology. Beyond the Logos Christology he did not purposely advance. It remained for him to the end the great instrument for the understanding of Scripture. But it happened to him, as it has happened to many besides him, that the process of pouring so much new wine into old bottles had an unhappy effect upon the bottles. This great adherent of the Logos speculation became the prime instrument of its destruction.

What is true in this matter of Tertullian is true also in his own measure of Hippolytus. Both stood firmly on the Rule of Faith: [31] and the instrument for its interpretation used by each alike was the Logos Christology, which both had adopted in its entirety from the Apologists. This accounts for the similarity of their teachings. The difference of their teachings is due very largely to the unequal ability of the two men.[32] Ter-

---

[30] He carries back the Rule of Faith to the teaching of Christ ("De Præscriptione," ix. xiii. Cf. xx. xxi. xxvii. etc.).

[31] In Hippolytus the term and its synonyms are of very important occurrence (see Kunze, p. 129), and except in the "Little Labyrinth" the form "Rule of Truth" is the one he employs.

[32] A similar judgment is expressed by Bethune-Baker, "The Meaning of Homoousios in the 'Constantinopolitan' Creed," in "Texts and Studies," J. A. Robinson, ed., vii. 1, pp. 73–74, note.

tullian was much the abler man and succeeded much better in making room in his construction for the elements of truth embedded in the Rule of Faith which the Logos Christology found difficulty in assimilating. Callistus was not without some color of justification in excommunicating Hippolytus as well as Sabellius, as alike with him defective in his teaching. Only, Callistus was incapable of perceiving that it was the Logos Christology, and not the facile methods of Monarchian Modalism, which was seriously seeking to embrace and explain all the facts; that in it alone, therefore, was to be found the promise of the better construction yet to come, toward which it was reaching out honest and eager hands. His own shallow opportunism prevented him from apprehending that what was needed was not denial of all real distinction between God and Logos, Father and Son, and therewith the confounding of the entire process of redemption, but the rescue of this distinction from its entanglement with cosmological speculation, and the elevation of it from a mere matter of degrees of divinity to the sphere of personal individualization, while yet it should be jealously guarded from the virtual division of the Godhead into a plurality of deities. Callistus, the politic ruler of a distracted diocese, intent above all on calming dangerous excitement and discouraging schism, ready to purchase peace at any cost, was not capable of such a feat of sound thinking. Hippolytus was too little independent of his inheritance to be capable of it. Even Tertullian was not capable of carrying through such a task to its end: though he was able to advance it a little stage toward its accomplishment. All the circumstances considered, this was a great achievement, and it could not have been accomplished had not Tertullian united to his zeal in controversy and his acumen in theological construction an essential broad-mindedness, an incorruptible honesty of heart and a sure hold on the essentials of the faith.

That the account thus suggested correctly represents the facts will appear upon a somewhat more detailed investigation of the exact attitude of Tertullian both to the Logos

Christology and to the Rule of Faith. To such an investigation we shall now address ourselves.

Even in his earliest writings there occur passages in which full and convinced expression is given to the speculations of the Logos Christology, from which it appears that from the beginning of his activity as a Christian writer these speculations supplied the molds in which Tertullian's thought ran. When, for example, in the twenty-first chapter of his " Apology," which was written about 197, he undertakes to expound to his heathen readers the deity of Christ,[33] he identifies Him out of hand with the Logos of Zeno and Cleanthes,[34] because, as he says, " we have been taught " (didicimus) as follows — whereupon he proceeds to set forth the Logos doctrine, thus declared to be to him the traditionary doctrine of the Church.[35] " We have been taught," says he, that the Logos " was produced (prolatum) from God (ex Deo) and in [this] production generated, and therefore is called the Son of God and God, because of (ex) the unity of the substance, since God also is Spirit. Just as when a ray is put forth (porrigitur) from the sun, it is a portion of the whole (portio ex summa), but the sun will be in the ray, because it is a ray of the sun, and is not separated from the substance, but stretched out (non separatur substantia sed extenditur); so Spirit [is extended] from Spirit and God from God, as light is kindled from light. The materiæ matrix (source of the material) remains entire and undiminished (integra et indefecta) although you draw out from it

[33] " Necesse est igitur pauca de Christo ut deo."

[34] " Your philosophers . . . Zeno . . . Cleanthes . . . and we too (et nos autem). . . ."

[35] Kunze, p. 197, has some excellent remarks on the relative places taken by philosophy and Scripture in the thinking of such men as Irenæus and Tertullian. They wished to be purely Biblical; and the influence of philosophy " was exerted only through the medium of their understanding of the Bible, through the filter of Bible intérpretation." " This was true, for example," he adds, " of their Logos theory. As certain as it is that in this matter extra-Christian influences are recognizable, it is equally certain that for Tertullian, and especially for Irenæus, the Logos idea and its corollaries would have formed no part of the regula had they not found word and thing alike in the Scriptures."

many branches of its kind (*traduces qualitatis*): thus also what
is derived (*profectum*) from God is God and the Son of God,
and the two are one. In this manner, then, He who is Spirit
from Spirit and God from God made another individual in
mode [of existence], in grade, not in state (*modulo alternum
numerum, gradu non statu fecit*), and did not separate from
but stretched out from the source (*et a matrice non recessit sed
excessit*). This ray of God, then, descended into a certain virgin, as it had always been predicted in times past. . . ." [36]

What we read in the tract " Against Praxeas " embodies the
same ideas in the same terms. We must, however, note in more
detail how far Tertullian here commits himself to the forms of
the Logos speculation. We observe, then, in the first place, that
Tertullian with complete conviction shares the fundamental
conception out of which the Logos doctrine grows — the conception of the transcendence of God above all possibility of
direct relation with a world of time and space. So axiomatic
did it seem to him that God in Himself is exalted above direct
concernment with the world-process, that when discussing the
temporal activities of our Lord, he permits himself to say that
such things, hard to believe of the Son and only to be credited
concerning Him on the authority of Scripture, could scarcely
have been believed of the Father, even if Scripture had explicitly affirmed them of Him.[37] That is to say, the doctrine of
the transcendence of God, or as Tertullian phrases it, in Scriptural language which had become traditional in this school, of
the " invisibility " of God " in the fulness of His majesty," [38]
stood, as a fixed datum, at the root of Tertullian's whole
thought of God. In the second place, we observe that Tertullian shared with equal heartiness the current conception of the
Logos as, so to speak, the world-form of God. It was, indeed,
only in connection with the world, and as its condition, both
with respect to origin and government, that he was accustomed

[36] Cf. the parallel statements in " De Præscriptione " 13.

[37] " Against Praxeas," chap. xvi.: " Fortasse non credenda de patre, licet
scripta."

[38] Chap. xiv.

to think of a Logos at all. The prolation of the Logos took place, in his view, only for and with the world, as a necessary mediator, to perform a work which God as absolute could not perform. It was "*then,*" says Tertullian with pointed emphasis,[39] that the Word assumed "His own form," when God said, "Let there be light!" It was only when God was pleased to draw out (*edere*) into "their own substances and forms" (*in substantias et species suas*) the things He had planned within Himself, that He put forth (*protulit*) the Word, in order that all things might be made through Him.[40] We observe, in the third place, that Tertullian, with equal heartiness, shared the consequent view that the Logos is not God in His entirety, but only a "portion" of God — a "portion," that is, as in the ray there is not the whole but only a "portion" of the sun. The difference seems to be not one of mode only, but of measure. "The Father," he says, "is the entire substance, but the Son is a derivation and portion of the whole."[41] He speaks "of that portion of the whole which was about to retire into the designation of the Son."[42] To Tertullian this idea was self-evident inasmuch as the Logos was to him necessarily produced, or, rather, reduced Divinity — Divinity brought to a level on which it could become creator and principle of the world of time and space.[43] We observe, in the fourth place, that Tertullian also accorded with the current conception in thinking of the prolation of the Logos as a voluntary act of God rather than a necessary movement within the divine essence.

[39] *Loc. cit.,* chap. vii.: "Tunc igitur etiam ipse sermo speciem et ornatum suum sumit, sonum et vocem, cum dixit deus: fiat lux."

[40] Chap. vi.: "Iam, ut primum deus voluit ea, quæ cum sophiæ ratione et sermone disposeuerat intra se, in substantias et species suas edere, ipsum primum protulit sermonem, habentem in se individuas suas, rationem et sophiam, etc. So also chap. xii. "The first statement of Scripture is made, indeed, when the Son had not yet appeared: 'And God said, "Let there be light," and there was light.' Immediately there appears the Word, 'that true light. . . . From that moment God willed creation to be effected in the Word, Christ.' . . ."

[41] Chap. ix.

[42] Chap. xxvi.

[43] The real meaning of this phraseology will be discussed further on in this article.

As there was a time before which the Son was not,[44] so He came into being by the will of God,[45] and remains in being to fulfill the will of God, and at last when He has fulfilled the will of God retires once more into the divine unity.[46] All this, of course, applies only to the prolate Logos.[47] This whole development of the prolate Logos, therefore, is not only a temporal but a temporary expedient, by means of which God, acting voluntarily, accomplishes a work. When this work is accomplished the arrangements for it naturally cease. The Logos mode of existence thus emerges as an incident in the life of God which need not, perhaps, find a necessary rooting in His nature, but only a contingent rooting in His purposes. In the very nature of the case, therefore, the prolate Logos is dependent on the divine will.[48] It is hardly necessary to make a separate fifth observation, therefore, that Tertullian thoroughly shared the subordinationism inherent in the Logos Christology.[49] To him the Son, as prolated Logos, was self-evidently less (*minor*) than the Father, seeing that His prolation occurred by the Father's will, and in order to do His will. He remains subject to His will,[50] and when that will is accomplished returns into the divine

[44] Chap. v.: God was alone " up to the generation of the Son." Cf. chaps. vi. xiii. Cf. " Against Hermog.," iii.: Fuit autem tempus cum . . . Filius non fuit . . . ; and see Bull's long discussion of this passage in his " Denfensio Fidei Nicaenæ," iii. x. (E. T. 1851, pp. 509 f.). The real meaning of this too will be discussed later.

[45] Chap. xvi.: " The Scripture informs us that He who was made less (than the angels) was so affected by another and not Himself by Himself." Cf. chaps. iv. xxiii. The insistence of the Apologists on the origination of the Logos in an act of the will of God was their protest against the blind evolutionism of the Gnostics, and often was but their way of saying that creation was not a necessary process but a voluntary act on God's part; that is to say, it hangs together with their cosmological conception of the Logos. Cf. Hagemann, " Die Römische Kirche," p. 194. On the whole subject compare Dorner, " Doctrine of the Person of Christ," Div. I. ii. p. 460, and Bethune-Baker, " An Introduction to the Early History of Christian Doctrine," p. 159, note,[2] and pp. 194–195.

[46] Chap. iv. Cf. chaps. xxii. xxiii.

[47] The as yet unprolated Logos Tertullian wishes to distinguish from the uttered Logos or Sermo, as the unuttered Logos or Ratio; cf. chap. v.

[48] Cf. Stier, p. 100.

[49] Cf. Stier, p. 71.

[50] Chaps. iv. xvi. xviii.

bosom. The invisible Father alone possesses the fullness of the divine majesty: the Son is visible *pro modulo derivationis* — by reason of the measure of His derivation — and stands related to the Father as a ray does to the sun.[51] He is the *second,* in every sense of the term.

Even such a brief survey as this of the natural forms in which Tertullian's thought ran makes it exceedingly clear that the prime instrument in his hands for the interpretation of the facts of the Christian revelation was just the Logos Christology taken over in its entirety from his predecessors.

But if the Logos Christology thus supplied to Tertullian the forms of thought with which he approached the problems now brought into renewed prominence, the matter of his thinking was derived from another source, and from a source that lay even more deeply embedded in his convictions. If the Logos Christology was the instrument by means of which he sought to interpret the Rule of Faith, the Rule of Faith supplied the matter to be interpreted. The question that was always pressing upon him, therefore, was whether this matter in its entirety could be interpreted by the Logos Christology. Certainly Tertullian must be credited with a loyal effort to preserve all its data in their integrity, as even his most cursory reader will at once perceive; [52] and in making this effort, largely under the

[51] Chap. xiv.

[52] The Rule of Faith, which originates in the teaching of Christ and comes to us in the apostolic proclamation, and which is, therefore, " absolutely one, alone, immovable and irreformable," according to " De Vel. Virg.," 1, " prescribes the belief that there is one only God . . . who produced all things out of nothing through His own Word first of all sent forth; that this Word is called His Son . . . was made flesh and . . . having been crucified, rose again the third day, ascended into the heavens, sat at the right hand of the Father; sent instead of Himself the power of the Holy Ghost to lead such as believe on Him " (" De Præscriptione," xiii.). Or as Tertullian sets forth the items in " Against Praxeas," 2, relatively to the matters in hand in that tract, this aboriginal Rule of Faith teaches that " there is one God "; that " this one only God has also a Son, His Word, who proceeded from Himself, by whom all things were made and without whom nothing was made "; and that this Son has " sent also from heaven from the Father, according to His own promise, the Holy Ghost, the Paraclete, the Sanctifier of the faith of those who believe in the Father, and in the Son and in the Holy Ghost." Tertullian obviously looks

influence of the Monarchian controversy, he found himself compelled to enlarge and modify the contents of the Logos speculation, in order to embrace the data of the Rule of Faith.

In the first place, the Rule of Faith imposed on Tertullian the duty of framing a doctrine of the Holy Spirit as well as of the Son of God. For this, of course, the Logos Christology did not necessarily provide. But it pointed out a road to it by way of analogy. The Apologists, accordingly, though they were absorbed in the doctrine of the Logos and did not always know what to do with the Spirit, yet did not leave the subject so entirely to one side but that they handed down to their successors the beginnings of a doctrine of the Spirit framed on the analogy of this Christology.[53] They had already made it a matter of traditionary doctrine, for example, that the Spirit is related to the Son much as the Son is to the Father, and makes a third alongside of the Father and Son.[54] Tertullian takes up these somewhat fluid elements of traditional teaching and gives them sharpness and consistency.[55] He looks upon the Spirit apparently as a prolation from the Son, as the Son is from the Father, thus preserving, so to speak, a linear development in the evolution of God:[56] but he carefully preserves the

---

upon the Rule of Faith as originating in the baptismal formula given by our Lord, and as finding its normal succinct expression in the Baptismal Creed, commonly known as the Apostles' Creed.

[53] On the early opinions as to the Spirit, besides Dr. Swete's book on this precise subject, see Kahnis, " Lehre vom heiligen Geiste," pp. 168 f.; Nösgen " Geschichte der Lehre vom heiligen Geiste," chap. i.; Harnack, i. p. 197, note, and ii. p. 209, note [1]; Scott, " Origin and Development of the Nicene Theology," Lecture V.

[54] Scott, pp. 274, 284. " The doctrine of the Holy Spirit," says Scott, p. 285, note, " was not developed in the second century, but it was plainly present in the Church, both East and West. The theological statement of the Spirit in the second century did not use the term *hypostatic;* but all that was meant later by that term is clearly involved in the teachings of the Apologists and the anti-Gnostic writers." Tertullian " first called the Spirit ' God,' but he only uttered what the Church had ever believed."

[55] On Tertullian's doctrine of the Spirit, see Kahnis, pp. 255 f.; Scott, p. 284; Harnack, ii. p. 261, note [4]; Stier, p. 92, note. The most distinctive passages seem to be found in " Against Praxeas," ii. iii. iv. viii. ix. xi. xiii. xxvi. xxx.

[56] This characteristic of the Apologists' construction is its most marked

conception of the Father as *fons deitatis,* and thus frames as his exact formula the assertion that the Spirit, being the third degree in the Godhead, proceeds "from no other source than from the Father through the Son " (chap. iv.). In his familiar figures, as the Father and Son are represented by the root and the stem of the tree, by the fountain and the river, by the sun and its ray, so the Spirit, being " third from God and the Son," is as the fruit of the tree, which is third from the root, or as the stream from the river, which is third from the fountain, or as the apex from the ray, which is third from the sun (chap. viii.).[57] All flows down from the Father through colligated and conjoined grades (*per consertos et conexos gradus,* chap. viii. *ad fin.*), but the immediate connection is of the Father in the Son and the Son in the Paraclete (chap. xxv. *ad init.*), and thus it may be truly said that the Son received the Spirit from the Father and yet Himself shed Him forth — this " Third Name in the Godhead and Third Grade in the Divine Majesty, the Declarer of the One Monarchy of God and yet, at the same time, the Interpreter of the Economy " (chap. xxx.). Under the guidance of the Logos speculation Tertullian thus, in the first instance, conceives the Spirit apparently as a prolation of the Son as the Son is of the Father, and as therefore subordinate to the Son as the Son is to the Father: but nevertheless as ultimately deriving from the *fons deitatis* itself, through the Son, and through the Son subject ultimately to it.[58]

The consistent extension of the Logos speculation to cover the Third divine Person confessed in the Rule of Faith was, however, only a short step toward embracing the data included in that formula under the categories of the Logos speculation. The really pressing problem concerned the relations in which

---

trait, and is therefore frequently noted. Thus Hagemann, p. 139, when speaking of Hippolytus, adverts to the difference between the Church's construction and his, that the one thought of the trinitarian relationships " after the analogy of a circular motion (Kreisbewegung) and the other as *advancing in a straight line.*"

[57] Tertius enim est spiritus a deo et filio, sicut tertius a radice fructus ex frutice, et tertius a fonte rivus ex flumine, et tertius a sole apex ex radio.

[58] Stier, p. 92, note; Harnack, ii. p. 261, note [4].

the Father, Son, and Holy Spirit stand to one another. In the Rule of Faith — in the Baptismal Formula — they appear as coördinate persons, to each of whom true deity is ascribed, or, rather, to all three of whom the Name is attributed in common. Was the Logos speculation capable of taking up these data into itself and doing full justice to them? Tertullian must be credited with a sincere and a fruitful effort to make it do so. So far as the mere inclusion of the data under a single formula is concerned he found little difficulty. His formula is that the Father, Son, and Spirit are one in substance and distinct in person. In this formula he intrenches himself and reiterates and illustrates it with inexhaustible zest. He opens the serious discussion of the tract with a clear enunciation of it drawn out in full detail — crying out against the Monarchian assumption that the unity of the Godhead implies unity of Person, " as if One might not be All in this way also — viz., in All being of One, by unity of substance, while the mystery (*sacramentum*) of the οἰκονομία is still preserved, by which the unity is distributed into a Trinity, ordering (*dirigens*) the three — Father, Son, and Holy Ghost — three, however, not in status but in grade, not in substance but in form, not in power but in aspect (*species*); yet of one substance, and of one status, and of one power, inasmuch as He is one God from whom are reckoned these grades and forms and aspects under the name of the Father and Son and Holy Ghost." This is Tertullian's complete formula of Trinity in unity, which he promises to explicate more fully in the remainder of the treatise. This promise he very fairly fulfills — now repeating the entire statement more or less fully and now insisting on this or that element of it.[59] One of his favorite methods of indicating briefly the combined sameness and distinction is by employing distinctively the neuter and masculine forms of the words. " I and the Father are one," says our Lord; and Tertullian lays stress not only on the plural verb — " I and the Father *are*," not " *am*," one — but on the neuter form of the adjective — " unum," not " unus " — as implying " not singularity of number but unity

[59] E.g., chaps. iv. viii. ix. xi. xii. xxi. *sq.*

of essence," and the like (chap. xxii.). " These Three," he says again (chap. xxv.), " are unum, not unus, in respect of unity of substance, not singularness of number." So he rings the changes constantly on the unity of substance and distinction of persons.

So far, we shall easily say, so good. For so much the Logos speculation opens the way without straining. It is inherent in it that the divine prolations should be of the very essence of God, while, on the other hand, capable as prolations of acting in some sense as distinct beings. The tug comes when we ask whether this asserted unity of substance provides for the supreme deity of the prolations, so that we can say that Jesus Christ, for example, is all that God is; and whether this asserted distinctness of persons provides for a real individualization of personality, so that each so-called person stands over against the others in permanent distinctness and not in merely apparent and in its very nature temporary objectivation. Certainly the Logos speculation suggests a reduced deity for the prolations, and that in diminishing grades: and a temporal rather than an eternal — whether *a parte ante* or *a parte post* — distinction between them. Does Tertullian see glimpses beyond? In such glimpses beyond we shall discover whatever approach he has made to constructing a doctrine of a real Trinity. The hinge of the problem turns on the answers we shall be compelled to give to five questions: (1) Whether Tertullian by his distinction of " persons " intends a distinction which is really personal in the philosophical sense of that term; (2) whether Tertullian supposes this distinction of persons to have been constituted by the prolations of the Logos and Spirit, which, he teaches, took place in order to the creation and government of the world, or to belong rather to the essential mode of existence of God; (3) whether he succeeds in preserving the unity of God despite the distinction of persons which he teaches; (4) whether he is able to ascribe such deity to Christ as to say of Him that He is all that God is; (5) whether he accords to the Holy Spirit also both complete deity and eternal distinctness of personality. We shall need to look at his response to these five questions in turn.

But we shall reserve this for the Second Article.

IN the First Article it was pointed out that any approach which Tertullian may have made toward formulating a doctrine of a really immanent Trinity will be revealed by attending to the responses he makes to five questions. These questions are: (1) Whether he intends a real distinction of persons, in the philosophical sense of the term, by the distinction he makes between the divine "persons"; (2) whether he supposes this distinction of persons to belong to the essential mode of the divine existence, or to have been constituted by those prolations of the Logos and Spirit which, according to his teaching, took place in order to the creation and government of the world; (3) whether he preserves successfully the unity of God in the distinction of persons which he teaches; (4) whether he conceives deity in Christ to be all that it is in the Father; (5) whether he accords to the Holy Spirit also both absolute deity and eternal distinctness of personality. We shall endeavor now to obtain Tertullian's responses to these questions.

(1) The interest with which we seek Tertullian's answer to the first of these questions, great enough in itself, has been largely increased by a suggestion made by Dr. Charles Bigg, which has been taken up and given additional significance by Prof. Adolf Harnack. Dr. Bigg suggested [61] that Tertullian may have borrowed the word "persona" which he applies to the distinctions in the deity, not from the schools, but from the law courts. Harnack added to this the further suggestion [62] that the term "substantia" in Tertullian may well have had a similar origin. On these suppositions it was thought possible

[60] As originally printed in *The Princeton Theological Review*, January, 1906.

[61] "The Christian Platonists of Alexandria," p. 165.

[62] *Theolog. Litteraturzeitung*, 1887, No. 5, p. 110.

that Tertullian by his formula of three persons in one substance may have meant very little more than the Monarchians themselves might supposedly be able to grant. In his " History of Dogma " Harnack returns to the matter [63] with some persistency and, we might almost say, dogmatism. Tertullian he asserts, (iv. p. 144),[64] was not dealing with philosophical conceptions, but employing rather " the method of legal fictions." " It was easy for him," continues Harnack, " by the help of the distinction between ' substance ' and ' person ' current among the jurists, to explain and establish against the Monarchians, not alone the old, ecclesiastical, preëminently Western formula, ' Christus deus et homo,' but also the formula, ' pater, filius et spiritus sanctus — unus deus.' ' Substance ' (Tertullian never says ' Nature ') is, in the language of the jurists, nothing personal; it rather corresponds to ' property ' in the sense of possession, or ' substance ' in distinction from appearance or ' status '; ' Person,' again, is in itself nothing substantial, but rather a subject having legal standing and capable of holding property (*das rechts- und besitzfähige Subject*), who may as well as not possess various substances, as, on the other hand, it is possible that a single substance may be found in the possession of several persons." " Speaking juristically," he remarks again (iv. p. 122),[65] " there is as little to object to the formula that several persons are holders of one and the same substance (property), as to the other that one person may possess unconfused several substances." That is to say, apparently, when Tertullian describes God as " one substance in three persons," we may doubt whether any other conception floated before his mind than that one piece of property may very well be held in undivided possession by three several individuals; and when he speaks of our Lord as one person with two substances, we may question whether he meant more than that the same individual may very well appear in court with two distinct " properties."

[63] See especially E. T. ii. p. 257, note, 282; iv. pp. 57, 122 *sq.*, 144 *sq.*
[64] German 1st ed., 1887, ii. p. 307.
[65] German, as above, p. 288.

The theory certainly lacks somewhat in definiteness of statement,[66] and leaves us a little uncertain whether its application to Tertullian's teaching results in lowering the conception we suppose him to have attached to the term " person " or that we suppose him to have attached to the term " substance." The fact seems to be that Harnack, at least, himself vacillates in his application of it. Despite the passages already quoted, he sometimes speaks as if when Tertullian says that " Father, Son and Holy Ghost are three persons in the unity of the Godhead," we should raise the question whether by " persons " he means anything more than " capacities " — that is, whether the persons were conceived by him as much more than simply " nomina " (Harnack, iv. p. 57; " Against Praxeas," 30), and whether, therefore, his doctrine was not at least as nearly related to Monarchianism as to Nicene Trinitarianism (so Harnack, iv. p. 57, note). On the other hand, when he says that " God and man, two substances, are one Christ," we seem to be expected to raise the question whether by " substance " he means much more than " status, virtus, potestas " — that is, whether he really conceived the individual Jesus Christ as including in Himself two unconfused natures, or only two aspects of being. The sense of confusion produced by this attempt so to state the theory as to make it do double duty — and that, in each instance of its application — is already an indication that it is not easy to adjust it precisely to the facts it is called in to explain. What we are asked to do apparently is not merely to presume that Tertullian derived his nomenclature from the law courts; but to suppose that he was not quite sure in his own mind in what sense he was borrowing it. In other words, we are to suppose that he began by borrowing the terms, leaving the senses in which he should employ them to be fixed afterward; instead of beginning, as he must have done,

[66] Bethune-Baker, in his " The Meaning of Homoousios in the ' Constantinopolitan ' Creed," in " Texts and Studies," J. A. Robinson, ed., vii. 1, pp. 21 *sq.*, and especially in his " An Introduction to the Early History of Christian Doctrine," pp. 138 *sq.*, gives a lucid statement of the theory, and adopts it up to a certain point, but remarks that " the conceptions and expressions of Tertullian were by no means entirely controlled by legal usage. . . ."

with the conceptions to express which he borrowed or framed terms.

The real difficulty with the theory, however, is that it seems to be entirely without support in Tertullian's own usage of the words, and much more in his definitions and illustrations of their meaning. Harnack urges in its support little beyond the two somewhat irrelevant facts that Tertullian is known to have been a jurist, and so might well be familiar with juristic language, and that he used by predilection the term " substance " rather than " nature." [67]   On the other hand, that Tertullian is

[67] The introduction of " substance " instead of " nature " appears to have been due to an attempt to attain greater precision of terminology. Augustine, " De Trinitate," Book VII. chap. vi. § 11 (" Nicene and Post-Nicene Fathers," Series I. iii. p. 112), explicitly testifies that this use of " substance " was of comparatively recent origin: " The ancients also who spoke Latin, before they had these terms, *which have not long come into use,* that is, essence or substance, used for them to say nature. In an earlier treatise, " De Moribus Manichaeorum " (A.D. 388), chap. ii. § 2, Augustine had made the same remark (" Nicene and Post-Nicene Fathers," Series I. iv. p. 70): " Hence is the new word which we now use derived from the word for being — essence namely, or, as we usually say, substance — while, before these words were in use, the word nature was used instead." The whole matter is exhibited again in " De Haer.," xlix.: " The Arians, from Arius, are best known for the error by which they deny that the Father, Son and Holy Spirit are of one and the same nature and substance, or to speak more precisely, essence, called in Greek οὐσία"; and again, in the " Contra Sermon. Arian." xxxvi., " The Arians and Eunomians dub us Homoousiani, because against their error we defend the Father, Son and Holy Spirit by the Greek word ὁμοούσιον, that is, as of one and the same substance, or to speak more precisely, essence, which is called οὐσία in Greek; or, as it is more plainly (planius) expressed, of one and the same nature." That is Nature is the *common* word; Essence the *exact* one but stilted; Substance the nearest natural equivalent of Essence. The word " essentia " was as old as Cicero (Seneca, " Epistulae Morales.," lviii., *ad init.;* cf. Quintilian, " Inst.," 2. 14. 2; 3. 6. 23; 8. 3. 33), but never commended itself to the Roman ear, which esteemed it harsh and abstract: it was left, therefore, to an occasional philosopher to employ and then scarcely without apologies (Seneca, " Epistulae Morales," lviii. § 6; Quintilian, 2. 14, 1. 2). The more concrete " substantia " (apparently a post-Augustan word, cf. Quintilian, 2. 15. 34) became, therefore, the usual term in careful writing. The two are constantly used as exact synonyms: e.g., Apuleius, " De Platone et eius Dogmate," I. vi. writes: " The οὐσίαι which we call essentiæ, [Plato] says are two, by which all things are produced, even the world itself. Of these one is conceived by thought only, the other may be attained by the senses. . . . And *primæ quidem substantiæ vel essentiæ.* . . ." Nature was simply the popular term and was held to be less exact, and

here speaking as the heir of the Apologists and is dealing with conceptions not of his own framing, that, moreover, the whole drift of his discussion is philosophical, and that, above all, his own explanations of his meaning — as, for example, in the illustrations he makes use of — fix on the terms he employs a deeper sense, put this whole theory summarily out of court. It has accordingly made very few converts, and has more than once been solidly refuted.[68] In the aspect of it in which it comes especially before us in our present discussion, it certainly seems impossible to give it a hospitable reception.

If there is anything, indeed, that seems clear in Tertullian's exposition it is that he deals seriously with the personality which he attributes to the three distinctions of the " economy." [69] This is indeed the very hinge on which the whole controversy which he was urging so sharply against the Monarchian conception turns. Whatever care he exhibits in guarding the unity of the divine substance, therefore, by denying that

---

was therefore avoided by careful writers. Harnack's notion that Tertullian's preference of substantia has some deep theological significance seems, therefore, peculiarly unfortunate. For a refutation of it on its merits see Stier, *as cited*, pp. 76 *sq.* Bethune-Baker ("The Meaning of Homoousios in the ' Constantinopolitan ' Creed," in " Texts and Studies," J. A. Robinson, ed., vii. 1, pp. 16 and 65; cf. also *Journal of Theological Studies*, iv. p. 440) also appears to overstrain the distinction between " Substance " and " Nature " in Tertullian and his successors. Their preference for " substantia " is sufficiently accounted for by the greater precision of the word and its freedom from *qualitative* implications (cf. Quintilian's distinction of " substantia " and " qualitas " in 7. 3. 6). The " natura " of a thing suggests implications of kind; " substantia " raises no question of kind and asserts merely reality.

[68] E.g., briefly, by Seeberg, " Lehrbuch der Dogmengeschichte," 1895, i. pp. 85–87; and very copiously by J. Stier, " Die Gottes- und Logos-Lehre Tertullians," 1899, pp. 74–78. Even Loofs says ("Leitfaden zum Studium der Dogmengeschichte," 2d ed. p. 87): " These formulas show that [Tertullian] learned something in the course of his polemics, but are so thoroughly explicable as formalistic reworking of the Apologetic and Asian Tradition, that there is no need to derive them artificially from the juristic usage (against Harnack, ii. p. 288)."

[69] Cf. Dorner, " Doctrine of the Person of Christ," I. ii. p. 59: " As he gazed on the incarnate Logos, he felt certainly convinced of His personality. For it was not a mere impersonal power, but a divine subject, that had become man in Christ," etc. Cf. also p. 24, note 2.

any *separatio,* or *divisio,* or *dispersio* [70] has taken place or could take place in it, is necessarily matched by the equal emphasis he places on the reality of the *distributio, distinctio, disposi-tio* [71] that has place in it, and by virtue of which He who is eter-nally and unchangeably one (unum) is nevertheless not one (unus), but three — not, indeed, in status, substance, power, but in grade, form, species, aspect.[72] The point of importance to be noted here is not merely that Tertullian calls these dis-tinctions " persons " (which he repeatedly does),[73] but that he makes them persons by whatsoever designation he marks them. The whole of Scripture, he declares, demands this of its read-ers: it attests clearly the existence and distinction of the Trin-ity, and indeed establishes the Rule that He who speaks and He of whom He speaks and He to whom He speaks cannot pos-sibly be the same; nor does it fail to place thus by the first and second the third person also.[74] Only on the basis of this tri-personality of God, he urges, can the plural forms in which

[70] Chaps. iii. viii. ix.

[71] Chaps. ix. xiii.

[72] Chap. ii.: " Custodiatur οἰκονομίας sacramentum, quæ unitatem in trinitatem disponit, tres dirigens patrem et filium et spiritum, — tres autem non statu, sed gradu, nec substantia, sed forma, nec potestate, sed specie, — unius autem substantiæ et unius status et unius potestatis."

[73] Bethune-Baker, " An Introduction to the Early History of Christian Doctrine," p. 139, note [2] (cf. " The Meaning of Homoousios in the ' Constanti-nopolitan ' Creed," in " Texts and Studies," J. A. Robinson, ed., vii. 1, pp. 17–18), remarks, to be sure: " Tertullian seems, however, to avoid the use of *personæ* in this connexion " — that is to say, when " speaking as regards the being of God of one substance and three persons " — " using *tres* alone to express ' the three ' without adding ' persons ' in the case of the Trinity; just as later Augustine, while feeling compelled to speak of three ' persons,' apologized for the term and threw the responsibility for it upon the poverty of the language (" De Trini-tate," v. 10, vii. 7–10). Tertullian has the definite expression only when it can-not well be omitted — *e.g.* when supporting the doctrine of the Trinity from the baptismal commission, he writes, ' nam nec semel, sed ter, ad singula nomina in personas singulas tinguimur ' (" Against Praxeas," chap. 26)." There seems, however, to be as frequent use of the term as there would be any reason to ex-pect, and Tertullian explains (ch. xii.) that when he speaks of the distinction as " one " or " another " it is on the ground of " personality." See the long list of passages in Harnack, iv. p. 123.

[74] Chap. xi.

God speaks of Himself in Scripture be explained: [75] and how
can one issue what can justly be called a command except to
another? " In what sense, however, you ought to understand
Him to be another," he adds, " I have already explained — on
the ground of personality, not of substance — in the way of distinction not of division." [76]

In this whole discussion, Tertullian's watchword was necessarily *the economy:* and the economy was just the Trinity in
the unity. Had he not felt bound to assert the economy, there
had been no quarrel between him and the Monarchians, whose
watchword was the unity. As it was, he required to begin his
polemic against them with the distinct positing of the question: and this involved the distinct enunciation of the doctrine
of plural personality in the Godhead. We have always believed
and do now still believe, he says,[77] that there is one only God
— *but* — and it is in this "but" that the whole case lies —
but "under the following dispensation, or οἰκονομία, as it
is called — that this one God has also a Son, His Word, who
proceeded from Himself . . . who also sent from heaven, from
the Father, according to His own promise, the Holy Ghost,
the Paraclete, the Sanctifier of the faith of those who believe
in the Father and in the Son and in the Holy Ghost." This is
Tertullian's anti-Monarchian Confession of Faith. His complaint is that men behaved as if the unity of the Godhead
could be preserved in no other way than by representing the
Father, the Son, and the Holy Ghost as the very selfsame person, thus in their zeal for the unity neglecting the *sacramentum
oikonomiae,*[78] which distributes the unity into a Trinity. On
the contrary, he insists,[79] although the true God is one only
God, He must yet be believed in with His own οἰκονομία —
which with its numerical order and distribution of the Trinity
is a support to, not a breach of, the true unity; because, he ex-

[75] Chap. xii. *ad init.*
[76] Chap. xii. *ad fin.* Cf. xiii., near the beginning. Cf. Dorner, as cited, Div. I.
vol. ii. p. 24, note.[2]
[77] Chap. ii.
[78] Chap. ii.
[79] Chap. iii.

plains,[80] such a Trinity, flowing down from the Father through intertwined and connected steps does not at all disturb the monarchy, while it at the same time guards the state of the economy. Men must not be permitted to extol the monarchy at the expense of the economy, contending for the identity of the Father and Son, whereas the very names, Father and Son, plainly declaring their distinct personality, proclaim the economy [81] — lest under pretense of the monarchy men come to hold to neither Father nor Son, abolishing all distinctions in the interest of their monarchy.[82] Thus the discussion runs on, upholding the economy against the falsely conceived monarchy, to end in the same note [83] — in the declaration that the Son, the second name in the Godhead, and the second degree of the divine Majesty, has shed forth on the Church in these latter days the promised gift, "even the Holy Spirit — the Third Name in the Godhead and the Third Degree of the Divine Majesty, the Declarer of the One Monarchy of God, but at the same time the Interpreter of the *Economy,* to every one who hears and receives the words of the new prophecy; and the ' Leader into all truth,' such as is in the Father, and the Son, and the Holy Ghost, according to the mystery of the doctrine of Christ." To reject the economy is, in effect, he charges, to revert to Judaism — for to Jews not to Christians it belongs " so to believe in one God as to refuse to reckon the Son besides Him, and after the Son the Spirit." [84] The distinctive mark of Christianity to him, thus, is that the unity of God is so held that God is now openly known in His proper names and persons.[85]

Among the passages in which Tertullian exhibits with especial emphasis the distinction which he erects between the Father, Son, and Spirit under the name of persons there is a striking one [86] in which he is replying to the Callistan formula which made the Father not indeed suffer in and of Himself, but

---

80 Chap. viii. end.   84 Chap. xxxi.
81 Chap. ix.   85 Chap. xxxi.
82 Chap. x.   86 Chap. xxix.
83 Chap. xxx.

participate in the suffering of the Son. He makes his primary appeal here to the impassibility of God as such, and then falls to magnifying the distinction between the Father and the Son. " The Father," he asserts, " is separate from the Son, though not from God." The meaning seems to be that the Son is the name specifically of the incarnated Logos, and the incarnated Logos — as God, indeed, one in substance with the Father — is, as incarnated, something more, viz., flesh as well; and on this side of His being, which is the only side in which He suffered (for the Son, under the conditions of His existence as God, Tertullian allows, is as incapable of suffering as the Father) is not one with God, but separate from Him. The Monarchian might certainly reply that on this showing the Father Himself, if conceived to be incarnate, might be as truly said to share in the sufferings of the Son, or the flesh, as the Son, incarnated, could be said to have suffered. If the sufferings of the flesh were not of the flesh alone, but the incarnated deity stood in some relation to them, this would be, on Tertullian's own showing, as conceivable of the Father, deemed incarnate, as of the Son. Tertullian, therefore, attempts to help his answer out by means of a simile. If a river, he says, is soiled with mud, this miring of the stream does not affect the fountain, though the river flows from the fountain, is identical in substance with it, and is not separated from it: and although it is the water of the fountain which suffers in the stream, yet since it is affected only in the stream and not in the fountain, the fountain is not contaminated, but only the river that has issued from the fountain. We are not concerned now with the consistency of Tertullian: how he could say in one breath that the Son as God is as impassible, being God Himself, as the Father, and in the next that it is the very water from the fountain — the very substance of God in its second distinction — that is affected by the injury which has befallen it. What it concerns us to notice is, that in this illustration Tertullian very much magnifies the distinction between the persons of the Godhead. The Son is so far distinct from the Father that He may be involved in sufferings which do not reach back to or affect the

Father. The stream may be the fountain flowing forth: but the stream is so far distinct from the fountain, that what affects it is no longer felt in the fountain. Here is the individualization of personal life in an intense form, and an indication of the length to which Tertullian's conception of the personal distinction went.

In another passage [87] Tertullian announces the same results without the aid of a figure. He is engaged in discriminating between mere effluxes of power or other qualities from God and the prolation of a real and substantial person: in doing this, he magnifies the distinction between the original source and the prolation. Nothing that belongs to another thing is precisely that thing: and nothing that proceeds from it can be simply identified with it. The Spirit is God, no doubt; and the Word is God; because they proceed from God, from His very substance. But they are not actually the very same as He from whom they proceed. Each is God of God: each is a *substantiva res;* but each is not *ipse Deus;* but only " so far God as He is of the same substance with God Himself, and as being an actually existing thing, and as a portion of the Whole."

In still another passage Tertullian is repelling the Monarchians' scoff that as a word is no substantial thing, but a mere voice and sound made by the mouth, merely so much concussed air, intelligible to the ear as a symbol of thought, but in itself nothing at all: therefore (so they argued) the Word of God — the Logos — is to be conceived not as a substantial thing distinguishable from the Father, but only as a symbol of intelligible meaning. Tertullian reproaches them for being unwilling to allow that the Word is a really substantive being, having a substance of its own — an objective thing and a person — who, by virtue of His constitution as a second to God, makes, with God, two, the Father and the Son, God and the Word. He argues on two grounds that the Logos must have this substantial existence. The one is that He came forth from so great a substance: God who is Himself the fullness of Being, cannot be presumed to prolate an empty thing. The other is

[87] Chap. xxvi.

that He is Himself the author of substantial things: how could He, who was Himself nothing, produce things which are realities, with substantial existence? Whatever else this argument proves, it certainly proves that Tertullian conceived of the distinction between God the Father and God the Son as attaining the dignity of distinct individuality. " Whatever, therefore " — he closes the discussion with these words — " Whatever, therefore, has the substance of the Word, that I designate a Person. I claim for it the name of Son, and, recognizing the Son, I assert His distinction as second to the Father."

(2) It may remain, no doubt, a question whether Tertullian did not conceive this distinction of persons to have been the result of those movements of the divine substance by which successively the Logos and the Spirit proceeded from the fontal source of deity, so that the economy was thought of as superinduced upon a previous monarchy. It is thus, indeed, that he has been commonly understood.[88] In this case, while certainly he would take the personal distinctions seriously, he might be supposed not to look upon them as rooted essentially in the very being of God. God in Himself would be conceived as a monad: God flowing out to create the world and to uphold and govern it, as becoming for these purposes a triad. The " invisible God " would be a monad; the " visible God " — the God of the world-process — would become a triad.

It may be that it was after a fashion somewhat similar to this that Tertullian was naturally inclined to think of God and the distinctions he conceived to exist in His being; that is to say, his thought may have run most readily in the molds of what has come to be called an economic as distinguished from what is known as an immanent Trinitarianism. It was along these lines that the Logos speculation tended to carry him, and his hearty acceptance of that speculation as the instrument with which to interpret the deposit of Christian truth might well lead him to conceive and speak of the Trinitarian distinctions as if they were merely " economical." But the deposit of

[88] So, e.g., Dorner, Hagemann, Harnack, Stier.

truth subjected to interpretation by the Logos speculation was not quite tractable to it, and it is interesting to inquire whether Tertullian betrays any consciousness of this fact — whether in his dealing with the data embedded in the Rule of Faith he exhibits any tendency to carry back the distinction of persons in the Godhead behind the prolations by which the Logos and Spirit proceeded from it for the purpose of producing the world of time and space. So loyal an adherent of the Rule of Faith might well be expected to deal faithfully with its data, and to seek to do something like justice to them even when they appeared to be intractable to his ordinary instrument of interpretation. And so bold a thinker might well be incited by the pressure of such data to ask himself if there were nothing in the *fons deitatis* itself which might be recognized as a kind of prophecy or even as a kind of predetermination of the prolations which ultimately proceeded from it — if the very issue of these prolations do not presuppose in the Godhead itself a certain structure, so to speak, which involved the promise and potency of the prolations to come — if, in a word, the distinctions brought into manifestation by the prolations must not be presumed to have preëxisted in a latent or less manifest form in the eternal monad, out of which they ultimately proceeded.

That some indications exist of such a tendency on Tertullian's part to push the personal distinctions behind the prolations into the Godhead itself is perhaps universally recognized. It is frequently denied, to be sure, that this tendency goes very far. Harnack's form of statement is that it gives to Tertullian's teaching " a strong resemblance to the doctrine of an immanent Trinity, without being such." [89] Tertullian, he says, knew " as little of an immanent Trinity as the Apologists," and his Trinity " only *appears* such, because the unity of the substance is very vigorously emphasized." [90] Johannes Stier holds

---

[89] *Op. cit.,* iv. p. 122.

[90] *Op. cit.,* ii. pp. 260–261. Similarly Loofs remarks: " These formulas anticipate the later orthodoxy: it is all the more necessary to emphasize how strongly subordinationist they are: . . . the ' economical ' trinity here is just as little an eternal one as in the case of the older theologians of Asia Minor " (" Leitfaden zum Studium der Dogmengeschichte," 2d ed., p. 89).

essentially the same opinion. " Of an immanent Trinity in Tertullian," [91] he argues, " there can be no talk, because he is absolutely explicit that a plural personality came into existence for
the purpose of the world. Without the world, the primal unity
would have abided. It is indeed true that the Logos and the
Spirit were immanent in the unity of the divine original essence from the beginning, but nevertheless not — and this is
the point — in a *personal* manner! From the beginning God,
the divine original-essence, was alone; alone precisely as person (cf. " Against Praxeas," chap. v). From this (first) person,
no doubt, absolutely immediately, the Logos (*ratio, sermo*)
was distinguished as *subject,* but not yet as (second) *person* —
he became person only pretemporally-temporally. And as for
the Spirit, the matter is perfectly analogous in His case (cf.
" Against Praxeas," chap. vi). The Trinity of Tertullian is
purely (against Schwane, p. 164, and others) economical, conceived solely with reference to the world; nothing is easier to
see if we have the will to see it (cf. also Gieseler, p. 137; Harnack, i. p. 536; Huber, p. 117)." Nevertheless Harnack not only
can speak of Tertullian as " creating the formulas of succeeding orthodoxy," but can even declare that " the orthodox doctrine of the Trinity already announced its presence even in its
details, in Tertullian." [92] And Stier is forced to acknowledge
that Tertullian came within a single step of an immanent
Trinity.[93] " There needed, we must admit," he remarks, " only
a single step more to arrive at the eternal personal being of the
sermo in God, to establish an eternal, immanent relation between the divine original-essence and His Logos as *two divine
personalities,* to advance thence to the immanent Trinity. But
Tertullian stopped with conceiving the *sermo* from eternity,
it is true, along with the *ratio* — and the discernment of this
already itself means something — but still only as the *impersonal* basis (*Anlage*) of a future *personal sermo.*" The reason of Tertullian's failure to take the last step Stier, like

[91] *Op. cit.,* p. 95, note.
[92] iv. p. 121.
[93] P. 81.

Hagemann [94] and others before him, finds in the fact that Tertullian connected the personal *sermo* so intimately with the world that had he conceived the one as eternal, he must needs have conceived the other as eternal also: and as he was not prepared to think of the world as eternal, neither could he ascribe eternity to the personal Logos (cf. " Against Praxeas," chap. vi. *sq.*).

Possibly there is a *petitio principii* embedded in the terms in which this reason is stated. Tertullian certainly connected the prolate Logos so closely with the world that we could scarcely expect him to separate the two. But whether that involves a similar inseparable connection between the personal Logos and the world is precisely the question at issue. The prolation and the personality of the Logos seem to be for the moment confused by our critics, doubtless because it is judged that the two went together in Tertullian's mind: but this judgment cannot be justified by merely repeating it. Meanwhile we note that it is allowed that Tertullian did conceive the *sermo* as eternally existent along with the *ratio,* and this is rightly re-

---

[94] " Die Römische Kirche," pp. 173 *sq.* On p. 175 Hagemann writes as follows: " With the last idea " — the idea namely that the *sermo* is inseparable from the *ratio,* and therefore even *before* creation God was not " alone," but His " Word " included in his " reason " was with him — " Tertullian was advancing on the right road to the recognition of the eternal and personal existence of the Word in God. The Word has its ground in the Being of God, falls in the circle of His inner life, is inseparably given with Him. But he had shut himself off from the full and right understanding of the manner itself, by introducing into the investigation from the start the world-idea. He could not maintain, therefore, the full and eternal existence of the Word, without at the same time admitting the full and eternal existence of the world itself; and since this was to him an impossible idea, he could not carry through the former in its whole strictness. To him the Logos hung together with the world, and his conception of the latter was decisive for the conception of the former also. To be sure, he came near to the conviction of the eternity and the full divine nature of the Logos; but just as he was about to reach the goal, the world-idea hinderingly intruded in the way. No doubt it is to be said that his insight in this matter was injuriously affected by too great dependence on the Apologists." Again, on p. 177, summing up: " Enough: in order not to allow also the eternity of the world, he had sacrificed the eternity of the Son and taught, as a progressive realization of the world-idea, so also a progressive hypostatizing of the Logos."

garded as a matter of some significance and as equivalent at least to the postulation of something in the eternal mode of existence of God which supplies the basis (*Anlage*) for a future personal Logos. What this something was Stier does not indeed tell us, contenting himself merely with denying that it amounted in Tertullian's thought to a *personal* distinction, prior to the prolation of the Logos. He uses a German term to designate it — *Anlage* — which might be fairly pressed to cover all that Tertullian expresses as to his personal Logos, when he speaks of it as a *distributio, distinctio, dispositio, dispensatio:* and Stier can scarcely mean less than that Tertullian recognized in the eternal mode of existence of the Godhead such a distinction, disposition, distribution, dispensation, as manifested itself in the outgoing from Him of a *portio* into a truly personal distinction when He was about to create the world. Less than this would come perilously near to saying merely that the Son was potentially in the Father before He actually came into existence from the Father, which, as George Bull repeatedly points out, is no more than can be said of all created beings, all of which (according to Tertullian also), before they were produced actually, preëxisted in the thought and power of God.[95] By as much as Stier cannot mean that Tertullian recognized in the original mode of the divine existence no deeper basis for the personal prolation of the Word than there was for the production of the creature-world, by so

[95] e.g., "Defensio Fidei Nicaenæ," III. ix. 3 (E. T. 1730, p. 419). Dorner does not shrink from this assimilation of the preëxistence of the Logos and of the world: to Tertullian, he affirms explicitly. " In the first instance He has a mere ideal existence in the inner essence of God, like the world-idea itself " (Div. I. vol. ii. p. 64), and therefore " became a person for the first time, at, and for the sake of, the creation of the world " (pp. 73–74). " There is no place," in Tertullian's view, he says, " for a real, hypostatic Sonship in the inner, eternal essence of God: all that he has tried to point out, is the existence in God of an eternally active potence of Sonship " (p. 63), a " real potence of Sonship, . . . impersonal but already a personific principle " (p. 69). It does not appear what purpose these latter phrases serve beyond exhibiting a possible doubt in Dorner's own mind whether it is quite adequate to Tertullian's thought to represent him as assigning no more real preëxistence to the Logos than to the world — whether, in other words, the Logos, in his view, did not exist in some more real form than mere potentiality.

much must he be supposed to mean that Tertullian recognized that the very structure, so to speak, of the Godhead, from all eternity, included in it some disposition by virtue of which the prolation of the Logos, and afterward that of the Spirit, were provided for as manifestations of an eternal distinction in the Godhead. This certainly leaves only a short step to the recognition of an immanent Trinity; so short a step, indeed, that it is doubtful whether it does not lead inevitably on to it. The question is narrowed down at any rate to whether distinctions eternally existent in the Godhead, and afterward manifested in the prolate Logos and the prolate Spirit as truly personal, were conceived as already personal in the eternal mode of existence of God or as made such only by the acts of prolation themselves. We imagine that the average reader of Tertullian, while he will not fail to note how much the prolations meant to Tertullian's thought, will not fail to note, on the other hand, that these prolations rested for Tertullian on distinctions existent in the Godhead prior to all prolation, as the appropriate foundations for the prolations; nor will he fail to note further that Tertullian sometimes speaks of these ante-prolation distinctions in a manner which suggests that he conceived them as already personal.

The whole matter has been solidly argued, once for all, in the tenth chapter of the third book of George Bull's " Defensio Fidei Nicaenæ " (written in 1680, published in 1685). That this notable book is marred by special pleading, and that Bull shows a less keen historical conscience, as Baur puts it,[96]

[96] " Die christliche Lehre von der Dreieinigkeit und Menschwerdung Gottes," i. p. 110, where a sober estimate of the value of the work may be found. Cf. also Schaff, " History of the Christian Church," ii. p. 544. Meier (" Die Lehre von der Trinität," ii. pp. 76–77) looks upon Bull's effort to save the doctrine of the Trinity as a counsel of despair in the midst of a general decline of faith in this doctrine. Under the feeling that the doctrine could not be based on Scripture, since it is nowhere taught explicitly in Scripture, Bull undertook to show that it had for it at least the consistent testimony of antiquity. Even so, however, it was only a curtailed doctrine that he undertook the defense of. " Bull found himself also forced to make concessions; he perceived himself that he could maintain only the consubstantiality and the eternity of the Son, while allowing that differences existed as to special points —

or as we should rather say, a less acute historical sense, than
Petavius, his chief opponent in this famous debate, we suppose
can scarcely be denied. In the main matter of dispute between
these two great scholars, we can but think Petavius had the
right of it. The position which Petavius takes up,[97] indeed, appears to involve little more than recognizing that the literary
tradition of the Church, prior to the Council of Nice, was committed to the Logos Christology: while Bull undertakes the impossible task, as it seems to us, of explaining the whole body
of ante-Nicene speculation in terms of Nicene orthodoxy. The
proper response to Petavius would have been to point out that
the literary tradition, running through " Athenagoras, Tatian,
Theophilus, Tertullian, Lactantius," together with " certain
others, such as Origen," [98] is not to be identified at once with
the traditionary teaching of the Church, but represents rather a
literary movement or theological school of thought, which attempted with only partial success a specific philosophizing of
the traditionary faith of the Church. The measure of success
which Bull achieved in explaining this literary tradition in harmony with the traditional faith of the Church — which was
rather to be sought in the Rule of Faith and the naïve Christian consciousness of the times — is due to the constant refer-

---

es *e.g.*, whether the Son was begotten from the Father as respects substance:
and he considers that the ground of the differences among the Fathers which
Petavius adduced was due to an attempt to find scholastic definitions among
them. In his own faith he reverts to the pre-Augustinian period, . . . and sees
himself driven back upon the Logos-idea, . . . and in this driftage we see
the beginning of the destruction of the dogma even in the Church itself." It
probably is a fact that every attempt to revert from the Augustinian to the
Nicene construction of the Trinity marks a stage of weakening hold upon
the doctrine itself. With all Bull's zeal for the doctrine, therefore, his mode of
defending it is an indication of lack of full confidence in it, and in essence
is an attempt to establish some compromise with the growing forces of unbelief. The same phenomenon is repeating itself in our own day: cf. Prof.
L. L. Paine's " The Evolution of Trinitarianism," the assault of which on the
Augustinian construction of the doctrine is a sequence of a lowered view of
the person of Jesus gained from a critical reconstruction of the Bible.

[97] " De Trinitate," I. v. 8, quoted in Bull, " Introduction," 7 (E. T. 1851,
p. 9).

[98] This is the enumeration given by Petavius, " De Trinitate," I. v. 8.

ence which the writers with whom he deals made in their thinking to the Rule of Faith, of which they were always conscious as underlying their speculations and supplying the norm to which they strove to make their conclusions as far as possible conform; as well as to the survival in the final product which we know as Nicene theology of such elements of the Logos speculation as could be assimilated by it. He was able, therefore, to show repeatedly that the very men whom Petavius adduced as teachers of the inadequate formula betrayed here and there consciousness of elements of truth for which this formula, strictly interpreted, left no place; and also that language much the same as theirs — and conceptions not far removed from theirs — might easily be turned up in writers of unimpeachable orthodoxy living after the Council of Nice. In both matters he has done good service. It is unfair not to remember that these earlier writers wished to be and made a constant effort to remain in harmony with the Rule of Faith; and that we do not obtain their whole thought, therefore, until we place by the side of their speculative elaborations the elements of truth which they also held, for which these speculations nevertheless made no place. They were in intention, at all events, orthodox; and the failure of their theory to embrace all that orthodoxy must needs confess was an indication rather of the inadequacy of the theory to which they had committed their formal thinking, than of any conscious willingness on their part to deny or neglect essential elements of the truth. And it is useful, on the other hand, to be reminded that their unwearying effort to do justice — as far as their insight carried them — to the whole deposit of the faith bore its appropriate fruit, first, in the gradual, almost unnoted passing of their theory itself into something better, as the Nicene orthodoxy supplanted because transcending it, and next in the projection into the Nicene orthodoxy itself of many of the characteristic modes of thought and forms of expression of the earlier theory — conditioning both the conceptions and the terms used to embody them which entered as constituent elements into the new and better construction. Meanwhile, to fail to appreciate this historic evolution, and to attempt to interpret the inadequate conceptions of the earlier thinkers as only somewhat clumsily expressed enunciations of Nicene orthodoxy, is a grave historical fault, and could not fail to fill Bull's book with expositions which give it as a whole the appearance of an elaborate piece of special pleading. Only when the writer with whom he chances in any given passage to be dealing had become sharply aware — or at least uneasily conscious — of one or another of the elements of truth embodied in the Rule of Faith for which the speculation he had adopted as yet provided no place, and was really striving to take it up into his theory, make even by violence a place for it, and do justice to it, is Bishop Bull's exposition altogether admirable. This is the case with Tertullian in the matter of the eternal distinctions in the Godhead, and the result is that Bishop Bull, in the chapter in which he deals with this subject, has performed a delicate piece of expository work with a skill and a clearness which leave little to be desired.

He begins the discussion by adducing what is perhaps the most striking of the passages in which Tertullian appears explicitly to deny the eternity of the personal distinctions in the Godhead. It is to be found in the third chapter of his treatise against Hermogenes and runs as follows: " Because God is a Father and God is a Judge, it does not on that account follow that, because He was always God, He was always a Father and a Judge. For He could neither have been a Father before the Son, nor a Judge before transgression. But there was a time when there was no transgression, and no Son, the one to make the Lord a Judge, and the other a Father." Here certainly, apart from the context, and that wider context of the author's known point of view, there appears to be a direct assertion that there was a time before which the Son was not: and this falls in so patly with the Logos speculation which assigns a definite beginning to the prolated Logos, that it is easy to jump to the conclusion that Tertullian means to date the origination of the Logos at this time. Such a conclusion would, however, be erroneous; and it is just in the doctrine of the prolation of the Logos at a definite time that the passage finds its juster ex-

planation. It emerges that the term " Son " in Tertullian's nomenclature designates distinctively the prolate Logos. He
therefore asserts nothing in the present passage concerning the
eternity or non-eternity of personal distinctions in the Godhead. He affirms only that God became Father when the Logos
was prolated, seeing that the Logos became Son only at his prolation. Bishop Bull animadverts not unjustly on a tendency of
Tertullian exhibited here to overacuteness in argument and to
readiness to make a point at some cost: but he fairly makes
out his case that in the present instance Tertullian is to be
interpreted in this somewhat artificial sense — as if one should
say there was a time when God was not the Creator, because
creation occurred at a definite point of time, before which
therefore God was existent indeed, but not as Creator.[99] So
God became Father, not when the Logos came into existence,
but when He became a Son. By this neat piece of exposition
Bishop Bull seeks to remove the antecedent presumption
against Tertullian's admission of eternal distinctions in the
Godhead, which would arise from an explicit assertion on his
part that there was a time before which the Logos was not —
that is to say, the prolate Logos. He shows that this is only
Tertullian's way of saying that the Logos was not always
prolate.

He then wisely proceeds at once to a discussion of the prin-
cipal passage, wherein Tertullian seems to recognize personal
distinctions in the Godhead prior to the prolations of Logos
and Spirit. This is, of course, the very remarkable discussion in
the fifth chapter of the tract, " Against Praxeas," in which Tertullian gives, as it were, a complete history of the Logos.[100] In
this passage Tertullian begins by affirming that " before all
things " — alike before the creation of the world and the generation of the Son, that is to say, the prolation of the Logos —
God was alone (*solus*). He immediately corrects this, however,

[99] See above, pp. 30–31.
[100] This passage is discussed by Bull in Book III., chap. x., §§ 5–8. At an
earlier point — III. v. 5 — he had expounded the same passage more briefly,
but not less effectively.

by saying that by " alone " he means only that there was nothing extrinsic to God by His side: for not even then was He
really alone (*solus*), seeing that He had with Him that which
He had within Himself, namely, His Reason. This Reason, he
continues, is what the Greeks call the Logos, and the Latins are
accustomed to call Sermo — though Sermo is an inadequate
translation, and it would be better to distinguish and say that
Reason must antedate Speech, and that God rather had Reason with Him from the beginning, while He had Speech only
after He had sent it forth by utterance — that is to say, at the
prolation. This distinction, however, adds Tertullian immediately, is really a refinement of little practical importance. The
main thing is that " although God had not yet sent His Word,
He nevertheless already had Him within Himself, with and
in Reason itself, as He silently considered and determined with
Himself what He was afterward to speak through the Word."
Thus even in the silence of eternity, when God had not yet
spoken, the Word in its form of Reason was with God, and
God was therefore not alone. To illuminate his meaning, Tertullian now introduces an illustration drawn from human
consciousness. He asks his readers to observe the movements
that go on within themselves when they hold silent converse
with themselves; whenever they think, there is a word; whenever they conceive, there is reason. Speaking thus in the mind,
the word stands forth as a " conlocutor," in which reason
dwells.[101] " Thus," adds Tertullian, " the word is, in some sort,
a second within you, by means of which you speak in thinking,
and by means of which you think in speaking: this word is another." [102] Now, he reasons, all this is, of course, carried on in
God on a higher plane (*plenius*), and it is not venturesome to
affirm that " even before the creation of the universe [103] God

[101] There may be a reminiscence here, and there certainly is a parallel,
of the passage in Plato's " Sophist," § 263 E, where thought is called " the
unuttered conversation of the soul with itself," and we are told that " the
stream of thought flowing through the lips is called speech."

[102] " Ita secundus quodammodo in te est sermo, per quem loqueris cogi-
tando, et per quem cogitas loquendo; ipse sermo alius est."

[103] " Ante universitatis constitutionem."

was not alone, seeing that He had within Him both Reason and, intrinsic in Reason, His Word, which He made a second to Himself by agitating it within Himself." This Word, having within Himself Reason and Wisdom, His inseparables, He at length put forth (*protulit*) when it at length pleased Him to create the universe, that is, to draw out (*edere*) into their own substances and kinds the things He had determined on within Himself by means of this very Reason and Word.[104]

Nothing can be clearer than that in this passage Tertullian carries back the distinction manifested by the prolate Logos into the depths of eternity. It already existed, he says, within the silent God before the generation of the Word, that is, before the prolation of the Logos. He explicitly distinguishes its mode of preëxistence from that of things to be created, which " having been thought out and disposed," by means of that Word who was also the Reason of God, existed " in Dei sensu," and only needed to be drawn out in their substances and kinds — whereas He, the Word, from eternity coexisted with God as " a second," " another." All this Bishop Bull points out with great lucidity. He directs attention first to Tertullian's sharp discrimination at the outset between God's eternal existence " alone," so far as external accompaniment is concerned, and his inner companionship — so that He was never " alone," but ever had with Him, i.e., within Him, His " fellow," the Logos.

---

[104] It is interesting to observe how closely Marcellus of Ancyra, in this portion of his system, reproduced the thought of Tertullian in this chapter. To Marcellus, says Loofs (*Sitzungsberichte der königlich preussischen Akademie der Wissenschaften zu Berlin*," 1902, i. pp. 768–769), " the Logos is eternal. . . . And this Logos of God is without any γένεσις. Before the time of the creation of the world, He was simply in God; the one God, along with whom was nothing, ' had not yet spoken ' (ἡσυχία τις ἦν). When, however, God addressed Himself to create the world, τότε ὁ λόγος προελθὼν ἐγίνετο τοῦ κόσμου ποιητής, ὁ καὶ πρότερον ἔνδον νοητῶς ὀνομάζων αὐτόν. This προελθεῖν in sequence to which came in the πρὸς τὸν θεὸν εἶναι of which Jno. i. 1 speaks, did not, however, bring to a close the ἐν θεῷ εἶναι: the Logos remains δυνάμει ἐν τῷ θεῷ, and only ἐνεργείᾳ was He πρὸς τὸν θεόν; προῆλθεν δραστικῇ ἐνεργείᾳ. How this is to be understood, Marcellus — with all sorts of cautions — has illustrated by the analogy of the human Logos: ἐν γάρ ἐστι καὶ ταὐτὸ τῷ ἀνθρώπῳ ὁ λόγος καὶ οὐδενὶ χωριζόμενος ἑτέρῳ, ἢ μόνῃ τῇ τῆς πράξεως ἐνεργείᾳ." This reads (so far) almost like an exposition of the fifth chapter of the tract, " Against Praxeas."

He next calls attention to the fact that by Reason in this context Tertullian does not mean God's faculty of ratiocination, by virtue of which He was rational, but a really subsisting ἔννοια — the *verbum mentis* of the schools. Still further, he animadverts on Tertullian's admission that the distinction he was drawing between the Reason and the Word was not drawn by Christians at large who, translating the Greek word " Logos " in John i. 1, by the Latin *Sermo,* were accustomed to say simply that " the Word was in the beginning," i.e., eternally, and that " with God." In doing this he adverts to Tertullian's admission that he lays little stress on this distinction himself, and is fain himself to allow that the " Word " is coeternal with " Reason " — that is to say, of course, the " inner Word," not yet uttered for the purpose of creation: and further, that he allows that the Word consists of Reason, and existed in this His hypostasis or substance before He became the Word by utterance. Then, arriving at the apex of his argument, he points out that " Tertullian teaches that the Word, even anterior to His mission and going out from God the Father, existed with the Father as a Person distinct from Him." This, (1) because God is said not to be " alone "; but He only is not alone with whom is another person present. If through all eternity God was unipersonal, and there was not in the divine essence one and another, then God was alone. Hence God was not unipersonal, since He is affirmed not to have been alone. (2) Because in the illustration from human experience Tertullian distinguishes between the quasi-personality of the human inner word and the real personality of the divine inner Word. The whole drift of the illustration turns on the idea that " what occurs in man, God's image, is merely the shadow of what occurs really and in very fact in God." Finally, Bull argues that Tertullian clearly identifies the " Reason that coexisted with God from eternity with the Word prolated from Him at a definite point of time, and makes one as much personal as the other, conceiving nothing to have occurred at the prolation but the prolation itself — the Word remaining all the while, because God, unchangeable. This argument is expanded in a supplementary reason which Bull gives for his conclusion by the help of a passage which occurs in the twenty-seventh chapter of the tract, "Against Praxeas." In this passage Tertullian argues that the Word, because God, is "immutabilis et informabilis" — unchangeable and untransformable: since God never either ceases to be what He was or begins to be what He was not. How, then, Bull asks, can Tertullian have believed that the Word, who is God, began to be a person only at His prolation, or, indeed, for that is what is really in question, began at that time only to be at all? [105]   From such passages, Bull justly suggests, we may learn that by all that Tertullian says of the prolations of the Logos and Spirit he does not mean to detract in any way from the unchangeableness of the divine persons concerned in these acts: nothing intrinsic was, in his view, either added to or taken from either of the two, seeing that each is the same God, eternal and unchangeable. "Tertullian does indeed teach" — thus Bull closes the discussion — "that the Son of God was made, and was called the Word (*Verbum* or *Sermo*), from some definite beginning; i.e. at the time when He went out from God the Father, with the voice, 'Let there be light,' in order to arrange the universe. But yet that he believed that that very hypostasis, which is called the Word (*Sermo* or *Verbum*) and Son of God, is eternal, I have, I think, abundantly demonstrated." [106]

(3) There has been enough adduced incidentally in the course of the discussion so far, to make it clear that Tertullian in insisting on the distinction of persons in the Godhead — and in carrying this distinction back into eternity — had no inten-

---

[105] In support of this take such a statement as the following from the thirteenth chapter: "You will find this," says Tertullian, "in the Gospel in so many words: 'In the beginning was the Word, and the Word was with God and the Word was God.' He who was is One: and He with whom He was is another." As it is probable that by the words "in the beginning" Tertullian understood eternity, here is an explicit assertion of a distinction of persons in eternity. Again, in chap. viii., he says: "The Word, therefore, was both in the Father always, as He says, 'I am in the Father,' and with the Father always, as it is written, 'And the Word was with God.'"

[106] E. T. p. 545.

tion of derogating in any way from the unity of God. If in his debate with the Monarchians his especial task was to vindicate the οἰκονομία, the conditions of that debate required of him an equal emphasis on the " monarchy." And he is certainly careful to give it, insisting and insisting again on the unity of that one God whom alone Christians worship. This insistence on the unity of God has come, indeed, to be widely represented as precisely the peculiarity of Tertullian's doctrine of God. Says Loofs: [107] " Tertullian's Logos doctrine waxed into a doctrine of the Trinity (*trinitas* occurs first in him) because Tertullian sought to bring the Apologetic traditions into harmony with the stricter monotheism of the Asiatic theology." Similarly Harnack supposes that Monarchianism exercised a strong influence on Tertullian, " spite of the fact that he is opposing it," and remarks in proof that " no thought is so plainly expressed " by him in his tract, " Against Praxeas " " as this, that Father, Son and Spirit are *unius substantiæ*, that is ὁμοούσιοι "; [108] and again, that " Tertullian in so far as he designated Father, Son, and Spirit as one substance expressed their *unity* as strongly as possible." [109] We may attribute the influence which led Tertullian to lay the stress he did on the unity of God to whatever source we choose, but we must acknowledge that Tertullian himself did not trace it to the Monarchians. Though, no doubt, the necessity he felt upon him not to neglect this great truth was intensified by the fact that it was just with Monarchians that he was contending, yet Tertullian is not himself conscious of indebtedness to them for either his conception of it or his zeal in its behalf. To him it is the very principium of Christianity and the very starting-point of the Rule of Faith. Though he recognizes a monadistic monarchy as rather Jewish than Christian, therefore, and is prepared for a certain pluralism in his conception of God, all this is with him conditioned upon the preservation of the monarchy, and he has his own way of reconciling the monarchy, in which all his Christian

---

[107] " Leitfaden zum Studium der Dogmengeschichte," p. 88.
[108] iv. p. 57, note: cf. ii., pp. 257, note,[2] 259.
[109] ii. p. 257 note.[2]

thinking is rooted, on the one side, with the economy, which he is zealous to assert, on the other.

This way consists, briefly, in insistence not merely that the three persons, Father, Son, and Spirit, are of one substance, but that they are of one undivided substance. Though there is a *dispositio, distinctio* between them, there is no *divisio, separatio.* It is not enough for him that the Three should be recognized as alike in substance, condition, power.[110] What he insists on is that the Father, Son, and Spirit are inseparable from one another and share in a single undivided substance — that it is therefore "not by way of diversity that the Son differs from the Father, but by distribution: it is not by division that He is different, but by distinction."[111] "I say," he reiterates, they are "distinct, not separate" (*distincte, non divise*)."[112] They are distinguished "on the ground of personality, not of substance — in the way of distinction, not of division,"[113] "by disposition, not by division." The ill-disposed and perverse may indeed press the distinction into a separation, but the procession of the Son from the Father "is like the ray's procession from the sun, and the river's from the fountain, and the tree's from the seed"[114] — and thus the distinction between them may be maintained "without destroying their inseparable union — as of the sun and the ray, and the fountain and the river."[115]

By the aid of such illustrations Tertullian endeavored to make clear that in distinguishing the persons he allowed no division of substance. His conception was that as the sun flows out into its beams while yet the beams remain connected inseparably with the sun, and the river flows out of the fountain but maintains an inseparable connection with it, so the Son and Spirit flow out from the Father while remaining inseparable from Him. There is, in a word, an unbroken continuity of substance, although the substance is drawn out into — if we may speak after the manner of men — a different mold. The con-

---

[110] Chap. ii.
[111] Chap. ix.
[112] Chap. xi.

[113] Chap. xii.; cf. xxi. xxii.
[114] Chap. xxii.
[115] Chap. xxvii.

ception is that the prolation of the Logos — and afterward of the Spirit proximately from the Logos — is rather of the nature of a protrusion than an extrusion: the Godhead is, now, of a new shape, so to speak, but remains the Godhead still in its undivided and indivisible unity. As Tertullian expresses it sharply in the twenty-first chapter of the " Apology ": " Just as when a ray is shot forth (*porrigitur*) from the sun, it is a portion of the whole, but the sun will be in the ray because it is a ray of the sun, and is not separated from the substance but is extended (*extenditur*), so from Spirit [is extended] Spirit, and from God, God, as light is kindled from light. The *materiæ matrix* remains *integra et indefecta,* although you draw out from it a plurality of *traduces qualitatis;* and thus what has come forth (*profectum*) out of God is God, and the Son of God, and the two are one. Similarly as He is Spirit from Spirit and God from God, he is made a second member in manner of existence, in grade not state, and has not receded from the matrix but exceeded beyond it (*et a matrice non recessit sed excessit*)." In a word, the mode of the prolation is a stretching out of the Godhead, not a partition of the Godhead: the unity of the Godhead remains *integra et indefecta.*

The unity of the Godhead is thus preserved through the prolations themselves, which are therefore one in a " numerical unity," as it afterward came to be spoken of — though in Tertullian's usage this language would not be employed, but he would rather say that the persons differ in number, as first, second and third, while the substance remains undivided. It is precisely on the ground that in their view the prolations involved a division and separation of substance that he separates himself from the Valentinians.[116] " Valentinus," says he, " divides and separates his prolations from their author. . . . But this is the prolation of the truth, the guardian of the unity, wherein we declare that the Son is a prolation of the Father without being separated from Him. For God sent forth the Word (as the Paraclete also declares [117]) just as the root puts

[116] Chap. viii.
[117] I.e., this is a doctrine supported by the Montanistic prophecies.

forth the tree, and the fountain the river, and the sun the ray. For these are προβολαί of the substances from which they proceed. . . . But still the tree is not severed from the root, nor the river from the fountain, nor the ray from the sun; and neither the Word separated from God. . . . In like manner the Trinity, flowing down from the Father, through intertwined and connected steps, does not at all disturb the monarchy, while it at the same time guards the state of the economy." [118]

Harnack, therefore,[119] does considerably less than justice to Tertullian's conception, when he represents it as substantially the same as that of Valentinus, differing only in the number of emanations acknowledged — because, as Hippolytus certifies, the Valentinians "acknowledge that the one is the originator of all " and " the whole goes back to one." Nor does he improve matters when he adds in a note that " according to these doctrines, the unity is sufficiently preserved (1) if the several persons have one and the same substance, (2) if there is one possessor of the whole substance, i.e., if everything proceeds from him." Tertullian, on the contrary, is never weary of asseverating that his doctrine of unity demands much more than this — not merely that it is out of the one God that all proceeds — nor merely that what thus comes forth from God is of His substance, so that all of the emanations are of the substance of God — but specifically that this going forth from God of His prolations is merely an *extension* of the Godhead, not a division from it. Thus the unity, he says, is preserved through the prolations; and no separation from God is instituted by the prolations. These abide unbrokenly " portions " of the deity, not fragments broken off from the deity. Nor is Harnack much happier when he goes on [120] to say that Tertullian conceived God up to the prolation of the Logos " as yet . . . the only *person*." According to his explicit exposition of the life of God in eternity, Tertullian held that there never was a time when God was alone, except in the sense that there was no created universe about Him: in the beginning

[118] Chap. viii.   [119] ii. p. 258.   [120] ii. p. 259.

itself that Reason which the common people, simply translating the Greek of John's Gospel, call the Word, was with
Him, though within Him, as Another. Thus in the unity of the
Godhead there always was a distinction of persons, even before,
by the prolations of Son and Spirit, this distinction was manifested *ad extra.*

The distinctions of persons in the Godhead, accordingly,
as Tertullian conceived them, were not created by the prolations of Son and Spirit. These prolations merely brought into
manifestation the distinctions of persons already existing in
the Godhead. Neither did he suppose that these distinctions
would cease on the recession of these prolations back into the
Godhead — as Tertullian anticipates will take place when
their end is served. It is the prolations, not the personal distinctions, which in his thought have a beginning and ending;
and when he teaches that these prolations come forth at the
Father's will, fulfill their purpose and retire back into the Godhead, this cannot in any way affect his doctrine either of the
unity of God or of the Trinity in the unity. In all this process,
rather, he is tracing out only an incident in the life of God, a
temporary outflowing of God to do a specific work. The whole
exposition which Harnack gives of this transaction is colored
by misapprehension of Tertullian's import. It is indeed more
infelicitous than even this circumstance would indicate. No
doubt Tertullian's subordinationism is very marked. Though
he conceives the prolate Logos and the Spirit as truly God,
they are, in his view, God at the periphery of His being, going
forth, in a certain reduction of deity, for the world-work.[121]
But to speak of even the prolate Logos as a " Being which must
be a derived existence, which has already in some fashion a
finite element in itself, because it is the hypostatized Word of
creation, which has an origin "; and to add, " From the stand-

[121] Cf. Dorner, " Doctrine of the Person of Christ," Div. I. vol. ii. pp. 108,
186, 460. Dorner somewhat misses the point by failing to see that Tertullian
recognized the eternity of the personal distinction and so distinguished between the unprolated and the prolated Logos (see below, pp. 69 *sq.*): but even
Dorner perceives that there was some limit to Tertullian's subordinationism:
" An Arian Subordinationism was . . . foreign to his mind " (p. 74; cf. p.
108).

point of humanity this deity is God Himself, *i.e.*, a God whom men can apprehend and who can apprehend them, but from God's standpoint, which speculation can fix but not fathom, this deity is a subordinate, nay, even a temporary one " — is to go beyond all warrant discoverable in Tertullian's exposition. It is of the very essence of Tertullian's thought that there was no " finite element " in the Logos, or in the Spirit which constitutes the third in the Godhead — " as the fruit of the tree is third from the root, or as the stream out of the river is third from the fountain, or as the apex of the ray is third from the sun "; [122] that these prolations are, in a word, nothing but God Himself extended for the performance of a work — nothing, if the simile can be allowed, but the hand of God stretched out for the task of bringing a world into existence and guiding its course to its destined end. As such the Logos mediated between God and the world; but to make Tertullian teach, to use words of Bull's,[123] that " the very nature of the Son in itself is a mean between God and the creatures," that is to say, is something distinguishable alike from the supreme nature of God on the one side, and from the rest of created beings on the other — is to confound his whole conception. He not only did not teach that the Logos is a creature of nature different from that of God, of a derived existence, having an absolute origin, and destined to reach an end: but he explicitly teaches the contradictory of these things. The Logos existed eternally, he asseverates, in God: the prolation of the Logos, indeed, had a beginning and will have an end; but the Logos Himself who is prolated, is so far from being a derived existence, which has a finite element in it, and has an origin and is to make an end — that He is just God Himself prolated, that is, outstretched like a hand, to His work. And what is true of the Logos is true of the Spirit. He is not, as the Arians imagined, the creature of a creature, but just the still further prolated God — the tips of the fingers of the hand of God.[124]

[122] Chap. viii. *ad fin.*

[123] III. ix. 11 (E. T. p. 503).

[124] Irenæus makes use of the simile of God's hands to explain his conception of the relation of the Son and Spirit to God. Cf. IV. praef. § 4: " Man

(4) With this conception of the relation of the prolations to the divine essence Tertullian was certainly in a position to do complete justice to the deity of our Lord. Had the prolate Logos been to him a " middle substance " — something between God and man in its very nature — then it no doubt would have been impossible for him to do full justice to our Lord's deity as the incarnation of this Logos. But seeing that the Logos was to him God Himself prolated, one in substance with the primal deity itself, no question of the complete deity of the incarnated Logos could arise in his mind. " Nor shall we approximate," he says,[125] " to the opinions of the Gentiles, who, if at any time they be forced to confess God, yet will have other Gods below Him. The Godhead, however, has no gradation, for It is only one " and can, therefore, " in no case be less than Itself." Accordingly he is constant in declaring the Son, as He is God, to be " equal with " the Father.[126] All that is true of the Father, therefore, he would have us understand, is true also of the Son: they are not only of the same substance, but of the same power also; and all the attributes of the one belong also to the other. " The names of the Father," he says[127] — " God Almighty, the Most High, the Lord of Hosts, the King of Israel, He that Is — inasmuch as the Scriptures so teach, these, we say, belonged also to the Son, and in these the Son has come, and in these has ever acted, and thus manifested them in Himself to men. . . . When, therefore, you read Almighty God, and Most High, and God of Hosts, and King of Israel, and He that Is, consider whether there be not indicated by these the Son also, who in His own right is God

---

. . . was moulded by God's hands, i.e., by the Son and Spirit to whom He said, Let us make," etc. Cf. also IV. 20. 1; V. 1. 3; V. 5. 1; V. 28. 4. At a later date the Sabellians employed the figure of the alternately outstretched and withdrawn arm and hand as a figure of their notion of the successive movements of the divine revelation (Dorner, Div. I, vol. ii. pp. 155, 159, 168). Augustine *in Joannem*, § 53. 2–3, in criticising this Sabellian use of it, recognizes the propriety of the figure in itself.

[125] " Against Hermogenes," vii. (Bull, E. T. pp. 580–581).

[126] " Against Praxeas," chaps. vii. xxii.; " De Resurrectione Carnis," chap. vi.

[127] " Against Praxeas," chap. xvii. (Bull, E. T. p. 198).

Almighty, in that He is the Word of God Almighty." Again,[128] "' All things,' saith He, ' are delivered unto Me of the Father.' . . . The Creator hath delivered all things to Him who is not less than Himself, — to the Son: all things, to wit, which He created by Him, i.e., by His own Word." Accordingly, Tertullian does not hesitate to speak of the Son as God or to attribute to Him all that is true of God. He does not scruple, for example, to apply Rom. ix. 5 to Him — affirming Him in the words of that text to be God over all, blessed for ever.[129]

If it be asked how Tertullian made this recognition of the full equality of the Son with the Father consistent with the subordinationism which he had taken over from the Apologists along with their Logos Christology, the answer appears to turn on the identification of the Son with the prolate Logos. The strong subordination of the Son belongs to Him as prolated, not specifically as second in the Godhead. " It will therefore follow," says Tertullian in an illuminating passage,[130] " that by Him who is invisible, we must understand the Father *in the fullness of His majesty,* while we recognize the Son as visible *by reason of the dispensation of His derived existence (pro modulo derivationis);* even as it is not permitted us to contemplate the sun in the full amount of his substance which is in the heavens, but we can only endure with our eyes a ray by reason of the tempered condition of this portion which is projected from him to the earth. . . . We declare, however, that the Son also, *considered in Himself,* . . . is invisible, in that He is God, and the Word, and Spirit of God." In this passage it is affirmed that in Himself, because He is God, the Son shares all the qualities of God, and becomes " reduced God," if we can be allowed such a phrase, only *pro modulo derivationis,* that is to say, as the result of the prolation by virtue of which He is extended outwards for the purpose of action in and on the world. This passage will aid us also in apprehending how we are to understand Tertullian when he

---

128 " Against Marcion," iv. 25 (Bull, *loc. cit.*).
129 " Against Praxeas," xiii. xv.
130 Chap. xiv.

speaks of the Son as a " portion " only of the Godhead. Again it is, of course, only as prolate Logos that He is so spoken of: and as prolate Logos He is conceived under the figure of the ray which as a " portion " of the sun is " tempered " to the eyes of men. Similarly the prolate Logos is a " portion " of the Godhead, that is to say, not a separated part or even a particular part of the Godhead, but the Godhead itself " tempered " for its mission relatively to the world. This " portion " is not to be conceived, then, as a fragment of Godhead; it is in and of itself all that God is. Tertullian not only distinctly affirms this on all occasions, but expressly explains that it is neither separated from the Godhead nor in anything less than it, but is " equal to the Father, and has and possesses all that the Father has." [131] Nay, Tertullian tells us with crisp directness that this " *portio* " of the Godhead is Itself " consort in Its

---

[131] We are here quoting Bull, II. vii. 5 (E. T. p. 200), where, as well as pp. 536 *sq.*, the meaning of " portio " is discussed. It is discussed also in Hageman, pp. 182 *sq.*, who suggests, with a reference to *De virg. vel.*, chap. 4, *ad fin.*, that it is a technical logical term, and imports the " specific " as distinguished from the " general," in which case the Logos as a *portio* of the deity would rather be a " particularization " of deity than a " fragment " of deity. Dorner (Div. I. vol. ii. p. 78) thinks that the employment of such " inappropriate physical categories of the Son " is due to the " somewhat physical character of [Tertullian's] view of God," and " should be set rather to the account of his mode of expression, than of his mode of thought ": it " really disguised Tertullian's proper meaning " (cf. pp. 121–122). From the manner in which Tertullian uses the term " portio " it would seem probably to be a technical term in the Logos Christology and that would imply its currency in the debates of the day. It is interesting to observe in a " Sermon of the Arians " in " Augustini Opera Omnia," Migne ed., 1841, viii. coll. 677–684, which was in circulation in North Africa early in the fifth century what looks very much like a repudiation of the phraseology by the Arians — for Arianism was very much only the Logos Christology run to seed, the " left " side of the developing schemes of doctrine. In this document, at chap. 23, it is said: " The Son is not a part or a portion of the Father, but His own and beloved, perfect and complete, only-begotten Son. The Spirit is not a part or a portion of the Son, but the first and highest work (*opus*) of the only-begotten Son of God, before the rest of the universe." Augustine (" Contra Sermon. Arian.," xxvii. 23) answers only: " But what Catholic would say the Son is a part of the Father or the Holy Spirit part of the Son? A thing they [the Arians] think is to be so denied as if there were a question between us and them on it." It looks very much as if the whole past history of the use of this phraseology was out of memory in the opening fifth century.

fullness " (*plenitudinis consors*). " If you do not deny," he argues with Marcion,[132] " that the Creator's Son and Spirit and Substance is also His Christ, you must needs allow that those who have not acknowledged the Father have likewise failed to acknowledge the Son, seeing that they share the same substance (*per ejusdam substantiæ conditionem*): for if It baffled men's understanding in Its Plenitude, much more has a portion of It, especially since It is consort in the Plenitude." [133]

It cannot surprise us, therefore, when we observe Tertullian representing a distinctive way of designating our Lord as in part due merely to a desire to be clear and to avoid confusion in language. He is speaking [134] of the habit of distinguishing between God the Father and the Son by calling the former God and the latter Lord. There is no foundation for the distinction, he tells us, in the nature of things. Any one of the persons of the Godhead may with equal propriety be called either God or Lord. He " definitely declares that *two* are God, the Father and the Son, and with the addition of the Holy Spirit, even *three,* according to the principle of the divine οἰκονομία, which introduces number." He will never say, however, that there are two Gods or two Lords, yet " not as if," he explains, " it were untrue that the Father is God, and the Son is God, and the Holy Ghost is God, and each is God." This apparently can only mean that the three are all together the one God — and, indeed, one of his characteristic phrases is the famous *deus ambo* or even *tres.*[135] But though Christ is thus rightly called God, it is best, he thinks, in order to avoid mistakes, to speak of Him as Lord when the Father is mentioned at the same time, and to call Him God only when He is mentioned alone. For there is no gradation in thé Godhead, as Tertullian elsewhere remarks,[136] although there are three " grades " in the Godhead: which is as much as to say that considered in themselves, those who are distinguished as

132 " Against Marcion," iii. 6, *ad fin.*
133 Cf. Bull, II. vii. 6 (E. T. pp. 201 *sq.*).
134 " Against Praxeas," chap. xiii.
135 " Against Praxeas," xiii. *med.*
136 " Against Hermogenes," vii. (quoted above).

first, second, and third — that is to say, in the modes of their
existence as source and prolations of the first and second order
— are yet consorts in the plenitude of God.[137]

On this basis Tertullian, in developing his doctrine of
the person of Christ in the formula of "Deus homo, unus
Christus," could strenuously insist on the complete deity as
well as perfect humanity of this one divine-human person.
And in this insistence we may find the culminating proof that
he sought to do full justice to the true deity of Christ. He
approaches this subject[138] in the course of a confutation of
the Monarchian attempt to find a distinction between Father
and Son by understanding the Father to be the divine Spirit
incarnated and the Son to be the incarnating flesh. Thus, says
Tertullian, while contending that the Father and Son are one
and the same, they do, in fact, divide them and so fall into
the hands of the Valentinians, making Jesus, the man, and
Christ, the inhabiting Spirit, two. Proceeding to expound the
true relation between the incarnated Spirit and the incarnating

---

[137] Bull, IV. ii. 5 (E. T. pp. 580–581) treats with great care the apparent
contradiction between Tertullian's assertion in "Against Hermogenes," vii.,
that "the Godhead has no gradations," and the assertion in "Against Praxeas,"
ii., that the persons of the Godhead are three "not in state but in gradation."
Tertullian, Bull tells us, means in the latter passage by "*gradation, order,* but
not greater or less Godhead." "For," continues Bull, "whom he acknowledges
to be three in gradation, Them he denies to be different in state. But with
Tertullian, as we have seen, for a thing not to be different from another
in state, means, not to be set under it, but to be on a par and equal to it.
Hence in the same passage, presently after, he expressly says, that the three
Persons of the Holy Trinity are all of *one power;* and consequently that no
One of Them is more powerful or excellent than Another. Therefore the Godhead 'has no gradation,' that is, 'is in no case less than Itself,' as Tertullian distinctly explains himself; yet there are gradations in the Godhead, that
is, a certain order of the Persons, of whom One derives His origin from Another; in such wise that the Father is the first Person, existing of Himself;
the Son second from the Father, whilst the Holy Ghost is third, who proceeds from the Father through the Son, or from the Father and the Son."
This is a very favorable specimen of Bull's reasoning: and Tertullian's language may be made consistent with itself on this hypothesis. On the whole,
however, it seems more likely that the real state of the case in Tertullian's
thought was that indicated in the text. In the Godhead there are no gradations: but after prolations grades of being are instituted.

[138] Chap. xxvii.

flesh, he next argues that the process of incarnation was not that of a transformation of the divine Spirit into flesh, because God neither ceases to be what He was nor can He be any other thing than what He is. Accordingly when the Word became flesh, this was accomplished not by His becoming transmuted into flesh but by His clothing Himself with flesh. No less is it insupposable, he argues, that the incarnation was accomplished by any mixture of the two substances, divine Spirit and flesh, forming a third substance intermediate between the two.[139] At that rate Jesus would have ceased to be God while not becoming man: whereas the Scriptures represent Him to have been both God and man. Accordingly we must believe that there was no confusion of the two in the person of Jesus, but such a conjunction of God and man that, the property of each nature being wholly preserved, the divine nature continued to do all things suitable to itself, while the human nature, on the other hand, exhibited all the affections that belong to it. Jesus, thus, was in one these two — man of the flesh, God of the Spirit: and in Him coexist two substances, viz., the divine and the human,[140] the one of which is immortal and the other mortal. Throughout this whole discussion the integrity of the divine nature — immortal, impassible, unchangeable — is carefully preserved and its union in the one person Jesus Christ with a human nature, mortal, passible, capable of change, is so explained as to preserve it from all confusion, intermixture or interchange with it. We could not have a clearer exhibition of Tertullian's zeal to do full justice to the true deity of Christ.

(5) It scarcely seems necessary to add a separate detailed statement of how Tertullian conceived of the Holy Spirit.

[139] Accordingly we must not understand the phrase " Homo Deo mixtus," which occurs in the " Apology," chap. xxi., to imply that the two substances were " mixed," so as to make a *tertium quid*. What he means to say is only that Jesus Christ was neither man nor God alone, but the two together. Cf. Bethune-Baker, " The Meaning of Homoousios in the ' Constantinopolitan ' Creed," in " Texts and Studies," J. A. Robinson, ed., vii. 1, p. 22, note.

[140] Chap. xxix. *ad init.*

While we cannot say with Harnack [141] that Tertullian exhibits no trace of independent interest in the doctrine of the Spirit, it is yet true that he speaks much less fully and much less frequently of Him than of the Logos,[142] and that his doctrine of the Spirit runs quite parallel with that of the Logos. He has spoken of Him, moreover, ordinarily in connections where the doctrine of the Logos is also under discussion and therefore his modes of thought on this branch of the subject have already been perhaps sufficiently illustrated. The *distinct personality* of the Spirit is as clearly acknowledged as that of the Logos Himself. In the οἰκονομία the unity is distributed not into a duality, but into a trinity, providing a place not for two only but for three — the Father, Son, and Holy Ghost; who differ from one another not in condition, substance, or power but in degree, form, and aspect.[143] And everywhere the third person is treated as just as distinct a personality as the second and first. There is no clear passage carrying this distinct personality back into *eternity*. That Tertullian thought of the personality of the Spirit precisely as he did of that of the Logos is here our only safe guide. On the other hand, there is no lack of passages in which the *unity of substance* is insisted upon relatively to the Spirit also.[144] After explaining that the substance of the Son is just the substance of the Father, he adds: " The same remark is made by me with respect to the third degree, because I believe the Spirit to be from no other source than from the Father through the Son." [145] So again: " The Spirit is the third from God and the Son, as the fruit from the tree is the third from the root, and the stream from the river is third from the fountain, and the apex from the ray is third from the sun. Nothing, however, is separated from the matrix from which it draws its properties; and thus, the

---

[141] ii. p. 261, note [4].

[142] Cf. Nösgen, " Geschichte der Lehre vom heiligen Geiste," p. 21.

[143] " Against Praxeas," chap. ii. *ad fin.*, cf. chap. iii. near end, chaps. viii. xi. *ad fin.*, xiii. xxx. Cf. Stier, *op. cit.*, p. 92, note.

[144] " Against Praxeas," chaps. ii. *ad fin.*, iii. *ad fin.*, iv. *ad init.*, viii. ix. *ad init.*, etc.

[145] Chap. iv. *ad init.*

Trinity flows down from the Father through *consertos et conexos gradus* and in no respects injures the monarchy while protecting the economy." [146] On this view the *true deity* of the Spirit is emphasized as fully as that of the Logos, and Tertullian repeatedly speaks of Him likewise shortly as God,[147] as " the Third Name in the Godhead and the Third Degree of the Divine Majesty." [148] Accordingly when he " definitely declares that two are God, the Father and the Son," he adds,[149] " and with the addition of the Holy Ghost, even *three,* according to the principle of the divine economy, which introduces number, in order that the Father may not, as you perversely infer, be believed to have Himself been born, and to have suffered." To Tertullian, therefore, the alternative was not the complete deity of the Spirit or His creaturehood; but the unity of Monarchianism or the Trinity in the unity of the economy. He never thinks of meeting the Monarchian assault by denying the full deity of the Spirit, but only by providing a distinction of persons within the unity of the Godhead. The most instructive passages are naturally those in which all three persons are brought together, of which there are a considerable number.[150] To quote but one of these, he explains that " the connection of the Father in the Son, and of the Son in the Paraclete, produces three coherent Persons, [distinct, nevertheless] one from the other: these three are one substance, [*unum*], not one person, [*unus*], as it is said, ' I and my Father are one [*unum*],' in respect of unity of substance not singularity of number." [151] There can, in short, be no question that Tertullian had applied to the Spirit with full consciousness all that he had thought out concerning the Son, and that His doctrine of God was fully settled into a doctrine

---

[146] Chap. viii. *ad fin.*

[147] He seems to be the first in writings which have chanced to come down to us to apply the name " God " to the Spirit; but this is mere accident.

[148] Chap. xxx. *ad fin.*

[149] Chap. xiii. *med.*

[150] E.g., chaps. ii. *ad init., et fin.,* iii. *ad fin.,* viii. *ad fin.,* ix. *ad init.,* xiii. *med.,* xxv. xxx.

[151] Chap. xxv. *ad init.*

of Trinity. His mode of speaking of the Spirit introduces no new difficulty in construing his doctrine — which is something that cannot be said of all his predecessors.

By such expositions as these, Tertullian appears, in seeking to do justice to the elements of doctrine embalmed in the Rule of Faith, fairly to pass beyond the natural reach of the Logos speculation and to open the way to a higher conception. A symbol of this advance may not unfairly be discovered in the frequent appearance in his pages of the new term " Trinity." The Greek equivalent of this term occurs in his contemporary Hippolytus,[152] but scarcely elsewhere, at this early date, to designate the distinctions in the Godhead — unless indeed we account the single instance of its employment by Theophilus of Antioch a preparation for such an application of it.[153] In any event, there is a fine appropriateness in the sudden apparition of the term in easy and frequent use,[154] for the first time, in the pages of an author whose discussions make so decided an approximation toward the enunciation of that doctrine to denote which this term was so soon to become exclusively consecrated. The insistence of Tertullian upon the οἰκονομία in the monarchy — on unity of substance, with all that is implied in unity of substance, persisting in three distinct persons who coexist from eternity — certainly marks out the lines within which the developed doctrine of the Trinity moves, and deserves to be signalized by the emergence into literature of the term by which the developed doctrine of the Trinity should ever afterward be designated.

It is possible that something of the same symbolical significance may attach also to Tertullian's use of his favorite term οἰκονομία. Of course, οἰκονομία is not a new word; but it is used by Tertullian in an unwonted sense — a sense scarcely found

[152] " Contra Noëtum," chap. 14.

[153] " Ad Autol.," ii. 15. Here the term τρίας first occurs in connection with distinctions in the Godhead; and it is customary, therefore, to say that here first it is applied to express the Trinity. So, e.g., Kahnis, Harnack, Loofs, Seeberg. As Nösgen (pp. 13–14) points out, however, it is by no means certain that the word here has any technical import.

[154] E.g., " Against Praxeas," chaps. ii. iii. xi. xii. etc.

elsewhere except in his contemporary Hippolytus,[155] and, perhaps as a kind of preparation for their use of it, in a single passage of Tatian.[156] Tertullian constantly employs it, as we have seen, to designate, as over against the monarchy, the mystery of the Trinity in the unity. There can be no question of its general implication in his pages; but it is, no doubt, a little difficult to determine the precise significance of the term itself which he employs. The fundamental sense of the word is " disposition "; but in its application it receives its form either from the idea of " administration," or from that of " structure." If it is used by Tertullian in the former shade of meaning, its employment by him need not have great significance for his Trinitarian doctrine. He would, in that case, only say by it that the monarchy of God is administered by a disposition of the Godhead into three several personalities, Father, Son, and Holy Ghost, through whom the single Lordship is carried on, as it were, by deputy; while the precise relation of these personalities to one another and to the Godhead itself would be left to the context to discover.

An argument which occurs in the third chapter of the tract, " Against Praxeas," seems to many to suggest that it was in this sense that the term was employed by Tertullian. Tertullian here explains that " monarchy has no other meaning than single and unique rule "; " but for all that," he adds, " this monarchy does not preclude him whose government it is . . . from administering his own monarchy by whatever agents he will ": and much less can the integrity of a monarchy suffer by the association in it of a Son, since it is still held in common by two who are so really one (*tam unicis*). Applying these general principles to the monarchy of God, he argues that this monarchy is therefore by no means set aside by the circumstance that it is administered by means of legions and hosts of angels "; and much less can it be thought to be injured by the participation in it of the Son and Holy Spirit, to whom the second and third places are assigned, but who are in-

---

[155] " Contra Noëtum," chaps. 8 and 14.
[156] " Ad Græc.," 5.

separably joined with the Father, in His substance. " Do you really suppose," he asks, " that those who are naturally members of the Father's own substance, His congeners,[157] instruments of His might, nay, His power itself, and the entire system of His monarchy, are the overthrow and destruction thereof? " It seems tolerably clear that Tertullian is not here comparing the economy with the administrative agents of a monarchy: with them he rather compares the hosts of angels through whom the divine monarchy is administered. The economy is rather compared to the sharing of the monarchy itself between father and son as co-regents on a single throne. In that case, so far is economy on his lips from bearing the sense of administration that it is expressly distinguished from it, and referred to something in the Godhead deeper than its administrative functions. The illustration, therefore, emphasizes, indeed, the personal distinctions of the economy — they are comparable to the distinction between father and son in a conjoint rule — but it suggests equally the penetration of this distinction behind all matters of administration into the Godhead, the Ruling Being, itself.

Nor is this impression set aside by the implication of the other figures employed by Tertullian to explain the relations of the persons in the Godhead. When he compares them to the root, the tree, and the fruit, or to the fountain, the river, and the stream, or to the sun, the ray, and the apex, his mind seems undoubtedly to be upon the prolated Logos and Spirit; these figures indeed, so constantly upon his lips, seem inapplicable to eternal distinctions, lying behind the prolations. But it must be remembered, first, that these illustrations are not original with Tertullian, but are taken over by him from the Apologists along with their Logos speculation — although they are doubtless developed and given new point by him; next, that the precise point which he adduces them to illustrate is not the whole import of the economy, but the preservation of the unity of substance within the economy of three persons; and finally, that the ordinary engagement of his mind with the

---

[157] *pignora* = pledges of his love, i.e., his close relations.

Trinity of Persons, in what we may call its developed form — its mode of manifestation in God acting *ad extra* — need not by any means exclude from his thought a recognition of an ontological basis, in the structure of the Godhead itself, for this manifested Trinity. And if in one passage he presses his illustrations to the verge of suggesting a separation of the Son from the Father — intimating that the Son may be affected by the sufferings of the God-man while the Father remains in impassible blessedness;[158] in another, on the other hand, he seems expressly to carry back the distinction of persons into the eternal Godhead itself — affirming that God was never "alone" save in the sense of independence of all external existence, but there was always with Him, because in Him, that other self which afterward proceeded from Him for the making of the world.[159] The fullest recognition, therefore, that Tertullian habitually thought of the Trinity in, so to speak, its developed form — with the Logos and the Spirit prolate and working in the world — by no means precludes the possibility that the very term οἰκονομία connoted in his hands something more fundamental than a distinction in the Godhead constituted by these prolations.

And certainly the word was currently employed in senses that lent it a color which may very well have given it to Tertullian the deeper connotation of internal structure, when he applied it to the Godhead. To perceive this, we have only to recall its application to express the proper adjustment of the parts of a building, as Vitruvius, for example, uses it,[160] or to express what we call the disposition, that is the plan or construction of a literary composition, as it is used, say, by Cicero, when he speaks of the οἰκονομία *perturbatior* of his letter,[161] or by Quintilian,[162] when he ascribes to the old Latin comedies a better οἰκονομία than the new exhibited.[163] A very

[158] Chap. xxix.
[159] Chap. v.
[160] "De Architectura," I. ii. 1.
[161] "Ad Att.," vi. 1.
[162] "Inst.," I. viii. 9.
[163] This sense is discussed by Daniel, as below, note [166], under his divi-

interesting instance of the employment of the word in this sense of "structure" occurs in the *Letter of the Church of Smyrna,* giving an account of the martyrdom of Polycarp.[164] The martyrs were so torn by the scourge, says this passage, that "the οἰκονομία of their flesh was visible even so far as the inward veins and arteries." Lightfoot translates here, "*the internal structure and mechanism,*" and refers us to Eusebius' paraphrase, which tells us the martyrs were so lacerated that "the hidden inward parts of the body, both their bowels and their members, were exposed to view."[165] There can be no doubt that this very common usage of the term was well known to Tertullian the rhetorician, and it may very well be that when he adopted it to express the distribution of the Godhead into three persons it was because it suggested to him rather the inner structure, so to speak, of the Godhead itself, than merely an external arrangement for the administration of the divine dominion.

That Tertullian's usage of the term implies as much as this is recognized, indeed, by the most of those who have busied themselves with working out the interesting history of this word in the usage of the Fathers.[166] Dr. W. Gass, for example,

---

sion 4, p. 160, where a number of examples are given. See also Lightfoot, on Eph. i. 10, and the Lexicons.

[164] Chap. ii. See the note of Lightfoot on the passage in his great work on "Ignatius" (II. ii. p. 950).

[165] "Historia Ecclesiastica," iv. 15; McGiffert's Translation, p. 189*a*.

[166] An account of the several attempts to trace the history of the word is given by Gass in the article referred to in the next note. The more important are: von Cölln in Ersch and Gruber sub. voc. *Œconomia;* H. A. Daniel in his "Tatianus der Apologet," pp. 159 *sq.;* Münscher in his "Dogmengeschichte," iii. pp. 137 *sq.;* Gass's own extended article; and Lightfoot in his posthumously published volume entitled "Notes on Epistles of St. Paul," p. 319 (on Eph. i. 10), with which should be compared his notes on Col. i. 25, Ign. "ad Eph." xviii. (II. i. p. 75), and "Martyr. Polycarp.," ii. (II. ii. p. 950). The discussion of Gass is by far the fullest, but needs the preceding ones to supply the earlier philological development, and Lightfoot's clear statement as a supplement. See also the Bishop of Lincoln's (Kaye's) "Account of the Writings of Justin Martyr," pp. 173, *sq.,* and Baur's "Dreieinigkeit," i. p. 178, note. Hagemann "Die Römische Kirche," pp. 136, 150, 167, 175, etc., as per index) constantly represents the οἰκονομία as (even in Tertullian) merely "the sum of the divine acts which have reference to the government of the world," "the sum of the ex-

after tracing the word up to Tertullian and finding it employed up to that point to express " the outward-going revelatory activity of God, whether creative and organizing or redemptive," [167] remarks upon the sudden change that meets us in Tertullian. " It has been justly thought remarkable," he continues, " that this same expression is applied by Tertullian to the inner relations of the Godhead itself. He employs ' economy' as an indispensable organon of the Christian knowledge of God, in his controversy with Praxeas." Then, after quoting the passages in the " Against Praxeas," chaps. ii. and iii., he proceeds: " Monarchy and economy are therefore the two interests on the combination and proper balancing of which the Trinitarian conception of God depends; by the former the unity of the divine rule, by the latter the right of an immanent distinction is established, and it is only necessary that the latter principle should not be pressed so far as to do violence to the former." Without laying too much stress on so nice a point, it would seem not unnatural therefore to look upon Tertullian's predilection for the term οἰκονομία as, like his usage of the term *Trinitas*, symptomatic of his tendency to take a deeper view of the Trinitarian relation than that which has in later times come to be spoken of as " merely economical."

We derive thus from our study of Tertullian's modes of statement a rather distinct impression that there is discoverable in them an advance toward the conception of an immanent Trinity. The question becomes at once in a new degree pressing how far this advance is to be credited to Tertullian himself, and how far it represents only modes of thought and even forms of statement current in the Christianity of his

ternal revelations of God," " the internal distributions of the original unitary Godhead into a purely divine and a finite substance, and the division of the latter into a graded plurality of beings which make up the pleroma " — which last is the Gnostic way of expressing it.

[167] In an article on " Das patristische Wort οἰκονομία," in Hilgenfeld's *Zeitschrift für wissenschaftliche Theologie*, xvii. (1874), pp. 478 *sq.*

time, which push themselves to observation in his writings only because he chances to be dealing with themes which invite a rather fuller expression than ordinary of this side of the faith of Christians. We shall return to this question in the Third Article.

THIRD ARTICLE[168]

In the First and Second Articles it has been pointed out that there is discoverable in Tertullian's modes of statement a rather distinct advance towards the conception of an immanent Trinity. We wish now to inquire how far this advance is to be credited to Tertullian himself, and how far it represents modes of thought and forms of statement current in his time, and particularly observable in Tertullian only because he chances to be dealing with themes which invited a fuller expression than ordinary of this side of the faith of Christians.

We have already seen that there is a large traditional element in Tertullian's teaching; that even the terms, " Trinity " and " Economy," in which his doctrine of the distinctions within the Godhead is enshrined, are obviously used by him as old and well-known terms; and that he betrays no consciousness of enunciating new conceptions in his development of his doctrine, but rather writes like a man who is opposing old truth to new error. Indeed he openly asserts that this is the case. If we are to take his own point of view in the matter, we cannot hesitate to assert, then, that he has himself made no advance, but is simply enforcing the common Christian faith against the innovations of destructive heresy. Of course this common Christian faith, which he is zealous thus to enforce, is fundamentally the Rule of Faith. But it can scarcely be denied that it is more than this; Tertullian's own view clearly is that his expositions embody also the common understanding of the Rule of Faith. He is not consciously offering any novel constructions of it, or building up on his own account a higher structure upon it. No doubt he is doing his best to state the common faith clearly and forcibly, and to apply its elements tellingly in the controversy in which he was engaged; and he may certainly in so doing have clarified

[168] As originally printed in *The Princeton Theological Review*, April, 1906.

it, and even filled it with new significance, not to say devéloped from it hitherto unsuspected implications. How far, however, this can be affirmed of him can be determined only by some survey of the modes of thought and statement of his predecessors and contemporaries who have dealt with the same doctrines.

What first strikes us when we turn to the Apologists with this end in view is that most of Tertullian's modes of statement can be turned up, in one place or another, in the Apologetic literature. We say " in one place or another " advisedly, for the peculiarity of the case is that they do not all appear in the pages of a single writer, but scattered through the writings of all. Thus if the term τρίας appears in Theophilus, it is in Tatian that the term οἰκονομία meets us in a sense similar to that in which Tertullian uses it. If Athanagoras seems to struggle to carry back the divine relationships into eternity,[169] and Theophilus by the use of the distinction between the λόγος ἐνδιάθετος and the λόγος προφορικός at least seeks a basis for the distinction of God and His Logos prior to the prolation of the Logos, Justin leaves us uncertain whether he thought of the Logos as having any sort of being before the moment of His begetting. The simile by which the relation of the Logos to God is compared to the relation of the light to the sun is already found in Justin: but it is to Tatian that we must go to discover such a careful exposition of the relation of the Logos to God as the following: " He came into being by way of impartation (κατὰ μερισμόν) not of abscission (κατὰ ἀποκοπήν) ; for what is cut off is separated from the primitive (τοῦ πρώτου), but what is imparted, receiving its share of the Economy,[170] does not make him from whom it is taken de-

---

[169] Cf. Bethune-Baker, " An Introduction to the Early History of Christian Doctrine," p. 129.

[170] This is a very obscure phrase: οἰκονομίας τὴν αἵρεσιν προσλαβόν. Clericus declared that in his day it had never been successfully explained. Daniel (p. 164) explains: " What has arisen through participation, as one light is kindled from another, has of course part in the nature of the thing from which it is derived, and is of the same nature with it; but does not make the thing from which it is taken any poorer in this nature." Baur translates the whole passage thus: " What is cut off is separated from the substance, but what is distinguished as a portion, what by free self-determination receives the œconomy,

ficient." [171] The result is that while we could from fragments, derived this from one and that from another of the Apologists, piece together a statement of doctrine which would assimilate itself to Tertullian's, we could verify this statement from no one of the Apologists, but, on the contrary, elements of it would be more or less sharply contradicted by one or another of them. There are, in other words, hints scattered through the Apologists that men were already reaching out toward the forms of statement that meet us in Tertullian, but only in him are these hints brought together. We assent, therefore, when Harnack [172] says: "We cannot at bottom say that the Apologists possessed a doctrine of the Trinity." Only we must in this statement emphasize both the terms "at bottom" and "doctrine." There are everywhere discoverable in the Apologists suggestions of a Trinitarian mode of thought: but these are not brought together into a formulated doctrine which governed their thinking of the being of God.

The phenomena are such, in one word, as to force us to perceive in the writings of the Apologists — as has been widely recognized by students of their works — a double deposit of conceptions relative to the mode of the divine existence. There is their own philosophical construction, which is, briefly, the Logos speculation. And underlying that, there is the Christian tradition — to which they desired to be faithful and which was ever intruding into their consciousness and forcing from them acknowledgment of elements of truth which formed no part of their philosophical confession of faith. This divided character of the Apologetic mind is by no one more clearly expounded than by the late Dr. Purves in his lectures on "The Testimony of Justin Martyr to Early Christianity." Justin was, as Harnack remarks, [173] "the most Christian among

---

the plurality in the unity, causes no loss to that from which it comes." Bethune-Baker (p. 126) renders: "Receiving as its function one of administration," and explains: "The part of οἰκονομία, administration of the world, revelation."

[171] "Or. c. Gr." 8.
[172] ii. 209, note 1 at the end.
[173] ii. p. 203, note 2.

the Apologists," and this feature in his dealing with doctrine is perhaps especially marked in him: but it is shared also by all his congeners. Dr. Purves fully recognizes that Justin was, in his thinking about God, first of all the philosopher: and that his " own thought strongly *tended away from the doctrine of a Trinity* " [174] — toward a sort of ditheism which embraced a doctrine of " the consubstantiality of the Logos and the Father of all." And yet there crops up repeatedly in his writings testimony to the worship by the Christians of three divine persons. This testimony is particularly remarkable with reference to the Spirit. For " his own theology had really no place for the Spirit," and yet " Justin speaks of the Spirit as not only an object of worship but as the power of Christian life." " Thus Justin," concludes Dr. Purves,[175] " in spite of himself testifies to the threefold object of Christian worship. He even finds in Plato an adumbration of the first, second and third powers in the universe, though in doing so he misunderstands and misinterprets that philosopher. Justin's own conception is vague, or, when not vague, unscriptural in certain important points. . . . But . . . he . . . effectively testifies to the traditional faith of the Church in the Father, Son, and Spirit as the threefold object of Christian worship, and the threefold source of Christian life." What was true of Justin was true, each in his measure, of the other Apologists. " Two conceptions of Deity were struggling with each other " [176] in their minds. Dominated by their philosophical inheritance, they could only imperfectly assimilate the Christian revelation, which therefore made itself felt only in spots and patches in their teaching. What was needed that the Christian doctrine of God should come to its rights was some change in the conditions governing the conceptions of the leaders of Christian thinking by which they might measurably be freed from the philosophical bondage in which they were holden.

The appearance of juster views precisely in the expositions of Tertullian would seem thus to be connected ultimately with

[174] *Op. cit.,* p. 275.   [176] P. 145.
[175] P. 279.

a certain shifting of interest manifested in Tertullian as compared with the Apologists. The Apologists were absorbed largely in the cosmological aspects of Christian doctrine.[177] In Tertullian these retire into the background and the soteriological interest comes markedly forward. In their cosmological speculations, the Apologists, for example, scarcely felt the need of a Holy Spirit; all that they had clamantly in mind to provide for, they conceived of as the natural function of the Logos. Their recognition of the Holy Spirit was therefore largely conventional and due to allegiance to the Christian tradition. A new point of view has been attained when Tertullian, out of his soteriological interest, thinks of the Spirit profoundly as the sanctifier of men, the " vicarious power " of the Logos for applying His redemptive work. This shifting of interest inevitably led to a new emphasis on the distinctive personalities of the three persons of the deity, and to their separation from the world-process that justice might be done to their perfect deity as the authors — each in his appropriate sphere — of salvation.[178] It is instructive that in his " Apology," addressed like the chief works of the Apologists to the heathen, Tertullian still moves, like them, largely within the cosmological sphere: whereas in his tract, " Against Praxeas," addressed to fellow-Christians, the soteriological point of view comes more to its right. And it is equally instructive that among preceding writers it is in Irenæus who,

---

[177] General discriminations like this must, of course, not be pressed to extremes. See, e.g., Purves, op. cit., p. 277. Cf. Bethune-Baker, " An Introduction to the Early History of Christian Doctrine," p. 125.

[178] For the point of view of the text cf., e.g., Nösgen, " Geschichte .der Lehre vom heiligen Geiste," pp. 24 sq.: " Precisely with this Church father [Tertullian] there begins, on the ground of Christian experience, to break through the recognition of the inner necessity of the Holy Spirit for the nature of the Triune God. . . . His interest in the third Person of the Trinity hangs on the fact that the Holy Spirit leads the children of God (credentes agat). . . . Accordingly it must not be made a reproach to him that he permits the immanent relation statedly to shine through only as the background of the self-revelation of the Triune One. . . . It is precisely because he does this that he first marked out definitely the point of departure from which the peculiarity of the Holy Spirit as God and as trinitarian Person could be really grasped." Cf. Kahnis, p. 296.

with emphasis, eschewed philosophy and sought to build up a specifically Biblical doctrine, that we find forms of statement concerning the three persons whom Christians worshiped as the one God most nearly approaching the construction adumbrated by Tertullian. Perhaps it is not too much to say that the supplanting among Christian thinkers of the Logos speculation by a doctrine of immanent Trinity was largely mediated by the shifting of interest from the cosmological to the soteriological aspect of Christian truth, and that in Tertullian we see for the first time clearly marked the beginning of the process by which this change was wrought.

This suggestion receives notable support from a comparison of Tertullian's modes of statement with those of his contemporary Hippolytus, in his treatise, " Against Noëtus " — a treatise which, as it arose out of conditions remarkably like those which called out Tertullian's tract, " Against Praxeas," contains so much that is similar to what we find in that tract that it is hard to shake ourselves entirely free from the illusion that one borrows from the other. Hippolytus' relation as a pupil to Irenæus,[179] whose language in regard to the Trinitarian relationships approaches that of Tertullian most nearly of all previous writers, and from whom Tertullian himself frankly draws, is doubtless another factor of importance in accounting for the resemblance between the two tracts. But as we have already suggested, we are persuaded that this resemblance, so far as it is real, is mainly due to the fact that Tertullian and Hippolytus, alike heirs of the Logos-speculation, and alike determined to do justice to the deposit of truth in the Rule of Faith, were alike called upon in the new conditions of the early third century to uphold the common faith of Christendom against the subtlest form of the Monarchian attack. If this be true, nothing could hold out a better promise of enabling us to discriminate in Tertullian's statements the traditional element from his personal contribution than a comparison of them with those of Hippolytus.

The first thing that strikes us in attempting such a com-

[179] Cf., e.g., Harnack, " Chronologie," ii. pp. 213, 223.

parison is the extent of the common element in the two. We meet in Hippolytus the same terminology which we have found in Tertullian. He, too, employs the term Trinity; [180] and, as well, Tertullian's favorite term, " the Economy " [181] — although perhaps not with the same profundity of meaning; even Tertullian's phrase, " the mystery of the economy." [182] We almost feel ourselves still on Tertullian's ground when we read in Hippolytus: " For who will not say that there is one God? Yet he will not on that account deny the Economy." [183] This feeling is increased by the occurrence in Hippolytus of similar illustrations of the relations of the Logos to the primal Godhead. " But when I say *another*," he remarks, " I do not mean that there are two Gods, but that it is only as light of light, or as water from a fountain, or as a ray from the sun." [184] Even the same proof-texts are employed in the same manner. Thus the declaration in Jno. x. 30, " I and the Father are one," is treated quite in Tertullian's manner. " Understand that He did not say, ' I and the Father *am one*, but *are one*.' For the word *are* is not said of one person, but it refers to *two persons*, and one power." [185] So again, like Tertullian, Hippolytus insists strongly on the true deity of Christ and supports it after much the same fashion. He calls Him " God," [186] " the Almighty," [187] appeals just like Tertullian to Mt. xi. 27, and like Tertullian even applies to Him the great text, Rom. ix. 5, commenting: " He who is over all, God blessed, has been born; and having been made man, He is God for ever." [188] His doctrine of the Person of Christ, moreover, is indistinguishable from Tertullian's. " Let us believe, then, dear brethren," he says, " according to the tradition of the apostles, that God the Word came down from heaven, into the holy Virgin Mary, in order that, taking the flesh from her, and assuming also a human, by which I mean a rational soul, and becoming

[180] " Contra Noëtum," chap. 14.
[181] Chaps. 3, 4, 8, 14.
[182] Chap. 4, no fewer than three times.
[183] Chap. 3.
[184] Chap. 11.
[185] Chap. 7.
[186] Chap. 8.
[187] Chap. 6.
[188] Chap. 6.

thus all that man is with the exception of sin, he . . . was manifested as God in a body, coming forth too as a perfect man. For it was not in mere appearance or by conversion, but in truth, that He became man." [189] Underlying and sustaining all these detailed resemblances, moreover, is the great fundamental likeness between the two writers arising from their common application of the Logos speculation to the facts of the Christian tradition, and their common opposition to the Monarchian heresy.

With a little closer scrutiny, however, marked differences between the two writers begin to develop.

In the first place, we observe that Hippolytus does not very well know what to do with the Holy Spirit. He repeats the triune formula with great emphasis: " We cannot otherwise think of one God," he says, " but by believing in truth in Father and Son and Holy Spirit." " The Economy of agreement is gathered up into one God: for God is One: for He who commands is the Father, and He who obeys is the Son, and that which teaches wisdom is the Spirit." [190] " We accordingly see the Word incarnate, and through Him we know the Father, and believe in the Son and worship the Holy Ghost." [191] He manifestly desires to be led in all things by the Scriptural revelation: from no other quarter, he declares, than the oracles of God will he derive instruction in such things, and therefore as they declare to us what the Father wills us to believe, that will he believe, and as He wills the Son to be glorified, so will he glorify Him, and as He wills the Holy Spirit to be bestowed, so will he receive Him. [192] Nevertheless it is quite clear that he can hardly assimilate the Biblical doctrine of the Spirit, and when he comes to speak out his mind upon Him, he makes it apparent that he does not at all think of Him as a person. It is curious to observe, indeed, the circumlocutions he employs to avoid calling Him a person. " I shall not indeed say there are two Gods, but one; two persons, however, while the third economy is the grace of the Holy Spirit. For the Father indeed

[189] Chap. 17.
[190] Chap. 14.
[191] Chap. 12.
[192] Chap. 9.

is one, but there are two persons, because there is the Son also: and then there is the third, the Holy Spirit." [193] From a passage like this, Hippolytus' fundamental thought would seem to have been, like Justin's, a kind of ditheism, somewhat violently transformed into a tritheism under the pressure of the traditional faith.

When we look further we perceive that even this ditheism is far from pure. We observe a notable effort to avoid that clear assertion of substantial unity of the Father and Son which constitutes the very core of Tertullian's doctrine. When the declaration of our Lord in Jno. x. 30, " I and the Father are one," is quoted,[194] Hippolytus' exposition is: " It refers to two persons and one " — not substance, as Tertullian would have said, but — " *power.*" And then Hippolytus calls in illustratively Jno. xvii. 22, 23, where our Lord expresses His desire that His disciples may be one, even as He and the Father are one, and asks triumphantly, " Are all [the disciples] one body in respect of substance, or is it that we become one in the power and disposition of likemindedness? " [195] " In the same manner " — thus he applies the illustration — " the Son . . . confessed that He was in the Father in power and disposition." This view of the unity of Father and Son as consisting in unity in mind and power only is consistently preserved throughout; [196] and the revelatory character of the Son is in harmony with this hung, not on His identity with God, but on His character as the *image* of God.[197] Accordingly, we discover that the Logos is not thought by Hippolytus to have been eternally with God, but is assigned an absolute beginning at a definite point of time previous to the creation of the world. Like Ter-

---

[193] Chap. 14. That the personality of the Holy Spirit is here denied is held by Meier, " Die Lehre von der Trinität," i. p. 88; Harnack, E. T. ii. p. 262, note; Nösgen, " Geschichte der Lehre vom heiligen Geiste," p. 20. Cf. also J. Sjöholm, " Hippolytus och Modalismen," Lund: 1898. On the other hand, see Döllinger, " Hippolytus and Callistus," E. T. pp. 193–194, and Hagemann, " Die Römische Kirche," pp. 268 *sq.*

[194] Chap. 7.

[195] τῇ δυνάμει καὶ τῇ διαθέσει τῆς ὁμοφρονίας ἐν γινόμεθα;

[196] E.g., chaps. 8 and 16.

[197] Chap. 7 *ad fin.*

tullian, he tells us that God subsisted from all eternity alone, having nothing contemporaneous with Himself. But he does not, like Tertullian, tell us that though thus existing alone, so far as things external to Himself are concerned, there was within Him another, His fellow, His eternal Word, a second to Him. Quite differently, he tells us that though alone, He was many — a plurality.[198] And then he goes on to explain that this means that God was never " reasonless, or wisdomless, or powerless, or counselless, but all things were in Him and He was the all." [199] In other words, it is not of a personal Logos as the eternal Companion that Hippolytus is thinking, but of the ideal world, the κόσμος νοητός, as constituting an eternal " plurality " of God. Accordingly when in another place [200] he is again describing the origin of the Logos, the eternal existence which he attributes to Him is not an existence as a personal Logos, but only as the " indwelling rationality of the universe." The Logos thus for Hippolytus exists from all eternity only ideally. From this ideal existence He came into real existence for the first time when God, intending to create the world, begat Him " as the Author and Fellow-Counsellor and Framer of the things that are in formation," [201] and " thus," says Hippolytus,[202] " there appeared another beside Him " — thus and then only. Here it must be remarked is a doctrine of the absolute origination of the Logos by the will of the Father, so that the Logos appears distinctly as a creature of the Father's will.[203]

---

[198] Chap. 10, ad init., αὐτὸς δὲ μόνος ὢν πολὺς ἦν.

[199] οὔτε γὰρ ἄλογος, οὔτε ἄσοφος, οὔτε ἀδύνατος, οὔτε ἀβούλευτος ἦν, πάντα δὲ ἦν ἐν αὐτῷ, αὐτὸς δὲ ἦν τὸ πᾶν.

[200] " Philosophumena," x. 33 (xxix.) — ἐνδιάθετος τοῦ παντὸς λογισμός.

[201] " Contra Noëtum," chap. 10 — ἀρχηγὸν καὶ σύμβουλον καὶ ἐργάτην.

[202] Chap. 11.

[203] On the extreme emphasis put by Hippolytus on the divine will, cf. Hagemann, " Die Römische Kirche," p. 197 : " No one of the earliest representatives of Christian science lays such stress on the will of God as Hippolytus. With great emphasis, often several times in succession in almost identical phrases, he repeats, when speaking of the origin of the Logos or of creation in general, the formula in which he expresses his proposition that the whole revelation of God ad extra is grounded in His will, that He can create or not create,

Nor does Hippolytus in the least shrink from this conception. When explaining that Adam was made a man with the characteristics and limitations of a man, not by inadvertence or because of any limitation of power on God's part, but by design, he says: " The Creator did not wish to make him a God and failed in His aim; nor an angel — be not deceived — but a man. For if He had wished to make thee a God He could have done so: *you have the example of the Logos.*" [204] To Hippolytus, therefore, the Logos is distinctly a created God, whom God made a God because, shortly, He chose to do so. He has indeed preëminence above all other creatures, not only because He was made a God and they were not, but also because He alone of creatures was made by God Himself while all other creatures were made by Him the Logos; and because they all were made out of nothing, while " Him alone God produced from existing things (ἐξ ὄντων)," and, as God alone existed, that means from His own substance.[205] The Logos is therefore only in this sense of the substance of God, that He was framed

---

retain the Logos in Himself or permit Him to proceed out, as He wills. He even speaks once of the Logos himself as a product of the divine will (chap. 13; cf. chaps. 8, 9, 10, 11)." For the fundamental significance of this see above, p. 32 note [45], and the references there given. Natural as this stress on the voluntariness of the divine action, even in the prolation of the Logos, was on the lips of the Apologists in protest against the natural processes of emanation taught by the Gnostics, there underlay it in its application to the prolation of the Logos a view of the relation of the Logos to the Father which scarcely did justice to the real state of the case, and was near to a conception of the Logos as absolutely originating in this act of the divine will, and hence as of creaturely character. This point of view was that of some of the Apologists, and was revived by the Arians. In opposition to it the Nicene Fathers (Athanasius, " Or. cont. Ar.," III. xxx.; " De Decret. Nic. Syn."; Ambrose, " De Fide Chr.," iv. 9) learned to go behind the will of God in the generation of the Logos. There is a sense, of course, in which, as Döllinger points out (" Hippolytus and Callistus," E. T. p. 198), God as voluntary subject does all He does voluntarily; but after all said and done as the Arian contention that the Son owed His being to an act of will on the part of the Father was meant to imply that the Son was a creature, this mode of speech is Arian in tendency and it is best frankly to say — taking will in its natural sense — that the act of eternal generation is not an act of will but a necessary movement in the divine being. (Cf. Dorner, *op. cit.*, Div. I. vol. ii. p. 460.)

[204] " Philosophumena," x. 33. (xxix.).

[205] *Ibid.*

out of the divine substance; although what the process was by which God thus "begat Him as He willed," Hippolytus declines to inquire as too mysterious for human investigation.[206] He has no hesitation, however, in speaking of him as a creature who came into existence at a definite time, is only what His maker willed, and is God and possessor of the power of God and therefore almighty only by gift and not by nature.[207]

It is not necessary to pursue this inquiry further. Enough has been brought out to show that Hippolytus' Trinity consisted in a transcendent God who produced at a definite point of time a secondary divinity called the Logos, to whom He subjected all things; and along with these a third something not very definitely conceived, called by the Church the Holy Spirit. Here is not one God in three persons; here is rather one God producing a universe by steps and stages, to the higher of which divinity is assigned. In other words, we see in Hippolytus a clear and emphatic testimony indeed to a rich deposit of Christian faith, but overlying and dominating it a personal interpretation of it which reproduces all the worst defects of the Logos speculation. In this he forms, despite the surface resemblance of his discussion to Tertullian's, a glaring contrast with that writer. In Tertullian the fundamental faith of the Church comes to its rights and is permitted to dominate the Logos speculation. And it is just in this that his superiority as a theologian to Hippolytus is exhibited. Hippolytus' thought remains in all essential respects bound within the limits of the Logos speculation. Tertullian's has become in all essential respects a logical development of the Church's fundamental faith. It is therefore that it is he and not Hippolytus who became the Father of the doctrine of an immanent Trinity.

A comparison of Novatian's treatise " On the Trinity "[208]

---

[206] " Contra Noëtum," chap. 16.

[207] Cf. also chap. 6, where Christ is said to have been " appointed almighty by the Father."

[208] There seems no real reason for doubting the authorship of this book by Novatian, though Hagemann (pp. 371 sq.) doubts it, and Quarry even ascribes it to Hippolytus. Cf. Harnack, " Chronologie," ii. pp. 396 sq., note 1, and p. 400, note 2. Harnack dates it c. 240 (p. 399).

will still further strengthen our respect for Tertullian. Novatian seems to have been a diligent student of Tertullian;[209] it
might be presumed, therefore, that in this treatise he has
drawn upon the master whom he honored by his imitation but
never names. Despite, however, Jerome's declaration that the
book is only " a kind of epitome "[210] of Tertullian's work, and
the repetition of this judgment by a whole series of subsequent
writers,[211] we find ourselves doubting whether the presumed
fact is supported by the treatise itself. Novatian goes his own
way, and it is questionable whether there is much common to
his treatise and Tertullian's tract " Against Praxeas," which
may not be best accounted for on the ground of the traditional
elements of belief underlying both.[212] No doubt Novatian must
be supposed to have known Tertullian's treatise and his own
thinking may have been affected by its teaching. But there
seems little or no evidence that he has drawn directly upon it
for his own work. Novatian's tract, unlike those of Tertullian
and Hippolytus, is not in the first instance a piece of polemics
with only incidental positive elements; but is primarily a constructive treatise and only incidentally polemic; moreover, its
polemic edge is turned not solely against Monarchianism, but
equally against tritheism. In point of form it is an exposition
of the Rule of Truth,[213] which requires us to believe in God the

---

[209] Cf. Harnack in the *Sitzungsberichte der königlich preussischen Akademie der Wissenschaften zu Berlin*, 1895, ii. p. 562, and " Chronologie," ii. pp.
399–400.

[210] " De virr. inlust.," chap. 70.

[211] E.g., Loof's " Leitfaden zum Studium der Dogmengeschichte," p. 105:
" There is scarcely a thought that cannot be pointed out in Tertullian." But
Harnack, " Chronologie," ii. pp. 399–400, recognizes that in any event Jerome's
statement is overdrawn, though he finds a real connection between the two
books.

[212] We have the support in this, at least, of Hagemann, " Die Römische
Kirche," p. 379.

[213] Novatian's own phrase is always Rule of Truth, although the title of
his treatise has Rule of Faith, whence Kunze infers that the title is not from
his own hand (" Glaubensregel, Heilige Schrift und Taufbekenntnis," pp.
5–6). Novatian, remarks Kunze (p. 178), makes use of the Roman Baptismal
Creed (Apostolicum), but evidently " only the Trinitarian formula stood to
him as a formula, and we may even say that to him the notion of *regula*

Father and Lord Omnipotent, in the Son of God, Christ Jesus, the Lord our God, and in the Holy Spirit, once promised to the Church; and its disposition follows these three fundamental elements of the faith (chaps. i.–viii.; ix.–xxviii.; xxix.; with a conclusion, xxx.-xxxi.). To its expository task it gives itself with a conscious effort to avoid wandering off into the refutation of heresies, farther than may be necessary to subserve the purpose in view. " I could set forth the treatment of this subject," he remarks on one occasion when a heresy is engaging his attention, " by all the heavenly Scriptures . . . except that I have not so much undertaken to speak against this special form of heresy as to expound the Rule of Truth concerning the person of Christ." [214]

The positive exposition Novatian has set himself to give is very richly worked out and quite justifies Jerome's admiration of the book. In particular the exegetical demonstration of the divinity of Christ which it offers is very thorough and noble and can scarcely find its superior in ancient literature. Alongside of its zeal for the deity of Christ, its zeal for the unity of God burns warmly, and its Trinitarian doctrine seems to be dominated by the interaction of these two factors. The key to the whole is revealed by Novatian himself when he declares our chief duty to be to contend earnestly that Christ is God, but in such a way as not to militate against the Scriptural *fundamentum* that there is but one God.[215] It is indeed tritheism rather than Monarchianism which causes Novatian the deepest anxiety and though he argues stoutly against the latter, it is his opposition to the former which most decisively determines his own forms of statement. Thus, although he exhibits little vital interest in the Logos speculation for its own sake, and writes rather from the standpoint of the traditional

---

veritatis belonged only to it and not to the ' Apostles' Creed '; and to the ' Apostles' Creed ' only so far as it is built up upon the Trinitarian formula." This is, however, in effect the essential conception of all the early Fathers: that is to say, the Apostles' Creed to them is not the Rule of Faith, but only a commodious summary of it.

[214] Chap. xxi.

[215] Chap. xxx. near the beginning.

faith, he is thrown back strongly upon the linear development
of the Trinity which is the product of the Logos speculation.[216]
Laboring to secure the unity of God at all hazards, he feels that
he can do this only by emphasizing the origination of the Son;
and not attaining to a clear grasp of the conception of eternal
generation, he is led to protect the origination of the Son by
emphasizing His posteriority to the Father.[217] Amid these
ideas, it must be confessed, he somewhat flounders. He is earnestly desirous of doing full justice to the deity of Christ, and
he feels that in order to do so he must assimilate Him to the
eternal God. But he does not know quite how to do this consistently with a fitting proclamation of the unity of God. Accordingly he tells us, on the one hand, that the Son " was always in the Father " because the " Father was always Father ":
but he at once turns to argue, on the other hand, that the
Father must in some sense precede the Son, because it is " necessary that He who knows no beginning must precede Him that
has a beginning "; and to insist over and over again that there
would be two Gods, if there were two who had not been begotten, or two who were without beginning, or two who were
self-existent. The doctrine of " eternal generation " is here
struggling in the womb of thought: we do not think it quite
comes to the birth.

And thus Novatian seems to us to fall back essentially upon
the Logos construction, but on the Logos construction so far
purified that it is on the point of melting into Nicene orthodoxy. In order to protect the unity of God, in other words, he
was led to emphasize not the sameness of the Son and Spirit
with God the Father, as Tertullian did with his developed doctrine of the numerical unity of substance, but their difference
from Him. The nerve of Novatian's Trinitarianism thus becomes his strong subordinationism. Though he knows and emphasizes the difference between creation and procession,[218] and
urges as few others have urged the true divinity of Christ, yet
our Lord's deity is to Him after all only a secondary deity. He

---

[216] See above, pp. 34–36.   [218] Cf. Harnack, ii. p. 259, note 3.
[217] Chap. xxxi.

had a beginning; He was not self-originated; He was the product of His Father's will; He exists but to minister to that
will; though He be God, He is not God of Himself, but only
because "He was begotten for this special result, that He
should be God"; and though He is Lord, He is Lord only because the Father so willed and only to the extent the Father
willed.[219] When He says "I and the Father are one," therefore, "He referred to the agreement, and to the identity of
judgment, and to the loving association itself, as, reasonably,
the Father and Son are one in agreement and love and affection." [220] Tertullian would here have referred to sameness of
substance: even Hippolytus would have referred to sameness
of power: Novatian's zeal for the unity of God holds him back,
and though he believes the Son to be consubstantial with the
Father in the sense that as the son of a man is a man so the
Son of God is God,[221] yet he must believe also that He is second
to the Father in the strongest sense of that word. This subordination of the Son to the Father is repeated, in his view, in
the similar subordination of the Spirit to the Son. So clear is it
that, with all his good intentions and upward strivings, Novatian remains, in his theoretical construction of the relationships of the three persons he recognized as God, under the
Logos speculation and fails to attain the higher standpoint
reached by Tertullian. Revolting from the tritheism of Hippolytus, he yet does not know any other way to secure the
unity of God but Hippolytus' way — that is, by so sharply
emphasizing the subordination of the two objects of Christian worship additional to God the Father as to exalt the
Father into the sole Self-Existent, Beginningless, Invisible, Infinite, Immortal, and Eternal One. That he guards this subordination better than Hippolytus is a matter of degree and
does not erect a difference of kind between them. Novatian

[219] All these phrases are from chap. xxxi.
[220] Chap. xxvii.
[221] Cf. Bull, iii. 17, E. T. pp. 541 *sq.*, and see Nösgen, p. 26, note 2. Novatian is treated by Bull, especially pp. 131, 297, 479, 528, 582, 597, 607, E. T. The
best that can be said for him is there said.

marks, no doubt, the highest level of Trinitarian doctrine attainable along the pathway of subordinationism. That this level is lower than the level attained by Tertullian is only evidence that Tertullian's organizing principle had become no longer subordinationism but equalization. It is, in other words, Tertullian's formula of numerical sameness of essence with distinction of persons, not the formula of the Logos speculation in which the stress was laid on subordinationism,[222] that had in it the promise and potency of the better things to come.

From such comparisons as these we obtain a notion of the nature of the step toward the formulation of the Church's ingrained faith in an immanent Trinity which was made by Tertullian. The greatness of this step is fairly estimable from the fact that Tertullian's statements will satisfy all the points on which Bishop Bull laid stress in his famous effort to show " the consent of primitive antiquity with the fathers of the Council of Nice." These points he sums up in four:[223] " first, that Christ our Lord in His higher nature existed before [His birth of] the most blessed Virgin Mary, and, further, before the creation of the world, and that through Him all things were made; secondly, that in that very nature He is of one substance with God the Father, that is [that] He is not of any created and mutable essence, but of a nature entirely the same with the Father, and consequently very God; thirdly, which is a consequence of this, that He is co-eternal with God the Father, that is, a Divine Person, co-existing with the Father from everlasting; lastly, that He Himself is, nevertheless, subordinate to God the Father, as to His Author and Principle." Tertullian teaches, in other

---

[222] Speaking of the Logos doctrine, Prof. L. L. Paine says truly: " In this view the subordination element is vital, and it became the governing note of the whole Logos-school " (" Evolution of Trinitarianism," p. 31). Where Prof. Paine is wrong is in not perceiving how deeply this subordinationism was contrary to the fundamentals of the Christian faith: and by this failure he is led to do grave injustice alike to Athanasianism — in which he discerns more subordinationism than really existed in it — and to Augustinianism — whose reproach to him is that it is determined to be rid of subordinationism. Prof. Paine, in other words, misconceives both the historical development and its meaning.

[223] Bull, Defensio Fidei Nicaenæ," Conclusion, ad init., E. T. p. 655.

words, the preexistence, consubstantiality, eternity, and subordination of the Son, and likewise of the Spirit. What, then,
lacks he yet of Nicene orthodoxy? It is this question which
Bishop Bull presses; but, as he presses it, he only makes us
aware that Nicene orthodoxy cannot quite be summed up in
these four propositions. Meeting these four tests Tertullian yet
falls short of Nicene orthodoxy, retaining still too great a
leaven of the Logos speculation. But that he is able to meet
Bull's tests, which none of his predecessors or contemporaries
can meet, indicates the greatness of the step he marks toward
the Nicene orthodoxy.

That we may fairly call Tertullian the father of the Nicene
theology there seems to be wanting nothing but some clear
historical connection between his work and that of the Nicene
fathers. It is over-exigent no doubt to demand an external
proof of connection. The silent influence of Tertullian's discussion supplemented by that of Novatian [224] supplies a sufficient
nexus. But we naturally desire to trace in some overt manifestations the working of this influence. A step toward providing this is afforded by the episode of the " two Dionysii," in
which the Roman Dionysius out of his Western Trinitarian
consciousness corrects and instructs his less well-informed
Alexandrian brother, who had permitted himself to speak of
our Lord after a fashion which betrayed the most unformed
conceptions of the relations of the distinctions in the Godhead.
The letter of Dionysius of Rome (259–269 A.D.) *Against the
Sabellians,* a considerable portion of which has been preserved
by Athanasius in his " Letter in Defense of the Nicene Definition," [225] is very properly appealed to by Athanasius as an
instance of Niceneism before Nice. It seems clearly to be dependent on Tertullian, though, as Harnack puts it, " no single
passage in it can be pointed out which is simply transcribed
from Tertullian, but Dionysius has, rather in opposition to the

[224] On the great influence of Novatian's treatise see Bethune-Baker, (" An
Introduction to the Early History of Christian Doctrine," p. 191.

[225] Chap. vi. or §§ 26–27 (" Nicene and Post-Nicene Fathers," Second
Series, iv. pp. 167–168).

formula of Dionysius of Alexandria, developed further in the direction of orthodoxy Tertullian's Trinitarian doctrine." [226] Quite in the Roman manner [227] Dionysius turned the edge of his polemic as much against tritheism as against Monarchianism, and thus, by insisting on " the gathering up of the Divine Triad into a summit," preserved the unity of the common essence and so helped forward to the formulation of the *homoousios*. Similarly by his insistence that the Son was no " creature " ($\pi o\iota\eta\mu a$) and was not "made " ($\gamma\epsilon\gamma o\nu\acute{\epsilon}\nu a\iota$) but "begotten " ($\gamma\epsilon\gamma\epsilon\nu\nu\eta\sigma\theta a\iota$), he laid the foundations of the Nicene formula of " begotten, not made," which also thus goes back through him to Tertullian. Nothing could be more instructive than the emergence into the light of history of this instance in the latter half of the third century of the greater readiness of the West to deal with the Trinitarian problem than the East.

We need seek no other historical link, however, between Western orthodoxy and the East than that provided by " the great Hosius " himself, who was the channel by means of which the formulas beaten out in the West, primarily by Tertullian, were impressed on the East in the Nicene symbol. We are credibly told by Socrates [228] that Hosius disputed in Alexandria on " substance " ($o\dot{v}\sigma\acute{\iota}a$) and " person " ($\dot{v}\pi\acute{o}\sigma\tau a\sigma\iota s$) prior to the Nicene Council; and his dominant influence with the emperor as well as the prominent place he occupied in the Council itself afford sufficient account of the successful issue of that Council in establishing Tertullian's formula of " one substance and three persons " — the $\dot{o}\mu oo\acute{v}\sigma\iota os$ in effect — as the faith of the whole Church. [229] If despite Athanasius' hint that it

---

[226] *Sitzungsberichte der königlich preussischen Akademie der Wissenschaften zu Berlin*, 1895, ii. p. 563.

[227] Callistus, Novatian, Dionysius.

[228] " Historia," III. vii.

[229] Cf. Harnack, iv. pp. 5, 11 and 50, 121; and *Sitzungsberichte der königlich preussischen Akademie der Wissenschaften zu Berlin*, 1895, ii. p. 564, especially the former references where the matter is argued. See also Gams, " Kirchengeschichte von Spanien," II. i. p. 140. When Socrates (III. vii.) tells us that on Hosius' visit to Alexandria in 324 $\tau\dot{\eta}\nu$ $\pi\epsilon\rho\dot{\iota}$ $o\dot{v}\sigma\acute{\iota}as$ $\kappa a\dot{\iota}$ $\dot{v}\pi o\sigma\tau\acute{a}\sigma\epsilon\omega s$ $\tau\epsilon\tau o\acute{\iota}\eta\tau a\iota$ $\zeta\acute{\eta}\tau\eta\sigma\iota\nu$, we are tempted to see not only a priming of the Alexandrians

was Hosius who "set forth the Nicene Faith," [230] we cannot quite say that Hosius was the "draftsman" of the Nicene Creed,[231] since that Creed was formally framed by a series of amendments out of a formula offered by Eusebius of Cæsarea, yet what is implied in such a statement is essentially true. Hosius was the effective author of the Nicene Creed, and that is as much as to say that in its fundamental assertions that Creed is a Western formulary,[232] and its roots are set in the

---

for what was to come, by this Westerner, the heir of the Western Trinitarianism, but in the choice of the term "hypostasis" for "person" a reflection of Tertullian's *substantiva res* — especially as we are told that Hosius was on this occasion especially zealous in guarding against Sabellian tendencies. We must not, however, push the details of Socrates' report too far.

[230] "History of the Arians," chap. 42.

[231] Bethune-Baker, "The Meaning of Homoousios in the 'Constantinopolitan' Creed," in "Texts and Studies," J. A. Robinson, ed., vii. 1, p. 11, note: "That Hosius — for many years previously the most influential bishop in the West, the intimate friend and trusted adviser in ecclesiastical matters of Constantine — was the real 'draftsman' of the Creed seems certain." Loofs, in Herzog, "Realencyklopädie für protestantische Theologie und Kirche,³" viii. p. 378: "That Hosius, the confidant of the emperor, was of great influence here [at the Synod of Nice] lay in the nature of the circumstances, . . . and the statement of Athanasius that 'he set forth (ἐξέθετο) the faith at Nice' ("History of the Arians," § 42), although not exact in its affirmation — for the Nicænum was framed by amendments out of a draft offered by Eusebius of Cæsarea — nevertheless is in essence true." Zahn, "Marcellus von Ancyra," p. 23: "Hosius from the beginning of the Arian controversies exerted the most decisive influence on the course of external events, *i.e.*, on the Emperor. It was due to him that Constantine came forward so positively for the ὁμοούσιος, that Eusebius could speak as if the Emperor were the actual originator of that term. Hosius is said to have raised the question concerning οὐσία and ὑπόστασις on the occasion of his visit to Alexandria, and Athanasius makes his enemies declare of him, 'It was he that set forth the faith at Nice' ("History of the Arians," § 42) — by which he assigns him not merely a share in the development of the Nicene faith, as Hefele supposes (i. p. 280), but a controlling influence in the debates on the faith which took place at Nice, and that means nothing less than in the choice of the formula." Zahn adds that Socrates' statement of what happened in Alexandria finds support in the independent report of Philostorgius (i. 7), that Alexander had come to an understanding with Hosius as to the ὁμοούσιος before the Synod. It seems clear, in any event, that antiquity thought of Hosius as bearing the prime responsibility for the homoousios in the Nicene Creed.

[232] Loofs, in Herzog, "Realencyklopädie für protestantische Theologie und Kirche,³" ii. p. 15, line 16: "The Nicænum became what it is under Western

teaching of Tertullian. It was thus given to Tertullian to mark out the pathway in which the Church has subsequently walked and to enunciate the germinal formulas by means of which the Arians were ultimately overcome.

It would be wrong, of course, to derive from these facts, striking as they are, the impression that Tertullian's influence was the only important force operative in the Church for the formation of the doctrine of the Trinity. It would be truer to see in Tertullian and in his definitions only one manifestation of a universally working tendency making steadily toward this end. Wherever the Rule of Faith, which was rooted in the formula of the baptismal commission, formed the fundamental basis of Christian belief, and wherever the data supplied by this Rule of Faith were interpreted in the forms of the Logos speculation, there was constantly in progress a strenuous effort to attain clarity as to the relations of the distinctions in the Name designated by the terms Father, Son, and Holy Ghost. And this is as much as to say that every thinking man in the Church was engaged with all the powers of construction granted to him in working out this problem. Even the Monarchians themselves, to whom in the providence of God it was given to keep poignantly before the eyes of men the items of the faith which were likely to be neglected by the Logos speculation, were yet apt to express themselves more or less in its terms.[233] Accord-

influences "; ii. p. 14, line 53: " The positive declarations of the symbol can be historically understood only when we remember that the emperor was a Westerner and . . . was directed by the advice of Western counsellors, especially Hosius "; iv. pp. 45–46: " Only the influence of the West — Constantine (although he understood Greek) had Western counsellors — explains the acts of the Synod of Nice: the characteristic terminology of the Nicænum . . . fits, in its entirety, only Western conceptions."

[233] The same is true also of the Montanists — to whom the function was committed of emphasizing the doctrine of the Spirit in the Church — if we can judge by the example and trust the testimony of Tertullian. Harnack (E. T. iv. pp. 108 *sq.*) is right in assigning to them an important place in the development of the doctrine of the Spirit: he is wrong in the specific function assigned them in this development. If we can judge by the example of Tertullian, the

ingly from the very beginning Christian literature is filled with adumbrations of what was to come. Already in Athenagoras Tertullian's doctrine of eternal pre-prolate distinctions in the Godhead almost came to birth; already in Theophilus Origen's doctrine of eternal generation seemed on the verge of conception. Least of all did the great Alexandrian divines wait for Tertullian's initiative. Origen, for example, his younger contemporary, and at once the calmest and profoundest thinker granted to the Church in the Ante-Nicene age, went his own independent way toward the same great goal. Only, Origen sought the solution of the problem not with Tertullian by separating the Logos from the cosmic processes and thereby carrying the distinctions in the Godhead, freed from all connection with activities *ad extra,* back into the mysteries of the innermost modes of the divine existence, but by pushing the cosmic processes themselves, along with the Logos, back into, if not the immanent, at least the eternal modes of the divine activity. Thus he gave the Church in full formulation the doctrine of the eternal generation of the Son of God, indeed, but along with it also the doctrine of eternal creation: and by his failure to separate the Son from the world, with all that was, or seemed to be, involved in that, he missed becoming the father of the Christian doctrine of the Trinity by becoming instead — well or ill understood, but at least not unnaturally — the father of Arianism. It was not along this pathway that the Church doctrine of the Trinity was to be attained, but rather along that beaten out by the feet of Tertullian.[234] And this, simply because the Church doctrine of the Trinity could not come to its rights within the limits of the Logos specula-

---

effect of their movement was to elevate and deepen the conception of the Spirit and His work.

[234] Harnack (E. T. iv. p. 110), speaking of the development of the doctrine of the Spirit, although he recognizes that in his doctrine of the pre-temporal *processio* of the Spirit Origen is in advance of Tertullian, for Tertullian does not teach this *explicitly* (see above, pp. 70–71), yet remarks that "by the 'unius substantiæ,' which he regards as true of the Spirit also, Tertullian comes nearer the views which finally prevailed in the Fourth Century."

tion, and Origen's construction preserved the essential elements of the Logos speculation while Tertullian's prepared the way for transcending it.

To put the matter into somewhat abstract form, the immanent movement of Christian thought, we conceive, took some such course as the following. The Logos speculation laid its stress on the gradations of deity manifested in the Logos and the Spirit, and just on that account did less than justice to the Church's immanent faith in which the Father, Son, and Holy Ghost appeared as equal sharers in the Name. That justice might be done to the immanent faith of the Church, therefore, it was essential that the stress should be shifted from gradations of deity to the equality of the persons of the Godhead. This correction carried with it the confession not merely of the eternity of these persons, but also their unchangeableness, since not only eternity but also unchangeableness is an essential attribute of deity, and must belong to each person of the Godhead if these persons are to be seriously conceived to be equal. That justice might be done to these conceptions, it obviously was not enough, then, that a basis for the prolations should be discovered in the eternal existence form of God, nor indeed merely that personal distinctions underlying these prolations should be carried back into eternity, nor merely that the prolations themselves should be pushed back into eternity. In the last case the eternal prolates must further be conceived as in no sense inferior to the unprolate deity itself, sharers in all its most intimate attributes — not only in its eternity and unchangeableness, therefore, but also in its exaltation, or in the speech of the time, its " invisibility," including self-existence itself. But so to conceive them involved, of course, the evisceration of the entire prolation speculation of its purpose and value — as may be readily perceived by reading in conjunction the chapters of Tertullian (who is still so far under the control of the Logos speculation) in which he argues that " invisibility " is the peculiarity of the Father in distinction from the Son, the very characteristic of the Son being His " visibility," [235] and

[235] " Against Praxeas," chaps. xiv.–xvi.

the discussion of Augustine [236] in which he solidly argues that the Son and Spirit are, because equally God with the Father, also equally " invisible " with the Father.[237] The orthodox doctrine of the Trinity could not become complete, in other words, until, under the pressure of the demand of the Christian consciousness for adequate recognition of the true and complete

[236] " De Trinitate," ii.

[237] There is, of course, a stream of better teaching running through the very fathers who denied " invisibility " to the prolate Logos in the interests of the Logos speculation. The passage in Ignatius, " Ad Ephes." (end of chap. iii.) sets the norm of this better mode of speech. See also Melito, *Frag.*, § 13 (Otto, " Corpus Apologetarum Christianorum," ix. p. 419), and Tertullian himself who, despite his elaborate distinction of " the Father from the Son by this characteristic, that the Son is visible, the Father invisible," nevertheless, " in the very same book and chapter " — viz., the fourteenth chapter of the tract " Against Praxeas," remarks " that the Son also, considered in Himself, is invisible " (Bull, IV. iii. 9, E. T. pp. 609 *sq.*). But the doctrine of the like invisibility of the Son with the Father came to its rights only with Augustine. On the whole subject of the patristic ideas of the " visibility " of the Logos and the " invisibility " of God as such, the discussions — which certainly involve no little special pleading — of Bull, Book iv. chap. iii., are well worth consulting. To the general student of doctrine these discussions of Bull have an additional interest, inasmuch as — although it doubtless would have shocked him to have had it suggested to him — his defense of the subordinationism of the fathers on the ground that they conceived it due not to any difference between the Father and Son in essence or attributes but to an " economy," is equivalent to attributing to the fathers and adopting for himself the essential elements of what is known in the history of doctrine as the " Covenant Theology " — a theology that was being taught by many Reformed theologians in Bull's day. When Bull says of the fathers (IV. iii. 12, E. T. ii. p. 615) : " They by no means meant to deny that the Son of God, equally with the Father, is in His own nature immeasurable and invisible; but merely intimated this, that all such appearances of God, and also the incarnation itself, had reference to the economy which the Son of God undertook " — he has only in other words enunciated the Covenant idea. When he adds: " Which economy is by no means suited to the Father, inasmuch as He had not His origin from any beginning, and is indebted for His authorship to none " — apart from his unwonted phraseology, he does not necessarily go beyond the Covenant theologians, who were quick to contend that the terms of " the Covenant " are themselves grounded in the intrinsic relations of the three Persons. These, they taught, are such as made it proper and fit that each person should assume the precise functions He did assume — as, in a word, made it alone suitable that it should be the Son and Spirit who should be " sent " and not the Father, and the like. The alternatives, in a word, would appear to be either an Arianizing subordinationism or the Covenant theology: all other constructions are half views and inherently unstable.

deity of the Son and Spirit, the whole conception of prolations of deity for specific functions had been superseded by a doctrine of eternally persisting personal distinctions in the Godhead itself. The way was prepared for this historically, no doubt, in large measure, by pushing the idea of prolation back into eternity, as Origen did, where it took the form of a doctrine of eternal generation and procession, and in so doing lost its primary significance and grew nigh to vanishing away — for what is the value of an essential, eternal, and unchangeable prolation of deity which, just because essential, eternal, and unchangeable, can have no inherent relation to activities *ad extra?* But the real goal was attained only when the whole idea of prolation, thus rendered useless and meaningless, had fallen away, and the Logos speculation gave place to something better. And it was Tertullian's definitions, not Origen's speculations, which prepared the way for the attainment of this goal. So that it was not Origen but Tertullian who become the real father of the Christian doctrine of the Trinity.

It is, of course, quite possible to exaggerate the measure in which this revolution of thought is traceable in the pages of Tertullian. It is first discernible in its completeness in the expositions of Augustine two centuries later. But it seems sufficiently clear that the beginnings of the line of development which ended in Augustine are perceptible in Tertullian.[238] Their mark is his insistence on the equality of the Son and Spirit with the Father, an insistence in which he fairly enunciated the great conception afterward embodied in the term *homoousios*. Tertullian, however, still lived and moved and had his being under the spell of the Logos speculation; he did not even perceive, as did Origen, that the notion of prolations before time must give way to the higher conception of eternal generation and procession — much less that even this latter

---

[238] Even Dorner, who does not perceive that Tertullian had in principle separated the Divine Persons as such from the world-process, yet admits that in his " conception of the Three Persons as inwardly connected (as *consertos, cohœrentes*)" Tertullian's view " includes a speculative element, to which the later doctrine of the Church was long in attaining " (" Doctrine of the Person of Christ," Div. I. vol. ii. pp. 76–77).

conception is of doubtful utility. Athanasius himself, indeed, did not perceive this last — and therefore the Nicene doctrine of the Trinity, worked out under his inspiration, still preserves these shells of outlived speculation, the kernel of which has withered away.[239] The phraseology in which they are embodied keeps its place even in the forms of statement of Augustine. The hold which the Logos speculation had on the minds of men is in nothing made more manifest than in such persistence of its forms in subsequent thought, after they had lost all their meaning. In very truth the Logos speculation provided the common ground on which the whole world of fourth century Christian thought still stood; and Arian differed from Athanasian largely only as the left wing differs from the right wing of the same fundamental type of thinking.[240] The merit of Tertullian is that his definitions, though still adjusted to the forms of the Logos speculation, had in them the potency of a better construction and were sure sooner or later to burst the

[239] Cf. the very judicious remarks of Dorner ("Doctrine of the Person of Christ," Div. I. vol. ii. pp. 327 *sq*.) on the survivals in the Nicene construction; see also pp. 184, 203–204, 491.

[240] Cf. Hagemann, p. 134: "When the origin of the Son out of the essence of God is placed in immediate connection with the creation of the world, there is needed in the way of great logical acuteness only a single unimportant step to set the Son in the sense of an Arius alongside of the world, as creature and Creator. No doubt Origen had guarded against this by ascribing not to the Son only but to the world as well an eternal origin: but the latter necessarily fell away as an open contradiction to the Church, and so nothing remained except either to join the Son so essentially with the Father that now the idea of His deity would come to its full rights and He should be recognized as in His Being wholly independent of the origin of the world, by which there would necessarily be raised again the problem of the unity of essence of the Father and the Son; or else so to connect Him with the temporal origin of the world that He should fall thereby out of the circle of the divine life and be conceived as a kind of created God in Plato's sense, as an Under-God by the side of or rather beneath the Father, who would embrace the whole divine world in Himself, the one God over all. Already in the case of Dionysius of Alexandria we have noted in *theory* a tendency to this latter development, even though his faith-consciousness remained free from this evil. In the case of Arius the theory, however, obtained a decisive victory over the faith. . . ." In this passage, we conceive, the essential logical relations of Orthodoxy and Arianism to their common basis in the Logos speculation are lucidly set forth. Cf. Dorner, as cited, pp. 267–280, and pp. 454–455.

shell in which they were artificially confined. In his recognition of the eternity of the personal distinctions in the Godhead apart from all questions of prolation, and in the emphasis he laid upon the equal deity of these persons, he planted fruitful seed which could not fail of a subsequent growth. Men might still cling to the old forms and seek merely to match the downward development which emphasized the distinction of the prolations from the fontal deity until it had degraded them into temporal creatures of the divine will, by emphasizing for themselves rather their eternity and their equality with God.[241] But by this very movement upward it was inevitable that the very idea of prolation, which was the core of the Logos speculation, should lose its significance and be pushed first out of notice and then out of belief — until the whole conception of a linear trinity should disappear and there should emerge the completed Trinitarianism of an Augustine, to whom the persons of the Trinity are not subordinate one to another but coordinate sharers of the one divine essence.

It is, of course, not the close of this process of thought that we see in Tertullian, but its beginning. But in him already appears the pregnant emphasis on the equality rather than the graded subordination of the personal distinctions in the Godhead, by the logical inworking of which the whole change in due time came about. So far as we can now learn it was he first, therefore, who, determined to give due recognition to the elements of the Church's faith embodied in the Rule of Faith, pointed out the road over which it was necessary to travel in order to do justice to the Biblical data. Say that he was in this but the voice of the general Christian consciousness. It remains that it was left to him first to give effective voice to the Christian consciousness, and that it was only by following out the lines laid down by him to their logical conclusion that the great achievement of formulating to thought the doctrine of the triune God was at length accomplished.

[241] Cf. Dorner, as cited, p. 328.

II

AUGUSTINE

AUGUSTINE [1]

1. LIFE. — Aurelius Augustine (the prænomen " Aurelius "
is attested by contemporaries but does not occur in his own
works or in his correspondence) was born of mixed heathen
and Christian parentage November 13, 354 A.D., at Tagaste, a
small municipality in proconsular Numidia. He was taught in
his childhood the principles of Christianity, and great sacrifices
were made to give him a liberal education. From his youth he
was consumed by an insatiable thirst for knowledge, and was
so inflamed by the reading of Cicero's " Hortensius " in his
nineteenth year that he thenceforth devoted his life to the
pursuit of truth. The profession to which he was bred was that
of rhetorician, and this profession he practiced first at Tagaste,
and then successively at Carthage, Rome, and Milan up to the
great crisis of his life (386). In his early manhood he had fallen
away from his Christian training to the Manichæans, who were
the rationalists of the age (373); and subsequently (383) had
lapsed into a general skepticism; but he had already fought his
way out of this, under the influence of the Neo-Platonists, before his conversion to Catholic Christianity took place at Milan
in the late summer of 386. He spent the interval between this
crisis and his baptism (Easter, 387) in philosophical retirement at Cassiciacum, and then, after a short sojourn at Rome,
returned to Africa (autumn, 388) and established at his native
town a sort of religio-philosophical retreat for himself and his
friends. Early in 391 he was almost forcibly ordained presbyter
at Hippo Regius, and nearly five years later (shortly before
Christmas, 395) was raised to the rank of coadjutor-bishop.
From the first he sustained practically the entire burden of the
administration, and, soon succeeding to its sole responsibility,

[1] From " Encyclopaedia of Religion and Ethics," ed. by James Hastings,
ii. pp. 219–224. Used by permission of the publishers, Charles Scribner's Sons.

continued bishop of that second-rate diocese until his death, August 28, 430.

In this simple framework was lived out the life of one who has been strikingly called incomparably the greatest man whom, "between Paul the Apostle and Luther the Reformer, the Christian Church has possessed." [2] We cannot date from him, it is true, an epoch in the external fortunes of the Church in the same sense in which we may from, say, Gregory the Great or Hildebrand. He was not, indeed, without ecclesiastico-political significance. He did much to heal the schisms which tore the African Church. He regenerated the clergy of Africa by his monastic training school. And it must not be forgotten that the two great Gregorys stood upon his shoulders. But his direct work as a reformer of Church life was done in a corner, and its results were immediately swept away by the flood of the Vandal invasion.

2. WRITINGS. — It was through his voluminous writings, by which his wider influence was exerted, that he entered both the Church and the world as a revolutionary force, and not merely created an epoch in the history of the Church, but has determined the course of its history in the West up to the present day. He was already an author when he became a Christian, having published (about 380) an æsthetical study (now lost), on "De pulchro et apto." But his amazing literary productivity began with his conversion. His first Christian writings were a series of religio-philosophical treatises, in which he sought to lay the foundations of a specifically Christian philosophy. These were followed by a great number of controversial works against the Manichæans, Donatists, Pelagians, interspersed with Biblical expositions and dogmatic and ethical studies. The whole was crowned by four or five great books in which his genius finds perhaps its fullest expression. These are his "Confessiones" (397–400), in which he gives an analysis of his religious experience and creates a new *genre* in literary form; the "de Doctrina Christiana" (397–426), in which the

[2] Harnack, "Monasticism and the Confessions of St. Augustine," p. 123.

principles of his Biblical exposition are expounded; the "Enchiridion ad Laurentium" on Faith, Hope, and Charity (421), which contains his most serious attempt to systematize his thought; the "De Trinitate (395–420), in which its final formulation was given to the Christian doctrine of the Trinity; and the " De Civitate Dei" (413–426), in which are laid the foundations of a rational philosophy of history.

He seems to have been himself aware of the significance of the writings into which he had so unstintedly poured himself, and he devoted some of his last years to a careful survey and revision of them in his unique " Retractationes " (426–428), in which he seeks to compact them into an ultimate whole. The influence which they exerted from the beginning is attested no less by the spiteful comments on their volume which escaped from those less well affected to them (e.g., the interpolators of Gennadius), than by the wondering admiration of the better disposed (already, Possidius, "Vita," chap. vii.). In point of fact they entered the Church as a leaven which has ever since wrought powerfully towards leavening the whole mass.

3. INFLUENCE. — (a) *Its extent.* — The greatness of the influence exerted by Augustine is fairly intimated by the suggestion that the division between the Eastern and Western Churches may properly be represented as having been " prepared " by him.[3] No doubt, according to Renan's saying, the building of Constantinople contained in it the prophecy of the division of the Empire, and the division of the Empire the prophecy of the division of the Church. But it was Augustine who imprinted upon the Western section of the Church a character so specific as naturally to bring the separation of the Churches in its train. It must not be inferred, however, that his influence was felt only in the West. The prevailing impression to this effect implies some failure to appreciate not only the extent of the intercourse between the East and the West in Augustine's day, but also the indebtedness of the East to the West for its theological constructions. The interest of the An-

[3] Reuter, " Augustinische Studien," vii. p. 499.

tiochenes in Western Christological thought, as illustrated, for instance, in the " Eranistes " and the correspondence of Theodoret, is only one example of a much wider fact; and in any event, the great doctrines of the Trinity and the Person of Christ, which form almost the entirety of " dogma " in the East, so far from being a gift from the East to the West, as often represented, had their origin in the West, and were thence communicated to the East — the former through the intermediation of " the great Hosius," and the latter through that of Leo the Great. Augustine, through whom — working, no doubt, in full knowledge of what had been done by the Greeks, but in entire independence of them — the doctrine of the Trinity received its completed statement, came too late to affect the Greek construction of this doctrine, and accordingly gave form on this great topic only to the thought of the West. But his Christological conceptions underlay the formulations of Leo, as those of Ambrose underlay his, and through Leo determined the Christological definitions of the East as well as of the West. Accordingly, while the doctrines of the East and the West on the Person of Christ have remained identical, in their doctrines of the Trinity the two sections draw somewhat apart, not only with respect to that perennial bone of contention, the *filioque* clause in the definition of the procession of the Spirit, but in what underlies this difference — their general conception of the relations of the Trinitarian Persons. This in the East is ruled by subtle subordinational inheritances (embedded in the Nicene formulary in the phrase θεὸς ἐκ θεοῦ and its equivalents), while in the West it is dominated by that principle of equalization which found its sharpest assertion in the ascription of αὐτοθεότης to Christ by Calvin, whose construction marks the only new (subordinate) epoch in the development of the doctrine of the Trinity after Augustine. This complete determination of Western thought on the fundamental Christian doctrine of the Trinity fairly illustrates at once the place of Augustine in Western Christian thought, and the effect of his supreme influence there in creating a specifically Western type of Christianity.

It is worth while, no doubt, to distinguish between the actual influence exerted by Augustine in the West, and what may perhaps, in a more external sense, be called the authority enjoyed by his name in the Latin Church. To no other doctor of the Church has anything like the same authority been accorded, and it seemed for long as if his doctrine of grace at least was to be treated as a definitely defined dogma, *de fide* in the Church. Already in 431 Celestine sharply reproved the bishops of Gaul for permitting Augustine's authority to be questioned in their dioceses; and soon afterwards, Gelasius (493) addressed to the bishop of Picenum a similar letter of rebuke for the like carelessness. Subsequent deliverances of Hormisdas (520), and Boniface II (530–531), and John II (534) confirmed the authority thus assigned him; and their encomiums were repeated by many later Roman bishops. It very naturally became, therefore, the custom of the " Augustinians " in the Church of Rome — like Diego Alvarez, Jansen, Noris — to ascribe " irrefragable authority " to his teaching; and the question was gravely debated among the theologians whether a truly plenary authority were really to be attributed to him, or whether he were only to rank as the first of the Church's authorized teachers. The result was very naturally that every tendency of thought in the Church was eager to claim for itself the support of his name; and the extraordinary richness of his mind, and the remarkable variety of, so to say, the facets of his teaching, lent him more than ordinarily to the appeal of numerous and even divergent points of view. The possibility of this was increased by the long period of time covered by his literary activity, and the only gradual crystallization of his thought around his really formative ideas. The Augustine of Cassiciacum or even of the presbyterate was a somewhat different Augustine from the Augustine of the episcopate; and not even at his death had perfect consistency been attained in his teaching. Accordingly the most amazing variety of doctrine, on almost every conceivable subject, throughout the Middle Ages, and later in the Church of Rome, has sought support for itself in some saying or other of his; and both sides of almost every controversy have appealed with confidence to his teaching. Schools of thought which had drifted entirely away from his most fundamental postulates still regarded and represented themselves as " Augustinian "; and the Church of Rome itself, whose whole history since the second Council of Orange (529) has been marked by the progressive elimination of Augustinianism from its teaching, is still able to look upon him as the chief doctor of the Church, upon whom its fabric is especially built. Confusion became so confounded that the Confession of Faith which Pelagius presented to Innocent was inserted quite innocently into the " Libri Carolini," and was even produced by the Sorbonne in 1521 against Luther as Augustine's own.

Obviously this universal deference to the name of Augustine furnishes no accurate measure of his real influence. It supplies, however, a fair general reflection of its extent. In point of fact the whole development of Western life, in all its phases, was powerfully affected by his teaching. This, his unique ascendancy in the direction of the thought and life of the West, is due in part to the particular period in history in which his work was done, in part to the richness and depth of his mind and the force of his individuality, and in part to the special circumstances of his conversion to Christianity. He stood on the watershed of two worlds. The old world was passing away; the new world was entering upon its heritage; and it fell to him to mediate the transference of the culture of the one to the other. It has been strikingly remarked that the miserable existence of the Roman Empire in the West almost seems to have been prolonged for the express purpose of affording an opportunity for the influence of Augustine to be exerted on universal history.[4] He was fortunate even in the place of his birth and formative years; although on the very eve of its destruction, Africa was at this precise moment, in the midst of the universal decadence, the scene of intense intellectual activity — into which he entered with all the force of his ardent

---

[4] Harnack, " Grundriss der Dogmengeschichte," E. T. " Outlines of the History of Dogma," p. 335.

nature. He gathered up into himself all that the old world had to offer, and re-coining it sent it forth again bearing the stamp of his profound character. It belonged to the peculiarity of his genius that he embraced all that he took up into himself " with all the fibres of his soul "; not, as has been said, " with his heart alone, for the heart does not think, nor with the mind only; he never grasps truth in the abstract, and as if it were dead," [5] but with his whole being, giving himself to it and sending it forth from himself as living truth, driven on by all the force of his great and inspiring personality. Accordingly, when, having tested everything that the old world had to offer and found it wanting, he gave himself at last to Catholic Christianity, it was with no reserves. Catholicism, frankly accepted as such, became his passion, and into the enthusiastic maintenance of it he threw all his forces. It was primarily as a Catholic Christian, therefore, that he thought, and worked, and lived. But the man who threw himself with such zeal into the service of Catholic Christianity was a man who had already lived through many experiences and had gathered much spoil in the process. He had sounded the depths of heresy in its most attractive form and had drunk the waters of philosophy in its culminating development; life in the conventicles of the sects and in the circle of cultured heathenism was alike familiar to him. But, above all the spoil he brought from without, he brought with him himself. He was a man of the highest and most individual genius — intellectual, but far beyond that, religious — who had his own personal contribution to make to thought and life. If we cannot quite allow that there were in very truth many Augustines, we must at least recognize that within the one Augustine there were very various and not always consistent currents flowing, each of which had its part to play in the future. Within the Catholic Christian a philosopher of the first rank was restlessly active; and within both a religious genius of the highest order was working; while for the expression of the resulting complex of feelings and ideas a lit-

[5] Portalié, in Vacant-Mangenot, " Dictionnaire de la Théologie Catholique," i. col. 2453.

erary talent was available second to none in the annals of the Church.

It is no wonder, therefore, that the Western Church has felt the force of his influence in all the main lines of its development, and in no one of its prominent characteristics could it have been without him what it has become. In him are found at once the seed out of which the tree that we know as the Roman Catholic Church has grown; the spring or strength of all the leading anti-hierarchical and mystical movements which succeeded one another through the Middle Ages; at least the promise and pre-formation of the great types of Western philosophical thought; and, above all, the potent leaven of vital religion. Beginning in the first force of its fresh promulgation by overcoming the ingrained rationalism of the popular Christianity expressed in Pelagianism and its daughter movements, it refused to be bound by the compromises of the Council of Orange, compacted though they were into a system by the genius of a Thomas, and given irrefragable authority in the Church of Rome by the decrees of Trent, but manifested its power by outbreak after outbreak, from Gottschalk in the ninth to Jansen in the seventeenth century; and then burst all bonds and issued in the Protestant Reformation in the sixteenth century.

(b) *Augustine as a Church-teacher.* — No doubt it is preeminently as the great Catholic doctor that Augustine stands out on the page of history. To his own consciousness he was just a Catholic Christian; and the whole mass of his teaching was conceived by him as simply the body of Catholic doctrine. It is, accordingly, interesting to observe that it is precisely as the Catholic doctor that he has lived in the hearts of the people. The legends which have gathered around his name picture him preëminently as the expounder of the *principia* of the Christian faith, particularly of the mysteries of the Godhead, who abode continually *in excelsis disputans de gloria excellentissimæ Trinitatis,* and communicated to the Church the results of his high meditations "as he was able" — a note of humility caught from his own habitual tone when speaking of himself.[6] The task to which he consciously gave himself was to apprehend, so far as it was given to him to apprehend, to proclaim, maintain, and defend the Catholic truth; and from this task he never swerved. It was no empty formula with him when he declared, as he repeatedly declared, " This is the Catholic faith, and it is therefore also my faith "; and he was altogether in earnest when he exhorted his readers not to love him more than the Catholic faith, and his critics not to love themselves more than the Catholic truth.[7] The body of Catholic doctrine constitutes thus the traditional element in Augustine's teaching. But, of course, it by no means left his hands precisely as it entered them. Nor did he contribute to it merely intellectual precision and logical completeness; he impressed on it the stamp of his religious fervor, and transmuted its elements into religious entities.

It was particularly in the doctrine of the Church, which he thus took up and transfigured, that he became in a true sense the founder of Roman Catholicism, and thus called into being a new type of Christianity, in which " the idea of the Church became the central power in the religious feeling" and "in ecclesiastical activity," " in a fashion which has remained unknown to the East." [8] This idea of the Church was, to be sure, so little the creation of Augustine that he took it over whole from his predecessors, and in his innermost thought, indeed, never thoroughly homologated it. It was Cyprian, not Augustine, who identified the Church with the episcopate, and to whom the Church outside which there is no salvation was fundamentally the hierarchical institution. It was Gregory the Great who first spoke of the organized Church as the divine *civitas.* To Augustine the Church was fundamentally the *congregatio sanctorum,* the Body of Christ, and it is this Church which he has in mind when he calls it the *civitas Dei,* or the Kingdom of God on earth. He is, however, not carefully observant of the distinction between the empirical and the ideal

[6] Cf. Stilting, " Acta Sanctorum," Aug. vi.

[7] " De Trinitate," I. iv. 7; III. *præf.* 2.

[8] Reuter, *op. cit.,* p. 499.

Church, and repeatedly — often apparently quite unconsciously — carries over to the one the predicates which in his
fundamental thought, belonged properly to the other. Thus
the hierarchically organized Church tends ever with him to
take the place of the *congregatio sanctorum,* even when he is
speaking of it as the Kingdom or City of God in which alone
any communion with God is possible here, and through which
alone eternal blessedness with God is attainable hereafter.

In the Donatist controversy, although the distinction between *habere* and *utiliter* or *salubriter habere* is made to do
yeoman service, the conception of the Church as the sole
sphere of salvation, passing into the conception of the Church
as the sole mediatrix of grace, and therefore the sole distribu-
tor of salvation, was necessarily thrown into high emphasis;
and the logic of the situation too directly and too powerfully
identified this Church with the empirical Church for the
deeper-lying conception of the *congregatio sanctorum* to remain in sight. Thus Augustine, almost against his will, became the stay of that doctrine of the Church as the sole instrument at once of true knowledge of the divine revelation and
of saving grace which provides the two *foci* about which the
ellipse of Roman Catholic doctrine revolves. What before him
was matter of assertion became in his hands a religion and
went forth to conquer the world. His profounder conception
of the Church as the *congregatio sanctorum,* and the consequent distinction between the empirical and the ideal Church,
with all its implications with respect to the action of the Sacraments and the effect of ecclesiastical decrees, and even of ex-
communication, did not indeed remain unobserved or unutil-
ized when occasion demanded. Thus, for example, they came
forward in their completeness in the arguments of the Im-
perialists in the great controversies of the later eleventh century.[9] These also, and in a truer sense than the Papalists in
that debate, were " Augustinians." But the main stream of
Augustine's influence flowed meanwhile in the traditionalist

[9] Mirbt, " Die Stellung Augustins in der Publicistik des gregorianischen
Kirchenstreits," p. 80.

channel, and gave the world the Church as the authoritative organ of divine truth and the miraculous vehicle of saving grace, through which alone the assured knowledge of the revelation of God could be attained, or the effective operations of His redeeming love experienced. Many of the subsidiary conceptions which fill out the system of Roman Catholic doctrine also find their direct prop in his teaching — its doctrine of merit, the distinctions between precepts and counsels, mortal and venial sins, and particularly the elaborate sacramental system, with its distinction between matter and form, its assertion of *ex opere operato* action, and of the indelible character of baptism and ordination, and even the doctrine of intention. On this side of his teaching the Roman Catholic Church may well be accounted Augustine's monument.

(*c*) *As a thinker.* — But beneath Augustine the traditionalist lay Augustine the thinker, and as a thinker he gave law not only to the Church but to the world. From the moment of his conversion, to be sure, religion became paramount with him. But this did not quench his philosophical impulse; it only made his specifically a religious philosophy, and himself, to adopt Rudolph Eucken's more precise definition,[10] " the single great philosopher on the basis of Christianity proper the world has had " — in the richness of his thought and poetry of his expression alike, not unworthy of comparison even with his great master Plato.[11] He brought with him into Catholic Christianity not only a sufficient equipment of philosophical knowledge, but a powerful and trained intelligence, and an intellectual instinct which had to find scope. It was in the rôle of Christian philosopher, seeking to give form and substance to fundamental verities from the Christian standpoint, that he first came forward in the service of faith; and though later the religious teacher and defender of the faith seemed likely to swallow up the philosophical inquirer, they never really did so, but

[10] Eucken, " Die Lebensanschauungen der grossen Denker [2], p. 216.

[11] Cf. E. Norden, in " Die Kultur der Gegenwart, i. 8, 1905, p. 394: " Augustine was the great poet of the ancient Church, though just as little as Plato did he write in verse. These two go together as the great poet-philosophers of all time."

his rich and active mind kept continually at work sounding all depths. Thus not only was there imparted to all his teaching an unwonted vitality, originality, and profundity, but "the activities set in motion were not confined to the narrow circle of theological science, but extended, directly or indirectly, to all forms of human life." [12] In every department of philosophical inquiry he became normative for the succeeding centuries; and until the rise of Aristotelianism in the twelfth century and its establishment in influence by the advocacy of such teachers as Albertus Magnus and Thomas Aquinas, Augustinianism reigned supreme. Throughout the remainder of the Middle Ages it contended masterfully with its great rival, forming many compromises with it, and tending to offset the rationalism into which Aristotelianism was ever degenerating by itself falling into mysticism. It thus became the support of the tendency towards mysticism which prevailed through the Middle Ages, or rather its protection from the pantheism into which, when drawing more directly from Neo-Platonic sources, it was ever liable to deteriorate. From it every Catholic reformer drew his strength, and to it the whole body of reformers before the Reformation made their appeal. From its partial obscuration it emerged at the Renaissance, and burst against into full view in the seventeenth century to lay the foundations of modern thought. Siebeck accordingly bids us see in Augustine "the first modern man"; [13] and, if Eucken questions the exactness of the designation, he is free to allow that the modern world finds in Augustine many points of contact, and, not only in questions of religious philosophy may wisely take its start from him rather than from Luther or Thomas, Schleiermacher or Kant, but in purely philosophical matters will find him in many respects more modern than Hegel or Schopenhauer.[14]

It was in the spheres of psychology and metaphysics that the dominion of Augustine was most complete. He aspired to

[12] Mirbt, *op. cit.*, p. 1.
[13] *Zeitschrift für Philosophie und Pädagogik*, 1888, p. 190.
[14] Eucken, *op. cit.*, p. 249.

know nothing, he tells us, but God and the soul; but these he strove with all his might to know altogether. His characteristic mark as a thinker was the inward gaze; the realities of consciousness were the primary objects of his contemplation; and from them he took his starting point for reflection on the world. Antiquity supplies no second to him in the breadth and acuteness of his psychological observation. And in his establishment of "immediate certainty of inner experience," as Windelband calls it,[15] in "the controlling central position of philosophic thought" he transcended his times and became "one of the founders of modern thought." If he may truly be said to have derived from Plato and Plotinus, in a far truer sense he stood above his Neo-Platonic teachers, and of his lineage have come Descartes and Malebranche and all that has proceeded from the movements of thought inaugurated by them. Even the famous ontological argument for the being of God, and, indeed, the very *cogito, ergo sum* of Descartes, have not merely their material but their formal pre-formation in him. It was not, however, in abstract thought alone, or chiefly, that he made his mark on the ages; his own thinking was markedly concrete, and nothing characterized it more strongly than the firmness of its grasp upon the realities of life, to the understanding and direction of which it was held strictly ancillary.

His impact upon the world might accordingly not unfairly be summed up, from one point of view, in the ethical revolution which he wrought. "In essence," remarks Harnack,[16] "Augustine's importance in the history of the Church and dogma lies in his giving to the West in the place of the Stoic-Christian popular morals, as that was recapitulated in Pelagianism, a religious, specifically Christian ethics, and so strongly impressing this on the Church that at least its formulas maintain up to to-day their supremacy in the whole extent of Western Chris-

[15] "A History of Philosophy," pp. 264, 270, 276.
[16] "Dogmengeschichte" [E. T. v. p. 30]; cf. on Augustine's place in the history of ethics, Joseph Mausbach, in "Die Kultur der Gegenwart," i. 4, 1906, p. 526.

tianity." Indeed, we might do worse, in seeking an index of his influence as a thinker, than fix upon the place he has occupied in political theory and practice. The entire political development of the Middle Ages was dominated by him; and he was in a true sense the creator of the Holy Roman Empire. It was no accident that the *De civitate Dei* was the favorite reading of Charlemagne: " he delighted," Einhard tells us (*Vita Caroli*, 24), " in the books of St. Augustine, and especially in those that bear the title ' Of the City of God.' " And in the great struggle between the Empire and the Papacy in the later eleventh century it was expressly to him that the controversialists on both sides made their appeal. No Father is quoted by them as often as he, except, perhaps, Gregory the Great; and no series of documents is cited more frequently than his writings, except, perhaps, the pseudo-Isidorian decretals.[17] Not only do writers like Walram of Naumburg and Wido of Ferrara reflect accurately his conception of the Church, with its emphasis on unity and its vacillation between the ideas of the *congregatio sanctorum* and a hierarchical organization — echoes of which still sound in William of Occam's " Defensor Pacis "' and the discussions of the conciliatory party in the Roman Church whose ornament was Gerson — but they made their appeal to Augustine in their endeavors to give validity to their defense " of the State as a Divine institution, of the moral significance and relative independence of the earthly sovereignty, of the necessary concordance of the *Sacerdotium* and *Imperium*," and the like.[18]

On the theoretical side he must be accredited, in this aspect of his thought, with the creation of the science of the Philosophy of History. For the primary significance of the *De civitate Dei* lies in the fact that " in it for the first time an ideal consideration, a comprehensive survey of human history found its expression." [19] No doubt his external position at the division of the ages, when the Old World was dying and the New

[17] Mirbt, *op. cit.*, p. 75.
[18] Reuter, *op. cit.*, p. 508.
[19] Seyrich, " Die Geschichtsphilosophie Augustins," 1891, p. 68.

World, under the dominion of Christianity, was struggling into its place, supplied him with incitement for the creation of this new science; and the demands which the times, in the crash of the secular order, made for an apology for Christianity, powerfully determined him to a general historical philosophy. But it was Christianity itself, as the entrance into the world of a renovating force, and his own particular conception of Christianity (leading him to conceive the history of human society no less than the course of the individual life, as the continuous evolution of the divine purpose, and impeling him to interpret all the forces of time as working harmoniously onward towards that faroff divine event to which all creation moves) that gave him not only the impulse to work out a philosophy of history, but the elements of the particular philosophy of history which he actually presents in his epoch-making treatise, which, incomplete and perhaps one-sided as it is, still retains full validity in its fundamental traits.

(d) *As a regilious genius.* — Not even, however, in Augustine the philosopher do we find the Augustine whose influence has wrought most powerfully in the world. The crisis through which he passed at his conversion was a profound religious revolution; and if he gave himself at once to the task of constructing a philosophy, it was distinctively a Christian philosophy he sought to construct, built though it was largely out of Platonic materials: the authority of Christ, he tells us in the earliest of the writings in which this task was prosecuted, ranked with him even above that of reason. And if he devoted all his powers to the exposition and defense of the Catholic faith, it was because he saw in the Catholic faith the pure expression of religion, and poured into the Catholic faith all the fulness of his religious emotion. It is not Augustine the traditionalist, or Augustine the thinker, but Augustine the religious genius, who has most profoundly influenced the world. The most significant fact about him is that he, first among Church teachers, gave adequate expression to that type of religion which has since attached to itself the name of " evangelical "; the religion, that is to say, of faith, as distinct from the religion of works; the religion which, despairing of self, casts all its hope on God, as opposed to the religion which, in a greater or less degree, trusts in itself; in a word — since religion in its very nature is dependence on God — religion in the purity of its conception, as over against a *quasi*-religious moralism. What requires particularly to be noted is that he gave full expression to this type of religion both in its vital and in its thetical aspects — the former most adequately in that unique book in which he reveals his soul, and admits us as spectators to the struggles of his great heart as it seeks to cleanse itself of all trust in itself and to lay hold with the grasp, first of despair, next of discerning trust, and then of grateful love, on the God who was its salvation; and the latter most adequately in that long series of writings in which he expounds, defends, and enforces with logical argument and moving exhortation the fundamental elements of the theology of grace, as against the most direct assailants which that theology has been called upon to meet in the whole history of Christian thought. The great contribution which Augustine has made to the world's life and thought is embodied in the theology of grace, which he has presented with remarkable clearness and force, vitally in his " Confessions," and thetically in his anti-Pelagian treatises.

It would be altogether a mistake to suppose that Augustine consciously discriminated between the theology of grace, which was his personal contribution to Christian thought, and the traditional Catholicism, which he gave his life to defend and propagate. In his own consciousness, the two were one: in his theology of grace he was in his own apprehension only giving voice to the Catholic faith in its purity. Nevertheless, however unconsciously, he worked with it a revolution both in Christian teaching and in Christian life, second in its depth and its far-reaching results to no revolution which has been wrought in Christian feeling and thought in the whole course of its history. A new Christian piety dates from him, in which, in place of the alternations of hope and fear which vex the lives of those who, in whatever degree, hang their hopes on their own merits, a mood of assured trust in the mercy of a gracious God is substituted as the spring of Christian life. And a new theology corresponding to this new type of piety dates from him; a theology which, recalling man from all dependence on his own powers or merits, casts him decisively on the grace of God alone for his salvation. Of course, this doctrine was not new in the sense that it was Augustine's invention; it was the doctrine of Paul, for example, before it was the doctrine of Augustine, and was only recovered for the Church by Augustine, though in that age, dominated in all its thinking by the dregs of Stoic rationalism, it came with all the force of a new discovery. And, of course, Augustine did not discover it all at once. Because his conversion was a vital religious experience, in which the religious relation was realized in thought and life in unwonted purity and power, the fundamental elements of his religious revolution were from the first present in his mind and heart; in his earliest Christian writings he already gives expression to both the formal and the material principles, as we may term them, of the theology of grace. The authority of the divine revelation in and through Christ, embodied in the Scriptures, and the utter dependence of man on God for all good (*potestas nostra Ipse est, da fidem*), are already the most intimate expression of his thought and life. But just because the religious system to which he gave himself on his conversion was taken over by him as a whole, time was requisite for the transfusion of the whole mass by the consistent explication and conscious exposition of the " Augustinianism " implicitly summed up in such maxims. The adjustment went on slowly, although it went on unbrokenly. It required ten years before the revived Paulinism attained even a fully consistent positive enunciation (first in the work, " De diversis quæstionibus ad Simplicianum," A.D. 396); and, though the leaven worked steadily thereafter more and more deeply and widely into his thought, death intervened before all the elements of his thinking were completely leavened. That is the reason why Augustine was both the founder of Roman Catholicism and the author of that doctrine of grace which it has been the constantly pursued effort of Roman Catholicism to neutralize, and which in very fact either must be neutralized by, or will neutralize, Roman Catholicism. Two children were struggling in the womb of his mind. There can be no doubt which was the child of his heart. His doctrine of the Church he had received whole from his predecessors, and he gave it merely the precision and vitality which insured its persistence. His doctrine of grace was all his own: it represented the very core of his being; and his whole progress in Christian thinking consists in the growing completeness with which its fundamental principles applied themselves in his mind to every department of life and thought. In this gradual subjection to them of every element of his inherited teaching, it was inevitable, had time been allowed, that his inherited doctrine of the Church, too, with all its implications, would have gone down before it, and Augustine would have bequeathed to the Church, not " problems," but a thoroughly worked out system of evangelical religion.

(e) *Augustine and Protestantism.* — The problem which Augustine bequeathed to the Church for solution, the Church required a thousand years to solve. But even so, it is Augustine who gave us the Reformation. For the Reformation, inwardly considered, was just the ultimate triumph of Augustine's doctrine of grace over Augustine's doctrine of the Church. This doctrine of grace came from Augustine's hands in its positive outline completely formulated: sinful man depends, for his recovery to good and to God, entirely on the free grace of God; this grace is therefore indispensable, prevenient, irresistible, indefectible; and, being thus the free grace of God, must have lain, in all the details of its conference and working, in the intention of God from all eternity. But, however clearly announced and forcefully commended by him, it required to make its way against great obstacles in the Church. As over against the Pelagians, the indispensableness of grace was quickly established; as over against the Semi-Pelagians, its prevenience was with almost equal rapidity made good. But there advance paused. If the necessity of prevenient grace was thereafter (after the second Council of Orange, 529) the established doctrine of the Church, the irresistibility of this prevenient grace was put under the ban, and there remained no place for a complete " Augustinianism " within the Church, as Gottschalk and Jansen were fully to discover. Therefore, when the great revival of religion which we call the Reformation came, seeing that it was, on its theological side, a revival of " Augustinianism," as all great revivals of religion must be (for " Augustinianism " is but the thetical expression of religion in its purity), there was nothing for it but the rending of the Church. And therefore also the greatest peril to the Reformation was and remains the diffused anti-" Augustinianism " in the world; and, by a curious combination of circumstances, this, its greatest enemy, showed itself most dangerous in the hands of what we must otherwise look upon as the chief ally of the Reformation — that is to say, Humanism. Humanism was the ally of the Reformation in so far as it, too, worked for the emancipation of the human spirit; and, wherever it was religious, it became the seed-plot of the Reformation. But there was a strong anti-" Augustinian " party among the Humanists, and from it emanated the gravest danger which threatened the Reformation. Where this tone of thought was dominant the Reformation failed, because religious depth was wanting. What Spain, for example, lacked, says R. Saint-Hilaire justly, was not freedom of thought, but the Gospel. In the first stages of the Reformation movement in the North, this anti-" Augustinianism " may be looked upon as summed up in Erasmus; and Erasmus, on this very ground, held himself aloof from the Reformation movement, and that movement held itself aloof from him. " I am at present reading our Erasmus," wrote Luther six months before he nailed his theses on the door of the Schloss-Kirche at Wittenberg, " but my heart recoils more and more from him. . . . Those who ascribe something to man's freedom of will regard these things differently from those who know only God's free grace." Do we realize how much we owe to Erasmus and his friends that they remained Roman Catholics, and thus permitted the " Augustinianism " of the Reformation to plant its seed and to bear its fruit?

LITERATURE. — The literature upon Augustine is immense.

An excellent selection from it is given by Loofs at the head of the article " Augustinus " in Herzog, " Realencyklopädie für protestantische Theologie und Kirche," [3] ii. pp. 257 ff., with which should be compared that given by Harnack, " History of Dogma," v. pp. 61 f. The following deal directly with the influence of Augustine: Feuerlein, " Ueber die Stellung Augustins in der Kirchen- und Kulturgeschichte," in von Sybel's " Historische Zeitschrift," 1869, xxii. pp. 270–313; Reuter, " Augustinische Studien," Gotha, 1887, vii. pp. 479–516; Cunningham, " S. Austin and his place in the History of Christian Thought " (Hulsean Lectures for 1885), London, 1886; Schaff, " History of the Christian Church," iii., New York, 1884, § 180, pp. 1016–1028; Eucken, " Die Lebensanschauungen der grossen Denker," Leipzig, 1890 (2nd ed. 1897, pp. 216–250; 4th ed. 1902, pp. 210, etc.); Nourrisson, " La Philosophie de Sant Augustin," Paris, 1866, ii. pp. 147–276; Werner, " Die Scholastik des späteren Mittelalters," iii., Vienna, 1883, and " Die Augustinische Psychologie in ihrer mittelalterlich-scholastischen Einkleidung und Gestaltung," *Sitzungsberichte der phil.-hist. Classe der kais. Akademie der Wissenschaften,* Vienna, 1882, pp. 435–494; Siebeck, " Die Anfänge der neueren Psychologie," in *Zeitschrift für Philosophie und Pädagogik,* 1888, pp. 161 f., cf. his " Geschichte der Psychologie "; Ehrle, " Der Augustinismus und der Aristotelismus in der Scholastik gegen Ende des xiii. Jahrhundert," " Archiv für Literatur- und Kirchengeschichte des Mittelalters," 1889, v. pp. 603–635, cf. also *Zeitschrift für Katholische Theologie,* Innsbruck, 1889, xiii. pp. 172–193; Mirbt, " Die Stellung Augustins in der Publicistik des gregorianischen Kirchenstreits," Leipzig, 1888; Koch, " Der heilige Faustus, Bischof von Riez," Stuttgart, 1895, pp. 129–191; Gwatkin, " The Knowledge of God," [2] 1908, ii. p. 179; Portalié, " Augustine," in " Catholic Encyclopædia," ii. pp. 84–104, New York, 1907. The text of Augustine is most generally accessible in " Patrologia Latina," xxxii.-xlvii.; and his chief writings are translated in " Nicene and Post-Nicene Fathers," First Series i.–viii., Oxford and New York, 1886–1888.

III

AUGUSTINE'S DOCTRINE OF KNOWLEDGE AND AUTHORITY

AUGUSTINE'S DOCTRINE OF KNOWLEDGE AND AUTHORITY[1]

FIRST ARTICLE

AUGUSTINE marks almost as great an epoch in the history of philosophy as in the history of theology. It was with him that the immediate assurance of consciousness first took its place as the source and warrant of truth. No doubt there had been a long preparation for the revolution which was wrought by his announcement of " the principle of the absolute and immediate certainty of consciousness," as Windelband calls it, and his establishment of it in " the controlling central position of philosophic thought." But the whole preceding development will not account for the act of genius by which he actually shifted the basis of philosophy, and in so doing became " the true teacher of the middle ages," no doubt, but above and beyond that " one of the founders of modern thought." [2] He may himself be said to have come out of Plato, or Plotinus; but in even a truer sense out of him came Descartes and his successors.[3] When he urged men to cease seeking truth without them, and to turn within, since the home of truth is inside of man, he already placed them upon the firm footing which Descartes sought with his *cogito ergo sum*.[4]

[1] From *The Princeton Theological Review*, v. 1907, pp. 353–397.

[2] Windelband, " A History of Philosophy," E. T. pp. 276, 264, 270.

[3] Leder, " Augustins Erkenntnistheorie," p. 76: " If we must see in Plotinus the father of Augustine's Platonism, we may yet recognize it as an especially original service of the Church Father, that he established over against all scepticism the first point of all certitude in self-consciousness. He found in Plotinus no guidance for this: rather by an act of genius he anticipated in it the line of thought which Descartes (1640) made in his *Meditationes* the starting point of his expositions."

[4] " De vera religione," 39.72: " Noli foras ire, in te ipsum redi, in interiore homine habitat veritas."

If Augustine can be said to have had a philosophical master before he fell under the influence of the Neo-Platonists, that master must be discerned in Cicero. And from Cicero he derived rather a burning zeal in the pursuit of truth than a definite body of philosophical tenets or even a philosophical point of view. It is a mistake to think of him as ever surrendering himself to the skepticism of the New Academy. He does, indeed, tell us that, in his disillusionment with Manichaeism and his increasing despair of attaining the truth, the notion sprang up within him that the so-called Academics might after all prove the best philosophers, contending as they did that everything hangs in doubt and truth cannot be comprehended by men.[5] It is not strange that at such moments his thoughts surged in great waves towards their teachings.[6] But he tells us also that he could not commit himself to them; not only because he was repelled by their heathenism,[7] but also because he was shocked by their skepticism.[8] His difficulty at the time lay, in fact, in another quarter. He found no obstacle in the attainment of certitude: but nothing but apodeictic certitude satisfied him. He entertained no doubt, for example, that seven and three make ten; what he demanded was the same kind and degree of certainty he had here, for everything else. In other words, he would not commit himself to any truth for which he did not have ready at hand complete demonstration.

[5] " Confessiones " v. 10. 19.

[6] " De ultilitate credendi," viii. 20: " Saepe mihi videbatur [verum] non posse inveniri, magnique fluctus cogitationum mearum in Academicorum suffragium ferebantur." He proceeds to say that so often as he was thus tempted, he reacted on considering the vivacity, sagacity, perspicacity of the human mind; he could not believe this mind so much incapable of truth as ignorant as yet of the right way of going about its discovery: thus he was led to meditate on the problem of authority. " De beata vita," i. 4: " at ubi discussos eos [Manichaeos] evasi, maxime trajecto isto mari, dui gubernacula mea repugnantia omnibus ventis in mediis fluctibus Academici tenuerunt."

[7] " Confessiones " v. 14. 25: " I utterly refused to commit the healing of my soul to these philosophers, because they knew not the saving name of Christ."

[8] " Confessiones " vi. 4. 6: " I was not so insane as to fancy that not even this " — mathematical truth — " could be comprehended."

Augustine's point of departure was therefore the precise contradictory of that of the Academics. They asserted that we can never get beyond suspense because we lack all criterion of truth. The best we can do is to say that this or that looks like truth; that it is *verisimile* or *probabile:* we can never affirm that it is truth, *verum;* though, of course, we can as little affirm that it is not truth. Lacking all *signum,* we are left in utter and hopeless uncertainty. Augustine, on the contrary, in the apodeictic certainty of, say, mathematical formulas, was in possession of a sure criterion on the basis of which he could confidently assert truth. His difficulty was that he wished to apply this *signum* mechanically to every sphere of truth alike, and could content himself with no other kind of certitude. He was tempted to declare that nothing resting on less cogent grounds is known, or can be known, at all. What he needed yet was to learn that so far from the possession of apodeictic certitude for some things throwing into the shadow of doubt all for which it cannot be adduced, it provides a basis for valid assurance with respect to them, too. On the basis of this *signum* we may obtain in every sphere at least the *verisimile,* the *probabile* — a sufficient approach to truth to serve all practical purposes; or rather truth itself though not truth in its purity, free from all admixture of error. In other words, in every department of investigation there is attainable real and clear, if somewhat roughly measured, knowledge. What we currently call a yard of muslin, for example, though shown by the application of a micrometer not to be an exact yard, is yet by the self-same test just as truly shown to be a yard for all the practical ends for which muslin is used. The possession of a criterion gives validity to the *verisimile;* for who can declare that anything is like the truth unless he has the truth itself in mind with which to compare it and by which to judge it?

It was by a line of reasoning something like this that Augustine overthrew the Academics when, in his retirement at Cassiciacum, in the interval between his conversion and his baptism, he undertook to lay the foundations of a positive

Christian philosophy. It is absurd to talk of a *verisimile*, he urged, unless the standard, the *verum*, is in our possession. And not only is this standard, this *verum*, certainly in the possession of every man and instinctively employed by him; but no one can by any means rid himself of it. Do what we will, we cannot help knowing that the world is either one or not one; [9] that three times three are nine; [10] and the like; that is to say the principles which underlie, say for example, logic and mathematics. And in knowing these things, we know them not only to be true, but to be eternally and immutably true, quite independently of our thinking minds — so that they would be equally true if no human minds had ever existed, and would remain true though the whole human race should perish.[11] With this indefectible certainty of necessary truth the mind unavoidably knows, therefore, the laws of the true, the beautiful and the good,[12] according to which, as its criterion, it judges all of the true, beautiful, and good which is brought into observation in the experience of life. Nor can doubt be thrown upon these things by calling in question the reality of the very mind itself by which they are known, and therefore the validity of its convictions. Rather, the reality of the mind is given in the very act of knowledge: for what is not cannot act. Say even that this act is an act of doubt. If the mind did not exist, it could not even doubt.[13] The act of doubt itself becomes, thus, the credential of certitude. It is impossible even to doubt unless we are, and remember, and understand, and will, and think, and know, and judge: so that he that doubts must not and cannot doubt of these things, seeing that even if he doubts he does them.[14] Even he who says, "I do not know," thereby evinces not only that he exists and that he knows that he exists, but also that he knows what knowing is and that he

---

[9] "Cont. Acad." iii. 10. 23.

[10] "Cont. Acad." iii. 11. 25.

[11] "Cont. Acad." iii. 11. 25: necesse est, vel genere humano stertente, sit verum. Cf. "De lib. arbit." ii. 8. 21; "De Trinitate, ix. 6.

[12] "De lib. arbit." ii. 8, 9, 10, 15, 16; "De Trinitate," ix. 6; viii. 3; xiv. 15.

[13] "De lib. arbit." ii. 3, 7.

[14] "De Trinitate," x. 10. 14.

knows that he knows it.[15] It is impossible to be ignorant that
we are; and as this is certain, many other things are certain
along with it, and the confident denial of this is only another
way of demonstrating it.

What Augustine is doing in this reasoning, it will be observed, is withdrawing attention from the external world and
focusing it upon the inner consciousness. There, there alone,
he asserts, can truth be found. Those who seek it without,
never attain to it;[16] it is in the inner man that it makes its
home, and it can be discovered, therefore, only by those who
look within.[17] His polemic is turned upon that Sensationalism
in philosophy which had long reigned supreme in the schools,
and the dominion of which he was the first to break. In this
polemic, he considered himself to be building upon the New
Academy, whose mordant criticism of knowledge he persuaded
himself was only the negative side of a defense of an essential
Platonism which they kept, in its positive side, meanwhile in
reserve. In this judgment of fact he was certainly mistaken;
the Academy had itself fallen into the prevalent Sensationalism
and was itself, therefore, as truly as the Epicurean and Stoic
schools of the time the object of his confutation.[18] But to the
Sensationalistic maxim that " there is nothing in the intellect
which was not beforehand in the senses," by whomsoever
taught and in whatsoever forms, he opposes the direct contradiction that truth is to be sought, in the first instance, in
the intellect alone. As Robert Browning phrases it, " to know
rather consists in opening out a way whence the imprisoned
splendor may escape, than in effecting entry for a light supposed to be without." In other words, Augustine came forward
as a flaming Rationalist in the philosophical sense of that
term; in the sense, that is, in which it describes those thinkers
who hold that the " reason " is the fundamental source of

[15] " De Trinitate," x. 1. 3.

[16] " De vera religione," 49.94: . . . " veritas, ad quam nullo modo per-
veniunt qui foris eam quaerunt."

[17] " De vera religione," 39.72: " noli foras ire, in te ipsum redi, in interiore
homine habitat veritas." Cf. " Retractationes," i. 13.

[18] Cf. Leder, " Augustins Erkenntnistheorie," p. 35.

knowledge; and, in opposition alike to Sensationalism and Empiricism, which teach respectively that our knowledge is derived exclusively from sensation or experience (that is, sensation and reflection), contend rather that it is the " reason," acting under laws of its own, which supplies the forms of thought without which no knowledge can be obtained either by sensation or by experience.

Arnobius, his fellow African of a hundred years before, on the basis of the popular Stoicism was as flaming a Sensationalist as Augustine was a Rationalist, and it is interesting to contrast the strong expressions which the two give, each to his own point of view. Arnobius calls to the aid of his exposition the imaginary case of a man secluded from infancy to maturity in a dark cavern, guarded from every possible commerce with the external world. Such an one, he contends, would remain mentally empty; and, if confronted, not with some complicated problem, but with even the simple twice two are four, would stand like a stock or the Marpesian rock, as the saying is, dumb and speechless, understanding nothing.[19] In staring contrast with Arnobius, Augustine sometimes speaks as if contact with the external world and the intrusion of sensible images into the mind were a positive hindrance to the acquisition of knowledge; and as if the mind would do its essential work better if it could do it free from what, in that case, would be conceived as the distractions of sense; as if, in a word, something like the condition in which Laura Bridgman or Helen Keller were found were the most favorable for the development of human intelligence. This exaggeration, however, is no part of his system; and its occasional suggestion serves only to throw into a high light the strength and seriousness of his rationalism.

This rationalism, however, it may be observed, is never pressed to the extreme of conceiving the reason as the creator of its own object. That is to say, it never passes into the Idealism which in more modern times has lain so frequently in its

---

[19] Arnobius, " Adv. Gent." ii. 20 (American ed. of " The Ante-Nicene Fathers," vi. p. 442).

pathway. To Augustine the world of observation was far from being merely a " psychological phenomenon." Indeed, not only does he recognize the objectivity of the world of sense, but, with all the vigor of his contention that we must look within for truth, he insists equally on the objectivity of even the intelligible world. Man no more creates the world of ideas he perceives within him, than the world of sense he perceives without him. In his assertion that the objects of sensible and intellectual perception alike have indubitable objectivity lies, indeed, one of the main features of Augustine's philosophy.[20] Perhaps we may best catch his general idea, in the distinction he made between the two modes of knowledge — sense perception and intellection — corresponding to the two worlds, sensible and intelligible — if we represent him as thinking of the human soul as existing in a double environment, with both of which it is connected by appropriate organs of perception. On the one hand, it is connected with the sensible world by the external senses; on the other hand, with the intelligible world by the *sensus intimus* which is the intellect.[21] Augustine's notion is, essentially, that the soul, by these two modes of contact with its double environment, is enabled to read off the facts of each. His mode of statement commonly takes the form that as the sensible world impresses itself upon us through the external senses, so the intelligible world impresses itself upon us through the intellect: but we must not press the passivity of the soul to its several impressions which might seem

[20] Cf. Nourrison, " La Philosophie de Sant Augustin," ii. p. 295: " To affirm the certitude of consciousness is, for him, to affirm in the same act the certitude of the external world. . . . It is well to take note of the sagacity with which he distinguishes the phenomenon from the being and thus exonerates the senses from the errors which are commonly attributed to them. Organs and witnesses of what passes, and not of what does not pass, of the phenomenal and not the real, they are not the judges of truth — *judicium veritatis non esse in sensibus*. It is the intellect that knows or the intellect that deceives itself. Its knowledge is certitude. No Scotchman of our day could express it better."

[21] " Cont. Acad." iii. 17. 37: " Platonem sensisse duos esse mundos, unum intelligibilem, in quo ipsa veritas habitaret, istum autem sensibilem, quem manifestum esse nos visu tactuque sentire. Itaque illum verum, hunc verisimilem. . . ."

implied in this mode of statement. If, now, these two s, the sensible and the intelligible, stood contradictorily over against each other, the soul of man lying between them and invaded by impressions from each, would be in parlous case. Such, however, is not Augustine's conception. The sensible world is not thought of by him as itself independent of the intelligible. It not only has its source in the intelligible world, but derives its whole support and direction from it; and reflects, after its own fashion, its content. It cannot be perceived, therefore, save, so to speak, from the angle of the intelligible world; and in order that it may be understood, the soul must bring to its perception the principles derived from the intelligible world. In a word, the soul is caparisoned for the perception and understanding of the sensible world only by prior perception and understanding of the intelligible world. That is to say, the soul brings over from the intelligible world the forms of thought under which alone the sensible world can be received by it into a mental embrace.

This is, of course, a very developed form of Intuitionalism. According to the Stoics — those Sensationalists *a outrance* — the human mind is in the first instance a *tabula rasa,* on which outer things impress themselves ($\tau \acute{\upsilon} \pi \omega \sigma \iota \varsigma$). But even the Stoics could speak of truths of nature. In their most materialistic development they could find a place in their system for general ideas common to all men ($\kappa o \iota \nu \alpha \grave{\iota}$ $\check{\epsilon} \nu \nu o \iota \alpha \iota$, *communes notiones*), which they not only recognized as real, but valued as the best constituents of human knowledge. As men have practically the same environment, they explained, the sum of the impressions made by surrounding nature upon each, is practically the same as the sum of the impressions made upon all. Hence, peculiar confidence should be put in the ideas common to all men: they are the general teachings of nature, that nature life in conformity with which is the wise man's mark. "Natural ideas" are not foreign, then, to the Stoic system; but when the Stoics spoke of these ideas as "natural," they did not at all mean that they constitute a part of the nature with which man is endowed. Man was not supposed to bring them into life with him, but distinctly to acquire them in the process of living: they are impressed by nature on his soul. The transition is easy, however, from the conception of a body of ideas natural to man in this sense, to a conception of a body of ideas belonging to his nature as such, or, in other words, innate. Along with his reason, it is now said, every man possesses by nature, that is, by his constitution as man, a body of ideas: they belong to his nature as a rational being. In making this step we have definitely passed over from Sensationalism to Rationalism, and have so far approached Augustine's conception. But we have not yet reached it. The doctrine of innate ideas, strictly construed in that form is deistic. These ideas are ours because they have been from the beginning once for all impressed upon our nature by our Maker, who has made us thus and not otherwise — namely, so that by the action of our intellect we become aware of the principles thus made a part of our very structure. Augustine, however, was as little deistic as Sensationalistic in his thinking, and necessarily advanced a step further to a truly theistic Intuitionalism. These ideas, he teaches, are natural to man in the sense that they inhere in his nature as such, and are not impressed on him by external nature; and they are innate in the sense that they belong to his nature from the beginning of his being. But he cannot conceive them merely as impressed on the mind, or rather built into its structure, once for all at its creation. He thinks rather of the soul as constantly dependent on God, who is no more its Creator than its Upholder and Director; and of its intrinsic ideas as, therefore, continuously impressed on it by God. Thus its light is God alone; and the soul, in intellection, bears the same constant relation to God the Illuminator as in ethical action it bears to God the Sanctifier. God, he is never weary of saying, in his own adaptation of a Platonic formula, is at once the Author of all being, the Light of all knowledge, and the Fountain of all good; the God of creation, of truth, of grace: or, otherwise put, the *causa subsistendi*, the *ratio intelligendi*, and the *ordo vivendi*. His ontology of "innate ideas," accordingly, is that they are the immediate product in the soul of God the Illuminator, always present with the soul as its sole and indispensable Light, in which alone it perceives truth.

No doubt there is a Neo-Platonic factor in this construction, and possibly also the modes of expression employed may betray a reminiscence of Stoic τύπωσις — with the source of the impression elevated, however, from nature to nature's God. But we must beware of pushing it out of its theistic sobriety into the regions of an essentially pantheistic mode of thought, whether developed or only implicated. Nothing could be farther from Augustine's meaning than that God, as the Universal Reason and Sole Intelligence, comes to the knowledge of the truth in us, and we in and by Him, so that our knowledge simply coalesces with His. His doctrine of creation, by which the creature is set as an objective somewhat, with powers of its own, over against God the Creator, placed him at a whole diameter's distance from the pantheistic tendencies of Plotinus, otherwise so much his master.[22] But neither does the "ontologism" of William of Paris and Malebranche, Fenelon and Bossuet precisely reproduce his meaning. Augustine does not teach that we contemplate immediately the Divine Being, and in Him the intelligible world, that pleroma of eternal and immutable truths which constitutes the world of divine Ideas.[23] It would be much nearer his meaning to say that we see God in the eternal truths which by our *sensus intimus* we contemplate, than that we see them in Him. Undoubtedly he teaches that the soul has an immediate knowledge of God; and, in a sense, he does identify with God the intelligible world into contact with which the soul is brought by its *sensus intimus*. We should not be far from his meaning, however, if, reverting to a mode of representation we have already employed, we should say that the soul, set in its double environment, the sensible world on the one hand and the intelligible world on the

[22] Cf. Nourrison, *op. cit.*, ii. pp. 301, 334; Grandgeorge, "St. Augustine et le Néoplatonisme," p. 111; Portalié in Vacant-Mangenot, "Dictionaire de Théologie Catholique, i. col. 2330. *Per contra*, however, Ritschl, Loesche, etc.

[23] Cf. Portalié as cited, col. 2335; and Storz, "Philosophie d. hl. Aug.," pp. 65 *sq.*

other, as it knows the sensible world directly through the senses, so knows God in the intelligible world directly through the intellect. But God is not identified with the intelligible world, as it appears in the soul of man, except as its immediate author. He is in the soul of man not *substantialiter* but only *effective;* and it is precisely in this that the difficulty of the conception lies. If we may be permitted to employ theological conceptions here, we may say that Augustine's ontology of the intuition by which man attains intelligible truth, embraced especially two factors: the doctrine of the image of God, and the doctrine of dependence on God. To put it briefly, man's power of attaining truth depends, in his view, first of all upon the fact that God has made man like Himself, Whose intellect is the home of the intelligible world, the contents of which may, therefore, be reflected in the human soul; and then, secondly, that God, having so made man, has not left him, deistically, to himself, but continually reflects into his soul the contents of His own eternal and immutable mind — which are precisely those eternal and immutable truths which constitute the intelligible world. The soul is therefore in unbroken communion with God, and in the body of intelligible truths reflected into it from God, sees God. The nerve of this view, it will be observed, is the theistic conception of the constant dependence of the creature on God. This stands midway between the deistic conception, on the one side, that has no need of God except for the primal originating of the creature, and supposes that after that the creature's own powers suffice for all its acts; and the pantheistic view, on the other side, which substitutes the divine action for the creature's action and, having no need of a creature at all, transforms it into a mere simulacrum without reality of being or action. In the Theistic view, there is postulated the creature as the product of a real creation, by which it produced a real thing with real activities of its own; and alongside of this, the real dependence of this creature for the persistence and use of all its activities on the constant action of God. Applying this conception to the problem of intellection, Augustine conceives the soul as at once active and acted upon, but as active only because acted upon. It is only in the light of God, the sun of the soul, that the soul is illuminated to see light.

There was nothing novel in the ascription of all human knowledge to the illumination of God. It was not only Numenius who declared all knowledge to be but the kindling of a little light from the great light which lightens the world.[24] Platonist and Stoic alike offered a metaphysical and epistemological basis for such a representation. According to the one, knowledge is recollection; and Cicero had explained this — or explained it away — as meaning that right knowledge is implanted in the soul by God at its creation, and is, therefore, inherent in it; while Plotinus' language on the subject is scarcely distinguishable from Augustine's.[25] According to the other, the human *logos* is but a fraction of the universal *Logos* and reproduces in its thought His normative mind. In the mere matter of forms of statement, therefore, Augustine had harbingering enough. It was, nevertheless, quite a new spirit which informed his declarations, the spirit of a pure theism, derived, not from his philosophical predecessors, but from those Scriptures which themselves also told him of the true light that lighteth every man who cometh into the world.[26] It was the personal God, therefore, whom he spoke of as the " Sun of the soul, by whose illumination alone can intelligible verities be perceived," [27] the " Light of the truth," by which alone is knowledge of the truth awakened in the soul,[28] or — changing the figure only — the inner Monitor and Master of the soul.[29] It was the personal Logos that he had in mind, through whose immanent working all things that exist exist, all things that live live, all things that understand understand. Surely if it

[24] Eusebius, " Praep. Evang.," xi. 18.
[25] Cf. " De civitate Dei," x. 2.
[26] Cf. " Tract. in Joan." ii. 7; " Epist." 120. 4; " De pecc. merit." i. 25, 37, 48.
[27] " Solill.," i. 3.
[28] " De pecc. merit.," i. 25, 37.
[29] " De magistro."

be true even of the body that in Him we live and move and have our being,[30] it must much more be true of the mind, which, having been made in His likeness, lives and moves and has its being in Him in some more excellent, but of course not visible but intelligible way,[31] so that our spiritual illumination comes from the Word of God.[32]

We perceive that the outcome of this conception is that the condition of all knowledge is revelation. Accordingly, our action in seeking knowledge is represented as essentially a consultation of God; God's action in giving us knowledge as essentially a transference of truth to us by a divine imprinting of it on the soul. That mental act which we call understanding, Augustine explains,[33] is performed in two ways: either by the mind or reason within itself, as when we understand that the intellect itself exists; or on occasion of a suggestion from the senses, as when we understand that matter exists: in the first of which two kinds of acts we understand through ourselves, that is, by consulting God [34] concerning that which is within us; while in the second we understand by consulting God regarding that of which intimation is given us by the body and the senses. That is to say, in brief, knowledge of the sensible and of the intelligible alike is God-given, and in both instances is to be obtained only by referring to His teaching. He adds, in another place,[35] that this God who is so consulted, and who, being so consulted, teaches us, is none other than Christ, who dwells in the inner man — that is to say, " the incommutable Virtue of God, and His eternal Wisdom, which every rational soul, indeed, consults, though to each there is given only in proportion to his receptive capacity as determined by his own bad or good will." The divine act of giving, Augustine presents by predilection under the figure of an impressing as by a seal

---

[30] " Epist." 120. 4; " De Trinitate," xiv. 12.
[31] " De Trinitate, xiv. 12.
[32] Cf. " Tract. in Joan.," i.
[33] " Epist." xiii. (to Nebridius) 4.
[34] Deum consulendo.
[35] " De magistro," xi. 38.

or stamp, upon the soul. In what may be thought, perhaps, the classical passage on this subject,[36] he raises the question whence men obtain their knowledge of God and of the moral law. Not from memory, he answers, whether of their former existence in Adam or of any other state. Whence, then? Can we suppose that they can read off these immutable laws from their own mutable natures; these righteous laws from their own unrighteous hearts? "Where, then, do these rules stand written, whence even the unrighteous may recognize what is righteous; whence he that has not may learn what he ought to have? Where can they stand written save in the book of that Light which is called the Truth, whence every righteous law is transcribed, and transferred into the heart of the man who works righteousness, not by a process of transportation, but by a process of imprinting, as the device from a ring while it passes over into the wax, yet does not leave the ring." What the soul receives, therefore, is not the ring itself with its device; certainly not the device in the ring; but the device as impressed upon it from the ring, and the ring only in and through the device. The care which is taken here to represent the process as a transference of the laws without transfusion of the substance may be said to be the characteristic feature of this passage, as it is of the entire teaching of Augustine on the topic. The figure itself is in repeated use by him, and always with the same implication. Nowhere does he permit the reader to suppose either that God in His substance invades the soul, or that the soul sees in God the ideas which constitute the intelligible world: although he insists steadily that these ideas are the ideas that are in God and that he who sees them, therefore, so far sees God — but in a glass darkly. In a word, he preserves the distinctness of the human soul at the same time that he discovers in the intelligible world open to the soul a point of contact with God; and in the soul's perception of the intelligibles a perception at the same time of God, whose existence thus becomes to the soul as intuitively certain as is its own.

[36] "De Trinitate," xiv. 15. 21.

The effect of such an ascription of all human knowledge
to a revelation from God is naturally greatly to increase the
assurance with which truth is embraced. The ultimate ground
of our certitude becomes our confidence in God. In the last
analysis, God is our surety for the validity of our knowledge;
and that, not merely remotely, as the author of our faculties
of knowing, but also immediately as the author of our every
act of knowing, and of the truth which is known. We must
guard, indeed, against supposing that, in Augustine's view, the
human mind is passive in the acquisition of knowledge, or that
the acquisition of knowledge is unconditioned by the nature
or state of the acquiring soul. We have already had occasion
to quote passages in which the contrary is asserted, but we
must now emphasize it with some energy. We have been con-
templating thus far only Augustine's ontology of knowledge:
that we may be sure that we understand him aright we need
to attend also to his expositions of its mode. The fundamental
principle which rules his thought here may be brought into
relation with his favorite figure, if we bear in mind that an impression from a seal is conditioned not only by the device on
the seal from which the transference is made, but also by the
nature and state of the wax into which it is made — which
" takes " the impression, as we say. Suppose, for example, that
the wax is not of a quality, or is not in a condition, to take or
to retain with exactness or with clearness the device which is
impressed upon it? Augustine accordingly insists that, although
" every rational mind consults the eternal wisdom," that is to
say, by virtue of its very rationality is a recipient of impressions from the divine world of ideas, and thus has the acquisition of truth opened to it, or even, rather, thrust upon it: yet
this truth is " actually laid open to it (' unfolded to it,' pan-
ditur) in each case, only so far as it is able to lay hold of it
(' receive it,' ' take it,' capere) by reason of (propter) its own
will, whether evil or good." [37] In the interests of this point of

---

[37] " De magistro," xi. 38; cf. also " De Trinitate," xiv. 15. 21, ad finem;
" In Psalmos," iv. 8, med. et fin. Knowledge, therefore, with Augustine, is conditioned by the will; though we must be careful not to take the term " will "

view, Augustine made, in effect, a distinction between ideas, conceptions and perceptions. The ideas, which are reflections from the divine mind are always shining into the souls of men, unchangeable in the midst of men's multiform changes, whether these changes are due to their natural development from infancy to maturity, and on to old age, or to any other accident of life. But the perception of these ideas by the differing souls of men, or by the same soul in its varying stages or states, and, much more, the conceptions built up upon the foundation of these perceptions by the differing souls, or by the same soul in its varying states — obviously these are very different matters. In these things the soul itself comes into play, and the result will differ as soul differs from soul, or the soul in one of its states differs from itself in another of its states. If the condition of all knowledge, then, is revelation, and therefore all knowledge is in its source divine; yet it is equally true that the qualification of all knowledge is rooted in the human nature that knows, and in the specific state of the human being whose particular knowledge it is. It is in this fact that the varying degrees of purity in which knowledge is acquired by men find their explanation.

The underlying conception here is the very fruitful one that knowledge is not a function of the intellect merely but involves the whole man. There is nothing on which Augustine more strenuously insists; as, indeed, there is nothing upon which from his psychological or ethical point of view it became him more strenuously to insist. His psychological insight was too clear, and his analysis too profound, for him to lose sight of the simplicity of the soul and its consequent engagement

in too narrow a sense — as if it always must mean in Augustine the faculty of determination. It is, rather, quite frequently the whole voluntary nature; and what Augustine is really teaching is that the ethical state of the soul conditions knowledge. See the whole subject discussed from different points of view by W. Kahl, "Die Lehre vom Primat des Willens bei Augustinus, Duns Scotus und Descartes," 1886, and O. Zänker, "Der Primat des Willens vor dem Intellekt bei Augustin," in "Beiträge zur Förderung christlicher Theologie," xi. 1907. The literature of the subject is cited by these writers.

as a whole in all its acts; and the demands of his ethical nature were too clamant and his religious sense too lively to permit him to forget for an instant the determining effect upon every movement of the soul of the influences proceeding from them. Accordingly he does not content himself with declaring that no one can hope to see the truth without giving to philosophy his whole self.[38] Applying this conception in detail, he insists that God accords the truth only to those who seek it *pie, caste et diligenter*,[39] and urges therefore to a strenuous and devout pursuit of it, because it is only those who so seek whom God aids,[40] and the vision of the truth belongs only to those who live well, pray well, and labor well.[41] The conception includes more than a contention that for the actual framing of knowledge there is required no less than the action of God reflecting truth into the soul, an action of the soul's own in embracing this truth, and prior to that a preparation of the soul for embracing it. It seems to be further implied that the several orders of truth need different kinds or at least degrees of preparation for their reception. In proportion as we rise in the scale of knowledge, in that proportion embracing the truth becomes difficult and the preparation of the soul arduous. To attain the knowledge of God, which stands at the apex of achievement, demands therefore a very special purgation. Drawing near to Him does not mean journeying through space, for He is everywhere; it means entering into that purity and virtue in which He dwells.[42] " O God," he prays, " whom no one finds who is

---

[38] " Cont. Acad." ii. 3. 8: " ipsum verum non videbis, nisi in philosophiam totus intraveris."

[39] " De quantitate animae," xiv. 24.

[40] " De vera religione," x. 20: " intende igitur . . . diligenter et pie, quantum potes; tales enim adjuvat Deus."

[41] " De ordine," ii. 19. 51.

[42] " De doctrina Christiana," i. 10. 10: " The soul must be purified that it may have power to perceive that light and to rest in it when it is perceived "; this purification is journeying to God, for it is not by change of place that we draw near to Him who is everywhere, but by becoming pure and virtuous. Cf. " De Trinitate," iv. 18. 24: Sinful men need cleansing to be fitted to see eternal things; " De agone Christiano," xiii. 14: A vicious life cannot see that pure and sincere and changeless life.

not fully purged." [43] The influence of his Neo-Platonic teachers
is here very apparent, and is further manifested in a tendency
to represent the purgation of the soul for the higher knowledge
as consisting largely in its emancipation from sense. With
him as with them knowledge of the truth is constantly spoken
of as hanging essentially upon the escape of the soul from entanglement with the sensible.[44] This, as we have seen, is a
corollary of his rationalism and was perhaps inevitable with
his training. But these expressions which might be almost
exactly matched in Plotinus, have in Augustine, nevertheless,
an indefinitely deeper implication than in his Neo-Platonic
predecessors. With him the purely intellectualistic bearing
which they have with them, has noticeably given way to a
profoundly ethical one. Though he may still say that " the
filth of the soul " " from which filth the more one is cleansed,
the more readily he sees the truth," is shortly " the love of anything whatever except God and the soul ";[45] and though, therefore, he may still relatively depreciate all knowledge other than
that of God and the soul; yet after all, as he uses these terms,
it is of something far more profound than the relative intellectual rank of the several objects of knowledge that he is
thinking.

The implications of this general conception carried Augustine very far. Three of the corollaries which flow from it
seem especially worthy of attention here. The first of these is
that, the human soul being finite, it cannot hope to attain to
absolutely perfect knowledge. The second is that, the human
soul being subject to development, it can hope to attain to
anything like adequate knowledge only by a slow process, and
by means of aid from without. The third is that, the human
soul in its present condition being sinful, there is a clog upon
it in its aspiration to knowledge which it can never in its own
strength overcome. In order that we may apprehend Augustine's thought we must therefore attend to his doctrine of mystery as lying at the heart of all our knowledge; to his doctrine

[43] " Solil.," i. 3.   [45] " De utilitate credendi," 34.
[44] " Cont. Acad." II. ii.

of authority as the necessary pedagogue to knowledge; and to his doctrine of revelation as the palliative, and of grace as the cure, of the noetic effects of sin.

In his assertion of the certitude of human knowledge, Augustine is far from asserting that the human soul can know everything; or that it can know anything with that perfection of knowledge with which the infinite mind knows all things. It is impossible for the finite intelligence to comprehend in its mental embrace all that is the object of knowledge: it is as impossible for it to penetrate to the bottom of any object of knowledge which it embraces. For it, mystery not only surrounds the circle of knowledge illuminated by its intelligence, with a vast realm of impenetrable darkness; mystery equally underlies all that it knows as an unfathomable abyss which it cannot plumb. We know, then, and can know, only in part; only part of what there is to know, and what we do know only in part. This is true of all our knowledge alike, whether of sensible things or of intelligible things, whether of the world without us or of the world within us, or — in the highest measure — of the world above us, culminating in God, the mystery that surrounds whom dismays the intellect and compels us to exclaim that no knowledge can be had of Him beyond the knowledge of how ignorant we are of Him.[46] Of our very souls themselves, the very selves which know and which are known most intimately of all things, we know next to nothing. Augustine exhorts his somewhat bumptious young correspondent who fancied, apparently, that he knew all that was to be known of the soul, " to understand what he did not understand, lest he should understand nothing at all." [47] For who knows either how the soul comes into existence, or (that impenetrable mystery) how it is related to the body? So far is Augustine from supposing, therefore, that the soul is clothed in omniscience, or that it can know unto perfection any single object of its knowledge, that he rather teaches that all our knowledge rests

---

[46] " De ordine " ii. 18. 47: " cujus (Dei) nulla scientia est in anima, nisi scire quomodo eum nesciat." Cf. " De doctrina Christiana " i. 6. 6.

[47] " De anima et ejus origine," vi. 11. 15.

on mystery and runs up into mystery. What we know we know; and our certitude of that may be complete. But what we do not know surges all about us, an ocean of illimitable extent, and sinks beneath our very knowledge, a bottomless depth. We penetrate with our knowing but a very little way into the knowable before we lose ourselves in profundities which baffle all our inquisition.

The limitation which is placed upon our knowledge by our very nature as finite beings is greatly aggravated by the circumstance that we are not only finite but immature beings. We do not come into existence in the maturity of our powers; indeed, we remain throughout life, or we would better say throughout eternity, creatures whose very characteristic is change, or, to put it at its best, ever-progressing growth. At no given point in this development, of course, are we all that even we shall become. For the attainment, then, in our immaturity, of such knowledge as belongs to us as finite beings, there is obvious need of help from without. In other words, there is place for authority, and its correlate, faith. This is an ordinance of nature. Those who are first infants, then children, and only through the several stages of gradual ripening attain the maturity of their powers, will need at every step of their growth the guidance of those who are more mature than they, that they may accept on their authority, by faith, what they are not yet in a position to ascertain for themselves, by reason. And, as it is inevitable even among mature men, that some should outrun others in the attainment of knowledge; and especially that some should become particularly knowing in this or that sphere of knowledge, to which they have given unusual attention, or for which they have enjoyed uncommon facilities; there will always remain for creatures subject to change and developing progressively in their powers, not only a legitimate but a necessary place for authority on the one hand and for faith on the other. Not, of course, as if faith should, or could, supplant reason, or be set in opposition to reason. On the one hand, a right faith is always a reasonable faith; that is to say, it is accorded only to an authority which commends itself to reason as a sound authority, which it would be unreasonable not to trust. On the other hand, faith is in its idea not so much a substitute for reason as a preparation for reason; and the effort of the wise man should be to transmute his faith into knowledge, that is to say as his powers become more and more capable of the performance and opportunity offers, gradually to replace belief by sight. But in any event for such creatures as we are, our walk must largely be guided by faith, and it is only through faith that we can hope to attain to knowledge.[48]

Now add the factor of sin — sin which enters the soul of man, already, one would think, sufficiently handicapped in attaining truth by its finiteness and its immaturity, and refracts and deflects the rays of truth reflected into it from the divine source, so rendering the right perception of the truth impossible. The finiteness of the soul only so far limits it in the attainment of truth, that, being finite, it cannot know all truth nor all that is true of what it truly knows: what it does know is truth, and so far as it is known this truth is truly known. The immaturity of the soul passes gradually away as its powers develop, and therefore imposes only a temporary check upon the attainment of truth — determines that attainment to be a process of gradual advance instead of an instantaneous achievement. Neither the soul's finiteness, nor its mutability, accordingly, need more than warn us of the limitations of our powers and induce in us a becoming humility and patience. But the invasion of the soul by sin is a different matter. Here is a power which acts destructively upon the soul's native powers of apprehending truth, blinds the eyes of the mind, distorts its vision, fills it with illusions, so that it sees awry; and a power

[48] For this doctrine in its highest application, cf., e.g., "De Trinitate" xv. 27. 49: "But if they think they ought to deny that these things are, because they, with their blind minds, cannot discern them, then those who are blind from their birth, also, ought to deny that there is a sun. The light shines in darkness, and if the darkness comprehend it not, let them first be illuminated by the gift of God, that they may be believers: and let them begin to be light in comparison with unbelievers; and when this foundation has been laid, let them look up and see what they believe, that at some time they may be able to see."

which so far from passing away with time and growth, battens by what it feeds on and increases in its baleful influence until it overwhelms the soul with falsehood. No merely incomplete, or as yet uncompleted, knowledge accordingly results; but just no knowledge at all, or even anti-knowledge, positive error, vanity, and lies; and thus a condition is created which assuredly calls not for humility and patience, but for despair.

The question obtrudes itself whether such a doctrine does not render nugatory all of Augustine's carefully built up theory of the acquisition of knowledge. Granted that normal man may look within and find there impressed upon his very being the forms of thought by which God thinks, in the light of which he may see truth and know it to be divinely certain because certainly divine. Man as we know him is not normal man. Afflicted by the disease of sin which darkens the light that shines into him from God, clouding his vision of truth and deflecting all the activities of his mind — who will give him true knowledge? Surely, whatever may be true of abstract man, sinful man, which is the only man we know, is on this teaching condemned to eternal nescience. Must not Augustine, on his own showing, in the case of actual man, take his place, then, among the skeptics? It certainly is important for the understanding of Augustine's doctrine of knowledge to observe how he meets this obvious criticism.

Of the form in which the criticism itself is often urged, we may find a very instructive example in the formulation of it by Mr. John Owen, who, as an outcome of the very line of reasoning which we have suggested, formally classes Augustine not only among the skeptics, but among the skeptics of the worst order. Simple skepticism, he tells us, affects the basis of knowledge only; Augustine's variety of skepticism undermines the foundations, not only of truth but also of morals. For, according to Augustine, he continues —

By the disobedience of its ancestor the majority of the whole human race has become totally incapacitated for knowing or doing what is right and good. The faculties of every man, both of soul and body, have become perverted and misleading. It is needless to dwell on the theological aspects of this momentous doctrine; our present concern is with its philosophical bearings. We here see, as I have already suggested, the Augustinian theology in intimate relationship with Skepticism. With one voice the Greek Skeptics had declared the senses to be untrustworthy, the reason to be perverted, all the natural powers of man to be insufficient to attain knowledge, and precisely the same conclusions were arrived at by Augustine with the portentous extension of the incapacity to all right and good action. The latter fact renders, in my opinion, Augustine's theological Skepticism much more mischievous than any amount of mere speculative theoretical unbelief could possibly have been. . . . That man with all his efforts is unable to attain truth may conceivably be an unavoidable necessity of the only possible *modus operandi* of his faculties, and therefore the fact may not in the least detract from the beneficence of his Creator; but the moment we make his creation and fall, and perhaps his consequent eternal misery, indissoluble parts of the original intention of Omnipotence concerning him, that moment God is shorn of his attribute of goodness, man becomes the hapless victim of a caprice as unreasonable as it is irresistible, and the creation, so far as the majority of human beings is concerned, is a stupendous act of despotism and cruelty.[49]

We have required to quote so much of Mr. Owen's remarks in order to place his representation fully before us; and we require to say this much to exonerate ourselves from the suspicion of having quoted so much merely in order that we might stultify Mr. Owen's profession of concerning himself solely with the philosophical bearings of Augustine's doctrine of original sin. In point of fact he concerns himself with little except its theological aspects. After having barely remarked that it has philosophical bearings, he lapses at once into an assault on the doctrine on the ground that it contradicts the beneficence of God and indeed transmutes the good God into a cruel demon. We must refuse to be led off from our proper subject by this impertinent display of the *odium theologicum;* and we take note here accordingly merely of Mr. Owen's phil-

[49] John Owen, "Evenings with the Skeptics," ii. p. 196.

osophical criticism that Augustine's doctrine of original sin brings him into intimate relations with Greek skepticism.

Apparently what Mr. Owen means to suggest is that Augustine reached " precisely the same conclusions " with the Greek skeptics, and differed from them only in the grounds upon which he based these conclusions. They contended that human faculties are, as such, incapable of ascertaining truth; he, that human faculties have been so injured by sin as to have become incapable of ascertaining truth. That there is a sense in which this representation is perfectly just is obvious. Augustine did hold that the native depravity of man has noetic as well as thelematic and ethical effects: and that sinful man, as such, is therefore precluded by his sinfulness from that perception of truth which can be only *pie et caste* attained. To him it was therefore axiomatic that the natural man is incapable of attaining to true knowledge, at least in its highest reaches — those reaches in which the deflection of sin would be most apparent. But in his hatred of Augustine's doctrine of original sin, Mr. Owen has failed to observe that Augustine did not leave matters at that point. Where he differs by a whole diameter from the skeptics is that he knows a remedy for the dreadful condition in which human nature finds itself. When the skeptics declared that it belongs to human nature as such to be incapable of knowledge, there was an end of the matter. The condition of man is hopeless: he actually lacks faculty for knowing. Augustine's contention, on the contrary, is that it is knowledge, not nescience, which belongs to human nature as such. And if he finds human nature in a state in which it cannot fulfill its destiny of knowing, he knows how it may be recovered to itself and to the capacity for knowledge which properly belongs to it. In other words, the sinful condition of human nature is viewed by Augustine as abnormal; and all the results of this sinfulness as abnormalities which may be and are to be overcome. That Mr. Owen says nothing at this point of the provisions for overcoming these abnormalities cannot be set down to the credit of his account of Augustine's teaching.

At another point of Mr. Owen's discussion, no doubt, there does occur some suggestion of these provisions, though certainly a very insufficient one. He remarks [50] that " from the earliest history of Christianity the skeptical argument had been employed, for evidential purposes, as an *à priori* justification of divine revelation both in its ethical and intellectual acceptation." And he supports this by remarking further that " by the early Christian Fathers the confessions of ignorance, limitation, &c. on the part of Greek skeptics were put forward to show the necessity of superhuman knowledge." Even this suggestion is introduced, however, not to palliate but to accentuate Augustine's fault — not to point so much to the remedy which he offered for the noetic effects of sin, as to the excess of his " depreciation of human nature." Augustine had so low an opinion " of the intellectual imbecility of humanity," it seems, that he readily accepted the dogma " of the natural depravity of man " " as a complete solution of what would otherwise have been an enigma " to him. Nevertheless, it is not difficult to perceive that the postulation of a divine revelation comes in upon the conception of the sin-born " imbecility of humanity " as a mitigation of its otherwise hopeless condition. The proclamation of the provision of a divine revelation, if on the one hand it implies a need for it, on the other hand asserts a remedy for that need. Nor does the assertion of divine revelation cover the whole provision which Augustine offers for the removal of the natural incapacities of sinful man. He did not confine himself to pointing out a mitigation for the symptom; he sought and found also a remedy for the disease. If the noetic effects of sin might be neutralized by divine revelation, sin itself might be removed by divine grace. It is certainly grossly unfair to Augustine's teaching as to man's condition to focus attention upon the disease under which he holds that man suffers, and withdraw it entirely from the remedy which he asserts has been provided for this disease.

We must not, then, be misled into supposing Augustine

[50] *Op. cit.,* ii. p. 190.

to teach, even by remote implication, that man is hopelessly sunk in nescience or even in sin. Perfectly true as this is of his teaching of the condition of man considered in himself alone and so far as his own powers are concerned, it is considerably less than half the truth of Augustine's teaching of the condition of man. It means, no doubt, that Augustine, as he looked upon the virtues of the heathen as little more than *splendida vitia,* so looked upon the philosophy of the heathen as very much a farrago of nonsense. What a multitude of philosophers there have been, he exclaimed, in effect, and almost more opinions than philosophers! Who can find any two of them who perfectly agree? Varro enumerates not less than two hundred and eighty-eight possible sects. It would be easier to find a needle in a haystack than truth among these professional purveyors of truth.[51] But then Augustine knew something better than heathen thought to which to direct one in search of truth, as he knew something better than heathen ethics to which to direct one in search of holiness. His great word was *revelation;* and behind and above and all through revelation, there was the greater word still, *grace.* No doubt this means that he transferred dependence for truth, as for holiness, from man to God. He did distrust human nature as he found it. He did consider it in its own strength incapable of any good thing, and equally of any right thought. He did cast men back for all good on God's grace, for all truth on God's teaching. So far writers like Mr. Owen are quite right. Augustine did believe in the ingrained depravity of man in his present manifestation on earth; he did believe that this depravity renders him morally incapable and intellectually imbecile, if this somewhat exaggerated language pleases us. But he believed also in the goodness of God; and he believed that this good God has intervened with His grace to cure man's moral inability, and with His revelation to rescue man from his intellectual imbecility.

Nor was this doctrine of revelation and grace as remedies for man's sinful incapacities and condition a mechanical in-

---

[51] See "De Civitate Dei," xviii. 41.

trusion of an alien idea into Augustine's general conception. It rather stands in the most direct analogy alike with his whole conception of man's relation to God and with his particular view of man's natural needs and the natural provision for their satisfaction. Even had man not been sinful, Augustine would never have allowed that he was in a position of himself, apart from God, to do any good or to attain any truth. That would have seemed to him a crass deism, of which he would have been incapable. Even sinless man would have been to him absolutely dependent on God, the Author of all being, the Light of all knowledge, the Source of all good. We have seen him openly teaching that man as man can see light only in the Light; that all truth is the reflection into the soul of the truth that is in God; in a word, that the condition of all knowledge for dependent creatures is revelation, in the wider sense of that word. When now he teaches that revelation in a narrower sense and a more objective form is the condition of all right knowledge of higher things for sinful man — a revelation which is an integral part of a scheme of grace for the recovery of sinful man, not only from the effects of his sin but form his sin itself — he is speaking in close analogy with his fundamental theistic conception of the universe. He is but throwing sinful man back afresh on the God on whom men in all states and condition are absolutely dependent.

Similarly, the provision which Augustine makes, in revelation, to meet the sin-bred inability of men to attain right knowledge, is only an extension in a right line of the provision he discovered for meeting man's natural weakness growing out of his finiteness, and especially out of his only gradually attained maturity. In that case, we remember, he pointed to authority as the remedy for as yet ineffective reason. The child is naturally dependent on the authority of its elders, who offer to its faith the truth which its reason is as yet incapable of discovering or authenticating for itself. In every sphere of life we remain dependent on the authority of those who are in this or that or the other department of knowledge better instructed than we; and he who will be taught nothing, but insists on following his reason alone, is soon at the end of living in this world. Revelation plays precisely the same rôle for the mind darkened by sin. The heavenly Father intervenes to meet the needs of sin-blinded souls by offering to their faith, on the authority of God, the truth which they are as sinners incapable of ascertaining for themselves. This is the essence of Augustine's doctrine of revelation. Of course the condition of man as sinner determines as well the nature of the truths he needs to know as the manner in which alone he can come to the knowledge of them: the whole content of revelation is determined by the needs of those to whom it is made. But that may be left to one side here. What we are at present especially concerned with is that the need of revelation and the provision of revelation for sinful man stand in perfect analogy with the need and provision of instruction for, say, the immature child. The principle which governs in both cases is, not that reason is superseded by something better, but that, in default of reason due to special circumstances, provision is taken to supply the lack of reason, until reason may come to its rights. The lame man is supplied with a crutch until his lameness is healed. Here we have in brief Augustine's whole doctrine of revelation.

Clear and reasonable, however, as is Augustine's doctrine of revelation as the remedy for man's sin-bred disability to know aright, it seems to be very difficult for some writers to believe that it could have been a reality to him. It is not rare, therefore, to hear it intimated that he passed all his days under the torture of gnawing doubt, and flung himself upon the authority of the Church as some sort of palliation of his wearing despair. His permanent state of mind regarding Christianity, we are told, is much that which is exhibited in a certain class of Romish controversial literature, in which after every other support for human trust has been sedulously removed we are ultimately invited to take refuge in the authority of the Church as the sole haven of peace. This representation is given expression, as well as elsewhere, in some remarks of Prof. Adolf Harnack's, when he comes, in his

"History of Dogma," to deal with Augustine's attitude to the authority of the Church.[52] Here we are told that Augustine had become convinced, in his conflict with himself, " of the badness of human nature," and had been left by Manichæism " in complete doubt as to the foundations and truth of the Christian faith." And then:

> His confidence in the rationality of Christian truth had been shaken to the very depths, *and it was never restored.* In other words, as an individual *thinker* he never gained the subjective certitude that Christian truth, and as such everything contained in the two Testaments had to be regarded, was clear, consistent and demonstrable. When he threw himself into the arms of the Catholic Church, he was perfectly conscious that he needed its *authority* not to sink in scepticism or nihilism.

Dr. Harnack is too good a scholar to enunciate a historical judgment utterly without elements of truth. There are elements of truth of great importance even in this judgment, far from the mark as is the application which is made of them; and there are even points of great interest in the use which Dr. Harnack makes of these elements of truth. It is certainly true that in his experience with the Manichæans Augustine learned to distrust unaided reason as the source of religious truth; and discovered that there is a legitimate place for authority in religion. The Manichæans had promised him a purely rational religion; he found on testing it that what they gave him was a mass of irrationalities; and on feeling out for himself he discovered that unaided reason was inadequate to the task of meeting all the needs of man. There is truth, therefore, in saying that he once for all discarded reason as the sole instrument for the acquisition of truth in the religious sphere, and cast himself on instruction as the single hope of the soul in its longing after truth. But the sense in which this is true of Augustine is indefinitely different from the sense it takes upon itself in Dr. Harnack's representation. Beneath Dr. Harnack's representation there lies

[52] E. T. v. p. 79.

Dr. Harnack's own conception not only of the place of authority in religion, but of the nature of the Christian religion and its relation to authority, and of the nature of the particular source of authority to which he conceives that Augustine fled in his need, and of the rationality of Augustine's act in taking refuge with it. His whole statement, therefore, leaves the impression that Augustine in despair of reason renounced rationality, and gave himself over to an unreasoned authority for guidance; and never again recovered, we will not say objective rationality in his religious views, but even subjective confidence. The very interesting defense of authority in religion — from the historical point of view at least, if not from the intrinsic — with which Dr. Harnack closes his discussion [53] does nothing to modify this impression. It remains the gist of his exposition that Augustine took refuge in authority, because he despaired of reason, and therefore his attitude towards Christianity remained throughout life that of an irrationalist.

Nothing, however, could be less true than this of Augustine's real attitude. His appeal to authority was in his own mind not a desertion of reason but an advance towards reason. He sought truth through authority only because it became clear to him that this was the rational road to truth. It was thus not as an irrationalist, but as a rationalist, that he made his appeal to authority. His breach with Manichæism and his gradual establishment in Christian truth, in other words, was on this side of it merely the discovery that the Christian religion is not a natural religion and is therefore not either excogitable or immediately demonstrable by reason working solely on natural grounds; but is rather a revealed religion and therefore requires in the first instance to be told to us. It is thus in the last analysis, supernaturalism as versus naturalism that he turns to; [54] and this is far from the same

[53] Pp. 82–83.

[54] "De utilitate credendi," 29: "Therefore this so vast difficulty, since our inquiry is about religion, God alone can remedy: nor, indeed, unless we believe both that He is, and that He helps men's minds, ought we even to inquire of the true religion itself."

thing as irrationality as versus rationality — except, indeed, on the silent assumption that the supernatural is an absurdity, an assumption which was decidedly not Augustine's. In the sixth book of the " Confessions " he recounts to us the several steps by which he rose from the pure naturalism which had hitherto held him to this Christian supernaturalism. His disillusionment with Manichæism did not at once deliver him from his naturalistic point of view. He had found the tenets of the Manichæans irrational. But his rejection of them as such did not at once entail the adoption of another set of tenets as rational. His sad experience with them operated rather to make him chary of committing himself to any other body of conclusions whatever. He remained in principle a naturalist á outrance. He demanded the apodeictic certainty of mathematical demonstration for conviction; that is to say, he still depended for the discovery of truth upon immediate rational demonstration alone. This alone seemed to him adequate evidence upon which one could safely venture. All this time, says he, he was restraining his heart from believing anything, and thus in avoiding the precipice was strangling his soul: what he was demanding was that he should be made as certain of things unseen as that seven and three make ten.[55] He goes on to remark that a cure for his distress lay open before him in faith (credendo), had he chosen to take that road, since thus the sight of his mind might have been purged for vision of the truth. But as yet he could not enter that path. It was not long, however, before it began to invite his feet, slowly but surely. He could not avoid perceiving after a while that it is the path of nature. He reflected upon the host of things which he accepted on testimony. He reminded himself that in it lay the foundation of all history: and that life itself would soon come to a standstill if we refused to act on the credit of others. He meditated further upon the strength of the conviction which testimony produces when its validity and adequacy are beyond question. As the great place which faith fills in common life thus became more and more clear

[55] " Confessiones," vi. 4. 6.

to him, he could not escape the query why it should not serve a similar end in higher things. The principle of faith and its correlate authority, having once been recognized, it became, indeed, only a question of time before it should take its proper place in these higher concerns also. And, then, it was only a question of fact whether there existed in the world any adequate authority to guide men into the truth. Thus, says he, the Lord drew him on little by little, with a hand of infinite gentleness and mercy, and composing his heart gradually convinced him that in the Scriptures He had given to men an authority to which their faith is due, and through which they may attain by faith that knowledge of divine things to which they are as yet unable to rise through reason. " And also," he adds, " since we are too weak to search out the truth by mere (*liquida*) reason, and therefore need the authority of Holy Scriptures, I began to believe God never would have given such surpassing authority to those Scriptures throughout the whole world except that He wished to be believed through them and to be sought by their means." [56] There is depicted for us in this vital narrative, no despairing act of renunciation in which Augustine offered up his intellect a sacrifice upon the altar of faith, and sought peace from insatiable doubt in an arbitrary authority to which by an effort of sheer will he submits. What we see is a gradual advance under the leading of reason itself to a rational theory of authority in religion, on the basis of which rational certitude may be enjoyed in the midst of the weakness of this life.

What has been thus incidentally brought before us, it will be perceived, is Augustine's doctrine of faith and reason. The relations of faith and reason, as thus outlined, remained to him always a matter of sincere and reasoned conviction. We may read them so stated in the books " Against the Academics " and in the books " On the Predestination of the Saints " alike. It will be enough for our purpose, however, to observe how he deals with the matter in two or three treatises which are devoted expressly to elucidating certain aspects of it.

[56] " Confessiones," vi. 4. 8.

Take for example the treatises "On the Profit of Believing" (A.D. 391) and "On Faith in Things Not Seen" (A.D. 400), which were written not very far apart in time and in very similar circumstances. In both of these treatises he begins by setting himself sharply in opposition to the Sensationalists, "who fancy," says he,[57] "that there is nothing else than what they perceive by those five well-known reporters of the body," and "essay to measure the unsearchable resources of truth" by "the deceitful rule" of the "impressions (*plagas*) and images they have received from these"; whom, in a word, "folly has so made subject to their carnal eyes that whatsoever they see not through them they think they are not to believe."[58] From this starting point, in both alike, however, the advance is made at once to the defense of faith as a valid form of conviction, with respect not only to things not perceived by the bodily senses, but also to those lying beyond the reach of the intellect itself.[59] And in both alike the stress of the argument is laid upon the naturalness of faith and its indispensableness in the common life of men.[60] Why should that act of faith which lies at the very basis of human intercourse be excluded from the sphere of religion — especially in the case of one, say, of weak intelligence? Must a man have no religion because he is incapable of excogitating one for himself?[61] Certainly we must not confound faith with credulity: nobody asks that Christ should be believed in without due evidence that he is worthy of being believed in.[62] But, on the other hand, it is just as certain that we shall not attain to any real religion without faith. Say you are determined to have a religion which you can demonstrate. The very search for it presupposes a precedent faith that there is a God and that he cares for us; for surely no one will seek God, or inquire how we should

---

[57] "De utilitate credendi," 1.

[58] "De fide rerum quae non vid.," 1.

[59] *Ibid.* 2 *sq.*

[60] *Ibid.* 4; "De utilitate credendi," 23.

[61] "De utilitate credendi," 24.

[62] "De fide rerum quae non vid.," 5: cf. "De utilitate credendi," 22 *sq.*, and 25, where the necessary distinctions are drawn.

serve Him, without so much to go on.[63] And where and how
will you seek? Perchance you will inquire the way of those
who are wise? Who are the wise? How will you determine who
are wise in such things? In the manifold disagreements of
pretenders to wisdom, it will require a wise man to select the
really wise. We are caught in a fatal circle here; we must needs
be wise beforehand in order to discriminate wisdom.[64] There is
but one outlet; and that outlet is, shortly, revelation. For
revelation is a thing which can be validated by appropriate
evidence even to those who have not yet attained wisdom;
and which, when once trusted on its appropriate grounds,
gradually leads us into that wisdom which before was un-
obtainable. Thus, to man unable to see the truth, a justified
authority steps in to fit him to see it; and it is authority alone
which can bring such wisdom.[65] This is the reason the Lord
has chosen this method of dealing with us. Bringing us a
medicine destined to heal our corrupted condition, " he pro-
cured authority by miraculous works, acquired faith by authority, drew together numbers by faith, gained antiquity
by numbers, confirmed religion by antiquity: so that not only
the supremely inept novelty of heresy in its deceitful working,
but even the inveterate error of heathenism in its violent
antagonism can never root up this religion in any way whatever." [66] Here we have Augustine's golden chain. Miracles, authority, faith, numbers, antiquity, an absolutely established
religion: that is the sequence, traveling along which men arrive at a secure conviction which nothing can shake.

We may hear him argue the question with even more
specific application to the Christian religion in a notable
letter which he wrote about 410 to an eminent courtier and
scholar.[67] " The minds of men," he tells us here, " are blinded
by the pollutions of sin and the lust of the flesh "; they are
therefore lost in the mazes of discussion and are unable to

[63] " De utilitate credendi," 29.
[64] *Ibid.* 28.
[65] *Ibid.* 34.
[66] *Ibid.* 32 *ad fin.*
[67] " Epist." 118 (to Dioscorus), 5. 32–33.

discover the truth of things by reason. Therefore, that men may have the truth, Christ came — the Truth Itself, in union with a man — to instruct them in truth. Thus men are given the truth through faith, in order that "by instruction in salutary truth they may escape from their perplexities into the atmosphere of pure and simple truth." That is to say, we are introduced to truth by Christ's authority, so that, thus receiving it by faith, we may then be able to defend it by reason. " The perfection of method in training disciples," we read, " is, that those who are weak should be encouraged to enter the citadel of authority, in order that, when they have been safely placed there, the conflict necessary for their defence may be maintained by the most strenuous use of reason." " Thus," he adds, " the whole supremacy of authority and light of reason for regenerating and reforming the human race has been made to reside in the one saving Name, and in His one Church." For Christ has " both secured the Church in the citadel of authority . . . and supplied it with the abundant armor of equally invincible reason." The former He has done by means of the " highly celebrated ecumenical councils, and the Apostolic sees themselves " — which is as much as to say, apparently, that the authority of the Church finds expression through these organs. And the latter He has done " by means of a few men of pious learning and unfeigned spirituality " — that is to say, apparently, these are the organs through which the inherent rationality of Church teaching evinces itself. The entire sense seems, then, to be that what is taught by the Church on authority, through the appropriate organs of authority, is equally defended by the Church by reason, through the appropriate organs of reason. The Church as the pillar and ground of the truth commends it to faith; the Church, giving a reason for the faith that is in it, defends it to reason. The Doctor,[68] in other words, is as truly a manifestation of the Church's inherent life as the Bishop himself:

[68] On the " Doctor " in the early church, see Smith and Cheetham, " Dictionary of Christian Antiquities," 1876, i. p. 385a; and Harnack, in his larger edition of the " Didaché," 1884, pp. 131 sq.; and in his " Expansion of Christianity," E. T. i. pp. 444 sq.

reasoning is as inadmissibly her function as authoritative definition. Here is certainly an elevation of authority, properly
grounded, as a source of conviction; an elevation of faith,
properly placed, as a mode of conviction. But here is no depreciation of demonstration and reason to make way for
authority and faith. On the contrary, the two are placed side
by side, as joint methods and organs for attaining truth; and
the contention is merely that to each its own sphere belongs
into which the other cannot intrude.

It has seemed most convenient to present in the first instance Augustine's entire doctrine of faith and reason in concrete form, and in its application to the main problem to which
he applied it. But having in this way caught a glimpse of it
as a whole and in its ultimate bearings, it seems desirable to
pause and to glance in some detail at the main elements which
enter into it.

Let us first look at the doctrine in its most general aspects.
The fact of primary importance to note here is that with
Augustine faith and reason are never conceived as antagonists,
contradictories, but always as coadjutants, coöperating to a
common end. The thing sought is truth: what Augustine has
discovered is that there are two modes of mental action by
which truth may be laid hold of. It may be grasped by faith,
or it may be grasped by reason. " No one doubts," he tells us,
" that we are impelled to the acquisition of knowledge by a
double impulse — of authority and of reason." [69] And, though
we may be so constituted as eagerly to desire " to apprehend
what is true not only by faith but by the understanding "; [70]
and may, therefore, give to reason the primacy in rank, yet
we are bound to acknowledge for faith a priority in time.[71]
Granted that faith may seem to be a mode of conviction more
suitable for the ignorant multitude than for the instructed
few; yet there is no one who does not begin by being ignorant,
and there are many things great and good which we could

[69] " Cont. Acad.," iii. 20. 43, ad fin.; cf. " De ordine," ii. 9. 26, ad init.
[70] " Cont. Acad.," loc. cit.
[71] " De ordine," loc. cit.

never attain were the door not opened to us by faith.[72] Life
is too short to attempt to solve every question for ourselves,
even of those which are capable of being solved. We must be
content to accept many things on faith and leave difficulties
to be dealt with afterwards, or never to be dealt with.[73] And
surely it is the height of folly, because of insoluble difficulties,
to "permit to escape from our hands things which are altogether certain." [74] What is it but pride — which is the destruction of all true knowledge — that leads us to demand that
we shall, as we say, " understand everything "?

Not, of course, as if faith should be lightly or irrationally
accorded. If there is a sense in which faith precedes reason,
there is equally a sense in which reason precedes faith. That
mental act which we call faith is one possible only to rational
creatures; [75] and of course we act as rational creatures in performing it. " If, then," Augustine argues, " it is rational that,
with respect to some great concerns which we find ourselves
unable to comprehend, faith should precede reason; there can
be no question but that the amount of reason which leads us to
accord this faith, whatever that amount may be, is itself anterior to faith." [76] Faith is by no means blind: it has eyes of
its own with which, before it completes itself in giving that
assent which, when added to thinking, constitutes it believing,[77] it must needs see both that to which it assents and that
on the ground of which it assents to it. As we cannot believe
without knowing what it is to which we accord our faith, so
we cannot believe without perceiving good grounds for according our faith. " No one believes anything unless he has

[72] *Ibid.*

[73] " Epist." 102 (to Deogratias; 406 or 408 A.D.) chap. 38: " sunt enim in-
numerabiles [quaestiones] quae non sunt finiendae ante fidem, ne finiatur vita
sine fide."

[74] " De musica," vi. 5. 8.

[75] " Epist." 120 (to Consentius) chap. 3. " etiam credere non possemus,
nisi rationales animas haberemus."

[76] *Ibid.*

[77] " De praedest. sanctt." ii. 5: " Believing is nothing else than cum assensione cogitare "; " Enchirid." 20: " But if assent is taken away, faith too
falls; for sine assensione nihil creditur."

before thought it worthy of belief." [78] Reason, therefore, can never be " wholly lacking to faith, because it belongs to it to consider to whom faith should be given." [79] This function of reason, by which it considers to what men or writings it is right to accord faith is then precedent to faith; though faith is precedent to reason in the sense that, an adequate ground of credit having been established by reason, conviction must at once form itself without waiting for comprehension to become perfect.

Our knowledge thus embraces two classes of things: things seen and things believed. The difference between them is this: " with respect to things we have seen or see, we are our own witnesses; but with respect to those which we believe, we are moved to faith by other witnesses." [80] The distinction which Augustine erects between faith and reason, that is to say, is briefly that faith is distinctively that conviction of truth which is founded on testimony as over against that conviction which is founded on sight.[81] All the corollaries which flow from this distinction were present to his mind. He is found, for example, pointing out that all so-called knowledge itself rests on faith, so that in the deepest sense an act of faith precedes all knowledge. And on the other hand — and it is this point which is of most present interest to us — that all faith presupposes reason, and is so far from an irrational act that an unreasonable faith, a faith not founded in a reasonable authority demanding credit on reasonable grounds, is no faith at all, but mere " credulity," while what is thus unwarrantedly believed is mere " opinion." [82] As distinguished from knowledge on the one hand and credulity on the other, faith is that act of assent which is founded on adequate testi-

[78] " De praedest. sanctt." ii. 5.
[79] " De vera religione," xxiv. 45, also xxv. 46.
[80] " Epist." 147. 3. 8.
[81] " Epist." 147. 2. 7; " De Diversis Quaestionibus lxxxiii.," Quaest. 54. In " Retractationes," i. 14. 3 he allows that in such distinctions he is employing the word " knowledge " in a strict rather than a popular sense: in common speech we say " we know " even what rests on testimony.
[82] " De utilitate credendi," 11. 25; " De mendac.," 3.

mony; and the form of conviction which is so called may be free from all doubt whatsoever.[83] So far is faith thus from being a cloak for inexhaustible doubt, that doubt is inconsistent with it and is excluded just in proportion to the firmness of the grounding of faith, or, we may better say, just in proportion as faith fulfills its own idea. Its distinction from knowledge does not turn on the strength of the conviction it describes, but on the ground of this conviction. We know by sight; we believe on testimony.

We turn now to the application of this abstract doctrine of faith to the problem of the Christian religion. In this instance the testimony on which faith rests — on the basis of which that conviction we call faith is formed — Augustine supposed to be the testimony of God Himself. The grounds on which he accepted as such what he took to be a revelation from God may be assailed as insufficient; and the channels through which he considered that what he took to be a revelation from God asserts its authority over us, may be subject to criticism. But we can scarcely refuse to recognize the formal cogency of his reasoning. If it can be established that God, condescending to our weakness, has given us a revelation, then, undoubtedly, that revelation becomes an adequate authority upon which our faith may securely rest; and, as rational beings, we must accept as true what it commends to us as such, even though our reason flags in its attempts even to comprehend it, and utterly fails to supply an immediate rational demonstration of its truth. Here, above everywhere else, faith obviously must precede reason, and prepare the way for reason. It is here accordingly that Augustine's insistence on the priority of faith to reason culminates. It is with this application in mind that he repeats most assiduously that " before we understand it, it behooves us to believe "; [84] that " faith is the starting-point of knowledge "; [85] that we believe

---

[83] " De mendac." 3: " ille qui credit, sentit se ignorare quod credit; quamvis de re quam se ignorare novit, omnino non dubitet; sic enim firme credit. Qui autem opinatur, putat se scire, quod nescit."

[84] " De Trinitate," viii. 5. 8.

[85] *Ibid.* ix. 1. 1.

that we may know, not know that we may believe. Least of all, in this highest application of faith, does he mean that this faith does not itself rest upon reason, in the sense that it is accorded to an authority which is not justified to reason on valid grounds.[86] What he means is rather that the particular truths commended to us on the authority of a revelation from God, validated as such by appropriate evidence, are to be accepted as truths on that authority, prior to the action of our reason upon them either by way of an attempt fully to comprehend them, or by way of an attempt to justify them severally to our logical reason; and that this act of faith is in the nature of the case a preparation for these efforts of reason. The order of nature is, in other words, first, the validation of a revelation as such on its appropriate grounds; secondly, the acceptance by faith of the contents of this revelation on the sole ground of its authority; and, thirdly, the comprehension by the intellect of the contents of the revelation and the justification of them severally to reason so far as that may prove to be possible to us. This order of procedure Augustine defends against the Manichæans — who were the philosophic naturalists in vogue at the time — from every conceivable point of view and with endlessly varied arguments. The gist of the whole, however, is simply that when a revelation has been validated as such, we owe to the truths commended to us by it immediate credit, on the sole authority of the revelation itself, and neither need nor are entitled to wait until each of these truths is separately validated to us on the grounds of reason before we give our assent to it. In a word, the rational ground on which we accept each truth is the proof that the authority by which it is commended to us is adequate, and not a particular verdict of reason immediately passed upon each several truth. The particular verdict of reason on each several truth must wait on the act of faith by which we honor the general verdict of reason on the validity of the authority; and it may wait endlessly without invalidating or weakening the strength of conviction which we accord to the de-

[86] E.g., "Epist." 120. 1. 3 (as quoted above).

liverances of a revelation which has been really validated to us as such.

We may revert, of course, to the prior question, whether the assumed revelation on the authority of which faith is yielded has been soundly validated as such to reason. It is at this point that criticism of Augustine's system of faith becomes possible; and it is at this point that such criticism becomes sharp. We are told that Augustine accepted an alleged revelation on insufficient evidence; and that it is this fact which justifies the suspicion that his acceptance of it and the subjection of his reason to its authority were acts of violence done to his intellect in despair of ever attaining a solid basis in reason for religious conviction. It is quite possible to confuse in such a concrete judgment a number of suggestions, which we should discriminate if we are to form an estimate of the value of the criticism offered. We shall need to ask, for example, if what it is intended to suggest is that the evidence in existence for the reality of the revelation which Augustine accepted as a true revelation from God is insufficient to validate it; or only that the evidence which was actually before Augustine's mind and on which he personally depended in reaching his decision was insufficient. In the latter case we shall need to ask further if what is meant is that the evidence actually before Augustine's mind would be insufficient to convince us — seems to us in itself insufficient to command credit; or that it was actually insufficient to convince Augustine, so that, despite his protestations of conviction, he remained in reality unconvinced and at heart an actual skeptic all his days. It is the last of these propositions, it will be remembered, that Dr. Harnack affirms; although he does not keep it as rigorously separate from the others as would seem desirable. It is surely one thing to say that Augustine is open to criticism for giving credit to the Evidences of Christianity and recognizing the revelatory character of the Christian system; and quite another thing to say that Augustine is open to criticism for the particular conception he entertained of the Christian evidences — the selection he makes of the special items of evidence upon which he personally relies for the validation of the Christian system as a revealed religion; and still quite another thing to suggest that Augustine is open to criticism for his inaccessibility to the evidences of the Christian system as a revelation from God, and for remaining therefore all his life a doubter of the intellect, finding only a precarious peace for his distracted soul in an act of submission to an external authority arbitrarily yielded to in defiance of insatiable skepticism.

It can scarcely be expected that the whole body of the Christian evidences should be subjected to a new critical examination merely because a writer not himself able to look upon them as supplying a satisfactory proof of the divine origin of the Christian religion, blames Augustine for placing upon them a value beyond that which he is himself able to accord. We must be prepared to find those who resist the force of this evidence themselves, despising those who yield to it as superstitious, or even accusing them of intellectual dishonesty. It surely is enough at this point simply to recognize that this not unnatural tendency of the naturalistic mind is not without its influence upon the proneness in some quarters to speak of Augustine as making a sacrifice of his intellect in throwing himself upon authority in matters of religion. One thing is perfectly clear: if Augustine made such a sacrifice he was himself completely unconscious of doing so. He nowhere betrays the state of mind which is here attributed to him. He speaks always in terms of the most complete conviction of the truth of the Christian religion, and rests himself with entire confidence upon the evidences which appealed to him. To go behind his obviously sincere asseverations of security of mind and heart, because we are conscious that, in his place, we should have felt less secure, is to push the biographer's (and critic's) privilege of " imputing himself to his victim " to an unwarrantable extreme. Whatever we may feel Augustine ought to have done; whatever we may feel we, in his place, should have done; it certainly is a matter of historical fact that Augustine confidently accepted the Christian revelation as a genuine revelation, and found for his faith in it abundant justification. No fact in his mental history is more patent, or call it flagrant if you will. When in the closing words of his first Christian composition,[87] in the very act of consecrating himself to a life-long search of truth, he declares that "he certainly would never more give up the authority of Christ, because no stronger could be found," he speaks out of an unmistakably sincere conviction. And the note thus struck so far from fading away swells steadily to the end. Clearly the restless heart had found at last its rest: and rest is the characteristic of his Christian life. A skeptic, intellectual or moral, may be found in any man rather than in Augustine. He who in his despair as, in the crumbling of his former beliefs, he almost gave up hope of ever attaining assurance, yet could not fall in with the Academics because he still knew some things to be indisputably true, and only began to wonder whether the right way to truth was known to man — certainly could not lose his confidence after he had discovered the Way and established himself in it.

It remains a matter of interest of course to determine the nature of the grounds on which Augustine was convinced, or sought to convince others, of the truth of the Christian religion. To do so with any fullness would be, however, to write a section of the history of Apologetics, and would find its importance in that connection. We need not go so far afield in seeking to apprehend Augustine's doctrine of authority in religion. What is of primary importance here is merely to ascertain in a simple manner his conception of the sources, nature, and seat of this authority and the mode of its validation to men. In the Second Article we shall seek to do this with as much completeness as is requisite for our purpose.

---

[87] "Cont. Acad.," iii. 20. 43. It was the common sentiment of the men of the time: Paulinus of Nola says: "Plurima quaesivi, per singula quaeque cucurri, Sed nihil inveni melius quam credere Christo."

In the First Article we attempted to give a general exposition of Augustine's doctrine of knowledge and authority, which naturally ran up into some account of his doctrine of authority in religion. The more detailed study of this specific subject we were forced, however, to postpone to another occasion. We wish now to take up this topic and to make as clear as possible Augustine's teaching concerning it.

The cardinal facts to bear in mind are that, to speak broadly, with Augustine the idea of authority coalesces with that of revelation, the idea of revelation with that of apostolicity, and the idea of apostolicity with that of Scripture. With him, therefore, the whole question of authority in religion is summed up in the questions whether there is a revelation from God in existence, where that revelation is to be found, and how it is validated to and made the possession of men: while the master-key to these problems lies in the one word apostolicity. Whatever is apostolic is authoritative, because behind the apostles lies the authority of Christ, who chose, appointed, and endowed the apostles to be the founders of His Church; and Christ's authority is the authority of God, whose Son and Revelation He is. The great depository of the apostolic revelation is the Holy Scriptures, and these Scriptures become thus to Augustine the supreme proximate seat of authority in religion. The line of descent is, therefore, briefly, God, Christ, the Apostles, the Scriptures — the Scriptures being conceived as the embodied revelation of God, clothed with His authority as His inspired word, given to us by His accredited messengers, the apostles. Let us see how Augustine expresses himself on each of these points in turn.

On the actual authority of Scripture he certainly expresses himself in no wavering terms. The Holy Scriptures, he tells

[88] *The Princeton Theological Review*, July, 1907, pp. 353–397.

us, have been " established upon the supreme and heavenly
pinnacle of authority " [89] and should therefore always be read
" in assurance and security as to their truth " [90] and all their
statements accepted as absolutely trustworthy.[91] To them
alone among books had he learned to defer this respect and
honor — most firmly to believe that no one of their authors
has erred in any respect in writing: [92] for of these books of the
prophets and apostles it would be wicked [93] to have any doubt
as to their entire freedom from error.[94] " To these canonical
Scriptures only," he repeats,[95] " does he owe that implicit subjection so to follow them alone as to admit no suspicion whatever that their writers could have erred in them in any possible
respect, or could possibly have gone wrong in anything." The
accumulated emphases in such passages, no more than fairly
represent the strength of Augustine's conviction that, as he
puts it in another place, " it is to the canonical Scriptures
alone that he owes unhesitating assent." [96] It is this contention
accordingly in its most positive form which he opposes endlessly to the Manichæans in his long controversy with them.
He points out to Faustus, for example, that a sharp line of
demarcation is drawn between the canonical books of the Old
and New Testaments and all later writings, precisely in point
of authority. The authority of the canonical books, " confirmed
from the time of the apostles by the successions of the bishops
and the propagations of the churches, has been established in
so lofty a position, that every faithful and pious mind submits
to it." Other writings on the contrary, of what sort soever
they may be, may be read " not with necessity of believing

[89] " Epist." 82 (to Jerome), ii. 5: " sanctam Scripturam, in summo et
cœlesti auctoritatis culmine collocatam."
[90] *Ibid.:* " de veritate ejus certus ac securus legam."
[91] *Ibid.:* " veraciter discam."
[92] *Ibid.:* i. 3.
[93] " Nefarium."
[94] *Ibid., ad fin.*
[95] *Ibid.:* iii. 24: " sicut paulo ante dixi, tantummodo Scripturis canonicis
hanc ingenuam debeam servitutem, qua eas solas ita sequar, ut conscriptores
earum nihil in eis omnino errasse, nihil fallaciter posuisse non dubitem."
[96] " De natura et gratia," lxi. 71: " sine ulla recusatione consensum."

but with liberty of judgment." The same truth may indeed be found in some of these which is found in Scripture, but never the same authority, seeing that none of them can be compared with " the most sacred excellence of the canonical Scriptures." From what is said by other books we may accordingly withhold belief, unless indeed it is demonstrated " either by sound reason or by this canonical authority itself "; but " in this canonical eminence of the Holy Scriptures, even though it be but a single prophet, or apostle, or evangelist that is shown to have placed anything in his Scriptures, by this confirmation of the canon we are not permitted to doubt that it is true." [97] Similarly when writing to the Donatist Cresconius,[98] he refuses to treat even Cyprian as indefectible. " For," says he, " we do no injury to Cyprian when we distinguish his books — whatever they may be — from the canonical authority of the divine Scriptures. For not without reason has there been constituted with such wholesome vigilance that ecclesiastical canon to which belong the assured books of the prophets and apostles, on which we do not dare to pass any judgment at all, and according to which we judge with freedom all other writings whether of believers or of unbelievers." In a word, Augustine defends the absolute authority of every word of Scripture and insists that to treat any word of it as unauthoritative is to endanger the whole. This he argues to Jerome [99] and over and over again to the Manichæans, culminating in a most striking passage in which he protests against that subjective dealing with the Scriptures which " makes every man's mind the judge of what in each Scripture he is to approve or disapprove." " This," he sharply declares, " is not to be subject for faith to the authority of Scripture, but to subject Scripture to ourselves: instead of approving a thing because it is read and written in the sublime authority of Scripture, it seems to us written rightly because we approve it.[100]

[97] " Contra Faustum Man.," xi. 5.
[98] II. xxxi. 39.
[99] " Epist." 40. iii. 3.
[100] " Contra Faustum Man.," xxxii. 19.

With no less emphasis Augustine traces the supreme authority which he thus accords to the Scriptures to their apostolicity. Their authority is according to him due in the first instance to the fact that they have been imposed upon the Church as its *corpus juris* by the apostles, who were the accredited agents of Christ in founding the Church. In laying this stress on the principle of apostolicity, he was, of course, only continuing the fixed tradition of the early Church. From the beginning apostolicity had been everywhere and always proclaimed as the mark of canonicity,[101] and apostolicity remained with him the only consciously accepted mark of canonicity.[102] He says expressly that " the truth of the divine Scriptures has been received into the canonical summit of authority, for this reason — that they are commended for the building up of our faith not by anybody you please, but by the apostles themselves." [103] The proper proof of canonicity is to him therefore just the proof of apostolicity: and when it has been shown of a declaration that it has been made by an apostle, that is to give it supreme authority.[104] Though one declaration may be from the writings of one apostle and another " from any other apostle or prophet — such is the quality of canonical authority . . . that it would not be allowable to doubt of either." [105] To say " canonical " writings accordingly is to add nothing to speaking of them as genuine writings of the prophets and apostles.[106] The genuineness of the Christian Scriptures as documents of the apostolic age is, therefore, the point of chief importance for him. " What Scriptures can ever possess weight of authority," he asks with conviction in his voice, " if the Gospels, if the Apostolic Scriptures, do not possess it? Of what book can it ever be certain whose it is, if it

---

[101] This has recently been shown afresh by Kunze, " Glaubensregel, Heilige Schrift und Taufbekenntnis," 1899, pp. 114 *sq.*, 249 *sq.* Cf. Cramer, " Nieuwe Bijdragen," etc., iii. 155.

[102] Cf. Kunze, as cited, p. 302.

[103] " Epist." 82 (to Jerome), ii. 7: " non a quibuslibet, sed ab ipsis Apostolis, ac per hoc in canonicum auctoritatis culmen recepta."

[104] " Contra Faustum Man." xi. 5.

[105] *Ibid.*, 6.   [106] *Ibid.*: " vere.'

be uncertain whether those Scriptures are the Apostles', which are declared and held to be the Apostles' by the Church propagated from those very Apostles, and manifested with so great conspicuousness through all nations? " [107] We are not concerned for the moment, however, with the nature of the evidence relied on to prove these books apostolical: what we are pointing out is merely that to Augustine the point of importance was that they should be apostolical, and that this carried with it their canonicity or authority. Their authority was to him rooted directly in their apostolicity.

How completely Augustine's mind was engrossed with the principle of apostolicity as the foundation of authority is illustrated by a tendency he exhibited to treat as in some sense authoritative everything in the Church for which an apostolic origin can be inferred. The best example of this tendency is afforded by what we may call this doctrine of tradition.[108] This doctrine is, in brief, to the effect that where the guidance of the Scripture fails, the immemorial mind of the universal Church may properly be looked upon as authoritative, on the presumption that what has always been understood by the entire Church is of apostolic origin. Repeated expression is given to this position; for example, in his Anti-Donatist treatise " On Baptism " (A.D. 400) where he is seeking to defend the validity of heretical baptism and is embarrassed by Cyprian's rejection of it on the plea that Scripture is silent on the subject. Cyprian's principle, " that we should go back to the

[107] " Contra Faustum Man." xxxiii. 6.

[108] To Roman Catholic writers Augustine's doctrine of tradition seems that of the Church of Rome. Cf. Schwane, " Dogmengeschichte der patrist. Zeit," 1895, § 89.9 (pp. 703 sq.), and, though following Schwane closely, yet somewhat more dogmatically, Portalié in Vacant-Mangenot, " Dictionnaire de théologie Catholique, i. col. 2340. Schwane insists that Augustine joins oral Apostolic tradition to Scripture as necessary both for its completeness and for its interpretation, and that with reference to doctrine as well as usages; yet admits that to Augustine the Scriptures occupy the first place in authority and contain all things necessary to salvation, and that with adequate clearness; and that only the Scriptures are inspired and infallible (cf. loc. cit., pp. 713 sq.). Probably even this is assigning to tradition a much greater rôle than Augustine gave it, particularly with reference to doctrine.

fountain, that is to apostolical tradition, and thence turn the channel of truth to our own times" he of course heartily accepts; [109] he seeks only to turn it against Cyprian. "Let it be allowed," he says, that the "apostles have given no injunctions" on this point — that is to say, in the canonical Scriptures. It is not impossible, nevertheless, that the custom (*consuetudo*) prevalent in the Church may be rooted in apostolical tradition. For "there are many things which are held by the universal Church and are *on that account* (*ob hoc*) fairly (*bene*) believed to be precepts of the apostles, although they are not found written," *i.e.*, in the Scriptures: [110] or, as it is put in an earlier point, "there are many things which are not found in the letters of the apostles, nor yet in the councils of their followers, which yet *because they have been preserved throughout the whole church* (*per universam ecclesiam*) are believed to have been handed down and commended by them." [111]

Even when thus arguing for the apostolicity of tradition, however, Augustine never forgets the superior authority of Scripture. Perhaps the most instructive passage in this point of view is one in which he is investigating the value of baptism of infants. After appealing to the tradition of the universal Church he proceeds as follows: " And if anyone seeks a divine authority in this matter — although what is held by the universal Church, and that not as a thing instituted by councils but as of primitive inheritance (*nec conciliis institutum sed semper retentum est*) is most properly (*rectissime*) believed to have been handed down by apostolic authority — we are able in any case (*tamen*) to form a true conjecture of the value of the sacrament of baptism in the case of infants from the circumcision of the flesh . . . " [112] Here, in the very act of vindicating apostolicity, and therefore authority, for universal primitive custom, language is employed which seems to

[109] " De bapt. contra Donat.," V. xxvi. 37.
[110] *Ibid.*, V. xxiii. 31.
[111] *Ibid.*, II. vii. 12; cf. IV. vi. 9.
[112] *Ibid.*, IV. xxiv. 31.

betray that Augustine was wont to conceive "divine authority" (*auctoritas divina*) the peculiar property of Scripture.
In another Anti-Donatist treatise — the work against the
grammarian Cresconius (*c.* 406) [113] — we read somewhat similarly that "although no doubt no example" of the custom
under discussion "is adduced from the canonical Scriptures,
the truth of these Scriptures is nevertheless held by us in this
matter, since what we do is the *placitum* of the universal
Church, which is commended by the authority of these very
Scriptures; and accordingly since the Holy Scriptures cannot
deceive, whoever is afraid of being led astray by the obscurity
of this question should consult with respect to it that Church
which without any ambiguity is pointed out by the Holy
Scripture."

This care in preserving the superior right of Scripture is
not to be accounted for as due to the exigencies of the controversy with the Donatists. It reappears in more formal form
in purely didactic teaching — in a reply, for instance, which
Augustine made to a series of questions addressed to him by a
correspondent on matters of ritual observance.[114] Here Augustine distinguishes carefully between three varieties of such
observances: those prescribed by Scripture, those commended
by the practice of the universal Church, those of merely local
usage. When an observance is prescribed by the authority of
divine Scripture, no doubt can be admitted but that we must
do precisely as we read.[115] Similarly also only insane insolence
would doubt that we ought to follow the practice of the whole
Church, throughout the world.[116] In matters of varying usage
in different parts of the Church, on the other hand, we must
beware of erecting our own custom into a guide, and should
conform ourselves freely to the custom that obtains in the
Church where we may chance from time to time to be — in

[113] *Op. cit.,* i. 33. 39.

[114] " Epist." 54 and 55 (to Januarius — the 40th of that name in Smith and
Wace, "Dictionary of Christian Biography," — about 400).

[115] " Epist." 54, v. 6: "non sit dubitandum quin ita facere debeamus ut
legimus."

[116] *Ibid.;* "quid . . . tota per orbem frequentat ecclesia."

short, follow Ambrose's wise rule of "doing when we are in Rome as the Romans do." [117] There is nothing that Augustine deprecates more than the arbitrary multiplication of ordinances, by which, he says, the state of Christians which God wished to be free — appointing to them only a few Sacraments and those easy of observance — is assimilated to the burdensomeness of Judaism. He could wish therefore that all ordinances should be unhesitatingly abolished which are neither prescribed by the authority of the Holy Scriptures, nor have been appointed by the councils of bishops, nor have been confirmed by the custom of the universal Church [118] — in which sentence the selection of the terms so that "authority" is ascribed to Scripture alone is not unwitting.

Elsewhere, no doubt, Augustine uses the term "authority" more loosely of the other sources of "custom" also. This is true, for example, of the opening paragraphs of these very letters. Here he carefully draws out the threefold distinction among ordinances, which he applies throughout. The fundamental principle of the discussion on which he is about to enter, he tells us, is that our Lord Jesus Christ has subjected us to an easy yoke and a light burden, laying upon us only few Sacraments and those not difficult of observance. He then adds: "But with respect to those not written but traditional matters to which we hold, observed as they are throughout the whole world, what we are to understand is that they are retained as commended and instituted by the Apostles themselves, or by plenary councils, the authority of which in the Church is very useful." [119] The term "authority" happens to be employed here only of what the context tells us is the least weighty of the three "authorities" to the observances com-

[117] *Ibid.*, ii. 3, where a pleasant anecdote is told of Ambrose's advice to Monnica to follow his example in this.

[118] "Epist." 55, xix. 35; cf. 27, where the "authority" of the divine Scriptures and the "consent" of the whole Church are brought together.

[119] "Epist." 54. 1. 1.: "illa autem quae non scripta sed tradita custodimus, quae quidem toto terrarum orbe servantur, datur intelligi, vel ab ipsis apostolis, vel plenariis conciliis, quorum est in ecclesia saluberrima auctoritas commendata atque statuta retineri."

mended by which we should yield obedience: the Scriptures, universal primitive custom arguing apostolic appointment, and counciliary enactment. We may look somewhat roughly, perhaps, upon these three " authorities " as representing to Augustine respectively the authority of " Scripture," the authority of " tradition," and the authority of " the Church "; and if so, then these three " authorities " — the Scriptures, Tradition, the Church — took rank in his mind in that order. First and above all is the " authority " of Scripture, which is just the infallible Word of God, whose every word is to be believed and every precept obeyed just as it stands written. Then comes the " authority " of immemorial universal tradition, on the presumption that just because it is immemorially universal it may, or must, be apostolic; and if apostolic then also of divine appointment. Last of all comes the " authority " of the Church itself, for which no claim is made of divine infallibility, since that is an attribute of Scripture alone — nor even of such constructive apostolicity as may be presumed of immemorial tradition; but only of righteous jurisdiction and Spirit-led wisdom. Neither the individual bishop, nor any body of bishops assembled in council, up to the whole number in the plenary or ecumenical council, though each and all are clothed with authority appropriate to the place and function of each, is safeguarded from error, or elevated above subsequent criticism and correction. This high altitude of indefectible infallibility is attained by Scripture alone.[120]

An appropriate authority is granted of course to bishops,

[120] Cf. Reuter, " Augustin. Studien, p. 329: " There is not, to my knowledge, to be found in Augustine, any statement giving *un*ambiguous expression to this notion [of the infallibility of the Church]. We read, *Contra Cresconium* ii. 33. 39, ' Since Holy Scripture cannot err '; but I have sought in vain for any declaration corresponding to this with reference to the Church. The assertion, ' Outside the Church, there is no salvation' is nowhere complemented by this other one, ' The Church cannot err.' " Reuter proceeds to say that, although this precise formula does not occur, yet " important premises of it " may be found; but here opinions may lawfully differ. On what follows in the text Reuter, pp. 328 *sq.*, 333 *sq.*, may be profitably consulted; cf. also Schmidt, in Liebner's *Jahrbücher für deutsche Theologie* (1861), vi. pp. 197–255, especially 234 *sq.*

each in his proper sphere: but no one of them is free from error or exempt from testing and correction by the Holy Scriptures. Its own appropriate authority belongs similarly to councils of every grade: but no one of them can claim to have seen truth simply and seen it whole. If the Donatists appealed to Cyprian and his council, for example, Augustine, while ready to yield to Cyprian all the deference that was his due, did not hesitate to declare roundly, " The authority of Cyprian has no terrors for me," [121] and to assert that no council is exempt from error. For, he explains at length,[122] no one " is ignorant that the Holy Canonical Scriptures, as well of the Old as of the New Testament, are contained within their own determined (*certis*) limits, and that they are so set above all later letters of bishops that with respect to them it is not possible to doubt or to dispute whether anything that stands written in them is true or right, while all the letters of bishops which, since the closing of the canon have been written or shall be written, are open to confutation, either by the wiser discourses of some one who happens to be more skilled in the particular matter, or by the weightier authority or more learned prudence of other bishops, or by councils — if there chances to be anything in them that deviates from the truth." And as little is anyone ignorant

---

[121] " De Bapt. contr. Donat." ii. 1. 2: " non me terret auctoritas Cypriani." This does not mean, of course, that he denies all authority to Cyprian; but only that he knows the limits of Cyprian's authority. So, when he says, *op. cit.*, iii. 3. 5. *med:* " No authority (nulla auctoritas), clearly, deters me from seeking the truth," he is not proclaiming an abstract indefeasible liberty in seeking the truth, as A. Dorner (" Augustinus," p. 236) appears to suppose (cf. Reuter, *op. cit.*, p. 335, note 4), but means only to say that Cyprian expressly leaves the path open and does not interpose his authority (whatever that may amount to) to shut off free investigation. Accordingly, he repeats at the end of the paragraph more explicitly: " We have then liberty of investigation conceded to us by Cyprian's own moderate and truthful declaration." The assertion of a zeal for truth which takes precedence of all else, apparently wrongly attributed to this passage, may be more justly found in the remark which occurs in the " Contra Epist. Manich. Fundam." iv. 5, to the effect that " if the truth is so clearly proved as to leave no possibility of doubt, it takes precedence of all things which keep me in the Catholic Church." Cf. Schmidt, as cited above.

[122] *Ibid.*, ii. 3. 4.

" that the councils themselves which are held in the several regions and provinces must without any evasion yield to the authority of plenary councils which are assembled from the whole Christian world; and that even the earlier plenary councils themselves are corrected by later ones, when by some actual trial, what was closed has been opened, and what was hidden has come to light." We perceive accordingly that the limiting phrases in the famous passages in which Augustine declares the Holy Scriptures the sole infallible authority in the world are by no means otiose. He means just what he says when he writes to Jerome, " For I confess to your charity that I have learned to defer this respect and honor to those Scriptural books only (*solis*) which are now called canonical, that I believe most firmly that no one of those authors has erred in any respect in writing " ; [123] or again when he says in another place, " In the writings of such authors " — that is to say Catholic writers — " I feel myself free to use my own judgment, since I owe unhesitating assent *to nothing but the canonical Scriptures.*" [124] A presumptive apostolicity may lend to the immemorial customs of the universal Church an authority which only arrogance can resist; and to the Church which was founded by the apostles, and made by them a depository of the tradition of truth, a high deference is due in all its deliverances: but to the Scriptures alone belongs supreme authority because to them alone belongs an apostolicity which coalesces with their entire fabric. They alone present us with what we may perhaps call " fixed apostolicity."

The ground of this conception of apostolicity as the principle of divine authority lies ultimately in the relation in which the apostles stood to Christ. The apostles, as Christ's accredited agents, empowered by His Spirit for their work, are, in effect, Christ Himself speaking. This idea underlies the entirety of Augustine's reasoning, and is very fully developed in a striking passage which occurs at the close of the first book of the Harmony of the Gospels.[125] He tells us here that our

[123] " Epist." 82. 1. 3.   [124] " De natura et gratia," lxi. 71.
[125] " De consensu Evang.," i. 35. 54.

Lord, "who sent the prophets before His own descent, also despatched the apostles after His ascension. . . . Therefore, since these disciples have written matters which He declared and spoke to them, it ought not by any means to be said He has written nothing Himself; for the truth is that His members have accomplished only that which they became acquainted with by the repeated statements of the Head. For all that He was minded to give for our perusal on the subject of His own doings and saying, He commanded to be written by those disciples, whom He thus used as if they were His own hands. Whoever apprehends this correspondence of unity and this concordant service of the members, all in harmony in the discharge of diverse offices under the Head, will receive the account which he gets in the Gospel through the narrative constructed by the disciples, in the same kind of spirit in which he might look upon the actual hand of the Lord Himself, which he bore in that body that He made His own, were he to see it engaged in the act of writing." Apostolicity therefore spells authority because it also spells inspiration: what the apostles have given the Church as its law is the inspired Word of God. The canonical Scriptures are accordingly "the august pen of the Spirit" of God; [126] and in reading them we are, through the words written by their human authors, learning "the will of God in accordance with which we believe these men to have spoken," [127] seeing that it is "the Holy Spirit who with admirable wisdom and care for our welfare has arranged the Holy Scriptures" in all their details,[128] and has spoken in them in perfect foresight of all our needs and perplexities.[129] Accordingly Augustine makes the Lord declare to him, "O man, verily what my Scripture says, I say"; and this is the reason that we may be assured that the Scripture is true — because it is He that is true, or rather the Truth Itself, who has given it

[126] "Confessiones," vii. 21. 27: "venerabilem stilum Spiritus tui."

[127] "De doctrina Christiana," ii. 5. 6.

[128] *Ibid.*, ii. 6. 8.

[129] *Ibid.*, iii. 27. 38: "assuredly the Holy Spirit who through him [the human author] spoke these words, foresaw that this interpretation would occur to the reader. . . ."

forth.[130] Thus the circle of the authority of the Scriptures completes itself. The Scriptures occupy the pinnacle of authority because they are the Word of God, just God's congealed speech to us. We know them to be such because they have been given to us as such by the apostles who were appointed and empowered precisely for the task of establishing the Church of God on earth, and who are therefore the vehicles for the transmission to us of the will of God and the Word which embodies that will.

But have the Scriptures which we have and which have acquired canonical authority in the Church, really been given to us by the apostles as the Word of God? How shall we assure ourselves of these Scriptures that they possess that apostolicity which lends to them their revelatory character and makes them our supreme authority? The answer returned by Augustine to this question has been most variously conceived, and indeed, out of the several interpretations given it, heterogeneous traditions of his teaching have grown up as discordant at the extremes as the formal principles of Romanism and Protestantism. If we could content ourselves with a simple concrete statement, it doubtless would not be far astray to say briefly that Augustine received the Scriptures as apostolic at the hands of the Church; and that this is the meaning of his famous declaration, " I would not believe the Gospel except I were moved thereto by the authority of the Catholic Church." But the question at once arises whether this appeal to the Church is for conclusive testimony or for authoritative decision. Divergent interpretations at once intervene, and we find ourselves therefore little advanced by our concrete response. The precise question that is raised by these divergent interpretations is whether Augustine validated to himself the Scriptures as apostolic in origin and therefore the revealed Word of God by appropriate evidence, more or less fully drawn out and more or less wisely marshaled; or declined all argument and

---

[130] " Confessiones," xiii. 29. 44: " O Domine, nonne ista Scriptura tua vera est, quoniam tu verax et veritas edidisti eam? . . . O homo, nempe quod Scriptura mea dicit, ego dico."

cut the knot by resting on the sheer enactment of the contemporary Church. In the latter case Augustine would appear as the protagonist of the Romish principle of the supreme authority of the Church, subordinating even the Scriptures to this living authority. In the former he would appear as the forerunner of the Protestant doctrine of the supreme authority of Scripture.

The proper evidence of the apostolicity of the canonical Scriptures is, of course, historical. Apostolicity is a historical conception and its actuality can be established only on historical evidence. When Augustine declares of Scripture that it owes its authority to its apostolicity, he would seem, therefore, already to have committed himself to dependence for the validation of the authority of Scripture upon historical evidence. Many others than the Romanists, however, have found Augustine defective in his teaching or at least in his practice at this point. Neander remarks that Augustine having been brought by Manichæism into doubt as to which were the true documents of the Christian religion, and not being prepared for a historical investigation to determine the truth of the matter, had nothing left him but to fall back upon the tradition of the Church; [131] and this opinion is echoed by Reuter,[132] and sharpened by Harnack.[133] It is to be observed, however, that, when we have suggested that Augustine's dependence was placed wholly on the " tradition of the Church," [134] as Neander phrases it, we have not removed the ground of his conviction out of the sphere of historical judgments. To say " tradition " is indeed only to say " history " over again. And the question at this point is not whether the historical evidence which Augustine rested upon was good historical evidence, but whether he rested upon historical evidence at all, rather than upon the bare authority of the contemporary Church. It will be useful to

---

[131] " Katholismus und Protestantismus " (1863), p. 82.

[132] " Augustinische Studien," p. 491, note 1.

[133] " History of Dogma," v. p. 80; cf. Loofs, " Leitfaden zum Studium der Dogmengeschichte."

[134] " Die Ueberlieferung der kirche."

recall here Augustine's discussion of " tradition " to which we have just had occasion to advert. We will remember that he expressly distinguishes between " tradition " and " Scripture," and decisively subordinates the authority of " tradition " to that of " Scripture." It would certainly be incongruous to suppose him to be at the same moment basing the superior authority of Scripture on the inferior authority of tradition — in any other sense than that in which fact is based upon its appropriate evidence. We should bear in mind, moreover, that his appeal to " tradition " was in the instances brought before us distinctly of the nature of an appeal to testimony, and as such was distinctly discriminated from an appeal to the " Church," speaking, say, through a bishop or a council, and as distinctly preferred to it. His purpose was to validate certain customs prevalent in the Church as incumbent on all. This he does, not directly by asserting as sufficient the authority of the contemporary Church, as if the Church was as such clothed with the right to determine the practice of its adherents by a mere *ipse dixit*. He proceeds, rather, indirectly, by seeking to establish the apostolicity of these customs by an appeal to the immemorial universality of their tradition in the Church. Obviously " tradition " is treated here not as authority, but as evidence; and the " authority " thus validated by tradition is treated as superior to the " authority " of the contemporary Church speaking through whatever channels. It certainly would be incongruous to suppose that he was nevertheless consciously basing the authority of Scripture, which was to him superior to that of even tradition, on the bare authority of the Church, which he defines to be inferior to either. His appeal to the " Church," as by its " authority " moving men to believe the " Gospel " can scarcely be understood otherwise, therefore, than as a broad statement that the Scriptures are validated as apostolic and therefore authoritative in some way by the Church. What is meant, when this is made specific, is, obviously, that the testimony of the whole Church, borne unbrokenly from the beginning, to the apostolicity of the canonical Scriptures is conclusive of the fact.

In his appeals to the " Church " after this fashion Augustine certainly had in mind the Church as a whole, as extended through both space and time; and his fundamental contention is that the testimony of this Church is of decisive weight to the origin of her Scriptures in apostolic gift, and therefore to the authority of the Scriptures as an inspired revelation of the divine will. Such an appeal is distinctly of the nature of an appeal to historical testimony. But the nature of this appeal would not be essentially altered were we to omit consideration of the extension of the Church in time and focus attention on its extension in space alone, as many suppose Augustine to have done. To appeal to the testimony of the universal Church is to adduce historical evidence. Even if we do not accord such weight to this evidence as was obviously accorded to it by Augustine, this difference in our estimate of its conclusiveness should not blind us to its nature. We may smile if we will at the easiness of Augustine's historical conscience, and wonder that he could content himself with testimony so untested. But we ought to recognize that in so doing we are criticising his sense of historical values, not disproving that his resort to the Church was precisely for testimony.

Nor is it very difficult to do serious injustice to Augustine's sense of historical values in a matter of this kind. It is very much a matter of times and seasons. An appeal to the testimony of the universal Church at the close of the nineteenth or at the opening of the twentieth century is not altogether without historical value. But we must not fail to bear in mind that an appeal to the testimony of the universal Church at the close of the fourth or the opening of the fifth century is something very different from an appeal to its testimony at the close of the nineteenth or the opening of the twentieth century. Certainly the testimony of the universal Church at the close of the first or the opening of the second century is still treated in wide circles, as in such a thing as the apostolic gift of the Scriptures, conclusive. And it is not an easy matter accurately to estimate exactly the rate at which the value of this testimony decreases with the lapse of time. Are we so sure that its value had depreciated by the close of the fourth century to such an extent as to render an appeal to the Church as witness-bearer, at that period, absurd? The Church to which the Scriptures were committed by the apostolic college, by whom it was founded and supplied with its corpus juris — is not this Church the proper witness to the apostolicity of the Scriptures it has received from the hands of its apostolic founders? And is it strange that it has always been appealed to for its testimony to this fact? No doubt, as time passed and the years intervening between the commission of the Scriptures to the Church and its witness-bearing to them increased, this testimony became ever weaker as testimony. And no doubt as it became weaker as testimony it naturally took to itself more and more the character of arbitrary authentication. No doubt, further, it was by this slow transmutation of testimony into authentication that the Romish conception of Scripture as dependent upon the Church for its authentication gradually came into being. And no doubt still further the change was wrought practically before it was effected theoretically. Men came practically to rest upon the authority of the Church for the accrediting of Scripture, before they recognized that what they received from the Church was anything more than testimony. The theoretic recognition came inevitably, however, in time. So soon as the defect in the testimony of the Church arising from the lapse of time began to be observed, men were either impelled to cure the defect by an appeal to the Church of the past, that is to say by a historical investigation; or else tempted to rest satisfied with the authority of the living Church. The latter course as the line of easiest resistance, falling in, moreover, as it did, with the increasingly high estimate placed on the Church as mediatrix of religion, was inevitably ultimately taken; and the Romish doctrine resulted. Let it be allowed that in this outline we have a true sketch of the drift of thought through the Patristic Church. It still is not obvious that this development had proceeded so far by the close of the fourth century that Augustine's appeal to the " Church " to authenticate the " Gospel " must be understood as an appeal to the authority strictly so called rather than to the testimony of the Church. On the face of it, it does not seem intrinsically absurd to suppose that Augustine may still at that date have made his appeal to the Church with his mind set upon testimony. And when we come to scrutinize the actual appeals which he made, it seems clear enough that his mind rested on testimony.

Perhaps there is no better way to bring the fact clearly before us than to note the passages quoted by the Romish expositors with a view to supporting their view that Augustine based the authority of the Scriptures immediately upon the dogmatic authority of the Church. Thus, for example, Professor E. Portalié writes as follows: [135]

Above Scripture and tradition is the living authority of the Church. It alone guarantees to us the Scriptures, according to the celebrated declaration in the treatise " Against the Epistle of Manichæus called Fundamental," v. 6: " I indeed would not believe the Gospel except the authority of the Catholic Church moved me." Compare " Against Faustus the Manichæan " xxii. 79; xxviii. 2.

We reserve for the moment comment on " the celebrated declaration " from the " Contra Epist. Manich. Fundam.," and content ourselves with observing that if it indeed implies that Augustine based the authority of Scripture on that of the " living " Church, it receives no support from the companion passages cited. They certainly appeal to the " historical " Church, that is to say adduce the testimony of the Church extended in time rather than the bare authority of the Church extended in space. So clear is this in the latter case [136] that Augustine in it sets the testimony of the Manichæans to the genuineness of their founder's writings side by side, as the same in kind, with the testimony of the Church to the genuineness of the Apostolic writings. I believe, he says, that the book you produce is really Manichæus', because from the days of Manichæus until to-day it has been kept in continuous possession

---

[135] Vacant-Mangenot, " Dictionaire de théologie Catholique," i. col. 2341.

[136] " Contra Faustum Man.," xxviii. 2.

and estimation as his, in the society of the Manichæans: similarly you must believe that the book we produce as Matthew's is his on the same kind of testimony in the Church. To the fixed succession of bishops among the Christians is assigned no different kind of authority than is allowed to the fixed succession of presiding officers among the Manichæans; in both alike this succession is adduced merely as a safeguard for trustworthy transmission. No doubt Augustine represents the testimony of the Church as indefinitely more worthy of credit than that of the Manichæans, but this is a different matter: *gradus non mutant speciem.* Similarly, in the former citation [137] Augustine's appeal is not specifically to the Church of his time, but to the " holy and learned men " who were living in the time of the writers — real or alleged — of the books in question, who, he says, would be in position to know the truth of the matter. Nothing can be clearer in this case either, than that the point of Augustine's argument turns on the validity of the testimony of the Church, not on the dogmatic authority of the Church.

The note struck by these passages is sustained in all Augustine's discussions of the matter and sometimes swells to an even clearer tone. Take for instance the *argumentum ad absurdum* with which he plies Faustus [138] to the effect that we can never be assured of the authorship of any book " if we doubt the apostolic origin of those books which are attributed to the apostles by the Church which the apostles themselves founded, and which occupies so conspicuous a place in all lands." Clearly the appeal to the Church here is for testimony, not for authorization, as is evidenced very plainly in the sequel. For Augustine goes on to contrast the hardiness of the Manichæans in attempting to doubt the apostolicity of books so attested, with their equal hardiness in accepting as apostolic books brought forward solely by heretics, the founders of whose sect lived long after the days of the apostles; and then adduces parallels from classical authors. There are, he tells us, spurious books, in circulation under the

[137] " Contra Faustum Man.," xxii. 79.   [138] *Ibid.*, xxxiii. 6.

name of Hippocrates, known to be spurious among other things from the circumstance " that they were not recognized as his at the time when his authorship of his genuine productions was determined." And who doubts the genuineness of these latter? Would not a denial of it be greeted with derision — " simply because there is a succession of testimonies to these books from the time of Hippocrates to the present day, which makes it unreasonable either now or hereafter to have any doubt on the subject." Is it not by this continuity of the chain of evidence that any book is authenticated — Plato's, Aristotle's, Cicero's, Varro's — or any of the Christian authors' — " the belief becoming more certain as it becomes more general, up to our own day "? Is not the very principle of authentication this: the transmission of information from contemporaries through successive generations? How then can anyone be so blinded by passion as " to deny the ability of the Church of the apostles — a community of brethren as numerous as they were faithful — to transmit their writings unaltered to posterity, as the original seats of the apostles have been occupied by a continuous succession of bishops to the present day? " Are we to deal with the apostolic writings differently from the natural dealing we accord day by day to ordinary ones — whether of profane or religious authors? [139]

The matter is not different when at an earlier place in the same treatise [140] he takes up much the same point on which he is arguing in the famous passage " I would not believe the Gospel, etc." When Manichæus calls himself an apostle, he says, it is a shameless falsehood, " for it is well known that this heresy began not only after Tertullian, but after Cyprian." And what evidence can Manichæus or Faustus bring forward,

[139] Cf. *ibid.*, xxxii. 19: " Why not rather submit to the authority of the Gospel which is so well-founded, so confirmed, so generally acknowledged and admired, and which has an unbroken series of testimonies from the Apostles down to our own day, that you may have an intelligent belief? " Cf. also xi. 2, xiii. 4, xxxiii. 6 and 9. Because Augustine was deeply impressed by the catholicity of the Church's testimony (as e.g., " De morr. eccles. cath.," xxix. 61) is no reason why we should fail to see that he is equally impressed by its continuity — that is, by its historical character.

[140] xiii. 4, 5.

which will satisfy anyone not inclined to believe either their books or themselves? Will Faustus " take our apostles as witnesses? Unless he can find some apostles in life, he must read their writings: and these are all against him. . . . He cannot pretend that their writings have been tampered with; for that would be to attack the credit of his own witnesses. Or if he produces his own manuscripts of the apostolic writings, he must also obtain for them the authority of the Churches founded by the apostles themselves, by showing that they have been preserved and transmitted by their sanction. It will be difficult for a man to make me believe him on the evidence of writings which derive their authority from his own word, which I do not believe. . . . The authority of our books, which is confirmed by the agreement of so many nations, supported by a succession of apostles, bishops, and councils, is against you. Your books have no authority, for it is an authority maintained by only a few and these the worshippers of an untruthful God and Christ. . . . The established authority of the Scriptures must outweigh every other: for it derives new confirmation from the progress of events which happen, as Scripture proves, in fulfilment of the predictions made so long before their occurrence." Of course this is a piece of polemic argumentation, not a historical investigation: but the gist of the polemic is simply that the Scriptures of the Christians owe their authority to a valid historical vindication of them as of apostolic origin, while the Scriptures of the Manichæans lack all authority because they lack such a validation. Augustine does not think of such a thing as simply opposing the authority of the Church to the Manichæan contentions; and much less of course does he take a roundabout way to the same result, by opposing to them the authority of Scriptures which owe all their authority to the mere *ipse dixit* of the Church. If he speaks of authority as given to sacred books only " through the Churches of Christ," it is clear that this does not mean that these churches communicate to these Scriptures an authority inherent in the Churches, but only that it is by their testimony that that supreme authority which belongs to the Scriptures from their apostolic origin is vindicated to them, as indeed it is confirmed to them by other testimonies also, those, to wit, of miracles and fulfilled prophecy and the consent of the nations and the succession of apostles, bishops, and councils, to confine ourselves to items enumerated here. Surely it cannot be doubted that here also Augustine's appeal to the Church as authenticating the Scriptures is to the Church as a witness, not as an authorizer.

It is natural to turn from this passage immediately to the closely related one in the treatise " Against Manichæus' Epistle called Fundamental," in which the famous words, " I would not believe the Gospel, etc.," occur. If the passage which we have just had before us is rather a piece of sharp polemics than a historical investigation, much more this. Augustine proposes here to join argument with the Manichæans on the pure merits of the question at issue between them. He wishes to approach the consideration of their claims as would a stranger who was for the first time hearing their Gospel: and as they promise nothing less than demonstration he demands that they give him nothing less than demonstration before asking of him assent.[141] He warns them that he is held to the Catholic Church by many bonds, which it will be hard to loosen: so that their task of convincing him on the ground of pure reason will not be an easy one. He has found a very pure wisdom in the Catholic Church — not indeed attained to in this life by more than a few spiritual men, while the rest walk by faith, but nevertheless shining steadily forth for all who have eyes to see it. He has been deeply impressed by the wide extension of the Church. The authority it exercises — " inaugurated by miracles, nourished by hope, augmented by love, established by antiquity " — has very strongly moved him. The unbroken succession of rulers in the Church possesses for him a great weight of evidence. He confesses that the very name of " Catholic " — retained unchallenged amid so many heresies — has affected him deeply. What have the Mani-

---

[141] " Contra Epist. Manich. Fundam.," iii. 3.

chæans to offer him which would justify him in setting aside these and such inducements to remain a Catholic? Nothing but the " promise of the truth " (*sola veritatis pollicitatio*). The " promise " of the truth, observe: not " the truth " itself. If the latter — why, Augustine gives up the contest at once. For he allows without dispute, that if they give him truth itself — so clearly the truth that it cannot be doubted — *that* is something that is to be preferred to all these things which he has enumerated as holding him in the Catholic Church — these and all other things that can be imagined as holding him there. For nothing is so good as truth. But he persistently demands that there must be something more than a " promise " of truth before he can separate himself from the Catholic Church — or rather, as he puts it, before he can be moved " from that faith which binds his soul with ties so many and so strong to the Christian religion." It is, then, we perceive, strict demonstration which Augustine is asking of the Manichæans, and he conducts the argument on that basis.

Turning at once to Manichæus' " Fundamental Epistle " as a succinct depository of nearly all which the Manichæans believe, he quotes its opening sentence: " Manichæus, an apostle of Jesus Christ, by the providence of God the Father." There he stops immediately to demand proof — proof, remember, not mere assertion. You have promised me truth, he says — demonstrated truth: and this is what you give me. Now, I tell you shortly, I do not believe it. Will you prove it to me: or will you, in defiance of the whole claim of the Manichæans, that they ask faith of no man save on the ground of demonstration, simply demand of me belief without clear and sound proof? If you propose proof, I will wait for it. Perhaps you will turn to the Gospel and seek there a testimony to Manichæus. But suppose I do not believe the Gospel? Are you to depend for your proof — you who differentiate yourselves from Christians in this, that while they demand faith, you offer them demonstration and ask belief of nothing until you have demonstrated it — are *you* to depend for your proof on this very faith of the Christians? For observe, my faith in the Gospel rests on the authority of the Catholic Church. And moreover, I find myself in this quandary: the same Church that tells me to believe the Gospel tells me not to believe Manichæus. Choose, then, which you will. If I am to believe the Catholics, then I cannot believe Manichæus — for they tell me not to. If I am not to believe the Catholics, then, you cannot use the Gospel, because, it was out of the preaching of the Catholics that I have been brought to believe the Gospel. Or if you say I am to believe them in this one matter and not in the other — I am scarcely so foolish as to put my faith thus at your arbitrary disposal, to believe or not believe as you dictate, on no assigned ground. It was agreed that you should not ask faith from me without clear proof — according to your universal boast that you demand no belief without precedent demonstration. It is clear, then, that to render such a proof you must not appeal to the Gospel. " If you hold to the Gospel, I will hold to those by whose teaching I have come to believe the Gospel; by their instructions I will put no credit in you whatever. And if by any chance you should be able to find anything really clear as to the apostolicity of Manichæus you will weaken the authority of the Catholics for me, since they instruct me not to believe you; and this authority having been weakened I shall no longer be able to believe the Gospel for it was through them that I came to believe it." The upshot of it is that if no clear proof of Manichæus' apostleship is to be found in the Gospel, I shall credit the Catholics rather than you; while if there is such to be found in the Gospel I shall believe neither them nor you. Where then is your demonstration of the apostleship of Manichæus — that I should believe it? Of course I do not mean I do not believe the Gospel. I do believe it, and believing it I find no way of believing you. You can point out neither in it nor in any other book faith in which I confess, anything about this absurd apostleship of Manichæus. But it is certainly evident that your promise to demonstrate to me your tenets signally fails in this case on any supposition.

This is Augustine's argument in this famous passage. Undoubtedly the exact interpretation of its implications with respect to the seat of authority in Christianity is attended with considerable difficulty. And it is not altogether strange that the Romanists have seized upon it as subordinating the " Gospel " to the " Church ": nor even that they have been followed in this, not merely by extreme rationalists predisposed to every interpretation of a Patristic writer which tends to support their notion that the clothing of Scripture with absolute authority was a late and unhistorical dogmatic development,[142] but also by many scholars intent only upon doing complete justice to Augustine's opinions.[143] There are serious difficulties, however, in the way of this interpretation of the passage. One of them is that it would in that case be out of accord with the entirety of Augustine's teaching elsewhere. It is quite true that elsewhere also he speaks of the authority of the Church, and even establishes the Church on the " summit of authority." But in all such passages he speaks obviously of the Church rather as the instrument of the spread of the saving truth than as the foundation on which the truth rests — in a word, as the vehicle rather than the seat of authority.[144] And in general, as we have already seen, Augustine's allusions to the Church as " the pillar and ground of the truth " throw the stress on its function of witness-bearing to the truth rather than found the truth on its bare *ipse dixit*. It is scarcely likely that he has spoken in a contrary sense in our present passage. We must not permit it to fall out of sight that Augustine's point of view in this passage is that of one repelling the Manichæan claim of strict demonstration of the truth of their teaching. His rejoinder amounts to saying that they cannot ground a demonstration upon a Gospel accepted only on faith.

[142] Cf. e.g., H. J. Holtzmann, " Kanon und Tradition " (1859), pp. 2, 3.

[143] Cf. e.g., Harnack, " History of Dogma," v. 80; Loofs, " Leitfaden zum Studium der Dogmengeschichte "; Dorner, " Augustinus "; Kunze, " Glaubenslehre," etc.

[144] Portalié, as cited, col. 2413, adduces in proof that Augustine places the Church " above even Scripture and tradition," *De utilitate credendi,* xvii. 35, comparing " Epist." 118, 32.

The contrast at this point is not between the weakness of the basis on which they accept their tenets and the incomparable weight of the authority of the Church on which Christians accept the " Gospel." On the contrary, the contrast is between the greatness of their claims to demonstration and the weakness of its basis — nothing but the " Gospel " which is accepted on " authority " not on " demonstration " — on " faith " not on " reason " — in effect, on " testimony," not on " sight." In a word, the " authority of the Church " is adduced here not as superlatively great — so great that, in the face of it, the Manichæan claims must fall away let them be grounded in what they may; but rather as incongruously inadequate to support the weight the Manichæan must put on it if he is to build up his structure of demonstration. The Manichæan undertakes a demonstration, scorning a faith that rests on authority: and then actually wishes to rest that demonstration on a premise which has no other basis than a faith that rests on authority. He cannot *demonstrate* that Manichæus was an Apostle of Christ on the testimony of a " Gospel " which itself is accepted on the *authority* of the Catholic Church: " authority " being used here in its contrast with " reason," not with " testimony," and in pursuance of Augustine's general contention that all religious truth must begin with faith on authority and not with demonstration on reason. This being the case, so far is the passage from predicating that Augustine esteemed the " authority " of the Church as " the highest of all " as the Romish contention insists,[145] that its very gist is that the testimony of the Church is capable of establishing only that form of conviction known as " faith " and therefore falls hopelessly short of " demonstration."

Such being the case we cannot be surprised that in all ages there has been exhibited a tendency among those more or less emancipated from the Romish tradition to deny that even this famous passage asserts the supreme authority of the contemporary Church. Striking instances may be found

[145] Cf. Portalié, as cited, col. 2341 and col. 2413.

for example in William Occam [146] and Marsilius of Padua [147] in the fourteenth century and in John Wessel [148] in the fifteenth: and examples are not wanting throughout the whole period of papal domination.[149] Of course the early Protestant controversialists take their place in this series. With them the matter was even less than with William Occam and Marsilius a merely academical question. In their revolt from the dogmatic authority of the Church and their appeal to the Scriptures alone as the sole source and norm of divine truth, they were met by the citation of this passage from Augustine. As on its theological side the Reformation was precisely an "Augustinian" revival, the adduction of Augustine's authority in behalf of the subjection of Scripture to the Church, was particularly galling to them and amounted to a charge that they were passing beyond the limits of all established Christianity. They were indeed in no danger, in casting off the authority of the Church, of replacing it with the authority of any single father. Doubtless Luther spoke a little more brusquely than was the wont of the Reformers, in the well-known assertion: "Augustine often erred; he cannot be trusted: though he was

[146] Occam explains that the "ecclesia quae majoris auctoritatis est quam evangelista, est illa ecclesia cujus auctor evangelii pars esse agnoscitur" (Goldasti mon. tom. 1. fol. 402). That is to say, he understands the Church here as projected through time, and as including even Jesus Himself: the historical not the contemporary Church. But he takes "authority" strictly. Cf. Neander, "General History of the Christian Religion and Church," E. T. v. p. 40.

[147] Marsilius explains: "Dicit autem Augustinus pro tanto se credere evangelio propter ecclesiae catholicae auctoritatem, quia suae credulitatis initium inde sumpsit, quam Spiritu Sancto dirigi novit: fides enim quandoque incipit ex auditu" — in which he anticipates the general Protestant position. Cf. (quite fully) Neander, op. cit., E. T. v. pp. 27–28.

[148] De Potestate Ecclesiastica (Opp. p. 759): "We believe in the Gospel on God's account, and on the Gospel's account in the Church and the Pope; not in the Gospel on the Church's account: wherefore that which Augustine says ("Contra Epist. Manich. Fundam.," chap. 6), concerning the Gospel and the Church, originis de credendo verbum est, non comparationis aut praeferentiae. For the whole passage and others of like import, see Gieseler, "Lehrbuch der Kirchengeschichte," 1829, II, part 3, sect. 5, § 153, p. 495; E. T. "Ecclesiastical History," 1868, iii. 468; and cf. Schmidt, Jahrbücher für die Theologie, (1861), vi. 235.

[149] Cf., for example, the instances mentioned by Chamier, below.

good and holy, yet he, as well as other fathers, was wanting in the true faith." But the essential opinion here expressed was the settled judgment of all the Reformers and is by no means inconsistent with their high admiration of Augustine or with their sincere deference to him. The gist of the matter is that though they looked upon Augustine as their great instructor, esteeming him indeed the greatest teacher God had as yet given His Church; and felt sure, as Luther expressed it, that " had he lived in this century, he would have been of our way of thinking "; they yet knew well that he had not lived in the sixteenth century but in the fourth and fifth and that in the midst of the marvelous purity of his teaching there were to be found some of the tares of his time growing only too richly. Ready as they were to recognize this, however, they were not inclined to admit without good reason that he had erred so sadly in so fundamental a matter as that at present before us; and they did not at all recognize that the Romanists had made good their assertion that Augustine in saying that " he would not believe the Gospel except as moved thereto by the authority of the Catholic Church " was asserting the Romish theory that the authority of the Church lies behind and above all other authorities on earth — that, as even Schwane puts it, the Church is the representative of God on earth and its authority alone can assure us of the reality of a divine revelation.

Already at the Leipzig disputation with Eck, Luther had been triumphantly confronted with this statement of Augustine's; and in his " Resolutions " on that debate he suggests that Augustine was only giving what was historically true in his own case.[150] Augustine had himself been led to believe the Gospel through the ministration of the Church; and he adduces this fact only that he might bring to bear upon his heretical readers the impressive testimony of the whole Church, which was, of course, of much more moving weight than his own personal witness could be. As a matter of fact,

---

[150] See Köstlin, " The Theology of Luther," E. T. ii. pp. 224, 255, and especially i. pp. 320–321.

comments Luther, the Gospel does not rest on the Church, but contrariwise, the Church on the Gospel. It was not Luther's way to say his say with bated breath. This is the way he expresses his judgment in his " Table Talk ": [151] " The Pope . . . to serve his own turn, took hold on St. Augustin's sentence, where he says, *evangelio non crederem*, &c. The asses could not see what occasioned Augustin to utter that sentence, whereas he spoke it against the Manicheans, as much as to say: I believe you not, for ye are damned heretics, but I believe and hold with the Church, the spouse of Christ." It seemed to Luther, in other words, quite one thing to say that the credit of the Church ought to be higher than that of the Manichæans, and quite another to teach that the authority of the Church was needed to give authority to the Gospel. Perhaps the consentient opinion of the Reformers in this matter is nowhere better stated, in brief form, than in the Protestant " Objections " to the Acts of Ratisbon, which were penned by Melanchthon.[152] " Although therefore," we read here, " the conservation of certain writings of the Prophets and Apostles is the singular work and benefit of God, nevertheless there must be recognized that diligence and authority of the Church, by which it has, in part testified to certain writings, in part by a spiritual judgment separated from the remaining Prophetic and Apostolic Scriptures those that are unworthy and dissentient. Wherefore Augustine commends to us the authority of the primitive Church,[153] receives the writings that are approved by the Catholic consent of the primitive Church; (and) repudiates the later books of the Manichæans. Accordingly he says: ' *I would not believe the Gospel except the authority of the Catholic Church moved me.*' He means that he is moved by the consentient testimony of the primitive Church, not to doubt that these books were handed down from

---

[151] " Of the Fathers," near the beginning (chap. DXXX.). Augustine's statement is invoked in the bull, *Exsurge Domine,* published by Leo X in 1520 against Luther.

[152] *Corpus Reformatorum,* iv. 350. A French version is given in the Brunswick ed. of Calvin's works, v. 564 (*Corpus Reformatorum,* v. 33).

[153] " Auctoritatem primae Ecclesiae."

the Apostles and are worthy of credit (*fide*)." In a word, according to Melanchthon, Augustine is to be read as appealing to the testimony of the Church not as asserting its authority.

In the same line follow all the Reformers, and much the same mode of statement may be read, for example, in Butzer, or Calvin, or Bullinger, or Peter Martyr. " I will not now remember," writes Bullinger,[154] " how by manifest words the standard-bearers of that see do write, that the canonical scripture taketh her authority of the church, abusing this sentence of the ancient father St. Augustine, ' I would not have believed the Gospel, if the authority of the holy Church had not moved me.' . . ." How they abused it Peter Martyr tells us more fully: [155] " But they say that Augustine writes ' Against the Epistola Fundamenti,' ' I would not believe the Gospel except the authority of the Church moved me.' But Augustine wished to signify by these words nothing else than that much is to be attributed to the ministry of the Church which proposes, preaches, and teaches the Gospel to believers. For who of us came to Christ or believed the Gospel except as excited by the preaching of the Gospel which is done in the Church? It cannot be inferred from this, however, that the authority of the Gospel hangs on the Church in the minds of the auditors. For if that were true, long ago the Epicureans and Turks had been persuaded. . . ." As was to be expected it was Calvin who gives us the solidest piece of reasoning upon the subject. The gist of what he says is that Augustine was not setting forth the source whence the Gospel derives its authority, but the instrument by which men may be led to recognize that authority. The unbeliever, he remarks, may well be brought to trust the Gospel by the consent of the Church; but the believer's trust in the Gospel finds its authority not in the Church, but in the Gospel itself, and this is logically prior to that of the Church, though no doubt, it may be chronologically recognized last by the inquirer. The Church may thus

---

[154] " Decades," v. 2 (Parker Soc. ed. v. p. 67).
[155] " Loci Communes," Zurich, 1580, i. 251 (iii. 3. 3).

bring us to the Gospel and commend the Gospel to us; but when we have accepted the Gospel our confidence in it rests on something far more fundamental than the Church. Augustine, he insists, " did not have in mind to suspend the faith which we have in the Scriptures on the will and pleasure (*nutu arbitriove*) of the Church, but only to point out, what we too confess to be true, that those who are not yet illuminated by the Spirit of God, are by reverence for the Church brought to docility so as to learn from the Gospel the faith of Christ; and that the authority of the Church is in this way an introduction, by which we are prepared for the faith of the Gospel." Augustine is perfectly right, then, he continues, to urge on the Manichæans the universal consent of the Church as a *reason* why they should come believingly to the Scriptures, but the *ground* of our faith in the Scriptures as a revelation of truth is that they are from God.[156]

The Protestant scholastics, of course, developed what had by their time become the traditional Protestant contention, and defended it against the assaults of the Romish controversialists. Who first invented the philological argument that Augustine uses in this sentence the imperfect for the pluperfect " in accordance with the African dialect " — so that he says, not " I would not believe the Gospel," but, historically, " I would not have believed the Gospel " — we have not had the curiosity to inquire. If we may trust the English version of the " Decades," Bullinger already treats the tense as a pluperfect. Musculus,[157] who devotes a separate section of his *Locus de Sacris Scripturis* to the examination of Augustine's declaration lays great stress on this particular point, that in it *non crederem* is used for *non credidissem;* and Musculus is gen-

---

[156] " Institutes," i. 7. 3. Calvin very appositely points out that Augustine in the immediately preceding context represents the proper course to be to " follow those who invite us first to believe what we are not yet able to see, that, being made able by this very faith, we may deserve to understand what we believe, our mind being now inwardly strengthened and illuminated not by men but by God Himself." In these words, Calvin remarks, Augustine grounds our confidence in the Gospel on the internal operation of God Himself upon our minds. Cf. below, note 175.

[157] " Loci Communes," Basle, 1560, pp. 181–183 (Locus xxi).

erally cited by later writers upon it. This is true, for example, of both Whitaker and Chamier, who with Stillingfleet may be mentioned as offering perhaps the fullest and best discussions of the whole matter. Whitaker [158] devotes a whole chapter to it, and after adducing the arguments of Peter Martyr, Calvin, and Musculus, affirms that " it is plain that he (Augustine) speaks of himself as an unbeliever, and informs us how he first was converted from a Manichæan to be a Catholic, namely, by listening to the voice of the Church " — in which remark he appears to us to be quite wrong. Chamier's [159] treatment, which also fills a whole chapter, is exceedingly elaborate. He begins by calling attention to the singularity of the passage, nothing precisely to the same effect being adducible from the whole range of Augustine's writings. Then he cites the opinions of eminent Romanists divergent from the current Romish interpretation — those of John, Cardinal of Torre Cremara, Thomas Valden, Driedo, Gerson, who represent Augustine as assigning only a *declarative* authority to the Church, or as speaking not of the " living " but of the " historical " Church. " Augustine," says Driedo, " speaks of the Catholic Church which was from the beginning of the Christian faith ": " by the Church," says Gerson, " he understands the primitive congregation of those believers who saw and heard Christ and were his witnesses." All these are good staggers towards the truth, says Chamier: but best of all is the explanation of the passage which is given by Petrus de Alliaco, himself a cardinal, " in the third article, of the first question on the first of the sentences." In the judgment of this prelate Augustine's meaning is not that the Church was to him a *principium theologicum,* by which the Gospel was theologically proved to him to be true, but only a " moving cause " by which he was led to the Gospel — much " as if he had said, ' I would not believe the Gospel unless moved thereto by the holiness of the Church, or by the miracles of Christ: in which (forms of statement) though

[158] " Disp. on Holy Scripture " (1610), iii. 8 (Parker Society, E. T. p. 320).
[159] " Panstrat. Cathol." (Geneva, 1926), i. pp. 198 *sq.* (I. i. 7. 10).

a cause is assigned for believing the Gospel, there is no *principium prius* set forth, faith in which is the cause why the Gospel is believed." In a word, as it seems, Petrus de Alliaco is of the opinion that Augustine's appeal to the Church is to its testimony rather than to its authority. This opinion, now, continues Chamier, is illustrated and confirmed by weighty considerations brought forward by Protestant writers — whereupon he cites the arguments of Peter Martyr, Calvin, Musculus, Whitaker, and through them makes his way into a detailed discussion of the passage itself in all its terms. Rivaling Chamier's treatment in fullness if not equaling it in distinction is that given the passage in Stillingfleet's " Rational Account of the Grounds of the Protestant Religion," [160] under the three heads of (1) the nature of the controversy in which Augustine was engaged; (2) the Church by whose authority he was moved; and (3) the way and manner in which that Church's authority moved him — certainly a logically complete distribution of the material. The whole argument of scholastic Protestantism is brought before us in its briefest but certainly not in its most attractive form, however, in the concise statement given in De Moor's Commentary on John Marck's Compend.[161] According to this summary: (1) The Papists in adducing this passage to support their doctrine of the primary authority of the Church deceive themselves by a twofold fallacy — (A) They draw a general conclusion from a particular instance: it does not follow that because Augustine did not believe the Gospel except as moved by the authority of the Church, therefore no one can believe the Gospel whom the authority of the Church does not move; (B) They misunderstand Augustine, as if he were speaking of himself at the time of his writing, instead of at the time of his conversion. " For where he says, ' I would not believe were I not moved ' he is employing, as the learned observe, an African mode of speech, familiar enough to Augustine, in which the

---

[160] i. 7; " Works " (1709), iv. pp. 210 *sq.*

[161] " De Moor in J. Marck. Compend.," (1761), i. p. 160 (chap. ii. 7. *ad fin.*).

imperfect form is used for the pluperfect." . . . " His meaning then is not that believers should depend on the authority
of the Church, but that unbelievers should take their start
from it "; and in this sense he elsewhere speaks often enough.
(2) Augustine is not speaking here of *auctoritas praecipiens,
juris et imperii* (injunctionary authority, with a legal claim
upon us for obedience) " as the Papists insist, — as if Augustine would have believed solely because the Church pronounced
belief to be due ": but of *auctoritas dignitatis* (the authority
of observed desert), " which flows from the notable manifestations of Divine Providence observable in the Church, —
such as miracles, antiquity, common consent (chap. iv.), and
which may lead to faith though it is incapable of implanting
it in the first instance." (3) " What is noted here, then, is the
external motive of faith, but not at all the infallible *principium
credendi,* which he teaches in the fourth chapter is to be sought
in the truth alone. . . . And it is to be noted that the fathers
elsewhere rightly hold that the Holy Scriptures are superior
in authority both *in se* and *quoad nos* to the Church. . . ."

Of course it is observable enough from this survey, that
the interest of the Protestant scholastics was far more in the
dogmatic problem of the seat of authority in Christianity,
than in the literary question of the precise meaning of Augustine's words. We must bear in mind that the citations we have
made are taken not from studies in literary history but from
dogmatic treatises; and that their authors approach the particular question upon which we are interrogating them from
a dogmatic point of view, and in a doctrinal interest. There
would be a certain unfairness in adducing these citations in
a connection like the present, therefore, were there any real
occasion to defend the tone in which they are couched. This
is by no means the case. We need not hesitate to recognize
nevertheless at once that some of the reasoning employed
by them to support their interpretation will scarcely bear
scrutiny. It is a counsel of despair, for example, to represent
Augustine as employing — " in accordance with the usage of
the African dialect " — the imperfect in a pluperfect sense.

We may readily confess that the supposition does violence to the context of the passage itself, which requires the imperfect sense; it seems clearly to be the offspring of a dogmatic need rather than of a sympathetic study of the passage. And we are afraid the same must be said of the general conception of the meaning of the passage which has probably given rise to this philological suggestion — viz., that it is a historical statement of Augustine's own experience and means merely that he himself was led by the Church's authority to the Gospel. He is not writing his autobiography in this passage, but arguing with the Manichæans; and he is not informing them of what had been true of his own manner of conversion but confounding them by asserting what in a given case he, as a reasonable man, would do. There are elements enough of doubtful validity in the argument of the Protestant scholastics, therefore — as there could not fail to be in the circumstances. But it is quite another question whether their general conception of the passage is not truer than that of their Romish opponents, and whether they do not adduce sound reasons enough for this general conception to support it adequately. It is a matter of common experience in every department of life — and not least in judicial cases, where the experience has been crystallized into a maxim to the effect that it is best to announce decisions and withhold the reasons — that the decisions of men's judgment are often far better than the reasons they assign for them: and it may haply prove true here too, that the position argued for by the Protestant scholastics is sounder than many of the arguments which they bring forward to support it.

It must be confessed, meanwhile, that modern Protestant opinion does not show so undivided a front as was the case during the scholastic period. The majority of Protestant scholars, historical investigators as well as dogmatic systematizers, do, indeed, continue to defend the essential elements of the interpretation for which the Protestant scholastics contended; but even these ordinarily adopt a different line of argument and present the matter from a somewhat different point of

view; and there are many recent Protestant scholars, and they
not invariably those deeply affected by the rationalism of
the day, who are inclined to revert more or less fully to the
Romish interpretation. Even Dr. W. G. T. Shedd, who reproduces more of the scholastic argument than is now usual,[162]
shows the effect of the change. Even he quotes Hagenbach [163]
approvingly to the effect that Augustine " merely affirms " " a
subjective dependence of the believer upon the authority of
the Church universal, but not an objective subordination of
the Bible itself to this authority "; though he proceeds to
weaken the " subjective dependence of the believer upon the
authority of the Church " so as to leave room for a " private
judgment." What in his view Augustine is asserting is the
duty of the individual to respect the authority of the Church,
because the " Church universal had an authority higher than
that of any one member," and it is therefore unreasonable
for the individual, or a heretical party, to " oppose their private judgment to the catholic judgment." Or rather, what he
supposes Augustine to affirm is — as he fortunately weakens
the statement in the next sentence — " the greater probability
of the correctness of the Catholic Mind, in comparison with
the Heretical or Schismatic Mind, and thereby the *authority*
of the Church in relation to the individual, without dreaming,
however, of affirming its absolute *infallibility*, — an attribute
which he confines to the written revelation." Augustine's notion of " ecclesiastical authority " is by this expedient reduced
to " the natural expectation of finding that the general judgment is a correct one," coupled with " the right of private
judgment; the right to examine the general judgment and
to perceive its correctness with his own eyes." Thus, Dr. Shedd
supposes, " Augustine adopts the Protestant, and opposes the
Papal theory of tradition and authority." " The Papist's
method of agreeing with the catholic judgment," he explains,
" is passive. He denies that the individual may intelligently

---

[162] " History of Christian Doctrine," i. pp. 144–150. Cf. S. Baumgarten:
" Untersuchung. theol. Streitigkeiten," iii. pp. 2, 8.
[163] " Dogmengeschichte," § 119.

verify the position of the Church for himself, because the Church is *infallible,* and consequently there is no possibility of its being in error. The individual is therefore shut up to a mechanical and passive reception of the catholic decision. The Protestant, on the other hand, though affirming the high probability that the general judgment is correct, does not assert the infallible certainty that it is. It is conceivable and possible that the Church may err. Hence the duty of the individual, while cherishing an antecedent confidence in the decisions of the Church, to examine these decisions in the light of the written word, and to convert this presumption into an intelligent perception, or else demonstrate its falsity beyond dispute. ' Neither ought I to bring forward the authority of the Nicene Council,' says Augustine (" Contra Maximianum Arianum " II. xiv. 3), ' nor you that of Ariminum, in order to prejudge the case. I ought not to be bound (*detentum*) by the authority of the latter, nor you by that of the former. Under the authority of the Scriptures, not those received by particular sects, but those received by all in common, let the disputation be carried on, in respect to each and every particular.' " [164]

What strikes one most in these remarks of Dr. Shedd is that they begin by attributing to Augustine a doctrine of the authority of the Church universal over the individual, which forbids the individual to oppose his private judgment to the catholic judgment: proceed to vindicate to the individual a private judgment in the sense of a right to examine the general judgment that he may perceive its correctness with his own eyes — that is to say to an active as distinguished from a merely passive agreement with the catholic judgment: and end by somehow or other supposing that this carries with it the right to disagree with and reject the catholic judgment on the basis of an individual judgment. The premise is that it is not reasonable to erect the individual judgment against the catholic judgment: the conclusion is that it is the duty of the individual to subject the catholic judgment to his per-

[164] *Op. cit.,* pp. 148–149.

sonal decisions: the connecting idea is — that the individual ought to be able to give an active and not merely a passive reception to the catholic decision. The logic obviously halts. But it seems clear that what Dr. Shedd is striving to do is to give due validity to what he considers Augustine to assert in his famous declaration, viz., this, that the individual is subjectively under the authority of the Church; and yet at the same time to vindicate for Augustine a belief in the right of private judgment. He wishes to do justice to the conception of " authority " which he supposes Augustine to have had in mind in this expression, without doing injustice to Augustine's obvious exercise of freedom of opinion under the sole authority of the Scriptures. It cannot be said that he has fully succeeded, although there is much that is true in his remarks, considered as an attempt to give a general account of Augustine's estimate of the authority of the Church. But it is of no great importance for our present inquiry whether he has fully succeeded in this particular effort, or not; since, as has already been pointed out, Augustine does not seem to intend in this passage to place the individual subjectively under the " authority of the Church "; but appears to employ the term " authority " in an entirely different sense from that which it bears in such phrases — the sense namely in which it is the synonym of " testimony " and the ground of " faith," in distinction from the " demonstration " of " reason " which is the ground of that form of conviction which he calls " knowledge."

From another point of view of importance Dr. Shedd's instinct has carried him very near to the truth. We refer to the recognition that informs his discussion that Augustine did make more of the Church and of the authority of the Church than the Protestant scholastics were quite ready to admit. It is probably the feeling that this is the case which accounts for much of the tendency among recent scholars to concede something to the Romish interpretation of Augustine's doctrine of the authority of the Church. It certainly cannot easily be denied that Augustine does declare in this passage, that the credit we accord the Gospel hangs on the credit we give the Church. In this particular passage, this no doubt means no more than that we are dependent on the Church to accredit to us the Gospel; that it is from the Church's hands and on her testimony that we receive the Gospel as apostolic and divine. But, if we raise the broader question of Augustine's attitude towards the Church in its relation to the reception of the truth it cannot be successfully contended that it was solely as a *motivum credibilitatis* that he reverenced the Church. To him the Church was before all else the institute of salvation, out of which there is no salvation. And although it may be difficult to find expressed in language parallel to this crisp *extra ecclesiam nulla salus,* that outside of the Church there can be no right knowledge of God, it nevertheless certainly belongs to the very essence of his doctrine that outside of the Church there can be no effective knowledge of God. The Scriptures may be the supreme authority for faith, and it may be true, therefore, that wherever the Scriptures go, the salvatory truth will be objectively conveyed; but it is equally true that with Augustine this Word of truth will exert no saving power save in and through the Church.[165] As the Church is the sole mediatrix of grace and that not merely in the sense that it is through her offices alone that men are brought once for all to God, but also in the sense that it is through her offices only that all the saving grace that comes to men is conveyed to them — so that we are with Christ only when we are with His body the Church, and it is only in the Church that communion with God can be retained as well as obtained — it follows that the Word, however well known it may be and however fully it may perform its function of making known the truth of God, profits no man spiritually save in the Church.[166] It seems to be implicated in this that it is part of Augustine's teaching that the revealed truth of God, deposited in the Holy Scriptures, will not profit men

[165] The distinction between " habere " and " utiliter habere " or " salubriter habere " was made to do yeoman's service as regards baptism, in the Donatist controversy.

[166] Cf. A. Dorner, " Augustinus," pp. 233 *sq.,* and H. Schmidt, in *Jahrbücher für die Theologie* (1861), vi. 233.

even intellectually so that they may come by it to know God save in communion with the Church. Certainly he would never allow that an adequate knowledge could be obtained of that truth which must be chastely and piously sought and the key to which is love — access to which is closed to all but the spiritual man — outside the limits of that Church the supreme characteristic of which is that in it and in it alone is the love of God shed abroad in our hearts by the Holy Spirit which He has given unto us.[167]

The reverence which Augustine accordingly shows to the teaching of the Church is both great and sincere. It is no meaningless form when he opens his treatise on the " Literal Interpretation of Genesis " [168] or his great work on " The Trinity " [169] with a careful statement of the faith of the Church on the topics to be dealt with, to stand as a norm of teaching beyond which it would be illegitimate to go [170] — declaring moreover with complete simplicity, " This is my faith, too, since it is the Catholic faith." [171] There can be no question therefore that he accorded not merely a high value but also a real authority to the teaching of the Church, an authority which within its own limits may well be called a " dogmatic authority." But it needs also to be borne in mind that the organs of this authority were not conceived by him as official but vital — those called of God in the Church to do the thinking and teaching for the Church; [172] that the nature of this authority is never conceived by him as absolute and irreformable but always as relative and correctible — no teaching from any source is to be accepted unhesitatingly as above critical examination except that of the Scriptures only; and that as to its source this authority is not thought of by him

---

[167] " De unitate eccles." ii. 2: " The members of Christ are linked together by means of love that belongs to unity, and by means of it are made one with their Head."

[168] " De Gen. ad Lit. imperf.," *ad init.*   [169] " De Trinitate," i. 4. 7.

[170] " De Gen. ad Lit. imperf.," i. 1: " catholicae fidei metas; . . . praeter fidem catholicae disciplinae "; 2: " as the Catholic discipline commands to be believed."   [171] " De Trinitate," i. 4. 7, *ad fin.*

[172] " Epist." 118, v. 32: " armed with the abundant weapons of reason, by means of a comparatively few devoutly learned and truly spiritual men."

as original but derived, dependent upon the Scriptures upon which it rests and by which it is always to be tested and corrected. The Catholic faith as to the Trinity, for example, which is also his faith because it is the Catholic faith, is the faith that has been set forth, not by the organized Church on its own authority, but by "the Catholic expounders of the Divine Scriptures," intent upon teaching "according to the Scriptures"[173] and therefore only on the authority of these Scriptures. If there can be no question, therefore, that Augustine accorded a "dogmatic authority" to the Church, there can be no question either that the "dogmatic authority" he accorded to the Church was subordinated to the authority of the Scriptures, and was indeed but the representation of that authority in so to speak more tangible form. This, it is obvious, is in complete harmony with what we have already had occasion to note, in the matter of Christian observances, as to the relative authority Augustine accorded to the Scriptures, Tradition, the Church — in descending series. Only, it is to be noted that the dogmatic authority of the Church of which we are now specifically speaking expresses itself not merely, and not chiefly, through conciliar decrees, but rather through the vital faith of the people of God, first assimilated by them from the Scriptures, and then expressed for them by the appropriate organs of the expression of Christian thought, which in general are the Doctors of the Church. Such being the case, there can no question be raised whether or not the Church may be conceived as the supreme seat of authority in the dogmatic sphere. In many cases the proximate seat of authority it doubtlessly is; but never the ultimate seat of authority. That belongs with Augustine ever and unvaryingly to the Holy Scriptures,[174]

---

[173] "De Trinitate," i. 4. 7, *ad init.*

[174] "Epist." 164, iii. 6, offers a typical mode of statement: "And with respect to that first man, the father of the human race, that [Christ] loosed him from hell almost the whole Church agrees; and it is too considered that the Church does not believe this in vain — whencesoever it has been handed down, although the authority of the Canonical Scriptures is not expressly adducible for it (etiamsi canonicarum Scripturarum hinc expressa non proferatur auctoritas)."

witnessed to by the Church as given to it by the apostles as the infallible Word of God, studied and expounded by the Church for its needs, and applied by it to the varying problems which confront it with the measure of authority which belongs to it as the Church of God, the pillar and ground of the truth.

It is, however, in a deeper sense than even this that Augustine thought of the Church in relation to the acquisition of the knowledge of the truth. With Augustine the Church as it is the mediatrix of divine grace, is also the mediatrix of divine knowledge. As such the Church holds a position of the very highest significance between the supreme seat of authority, the Holy Scriptures, and the souls of men. Only in and through the Church can a sound as well as a saving knowledge of the contents of the Scriptures be hoped for; only in and through the Church can the knowledge of God enshrined in the Holy Scriptures avail for the illumination of the intellect with true knowledge of God, no less than for the sanctification of the soul for true communion with God. But, it must be remembered that in speaking thus, Augustine is thinking of the Church not mechanically as an organized body acting through official organs, say the hierarchy, but vitally, as the *congregatio sanctorum* acting through its vital energies as a communion of love. The Church in which alone according to Augustine true knowledge of God is to be had is fundamentally conceived as the Body of Christ. And this is as much as to say that the essence of his doctrine of the authority of the Church would not be inaptly expressed by the simple and certainly to no Christian thinker unacceptable formula, that it is only in Jesus Christ that God can be rightly known. The Church of Christ is the Body of Christ, and this Body of Christ is the real subject of the true knowledge of God on earth: it is only therefore as one is a member in particular of this Body that he can share in the knowledge of God, of which it is the subject. This is the counterpart in Augustine of that doctrine of the *Testimonium Spiritus Sancti* which was first formulated by Calvin and from him became the corner stone of the Protestant doctrine of authority: and it differs from that doctrine only because and as Augustine's doctrine of "the means of grace" differs from the Protestant.[175]

Augustine's doctrine of the Church is a fascinating subject on which it is difficult to touch without being carried beyond the requirements of our present purpose. Perhaps enough has already been said to indicate sufficiently for the end in view the place which the Church holds in Augustine's doctrine of authority. In the sin-bred weakness of humanity, the Church mediates between the divine revelation deposited in the Holy Scriptures and the darkened mind of man; and thus becomes a paedagogue to lead men to the truth. It is in the Church that the truth is known; and this not merely in the sense that it is in the hands of the Church that the Scriptures are found, those Scriptures in which the whole Truth of God is indefectibly deposited; but also in the sense that it is in the Church alone that the mysteries of the faith, revealed in the Scriptures, are comprehended: that it is only in the participation of the graces found in her that men may hope to attain to the vision which is the possession solely of saints. The true knowledge of God belongs to the fellowship of His people, and out of it cannot be attained. And therefore, although Augustine knows of many things which bind him to the Catholic Church and the adduc-

---

[175] On Augustine's conception of the Church as a communion of saints, see the fifth of Reuter's "Augustinische Studien"; and compare Schmidt as above cited, especially from p. 233. On Augustine's relation to the Protestant doctrine of the "testimony of the Holy Spirit" see Pannier, "Le Témoignage du Saint-Esprit" (1893), pp. 67–68. After citing "Tract. iii. in Ep. Joan. ad Parthos," ii. 13; "De Trinitate," iii. 1–2; "Confessiones," vi. 5, and xi. 3, he adds: "There certainly is not yet here the whole of the witness of the Holy Spirit. . . . But St. Augustine has the intuition of a mysterious work which is wrought in the soul of the Christian, of an understanding of the Bible which does not come from man, but from a power external to him and superior to him; he urges the rôle which the direct correspondence between the Book and the reader must play in the foundation of Christian certitude. In this, as on so many other points, Augustine was the precursor of the Reformation, and a precursor without immediate continuers." In point of fact Augustine is just as clear as the Reformers that earthly voices assail only the ears, and that cathedram in coelo habet qui cordia docet ("Tract. iii. in Ep. Joan. ad Parthos," ii. 13). He differs from them only in the place he gives the Church in communicating that grace out of which comes the preparation of the mind to understand, as well as of the heart to believe, and of the will to do.

tion of which as undeniable credentials giving confidence to
those who hold to that Church, he thinks should impress any
hearer — such as the consent of peoples and nations, the just
authority it enjoys among men, the unbroken succession of its
rulers from the beginning, and the very name of Catholic —
yet the real thing which above all others held him to the Catholic Church was, as he was well aware, that there was to be
found in it "the purest wisdom" (*sincerissima sapientia*). He
needs indeed to confess that to the knowledge of this wisdom
only a few spiritual men (*pauci spirituales*) attain in this life,
and even they (because they are men) only very partially (*ex
minima quidem parte*), though without the least uncertainty
(*sine dubitatione*).[176] The crowd (*turba*) meanwhile walk even
in the Church, by faith — since their characteristic is, not
vivacity of intellect, but simplicity in believing — the Church
performing its function to them in holding out the truth to
them to be believed. So that even the crowd are made in the
apprehension of faith — each according to his ability — to
share in the truth of which the Church is the possessor. All
the time, however, there is in the Church and in it alone for the
few spiritual men both the fullness of truth to be known and
the opportunity to know it. The underlying idea is clearly that
for the knowledge of the truth there are requisite two things
— the revelation of the truth to be apprehended and the preparation of the heart for its apprehension: and that these two
things can be found in conjunction only in the Church. Our
thought reverts at once to Augustine's fundamental teaching
that the remedy for the disabilities of sinful men is to be
found in the twofold provision of Revelation and Grace. In
the Church these two provisions meet, and it is therefore only
in the Church that the sin-born disabilities of men can be
cured: and only in the Church that men, being sinful, can
attain to that knowledge of divine things in which is life.

By this construction, it will not fail to be perceived, Augustine sets the Church over against the world — or, as he
would have phrased it, the glorious city of God over against

[176] "Contra Epist. Manich. Fundam.," i. 4, 5.

the earthly city — as the sole sphere in which true knowledge (*sapientia*) is found. Thus there is introduced a certain dualism in the manifestation of human life on earth. Two classes of men are marked off, separated one from another as darkness is separated from light. In the one, at the best only broken lights can play; because it is the natural development of sin-stricken humanity alone that it can offer. In the other may be found the steady shining of that true light which shall broaden more and more to the perfect day. The dualism of this conception of human life is resolved, however, by two considerations. In observing human life in its dualistic opposition we are observing it only in its process of historic development. The dualism is constituted by the invasion of the realm of darkness by the realm of light: and it exists only so long as the conquest of the darkness by the light is incomplete. A temporary dualism is the inevitable result of the introduction of any remedial scheme which does not act immediately and all at once. In the city of God — the Church of God's saints — we perceive the progress of the correction of the sin-born disabilities of men. Again the opposition of nature and the supernatural as the principles of the opposing kingdoms, must not be pressed to an extreme. With Augustine, as we have seen, all knowledge, even that which in contrast with a higher supernatural, may rightly be called natural knowledge, is in source supernatural: all knowledge rests ultimately on revelation. The problem to him was not, therefore, how to supplant a strictly natural knowledge by a strictly supernatural knowledge: but how to restore to men the power to acquire that knowledge which we call natural — how to correct sin-bred disabilities so that the general revelation of God may be reflected purely in minds which now are blinded to its reflection by sin. For this end, a special revelation, adapted to the needs of sin-disabled minds, is called in. Special revelation is not conceived here, then, as a substitute for general revelation, but only as a preparation for its proper assimilation. The goal is still conceived as the knowledge of God by direct vision; and special revelation is presented only as spectacles through which the blind may trace out the way to the cure. The intervention of God by a special revelation works, therefore, harmoniously into the general scheme of the production of knowledge of God through general revelation. The conception is that man being a sinner, and unable to profit by general revelation, God intervenes creatively by special revelation and grace — by special revelation enabling him to walk meanwhile until by grace he is once more prepared to see the Light in its own light. Special revelation, given through the prophets and apostles, is embodied in the Scriptures and brought to bear on man by the Church, in which is found the grace to heal men's disabilities. The Church therefore sets up in the world a city of God in which, and in which alone, man may live free from the disabilities that clog all action in the earthly city.

If we cry out that the remedy is incomplete, the answer is that it were better to say that the cure it is working is as yet uncompleted. So long as grace has not wrought its perfect work in our souls, there remains a dualism in all the 'functioning of our souls; so long as grace has not wrought its perfect work in the world there will remain a dualism in the world. But when grace has wrought its perfect work, then, as sin has been removed, the need of special revelation falls away, nay the need of all the instrumentalities by which grace is wrought falls away — the Church, the Scriptures, Christ the Mediator Himself — and God alone suffices for the soul's requirements. The end to which all is directed and in which all issues is not the destruction of nature but the restoration of nature: and when nature is restored, there is no longer need of the remedies. " There is nothing," says Augustine with emphasis, " that ought to detain us on the way " in our aspiration to God, in whom alone can we find our rest. And to put the sharpest possible point upon the remark he at once proceeds to apply it to our Lord Himself, who, says he, " in so far as He condescended to be our Way," wished not " to hold us " — the reference being possibly to Jno. xx. 17 — " but rather to pass away, lest we should cling weakly to temporal things, even though they had been put on and worn by Him for our salvation, and not rather press rapidly through them and strive to attain unto Himself who has freed our nature from the bondage of temporal things and set it down at the right hand of His Father." [177] The whole soteriological work of our Lord, in other words, is viewed by Augustine as a means to the end of our presentation, holy, and without spot, to the Father, and therefore as destined to fall away with all means when the end is attained.[178] When the Mediatorial Christ is viewed thus as instrument, of course the lower means also are so considered. Augustine, even, in a passage in the immediate neighborhood of what we have just quoted, speaks as if a stage of development might be attained even in this life in which the Scriptures, say, might fall out of use as a lame man healed would no longer need his crutch. "A man," says he,[179] "supported by faith, hope and love, and retaining these unshakenly, does not need the Scriptures except for instructing others." He adduces certain solitaries as examples: men in whom I Cor. xiii. 8 is already fulfilled — who "by means of these instruments" (as they are called) have had built up within them so great an edifice of faith and love that they no longer require their aid. So clear is it that by him all the means put in action by grace to cure the sin-bred disabilities of man were strictly conceived as remedies which, just because they work a cure, provide no substitutes for nature but bring about a restoration of nature.[180]

[177] "De Doctrina Christiana," i. 34, 38.

[178] Th. Bret, "La Conversion de S. Augustine" (Geneva, 1900), p. 64, generalizes as follows "We remark, however, that Augustine is affirmative only in what concerns the activity of Christ as reconciler. The rôle of eternal mediator, of perpetual friend, between the individual and God, was never clearly understood by Augustine. For him Christ came to restore man to his true condition, but, that once attained, the rôle of Saviour passed into the background. The sinner once cleansed of his sins, and placed in an atmosphere of the grace of God, found himself directly united with the Father without the intervention of the Son." This is only very partially correct; and its incorrectnesses touch on some important elements of Augustine's teaching. But it contains the essential matter.

[179] "De Doctrina Christiana," i. 39. 43.

[180] The general conception — but guarded from the fancy that attainment in this life can proceed so far as to be freed from the necessity of means

Augustine's whole doctrine thus becomes a unit. Man is to find truth within himself because there God speaks to him. All knowledge rests, therefore, on a revelation of God; God impressing on the soul continually the ideas which form the intellectual world. These ideas are taken up, however, by man in perception and conception, only so far as each is able to do so: and man being a sinner is incapacitated for their reception and retention. This sinful incapacity is met in the goodness of God by revelation and grace, the sphere of both of which is the Church. The Church is therefore set over against the world as the new Kingdom of God in which sinful man finds restoration and in its gradual growth we observe the human race attaining its originally destined end. The time is to come when the Kingdom of God shall have overspread the earth, and when that time comes, the abnormalities having been cured, the normal knowledge of God will assert itself throughout the redeemed race of man. Here, in a single paragraph, is Augustine's whole doctrine of knowledge and authority.

— is among the inheritances of Augustinians until this day. Cf., e.g., A. Kuyper, "Encyc. of Sacred Theology," E. T. pp. 368 *sq.;* and especially H. Bavinck, "Gereform. Dogmatiek," i. pp. 389 *sq.,* where the necessary cautions are noted. The misapprehensions of Harnack ("History of Dogma," E. T. v. pp. 99–100) will be obvious.

IV

AUGUSTINE AND HIS " CONFESSIONS "

AUGUSTINE AND HIS " CONFESSIONS "[1]

THERE is probably no man of the ancient world, of whose outward and inward life alike we possess such full and instructive knowledge as of Augustine's. His extraordinarily voluminous literary product teems with information about himself: and the writings of his contemporaries and successors provide at least the usual quota of allusions. But in his case these are supplemented by two remarkable books. For the whole earlier portion of his experiences, up to and including the great crisis of his conversion, we have from his own hand a work of unique self-revelation, in which he becomes something more than his own Boswell. And for the rest of his career, comprising the entire period of his activity as a leader in the Church, we have an exceptionally sober and trustworthy narrative from the hand of a pupil and friend who enjoyed a close intimacy with him for an unbroken stretch of nearly forty years. He is accordingly the first of the Christian fathers, the dates of whose birth and death we can exactly determine, and whose entire development we can follow from — as we say — the cradle to the grave.

The simple facts of his uneventful external life are soon told. He was born of mixed heathen and Christian parentage, in the small African municipality of Thagaste, on the thirteenth of November, 354. Receiving a good education, he was trained to the profession of rhetorician and practiced that profession successively at Thagaste, Carthage, Rome, and Milan, until his conversion, which took place at the last-named city in the late summer of 386. Baptized at Easter, 387, he returned to Africa in the autumn of 388, and established at his native town a sort of religio-philosophical retreat for himself and his friends. Here he lived in learned retirement until early in 391,

[1] From *The Princeton Theological Review*, iii. 1905, pp. 81–126.

when he was ordained a presbyter at Hippo — the sacred office being thrust upon him against his will, as it was later upon his followers, John Calvin and John Knox. Five years later (shortly before Christmas, 395), he was made coadjutor-bishop of Hippo, and from the first sustained practically the entire burden of its administration. He continued bishop of that second-rate sea-side town, until his death on August 28, 430, meanwhile having revolutionized the Church of Africa by his ceaseless labors and illuminated the world by his abundant writings. In this humble framework was lived a life the immediate products of which seemed washed out at once by the flood of disasters which instantly overwhelmed the African provinces, and with them the African Church which it had regenerated; but the influence of which is, nevertheless, not yet exhausted after a millennium and a half of years.

I. Possidius' Portrait of Augustine

The "Life" by Possidius is much briefer than we could have wished, but it presents a clear outline of Augustine's life drawn by the hand of one who worked in the full consciousness that he was handing down to posterity the record of a career which was of the first importance to the world. Augustine's literary activity by means of which he freed the Church from her enemies and built her up in the knowledge and service of God; Augustine's labors for the Church's peace by means of which he healed the schisms that divided the African community; Augustine's regeneration of the clergy of Africa through his monastic training-school: these are the points on which Possidius lays the greatest stress. In the meanwhile, however, he does much more than sum up for us what Augustine was doing for the Church and the world; though in doing this, he was speaking with a wisdom beyond his own knowledge, inasmuch as in a broader field than Africa Augustine has been a determining factor in precisely the matters here emphasized. He also paints for us a touchingly sincere portrait of the personality of his beloved master and enables us to see him at his daily work, submerged under superabundant labors, but always able to lift his heart to God, and already enjoying his rest with Him even in the midst of the clangor of the warfare he was ever waging for His Church and His truth.

Even as a presbyter, we read, he began to reap the fruit of his labors:

Alike at home and in the Church, he gave himself unstintedly to teaching and preaching the word of salvation with all confidence, in opposition to the heresies prevalent in Africa, especially to the Donatists, Manicheans and Pagans — now in elaborated books, and again in unstudied sermons — to the unspeakable admiration and delight of the Christians who as far as in them lay spread abroad his words. And thus, by God's help, the Catholic Church began to lift up its head in Africa, where it had long lain oppressed under luxuriating heresies, and especially under the Donatists, who had rebaptized the greater part of the people. And these books and tractates of his, flowing forth by the wonderful grace of God in the greatest profusion, instinct with sweet reasonableness and the authority of Holy Scripture, the heretics themselves, with the greatest ardor, vied with the Catholics in hearkening to, and moreover every one who wished and could do so brought stenographers and took notes even of what was spoken. Thus the precious doctrine and sweet savour of Christ was diffused throughout all Africa, and even the Church across the sea rejoiced when she heard it — for, even as when one member suffers all the members suffer with it, so when one member is exalted all the members rejoice with it.[2]

The labors he thus began as a presbyter, we are told, he but completed as bishop, the Lord crowning his work for the peace of the Church with the most astonishing success:

And more and more, by the help of Christ, was increased and multiplied the unity of peace and the fraternity of the Church of God. . . . And all this good, as I have said, was both begun and brought to a completion by this holy man, with the aid of our bishops.[3]

But alas! while man may propose it is God that disposes. Scarcely had this hard-won *pax ecclesiæ* been attained, when

[2] "Sancti Augustini Vita Scripta a Possidio Episcopo," chap. vii .
[3] Chap. xiii.

the Vandal invasion came and with it the ruin of the land. As the fabric he had built up fell about him, the great builder passes away also, and Possidius draws for us the picture of his last days with a tenderness of touch which only a true friend could show: [4]

We talked together very frequently and discussed the tremendous judgment of God enacted under our eyes, saying, " Just art Thou, O God, and Thy judgment is righteous." Mingling our grief and groans and tears we prayed the Father of mercies and Lord of all consolation to vouchsafe to help us in our trouble. And it chanced on a day as we sat at the table with him and conversed, that he said, " Bear in mind that I am asking God in this our hour of tribulation, either to deign to deliver this town from the enemy that is investing it, or, if that seems not good to Him, to strengthen His servants to submit themselves to His will, and in any event to take me away from this world to Himself." Under his instruction it became therefore our custom thereafter, and that of all connected with us, and of those who were in the town, to join with him in such a prayer to God Almighty. And behold, in the third month of the siege, he took to his bed, afflicted with a fever; and thus fell into his last illness. Nor did the Lord disappoint His servant of the fruit of his prayer. . . . Thus did this holy man, his path prolonged by the Divine bounty for the advantage and happiness of the Church, live seventy and six years, almost forty of which were spent in the priesthood and bishopric. He had been accustomed to say to us in familiar conversation, that no baptised person, even though he were a notable Christian and a priest, should depart from the body without fitting and sufficient penitence. So he looked to this in his last sickness, of which he died. For he ordered that those few Psalms of David called Penitential should be written out, and the sheets containing them hung upon the wall where he could see them as he lay in bed, in his weakness; and as he read them he wept constantly and abundantly. And that he might not be disturbed, he asked of us who were present, some ten days before he departed from the body, that no one should come in except at those hours when the physicians visited him or when food was brought him. This wish was, of course, observed, and he thus had all his time free for prayer. Unintermittently, up to the outbreak of this last illness, he had zealously and energetically preached

[4] Chaps. xxviii. xxix. xxxi.

in the church the Word of God, with sanity of mind and soundness of judgment. And now, preserved to a good old age, sound in all the members of his body, and with unimpaired sight and hearing, and with us, as it is written, standing by and watching and praying, he fell asleep with his fathers, having been preserved to a good old age: and we offered a sacrifice to God for the peaceful repose of his body and buried him.

His library, the biography proceeds, he left to the Church; and his own books, who that reads them can fail to read in them the manner of man he was? He adds: [5]

But I think that those could profit more from him who could hear and see him speaking as he stood in the church, especially if they were not ignorant of his walk among men. For he was not merely a learned scribe in the kingdom of heaven, bringing out from his treasury things new and old, and one of those merchantmen who, having found a pearl of great price, went and sold all that he had and bought it; but he was also of those to whom it is written, "So speak and so do," and of whom the Saviour says, "Whosoever shall do and teach men thus, he shall be called great in the kingdom of heaven.

What a testimony is this to Augustine's daily life before his companions! And how pathetic is this companion's parting request of his readers:

Pray with me and for me, that I may both in this world become the emulator and imitator of this man with whom for almost forty years, by God's grace, I lived in intimacy and happiness, without any unpleasant disagreement, and in the future may enjoy with him the promises of God Almighty.

II. THE "CONFESSIONS" OF AUGUSTINE

It is, however, to his own "Confessions," of course, that we will turn if we would know Augustine through and through. This unique book was written about 397–400, say about a dozen years after Augustine's conversion and shortly after his ordination as bishop of Hippo — at a time when he was al-

[5] Chap. xxxi.

ready thoroughly formed in both life and thought. There is laid bare to us in it a human heart with a completeness of self-revelation probably unparalleled in literature.

Jean Jacques Rousseau, to be sure, claims this distinction for his own " Confessions." " I have entered on a performance," says he, " which is without example, whose accomplishment will have no imitator. I mean to present my fellow-mortals with a man in all the integrity of nature; and this man shall be myself." Rousseau has at least the merit of perceiving what many have not recognized, that his book cannot be considered to belong to the same class of literature with Augustine's. But what we wish now to emphasize is that even as an unveiling of the soul of a man, which it makes its sole object, Rousseau's performance falls far behind Augustine's searching pages, although, as we shall see, self-revelation was in these merely an incidental effect. The truth is, Rousseau did not see deeply enough and could not command a prospect sufficiently wide to paint all that is in man, even all that is in such a man as he essayed to portray. Quite apart from the interval that separates the two souls depicted, Rousseau's conception of self-revelation rose little above exhibiting himself with his clothes off. To his prurient imagination nakedness, certainly unadorned and all the better if it were unadorning, appeared the most poignant possible revelation of humanity. It seemed to him, essential scandal-monger that he was, that he needed but to publish on the housetop all his " adventures " to enable the whole world to say of him in the Roman proverb, *Ego te intus et in cute novi;* and he was only too pleased to believe that the world, on so seeing his inward disposition at least if not his outward life, would be convinced that it agreed well with " loose Natta's." [6] He could feel no sympathy with Augustine's cry, " I became a mighty puzzle to myself." [7] The shallow self he knew only too well absorbed his entire attention and his one engagement was in presenting this self to the gaze of the public. What lay beneath the surface he passed by with

[6] Persius, " Satt.," iii. 30.

[7] " Confessiones," iv. 4. 9.: " factus eram ipse mihi magna quæstio."

the unconsciousness of an essentially frivolous nature.[8] No wonder that an air of insincerity hangs over the picture he has drawn. There will be few readers who will easily persuade themselves that what they read all happened, or happened as it is set down; they will rather be continually haunted with the suspicion that they are perusing not a veracious autobiography but a piccaroon novel. The interval that divides the " Confessions " of Rousseau from the " Adventures of Gil Blas of Santillane " is, in any case, narrower than that which separates it from the " Confessions " of Augustine.

It must be confessed, it is true, that, if not the sincerity, at least the trustworthiness of the portrait Augustine draws of himself also has not passed wholly unquestioned. It has of late become quite the mode, indeed, to remind us that the " Confessions " were written a dozen years after the conversion up to which their narrative leads; and that in the meanwhile the preceding period of darkness had grown over-black in Augustine's eyes, and as he looked back upon it through the intervening years he saw it in distorted form and exaggerated colors.[9] His is accordingly represented as " a prominent example

[8] James Russell Lowell, " Prose Works," 1891, ii. p. 261: " Rousseau cries, ' I will bare my heart to you! ' and throwing open his waistcoat, makes us the confidants of his dirty linen."

[9] See, e.g., Boissier, " La Fin du Paganisme," i. p. 293; Harnack, " Monasticism and the Confessions of Augustine," pp. 132, 141; Reuter, " Augustinische Studien," p. 4; Loofs, Herzog " Realencyklopädie für protestantische Theologie und Kirche," [3] ii. pp. 260–261, and especially pp. 266–267. Cf. also Gourdon, " Essai sur la Conversion de Saint Augustin," Cahors, 1900. R. Schmid in an article entitled " Zur Bebehrungsgeschichte Augustins " in the Zeitschrift für Theologie und Kirche, 1897, vii. pp. 80–96, has made the fact and extent of failure of the " Confessions" in trustworthiness the subject of a special study. No one doubts, he remarks, the subjective sincerity of the " Confessions "; and its objective trustworthiness can come into question only in minutiæ. The conclusion at which he arrives is that only in two points are the " Confessions " open to correction in their representation. Augustine was not led to give up his professorship by his conversion, but these two things fell together only by accident; and he still wished after conversion for a comfortable life, an otium cum dignitate, and loved to teach. " Thus in reality there remains, so far as the ' Confessions ' do not correct themselves — that is, permit the history to be seen through the veil of later reflections thrown over it — very little over. But even a little is, here, much. . . . In the main matter, however, the ' Con-

of a tendency frequently found in religionists of an effusive type, to exaggerate their infirmities in order to enhance their merits in having escaped them, or by way of contrasting present attainment with former unworthiness, just as a successful merchant sometimes boasts that he began his career with only sixpence in his pocket." [10] We are warned, therefore, not to take his descriptions of his youthful errors and of his fruitless wanderings in search of truth at the foot of the letter. A recent writer, for example, condemns all current biographies of Augustine because, as he says, they "all are constructed on the perverse type which is followed by Augustine himself in his seductive 'Confessions,'" in which he "is sternly bent on magnifying his misdeeds." Blinded by "the glare of his new ideal," as leading ecclesiastic and theologian of the West, his psychic perspective was foreshortened and he hopelessly misrepresented his unregenerate youth. "The truth seems to be," we are told, "that the book is a kind of theological treatise and work of edification. The Bishop of Hippo takes the rhetorician as an 'awful example' of nature without God. To point his dogmatic antithesis of nature and grace, philosophy and Christianity, nothing could be more forceful than his own career painted as darkly as conscience would permit. . . . But the fallacy of it all for us, reducing its value as a human document, is that Augustine examines his earlier life from a false point of view." [11]

Despite the modicum of truth resident in the recognition by the writer last quoted that the book is not formally an autobiography, but, as he terms it, "a kind of theological treatise and work of edification," this whole representation is fundamentally wrong. The judgment that Augustine passed on the misdeeds not merely, but the whole course, of his youth was

---

fessions' remain in the right — that it was a revolutionary inward experience, which brought him completely into the road on which he sought and found God and himself" (p. 96).

[10] See John Owen, "Evenings with the Sceptics," ii. p. 139.

[11] Joseph McCabe, "St. Augustine and His Age," pp. v., 24, 39, 41, 54, 69, 70, 195–198.

naturally essentially different at the time when he wrote his " Confessions " from what it had been during the life which is passed in review in them. He does not leave us to infer this — he openly declares it; or rather it is precisely this change of judgment which it is one of the chief purposes of the " Confessions " to signalize. We could hardly ask a man after he has escaped from what he has come to look upon as the sty to write of his mode of life in it from the point of view of one who loves to wallow in the mire. It is, however, something very like this that is suggested by our critics as the ideal of autobiographical narration. At least we read: " About the year 400, when they [the " Confessions "] were written, Augustine had arrived at a most lofty conception of duty and life; he commits the usual and inevitable fallacy of taking this later standard back to illumine the ground of his early career. In the glare of his new ideal, actions which probably implied no moral resistance at the time they were performed, cast an appalling shadow." [12] And again: " There is no trace in the ' Confessions ' that his conscience had anything to say at the time." [13]

Surely there is laid here a most unreasonable requirement upon the historian. We may or may not accord with the judgment that Augustine passes upon his early life. We may or may not consider that he who takes his knowledge of Augustine's youth from the " Confessions " must guard himself from accepting from them also the judgment they pass on the course of that youth as well as on the separate events that entered into it. For example, we may or may not believe that Augustine was right in attributing the passions of anger and jealousy manifesting themselves in infancy to the movements of inherent corruption derived from our first parents, or in representing the childish escapade of robbing a pear tree as an exhibition of a pure love of evil, native in men as men. But any such differences of moral standpoint of which we may be conscious, between ourselves and the Augustine who wrote the " Confessions," are one thing; and the trustworthiness of the record he has given us, whether of the external occurrences of

[12] *Op. cit.,* p. 24.   [13] *Ibid.,* p. 41.

his youth or of the inner movements of his soul during that period of restless search, which knew no rest because it had not yet found rest in God, is quite another thing. It is not merely the transparent sincerity of the " Confessions" which impresses every reader; it is the close and keen observation, the sound and tenacious memory, the sane and searching analysis that equally characterize them. " Observation, indeed," says Harnack, with eminent justice, " is the strong point of Augustine. . . . What is *characteristic* never escapes him " — and that is especially true of the secret movements of the heart.[14] The reader feels himself in the hands of a narrator not only whose will but whose capacity as well both to see and to tell the truth he cannot doubt. There is spread over the whole the evidence no more of the most absolute good faith than of the utmost care to distinguish between fact and opinion — between what really was and what the writer could wish had been. You may think " there is a morbid strain in the book "; you may accuse its author of " making a stage-play of his bleeding heart "; you may judge him " in many places overstrained, unhealthy, or even false." [15] All this will depend on the degree in which you feel yourself in sympathy with his standpoint. But " there is a look of intense reality on every page," as a careful student has put it; [16] and as you read you cannot doubt that here is not merely a sincere but a true record of the experiences of a soul, which you may — nay, must — trust as such without reserve.

It is important, however, in order that we may appraise the book properly, to apprehend somewhat more exactly than perhaps is common precisely what Augustine proposed to himself in it. It is inadequate to speak of it simply either broadly as an autobiography, or more precisely as a *vie intime*. Not to emphasize just here the decisive consideration that only nine of

[14] *Op. cit.*, pp. 128, 131. Cf. also T. R. Glover, " Life and Letters in the Fourth Century," p. 195.

[15] Harnack, *op. cit.*, p. 132.

[16] A. F. West, " Roman Autobiography, Particularly Augustine's Confessions," in *The Presbyterian and Reformed Review*, xii. No. 46 (April 1901) p. 183.

its thirteen books have any biographical content, it lies quite on the face of the narrative that even the biographical material provided in these nine books is not given with a purely biographical intent. Augustine is not the proper subject either of the work as a whole, or even of those portions of it in which his life-history is depicted. What he tells us about himself, full and rich and searching as it is, nevertheless is incidental to another end than self-portraiture, and is determined both in its selection and in its mode of treatment by this end. In sending a copy of the book, almost a generation later, to a distinguished and admiring friend who had asked him for it, he does indeed speak of it frankly as a mirror in which he himself could be seen; and, be it duly noted, he affirms that he is to be seen in this mirror truly, just as he was. "Accept," he writes to his correspondent [17] — "accept the books of my Confessions which you have asked for. Behold me therein, that you may not praise me above what I am. Believe there not others about me, but me myself, and see by means of myself what I was in myself; and if there is anything in me that pleases you, praise with me there Him whom I wish to be praised for me — for that One is not myself. Because it is He that made us and not we ourselves; nay, we have destroyed ourselves, but He that made us has remade us. And when you find me there, pray for me that I be not defective but perfected." Similarly in his "Retractations," [18] he says simply that the first ten books were "written about himself"; but he does not fail to declare also of the whole thirteen that "they praise the just and good God with respect both of his evil and his good and excite the human intellect and affection toward Him." This, he says, was their effect on himself as he wrote them, and this has been their effect on those that have read them.

From such passages as these we perceive how Augustine uniformly thought of his "Confessions" — not as a biography of himself, but, as we have commended a rather blind com-

[17] "Epist." 231, to Count Darius (§ 6).
[18] ii. 6: "a primo usque ad decimum de me scripti sunt."

mentator for seeing, rather as a book of edification, or, if you will, a theological treatise. His actual subject is not himself, but the goodness of God; and he introduces his own experiences only as the most lively of illustrations of the dealings of God with the human soul as He makes it restless until it finds its rest in Him. Such being the case the congeners of the book are not to be found in simple autobiographies even of the most introspective variety. The "Confessions" of Rousseau, of Hamann, of Alfred de Musset — such books have so little in common with it that they do not belong even in the same literary class with it. Even the similarity of their titles to its is an accident. For Augustine does not use the term "Confessions" here in the debased sense in which these writers use it; the sense of unveiling, uncovering to the sight of the world what were better perhaps hidden from all eyes but God's which see all things; but in that higher double sense in which we may speak of confessing the grace of God and our humble dependence on Him, a sense compounded of mingled humility and praise.

The real analogues of Augustine's "Confessions" are to be found not then in introspective biographies whose sole purpose is to depict a human soul, but in such accounts of spiritual experiences as are given us in books like John Newton's "Authentic Narrative," although the scope of this particular narrative is too narrow to furnish a perfect analogy. At the head of his narrative Newton has written this text: "Thou shalt remember all the way, by which the Lord thy God led thee through this wildness"; and the same text might equally well be written at the head of Augustine's "Confessions." We might almost fancy we hear Augustine explaining his own purpose when we hear Newton declaring that with him it was a question "only concerning the patience and long-suffering of God, the wonderful interposition of His providence in favor of an unworthy sinner, the power of His grace in softening the hardest heart, and the riches of His mercy in pardoning the most enormous and aggravated transgressions." Perhaps, however, the closest analogy to Augustine's "Confessions," among books, at least, which have attained anything like the same popular influence, is furnished by John Bunyan's " Grace Abounding to the Chief of Sinners." Bunyan's purpose is precisely the same as Augustine's — to glorify the grace of God. He employs also the same means of securing this end — an autobiographical account of the dealings of God with his soul. " In this relation of the merciful working of God upon my soul," says Bunyan, " it will not be amiss if, in the first place, I do, in a few words, give you a hint of my pedigree and manner of bringing up; that thereby the goodness and bounty of God toward me may be the more advanced and magnified before the sons of men." Just so Augustine, also, gave what he gave of " his pedigree and manner of bringing up"; and what he gave of his youthful wanderings in error and in sin; and what he gave of his struggles to find and grasp, to grasp and cling to what of good he saw and loved: only that " the goodness and bounty of God toward him might be the more advanced and magnified before the sons of men." We have said that the interval that divides Rousseau's " Confessions " from the " Adventures of Gil Blas of Santillane," is less than that which separates them from Augustine's. We may now say that the interval that divides Augustine's " Confessions " from the " Pilgrim's Progress " is less than that which separates them from any simple autobiography — veracious and searching autobiography though a great portion of it is. For the whole concernment of the book is with the grace of God to a lost sinner. It is this, and not himself, that is its theme.

This fundamental fact is, of course, written large over the whole work, and comes not rarely to explicit assertion. " I wish to record my past foulnesses and the carnal corruptions of my soul," says Augustine, " not because I love them, but in order that I may love Thee, O my God. For love of Thy love do I do this thing, — recollecting my most vicious ways in the bitterness of my remembrance, that Thou mayest become my Joy, Thou never-failing Joy, Thou blessed and sacred Joy; and collecting myself from the dissipation in which I was torn to pieces, when turned from Thee, the One, I was lost among the many." [19] "To whom do I relate this? . . . And why? Just that I and whosoever may read this may consider out of what depths we are to cry unto Thee. And what is nearer to Thy ears than a confessing heart and a life of faith? " [20] " Accept the sacrifice of my confessions from the hand of my tongue which Thou didst form and hast prompted that it may confess to Thy name. Heal all my bones and let them say, Lord, who is like unto Thee? . . . Let my soul praise Thee that it may love Thee, and let it confess to Thee Thy mercies that it may praise Thee." [21] "Why, then, do I array before Thee the narrations of so many things? . . . That I may excite my affection toward Thee, and that of those who read these things, so that we all may say, 'Great is the Lord and highly to be praised.'" [22] In these last words we observe that as he approaches the end of the book, he is still bearing in mind the words which he set at its beginning; [23] and by thus reverting to the beginning, he binds the whole together as one great volume of praise to the Lord for His goodness to him in leading him to His salvation. Accordingly he adds at once: "Therefore, we are manifesting our affection to Thee, in confessing to Thee our miseries and Thy mercies toward us, in order that Thou mayest deliver us altogether since Thou hast made a beginning, and we may cease to be miserable in ourselves and become blessed in Thee, since Thou hast called us to be poor in spirit, and meek and mourners, and hungerers, and thirsters after righteousness, and merciful and pure in heart and peacemakers." [24] Here the theme of the "Confessions" is clearly set before us. It is the ineffable goodness of God, which is illustrated by what He has done for Augustine's miserable soul, in delivering it from its sins and distresses and bringing it out into the largeness of the divine life and knowledge.

It is, obviously, only from this point of view that the unity of the book becomes apparent. For we must not fancy that

[19] ii. 1. 1.
[20] ii. 3. 5.
[21] v. 1. 1.
[22] xi. 1. 1.
[23] i. 1. 1.
[24] xi. 1. 1.

when Augustine has brought to a completion the narrative of the wonderful dealings of God with him, by which he was led to repentance, he has ended his "confessions"; to which he attaches the last four books therefore purely mechanically, without any rational bond of connection with their predecessors. To his consciousness, throughout the whole extent of these books, he continues to sound the voice of his confessions: and if we search in them for it we shall find the same note ringing in them as in the others. "Behold," he cries,[25] "Thy voice is my joy: Thy voice surpasses the abundance of pleasures. . . . Let me confess unto Thee whatsoever I have found in Thy books, and let me hear the voice of praise and drink Thee in and consider the wonderful things of Thy law, even from the beginning, in the which Thou didst make the heaven and the earth, down to the everlasting kingdom of Thy Holy City, that is with Thee." Not the least of the mercies that Augustine wished to confess to God that he had received from His hand was the emancipation of His intellect, and the freeing of his mind from the crudities with which it had been stuffed; and it is this confession that he makes, with praises on his lips, in these concluding books. The construction of the work, then, is something like the following: first Augustine recounts how God has dealt with him in bringing him to salvation (books i.–ix.); then what he has under the divine grace become, as a saved child of God (book x.); and finally what reaches of sound and satisfying knowledge have been granted to him in the divine revelation (books xi.–xiii.): and all to the praise of the glory of His grace. Body, heart, mind, all were made for God: all were incited to seek Him and to praise Him: and all were restless, therefore, until at last they found their rest in Him. Elsewhere than in Him had happiness, peace, knowledge been sought, but nowhere else had they been found. The proud was cast down: and he that exalted himself inevitably fell. But they whose exaltation God becomes — they fall not any more forever. This is the concluding word of the "Confessions."

[25] xi. 2. 3, *ad fin.*

Only in proportion as this, the true character of the book, is apprehended, moreover, does its true originality become evident. Even were it possible to think of it merely as an introspective autobiography, it would no doubt be epoch-making in the history of literary form. In an interesting paper on " Roman Autobiography," [26] Prof. A. F. West points out that this species of composition was especially Roman. " Autobiography, as well as satire," he remarks, " should be credited to the Romans as their own independent invention." " The appearance of Augustine's ' Confessions,' in 399 or 400," he continues, " dates the entrance of a new kind of autobiography into Latin literature — the autobiography of introspection, the self-registered record of the development of a human soul." It was characteristic of Augustine's genius that, in a purely incidental use of it, he invented an entirely new literary form and carried it at a stroke to its highest development. No wonder that Harnack falls into something like enthusiasm over this accomplishment.

The significance of the " Confessions," says he, " is as great on the side of form as on that of content. Before all, they were a literary achievement. No poet, no philosopher before him undertook what he here performed; and I may add that almost a thousand years had to pass before a similar thing was done. It was the poets of the Renascence, who formed themselves on Augustine, that first gained from his example the daring to depict themselves and to present their personality to the world. For what do the " Confessions " of Augustine contain? The portrait of a soul — not psychological disquisitions on the Understanding, the Will, and the Emotions in Man, not abstract investigations into the nature of the soul, not superficial reasonings and moralizing introspections like the " Meditations " of Marcus Aurelius, but the most exact portraiture of a distinct human personality, in his development from childhood to full age, with all his propensities, feelings, aims, mistakes; a portrait of a soul, in fact, drawn with a perfection of observation that leaves on one side the mechanical devices of psychology, and pursues the methods of the physician and the physiologist.[27]

[26] *Presbyterian and Reformed Review*, xii. No. 46 (April, 1901), p. 183.
[27] *Op. cit.*, pp. 127–128.

Obviously Harnack is thinking of the first nine books only. Otherwise he could scarcely speak so absolutely of the absence from the "Confessions" of "psychological disquisitions." For what is the great discourse on "Memory," embodied in the tenth book, but a psychological disquisition of the most penetrating kind, to say nothing now of the analysis of the idea of "Time," broached in the eleventh book? The achievement which he signalizes is, therefore, only part of the achievement of the book, and if Augustine in it has incidentally become the father of all those who have sought to paint the portrait of a human soul, what must be said of the originality of his performance when understood in its real peculiarity — as the dramatic portraiture of the dealing of divine grace with a sinful soul in leading it through all its devious wanderings into the harbor of salvation? Not in the poets of the Renascence — not even in Goethe's "Faust" in which Harnack strangely seeks the nearest literary parallel to the "Confessions" — can it now find its tardy successors. We must come down to the Reformation — perhaps to the "second Reformation" as the men of the seventeenth century loved to call their own times, and after that to that almost third Revolution which was wrought by the "Evangelical Revival" or "Great Awakening" — before we discover its real successors; and we must look through all the years, perhaps in vain, to find any successor worthy to be placed on a level with it.

We must avoid exaggeration, however, even with respect to the novelty of the book. Perhaps if we eliminate the question of value and think merely of the literary species which it so uniquely represents, it can scarcely be said that Augustine's performance was absolutely without forerunners, or remained absolutely without successors "for a thousand years." The greatness of its shining may blind our eyes unduly to lesser points of light, which, except for the glare of its brilliancy, might be seen to stud the heavens about it. A recent writer, for example, claims for a tractate of Cyprian's — the treatise or letter "To Donatus" — the honor of having pointed out the way in which Augustine afterward walked. He says:

Finally,[28] a great novelty appears in this little book. The pages on the conversion of Cyprian, which mark almost the advent of a new species of literature, directly herald the "Confessions" of St. Augustine. For a long time, a very profane manner of life, a passionate taste for pleasure, along with a sort of instinctive defiance of Christianity; subsequently, up to the very eve of the decisive event, incapacity to believe in the renewal promised in baptism, a very clear perception of the obstacles which a life so worldly opposed to so sudden a revolution; then, after many hesitations, grace, as startling as a clap of thunder, revolutionizing the whole being in its profoundest depths, to turn it toward a new destiny; and in the recollection left by this miraculous transformation, a fixed determination to refer all to God, to turn confession into acts of thankfulness: such are in Cyprian the essential traits that mark the steps of conversion. And these are precisely the ideas that dominate the "Confessions" of Augustine.

In effect, we have in this affected, mincing tract of Cyprian's, hidden as its lessons well-nigh are under the shadow of its rhetorical virtuosity, what may be called the beginnings of the Autobiography of Conversion — unless we prefer to penetrate yet a hundred years further back and see its beginnings in the beautiful description with which Justin Martyr opens his "Dialogue with Trypho" of how he found his way through philosophy to Christ. Both narratives have much in their substance that is fitted to remind of Augustine's. But both are too brief; the one is too objective and the other too affected; neither is sufficiently introspective or sufficiently searching to justify their inclusion in the same class with their great successor. A better claim, many will think, might be put in for the spiritual history which Hilary of Poictiers gives of his own former life in the splendid Latin of the first fifteen sections of his treatise "On the Faith" or, as it is commonly called, "On the Trinity." It is the story of a naturally noble soul, seeking and gradually finding more and more perfectly the proper aim of life as it rises to the knowledge first of the God of philosophy and then of the God of revelation, and ulti-

[28] Monceaux, "Hist. Lit. de l'Afrique Chrét.," II., "S. Cyprien et son temps," p. 266.

mately attains assured faith in the God and Father of our Lord Jesus Christ. Did it not move so exclusively on the intellectualistic plane, without depth of experimental coloring, its dignity of language and high eloquence might, despite its brevity, justify us in esteeming it no unworthy forerunner of the " Confessions."

Such predecessors, interesting as they are and valuable as marking the channels in which the new Christian literature naturally flowed, can hardly be thought of as having opened the way for Augustine — partly because their motive is too primarily autobiographical. Similarly he had few immediate successors who can be said to follow closely in his steps. Perhaps the " Eucharisticos Deo " of Paulinus of Pella — in which he essays to praise God for His preservation of him and for His numerous kindnesses through a long and eventful life — may not unfairly be considered a typical instance of such spiritual autobiographies as the next age produced. This poem is assuredly not uninteresting, and to the student of manners it has its own importance; but as a history of a soul it lacks nearly everything that gives to the " Confessions " their charm. That some resemblance should be discernible between the picture Augustine draws of his life and that which such writers draw of their own was unavoidable, since he and they were alike men and Christians and were prepared to thank God for making them both. But the resemblance ends very much at that point. The sublime depths and heights of Augustine and all that has made him the teacher of the world in this his most individual book is wanting, as well in his successors as in his predecessors. He had to wait for Bunyan before there was written another such spiritual " autobiography," or to be more precise, another such history of God's dealings with a soul: and even the " Grace Abounding " stands beside the " Confessions " only *longe intervallo*.

The attractiveness of the " Confessions " obviously lurks, not in its style, but in its matter — or rather in the personality that lies behind both style and matter and gives unity, freshness, depth, brilliancy to both matter and style. Harnack is quite right when he remarks that the key to the enduring influence of the book is found in the fact that we meet a person in it — a person " everywhere richer than his expression ": [29] that we feel a heart beating behind its words and perceive that this is a great heart, to whose beating we cannot but attend. Nevertheless the form of the " Confessions " is itself not without its fascination, and its very style has also its allurement. His rhetorical training had entered, to be sure, into Augustine's very substance and the false taste with which he had been imbued had become a second nature with him. Even in such heart-throes as express themselves in this book, he could not away with the frivolous word-plays, affected assonances, elaborate balancing of clauses and the like that form the hallmark of the sophistic rhetoric of the times. It has been remarked that " rhetorician as Augustine was, and master of several styles, he had a curious power of dropping his rhetoric when he undertook in homilies and commentaries to interpret Scripture." [30] Unfortunately, he also had a curious facility of dropping into offensive rhetorical tricks in the midst of the most serious discussions, or the most moving revelations of feeling. Apart from these occasional lapses — if lapses so frequent can be called occasional — the very form given this book as a sustained address to God is wearisome to many. M. Boissier [31] remarks that the transports and effusions with which Augustine addresses himself to God " end by seeming to us monotonous." Harnack thinks the book too long and too alien to modern thought ever to enter into really literary use in its entirety: and therefore welcomes the preparation of abridgements of it. [32] Prof. West [33] finds in it " ineptitudes and infelicities " which can be expected to shrink and permit " the central power " of the book to appear only for him who reads it in its original Latin. The merely English reader, he remarks, can

[29] *Op. cit.*, i. p. 136.

[30] E. W. Watson, *Classical Review*, February, 1901, p. 65, quoted in Glover, *op. cit.*, p. 195, note.

[31] *Op. cit.*, p. 292.

[32] *Theolog. Literaturzeitung*, 1903, No. 1, 12.

[33] As cited, pp. 184–185.

scarcely hope to find it very interesting. "The unchecked rhetoric, the reiterated calls on God, varied and wearisome, the shrewd curiosity in hunting down subtleties to their last hiding-places, the streaks of inane allegorizing,[34] and sometimes the violent bursts of feeling, — these are the things that frighten away readers and prevent them from reaching the real delights of the book."

It is difficult to draw up a catalogue of such defects without exaggeration: and in the present case an exaggerated impression, both with respect to quantity and quality, is almost certain to be conveyed. After all said, the "Confessions" are an eminently well and winningly written book. There is even in the mere style a certain poetic quality that gives it not merely character but beauty. Harnack justly speaks of "the lyricism of the style." There is certainly present in it, as Dr. Bigg points out,[35] something of "the same musical flow, the same spiritual refinement and distinction" that characterizes the "Imitation of Christ." It is not, indeed, as Dr. Bigg justly adds, either "so compact or so highly polished" as the "Imitation of Christ": "St. Augustine cannot give the time to cut each word as if it were an individual diamond, as a Kempis did." But Augustine more than compensates for this deficiency in preciosity by his greater richness, depth, and variety. There is nothing effeminate in Augustine's style, nothing over-filed, nothing cloying or wearisome. Here, too, indeed, it is true, as it generally is, that the style is the man. And Augustine is never an uninteresting person to meet, even through the medium of the written, or even of the translated, page. No more individual writer ever lived: and the individuality which was his was not only powerful and impressive, but to an almost unexampled degree profound, rich, and attractive. Harnack is right; the charm of the "Confessions" is that they are Augustine's and that he draws his readers into his life by

[34] Are these found to any appreciable extent outside the Thirteenth Book?

[35] Introduction to his version, published in Methuen's series, called the "Library of Devotion," 3d ed., 1900, p. 5.

them. Here are reflected, as in a mirror, the depth and tenderness of his ardent nature, the quickness and mobility of
his emotions and yet, underlying all, his sublime repose. He
who reads shares the conflicts and the turmoils depicted:
but he enters also into the rest the writer has found with
God.

It is in this fact that the unique attractiveness of the book
as a " work of edification " resides — an attractiveness which
has made it through a millennium and a half the most widely
read of all books written in Latin, with the possible exception
of the " Æneid " of Virgil.[36] He who reads these pages enters
as in none other into the struggles of a great soul as it fights its
way to God, shares with it all its conflict, and participates at
last with it in the immensity of its repose. As he reads, that
great sentence that sounds the keynote of the book and echoes
through all its pages, echoes also in his soul: " Thou hast made
us for Thyself, O Lord, and our heart is restless till it finds its
rest in Thee." The agonizing cry becomes his also, " O by Thy
loving-kindness, tell me, O Lord my God, what Thou art to
me: say unto my soul, *I am thy Salvation.*" And there likewise becomes his the childlike prattle of the same soul, stilled
in praise now that it has found God its salvation, as it names
over to itself as its dearest possession the sweet names by
which its God has become precious to it, " O Lord, my God,
my Light, my Wealth, my Salvation! " What is apt to escape
us who have, after so many years, entered into the heritage
which Augustine has won for us is that it was really he who
won it for us — that in these groans and tears into which we
so readily enter with him as we read, and in this hard-earned
rest in God into which we so easily follow him, he was breaking out a pathway not only for his own but for our feet. For
here is the astonishing fact that gives its supreme significance
to this book: it is the earliest adequate expression of that type
of religion which has since attached to itself the name of
" evangelical "; and, though the earliest, it is one of the fullest,
richest, and most perfect expressions of this type of religion

[36] Glover, *op. cit.*, p. 195.

which has ever been written. Adolf Harnack, realizing the immense significance of the appearance in Augustine of this new type of religion, consecrates a whole chapter in his "History of Dogma" to "The Historical Position of Augustine as Reformer of Christian Piety," as a preparation for the due exposition of his doctrinal teaching. In this chapter he makes many true and striking remarks; but he hardly exhibits a just appreciation of the intimate relation which subsists between Augustine's peculiar type of piety and his peculiar type of doctrine. Harnack, in fact, speaks almost as if it were conceivable that one of these could have come into existence apart from the other. The truth is, of course, that they are but the joint products in the two spheres of life and thought of the same body of conceptions, and neither could possibly have arisen without the other. If before Augustine alternating hope and fear were the characteristic sentiments of Christians and the psychological form of their piety was therefore unrest, while in Augustine the place of hope and fear is taken by trust and love, and unrest gives way to profound rest in God, this was because pre-Augustinian Christianity was prevailingly legalistic, and there entered into it a greater or less infusion of the evil leaven of self-salvation, while Augustine, with his doctrine of grace, cast himself wholly on the mercy of God, and so, as the poet expresses it,

> Turned fear and hope to love of God.
> Who loveth us.

The fact of the matter is that pre-Augustinian Christian thinking was largely engrossed with Theological and Christological problems and with Augustine first did Christian Soteriology begin to come to its rights. It was not he first, of course, who discovered that man is a sinner and therefore depends for his salvation on the grace of God; but in him first did these fundamental Christian truths find a soil in which they could come to their richest fruitage in heart and life, in thought and teaching. And here lies the secret of his profound realization (on which Harnack lays so much stress) that Christian happiness consists in "comforted remorse" (getrösteter Sünden-schmerz).[37] Before him men were prone to conceive themselves essentially God's creatures, whose business it was to commend themselves to their Maker: no doubt they recognized that they had sinned, and that provision had been made to relieve them of the penalty of their sins; but they built their real hope of acceptance in God's sight more or less upon their own conduct. Augustine realized to the bottom of his soul that he was a sinner and what it is to be a sinner, and therefore sought at God's hands not acceptance but salvation. And this is the reason why he never thought of God without thinking of sin and never thought of sin without thinking of Christ. Because he took his sin seriously, his thought and feeling alike traveled continually in this circle, and could not but travel in this circle. He thus was constantly verifying afresh the truth of the Savior's declaration that he to whom little is forgiven loves little, while he loves much who is conscious of having received much forgiveness: and as his trust increased and his love grew ever greater he realized better and better also that other saying that there is joy in heaven over one sinner that repents more than over ninety and nine righteous persons which need no repentance. So he came to understand that the heights of joy are scaled only by him who has first been miserable, and that the highest happiness belongs only to him who has been the object of salvation. Self-despair, humble trust, grateful love, fullness of joy — these are the steps on which his own soul climbed upward: and these steps gave their whole color and form both to his piety and to his teaching. In his doctrine we see his experience of God's seeking and saving love toward a lost sinner expressing itself in propositional form; in his piety we see his conviction that the sole hope of the sinner lies in the free grace of a loving God expressing itself in the forms of feeling. In doctrine and life alike he sets before us in that effective way which belongs to the discoverer, the religion of faith as over against the religion of works — the religion

[37] "Lehrbuch der Dogmengeschichte," iii. p. 59; E. T. "History of Dogma," v. p. 66.

which despairing of self casts all its hope on God as over against the religion that to a greater or less degree trusts in itself: in a word, since religion in its very nature is dependence on God, religion in the purity of its conception as over against a quasi-religious moralism. It is to the fact that in this book we are admitted into the very life of Augustine and are permitted to see his great heart cleansing itself of all trust in himself and laying hold with the grasp first of despair, then of discerning trust and then of grateful love upon the God who was his salvation, that the " Confessions " owe their perennial attractiveness and their supreme position among books of edification. In them Augustine uncovers his heart and lets us see what religion is in its essence as it works in the soul of one who has, as few have, experienced its power. He has set himself determinedly in this book to exhibit the grace of God in action. Elsewhere he has expounded it in theory, defended it against its assailants, enforced it with logical argument and moving exhortation. Here he shows it at work, and at work in his own soul.

It was only in his effort to show us the grace of God as it worked upon his own soul, that Augustine was led to set before us his life-history through all the formative years of his career — until, after long wandering, he at last had found his rest in God. This is the meaning and this is the extent of the autobiographical element in the " Confessions." Nine of the thirteen books are devoted to this religious analysis of his life-history; and although, of course, the matter admitted and its treatment alike are determined by the end in view, yet Augustine's analysis is very searching and the end in view involves a very complete survey of all that was especially determining in his life-development. In these pages we can see, therefore, just what Augustine was, and just how he became what he became. And the picture, almost extreme in its individuality as it is, is nevertheless as typical as it is individual. It is typical of the life of the ancient world at its best: for in his comprehensive nature Augustine had gathered up into himself and given full play to all that was good in the culture of the ancient world. And it is typical of what Christian experience is at its best: for in Augustine there met in unusual fullness and fought themselves out to a finish all the fundamental currents of thought and feeling that strive together in the human heart when it is invaded by divine grace, and is slowly but surely conquered by it to good and to God. It may repay us to run over the salient elements in this life-history as here depicted for us.

III. The Augustine of the "Confessions"

Augustine came into being at the "turn of the ages," just as the old world was dying, and the new was being born. He was the offspring of a mixed marriage, itself typical of the mixed state of the society of the times. His father, a citizen of importance but of straitened means, in a small African town, remained a heathen until his gifted son had attained his middle youth: [38] he appears to have been a man of generally jovial disposition, liable to fits of violent temper, possessing neither intellectual endowments nor moral attainments to distinguish him from the mass of his contemporaries: but he appreciated the promise of his son, and was prepared to make sacrifices that opportunity might be given for his development. His mother, on the other hand, was one of nature's noblewomen, whose naturally fine disposition had been further beautified by grace. Bred a Christian from her infancy, her native sensibility had been heightened by a warm piety: and her clear and quick intellect had been illuminated by an equally firm and direct conscience. Under her teaching her son was imbued from his infancy with a sense of divine things which never permitted him to forget that there is a God who governs all things and who is unchangeably good, or to find satisfaction in any teaching in which the name of Jesus Christ was not honored. He thus grew up in the nurture of the Lord,[39] but with the divided mind

---

[38] He became a catechumen shortly before Augustine's sixteenth year ("Confessiones," ii. 3. 6. Cf. ix. 9. 22). He died soon afterward.

[39] Cf. "De duabus anim.," i. 1: "The seeds of the true religion wholesomely implanted in me from boyhood."

which almost inevitably results from the divided counsels of a mixed parentage.

As his gifts more and more exhibited themselves worldly ambition took the helm and every nerve was strained to advance him in his preparation for a great career. His early piety, which had been exhibited in frequent prayer as a schoolboy [40] and in an ardent desire for baptism during an attack of dangerous illness,[41] more and more fell away from him, and left him, with his passionate temperament inherited from his father, a prey to youthful vices. An interval of idleness at home, in his sixteenth year (A.D. 370), brought him his great temptation, and he fell into evil ways; and these were naturally continued when, to complete his education, he went next year up to Carthage, that great and wicked city. But this period of unclean life was happily of short duration, lasting at the most only a couple of years. By the time Augustine had reached his seventeenth birthday (autumn of 371) we find him already attached to her who was to be the companion of his life for the next fourteen years, in a union which, though not marriage in the highest sense, differed from technical marriage rather in a legal than in a moral point of view. Though he himself, later at least, did not look upon such a union as true marriage,[42] it was esteemed its equivalent not only in the best heathen society of the time, but even in certain portions of the Church, perhaps up to his own day by the entire Church; [43] and it served to screen him from the multitudinous temptations to vice that

[40] " Confessiones," i. 9. 14: " For even as a boy I began to pray to Thee, my Help and my Refuge; to call upon Thee I burst the bonds of my tongue and prayed to Thee — child as I was, how passionately! — that I might not be flogged at school."   [41] " Confessiones," i. 11.

[42] " Confessiones," iv. 2. 2.: " One not joined to me in lawful wedlock"; x. 30. 41: " Thou hast commanded me to abstain from concubinage." Cf. " Apost. Constt.," viii. 32: " A believer who has a concubine — if she be a slave, let him cease, and take a wife legitimately: if she be free, let him take her as his legitimate wife; and if he does not, let him be rejected."

[43] Cf. the canons of the Council of Toledo of 400, can. 17: " Only let him be content with one woman, whether wife or concubine." Cf. Herzog, " Realencyclopädie für protestantische Theologie und Kirche ³," x. p. 746, and *The Princeton Theological Review*, i. No. 2 (April, 1903), pp. 309–10.

otherwise would have beset him. " I was faithful to her,"
he says.[44]

It was an overmastering and lofty ambition, not fleshly lust,
that constituted the real power in his life, and these years of
preparation at Carthage were years of strenuous labor, during
which Augustine was ever growing toward his higher ideals.
Already in his nineteenth year (373) he was incited to lay
aside his lower ambitions by the reading of a book of Cicero's,
since lost,[45] which had been designed to inflame the heart of
the reader with a love of philosophy and which wrought so
powerfully on Augustine that he resolved at once to make pure
truth thenceforward the sole object of his pursuit.[46] During
this whole period he must be believed to have remained nomi-
nally Christian; and perhaps we may suppose him to have continued in the formal position of a catechumen.[47]

He seems to have been a frequenter of the Church services,[48]
and he speaks of himself as having been during this time under
the dominance of " a certain puerile superstition " which held
him back from the pursuit of truth.[49] Accordingly, when the
" Hortensius " stirred his heart to seek wisdom and yet left him
unsatisfied, because the name of Jesus which, as he says, he
had " sucked in with his mother's milk," was not mentioned in
it, he turned to the Scriptures in apparently the first earnest
effort to seek their guidance he had made since his earliest
youth. But the lowly Scriptures — especially as read in the
rough Old Latin Version — had nothing to offer to the finical
rhetorician, and his eyes were holden that he could not penetrate their meaning: he was offended by their servant-form
and — seeking wisdom, not salvation — turned from them in
disgust. He had reached a crisis in his life, and the result was
that he formally broke with Christianity.

[44] Cf. especially " Solil.," iv. 2. 2. 17.

[45] His " Hortensius."   [46] Cf. especially " Solil." iv. 2. 2. 17.

[47] " De utilitate credendi," i. 2: " sed de me quid dicam, qui iam catholicus
christianus eram? "

[48] " Confessiones," iii. 3. 5. According to " Contra Epist. Manich. Fundam,"
viii. 9, ad fin., he had been accustomed to enjoy the Easter festival and missed
it sadly when he became a Manichæan.   [49] " De beata vita," 4.

It was eminently characteristic of Augustine both that throughout his years of indulgence and indifference he had maintained his connection with the Church, and that he broke with it when, having sloughed off his grosser inclinations, he turned to it in vain for the satisfaction of his higher aspirations. Essential idealist that he was, throughout the years in which he was entangled in lower aims the Church had stood for him as a promise of better things: now he felt that his spirit soared above all it had to offer him. But in breaking with the Church, he could not break with his conception of God as the good Governor of the world, nor with his devotion to the name of Jesus Christ. So he threw himself into the arms of the Manichæans. The Manichæans were the rationalists of the day. Professing the highest reverence for Christ and continually bearing His name on their lips, they yet set forth, under his cloak, a purely naturalistic system. The negative side of their teaching included a most drastic criticism of the Christian Scriptures, while on the positive side they built up a doctrine of God which seemed to separate Him effectually from all complicity with evil, and a doctrine of man which relieved the conscience of all sense of unworthiness and responsibility for sin, while yet proposing a stringent ascetic ideal. In all these aspects its teaching was attractive to the young Augustine, who, on fire with a zeal for wisdom, despised all authority, and, conscious of moral weaknesses, wished to believe neither God nor himself answerable for them. He not only, therefore, heartily adopted the Manichæan system, but entered apparently with enthusiasm into its propagation.

The change nearly cost him the chief saving external influence of his life — intercourse with his godly mother. Terrified by his open repudiation of Christianity and his ardent identification of himself with one of its most dangerous rivals for the popular favor, she forbade him her house, and was only induced to receive him back into the family circle when she became convinced that his defection was not hopeless. Monnica has been made the object of much severe and, as it seems to us, scarcely intelligent criticism for her action on this occasion. It has been sneeringly remarked, for example, that she did not object very much to Augustine's cherishing a concubine, but did object violently to his cherishing a heresy. " She seems to have accepted his companion without a murmur," says a recent writer,[50] " but the descent into heresy was an unpardonable depth." We shall raise no question here of the validity of Bacon's dictum, that " it is certain that heresies and schisms are of all others the greatest scandals; yea, more than corruption of manners." In any event the antithesis is unwisely chosen. We have seen that no great moral obliquity attached to such concubinage as Augustine's, which was, in fact, only an inferior variety of marriage: and though, no doubt, this entanglement was deeply regretted by Monnica, whose ambition for her son had earlier forbidden her providing him with a wife, yet it is quite likely that she saw no reason seriously to reprobate a relation which not only the law of the State, but probably that of the Church, too, acknowledged as legitimate. On the other hand, it is unfair not to recognize the immense change which Augustine's step wrought in his attitude to the religion which was his mother's very life. He may have been up to this moment both indifferent and even of evil life. But he had remained at least formally a Christian; he was still a catechumen; and there was ever hope of repentance. Now he had formally apostatized. He had not only definitively turned his back on Christianity, but was actively assailing it with scorn and ridicule, and that with such success that he was drawing his circle of friends away with him.[51] It was, says Augustine,[52] " because she hated and detested the blasphemies of his error " that she had broken off fellowship with him. Surely his mother's horror is not inexplicable; and it is to be remembered that her attitude of renunciation of intercourse was at once reversed on the reintroduction of hope for her son into

[50] McCabe, *op. cit.*, p. 66.

[51] In the " De duabus anim.," chap. ix., Augustine tells of the effect his easy victory over the ignorant Catholics had in hardening him in his error.

[52] " Confessiones," iii. 11. 19.

her heart. Nor did she ever cease to pursue him with her tears and her prayers.[53]

Despite the eagerness with which he cast himself into the arms of the Manicheans and the zeal with which he became their advocate, Augustine had had very little grounding in the debatable questions that lay at the base of the system. His studies in literature and the rhetorical art had been formal rather than philosophical. His sudden discovery in the teachings of the Manicheans, of the " wisdom " he had been inflamed to seek, was therefore liable to a rude shock of awaking when his studies in the liberal sciences, on which he now zealously entered, should begin to bear fruit. It was not, in effect, long before the sagacity of the good bishop's advice to Monnica, that he should not be plied with argument but left to the gradual effects of his own reading and meditation to open his eyes, began to manifest itself. He remained nine years — from the end of his nineteenth to the beginning of his twenty-ninth year (373–383) — in the toils of the Manichean illusion, exercising in the interval his function of teacher, first at Thagaste and then at Carthage. But by the end of this period the doubts which had early in it began to insinuate themselves, first as to the mythological elements, and then as to the whole structure of the system, had fulfilled themselves. He seems to have been no longer inwardly a Manichean when he went to Rome in the spring of 383, though throughout his one year's stay at that city he remained in outer connection with the sect. When he left Rome for Milan in the late spring of 384, as his thirtieth year was running its course, he left his Manicheism definitively behind him. Nothing had come, however, to take its place. His

---

[53] It is probably not necessary to revert here to the fact that Manichæism was not merely under the ban of the Church, but also under that of the State — that it was crime as well as heresy. The " severe and bloody laws enacted against them by Valentinian, A.D. 372, Theodosius, A.D. 381," repeating, possibly, the earlier proscription of Diocletian, A.D. 287 (see Stokes, " Smith & Wace," *op. cit.*, iii. p. 799), do not seem to have been executed with sufficient vigor in Africa to have made the profession of the heresy very dangerous (cf. Stokes as above: and Loofs, Herzog, " Realencyklopädie für protestantische Theologie und Kirche,[3] " ii. pp. 262, ll. 37 ff).

own experiences combined with his philosophical reading to cast his mind into a complete state of uncertainty, not to say of developed skepticism. He was half-inclined to end the suspense by adopting out of hand the opinions of " those philosophers who are called Academics, because they taught we must doubt everything, and held that man lacks the power of comprehending any truth." [54] But he revolted from committing the sickness of his soul to them, " because they were without the saving name of Christ." [55] And so, no longer a Manichean and yet not a Catholic, he hung in the balance, and " determined therefore to be a catechumen in ,the Catholic Church, commended to him by his parents, until something assured should come to light by which to steer his way." [56] Thus he reverted to the condition of his youth, but in a state of mind unspeakably different.

So far as his outward fortunes were concerned Augustine was now at last in a fair way to realize the ambitions which had been the determining force in his life.[57] Driven from Thagaste by a burning heart, racked with grief for a lost friend; and then successively from Carthage and Rome by chagrin over the misbehavior of his pupils; he cannot be said hitherto to have attained a position of solid consequence. Whatever reputation he may have acquired as a teacher, whatever applause he may have gained in the practice of his art, whatever triumphs he may have secured in public contests,[58] all were by the way, and left him still a " viator " rather than a " consummator." At Milan, however, as Government Professor of Rhetoric, he had at last secured a post which gave him assured social standing and influence, and in the fulfillment of the official duties of which he was brought into pleasant contact with the highest civic circles and even with the court itself. Now for the first time all that he had hoped and striven for seemed within his reach. His mother and brother came to him out of Africa; the circle of his old intimates gathered around him; new friends

[54] " Confessiones," v. 10. 19.
[55] " Confessiones," v. 14. 25.
[56] " Confessiones," v. 14. 25.
[57] Cf. Loofs, op. cit., pp. 265 ff.
[58] Cf. " Confessiones," iv. 2. 3; iv. 3. 5.

of wealth and influence attached themselves to him. It appeared no difficult matter to obtain some permanent preferment — through his host of influential friends a governorship might easily be had; and then a wife with a little money to help toward expenses could be taken; and the height of his desire would be reached.[59] Things were set in train to consummate this plan; a suitable maiden was sought and found and the betrothment concluded; [60] and everything was apparently progressing to his taste.

But, as so often happens, as the attainment of what had been so long and eagerly sought drew nigh, it was found not to possess the power to satisfy which had been attributed to it.[61] At no period of his life, in fact, was Augustine so far removed from complaceny with himself and his situation, inward and outward, as at this moment. His whole mental life had been thrown into confusion by the growth of his skeptical temper, and he had been compelled to see himself deprived of all rational basis for his intellectual pride. And now the very measures taken to carry his ambitious schemes to their fruition reacted to rob him of whatever remnants of moral self-respect may have remained to him. The presence in his household of his concubine was an impediment to the marriage he was planning: and accordingly she was, as he expresses it,[62] torn from his side, leaving a sore and wounded place in his heart where it had adhered to hers. This was bad enough: but worse was to follow. Finding the two years that were to intervene before his marriage irksome, he took another concubine to fill up the interval. He could conceal from himself no longer his abject slavery to lust. And he was more deeply shamed still by the contrast into which his degrading conduct brought him with others whom he had been accustomed to consider his inferiors. His discarded concubine to whom his heart still clung

[59] vi. 11. 19, *ad fin.*: " amicorum maiorum copia "; " præsidatus "; " cum aliqua pecunia."

[60] vi. 13. 23.

[61] Cf. Loofs, *op. cit.*, p. 265, and Bret, " La Conversion de St. Augustine," pp. 68–69.

[62] vi. 15. 25.

set him a better example; but, as he says, he could not imitate even a woman. The iron entered his soul; and his pride, intellectual and moral, was preparing for itself a most salutary fall. No doubt the precarious state of his health at this moment added something to increase his dejection. Possibly on account of the harshness of the northern climate of Milan, he had been seized with a serious affection of the chest, which required rest at least from his labors, and possibly threatened permanently his usefulness as a rhetorician. It tended at all events to cause deep searchings of heart in which he was revealed to himself in all his weakness.

Simultaneously with the growth of his better knowledge of himself, there was opening up to him also a better knowledge of Christianity. Received with distinguished kindness by Ambrose on coming to Milan and drawn by the fame of his oratory, he was accustomed to frequent the preaching services, with a view to estimating Ambrose's rhetorical ability. But as he listened, the matter of the discourses began also to reach his conscience, and he gradually learned not only that the absurdities of belief — such as, for example, that God had a physical form like a man's — which the Manicheans had charged upon the Catholics, but that the whole scheme of the baneful Biblical criticism he had learned from them lacked foundation. His prejudices having thus been removed he soon came to perceive that the Catholics had something to say for themselves worth listening to, and that there was an obvious place for authority in religion. By this discovery his mind was made accessible to the evidences of the divine authority of the Christian Scriptures, and he turned with new zest to them for instruction. Another discovery in his thirty-first year contributed powerfully to open his mind to their meaning. This was nothing less than the discovery of metaphysics. Up to this time Augustine's learning had been largely empirical and his thought was confined to crassly materialistic forms. Now the writings of the Neo-Platonists came into his hands and revealed to him an entirely new world — the world of spirit. Under these new influences his whole mental life was revolutionized: he passed from his divided mind with a bound, and embraced with all the warmth of his ardent nature the new realities assured to him at once by the authority of Scripture and the authentication of reason. To all intents and purposes he was already on the intellectual side a Christian, and needed but some determining influence to secure the decisive action of his will, for his whole life to recrystallize around this new center.

This determining influence was brought him apparently by means of a series of personal examples. These were given especial power over him by the self-contempt into which he had fallen through his discovery of his moral weakness. There was first the example of the rhetorician Victorinus, the story of whose conversion was related to him by Simplicianus, whom Augustine had consulted for direction in his spiritual distress. By this narrative Augustine was inflamed with an immense emulation to imitate his distinguished colleague, but found himself unable to break decisively with his worldly life. Then came the example of Anthony and the Egyptian monks, related to him by a fellow-countryman, Pontianus, on a chance visit; and with this the example also of their imitators in the West. This brought on the crisis. " A horrible shame," he tells us, " gnawed and confounded his soul " while Pontianus was speaking. " What is the matter with us? " he cried to Alypius. " What is it you hear? The unlearned rise and take heaven by storm, and we with all our learning, see how we are wallowing in flesh and blood! Are we ashamed to follow where they lead the way? Ought we not rather to be ashamed not to follow at once? " [63] We all know the story of the agony of remorse that seized him and how release came at length through a child's voice, by which he was led at last to take up the book that lay on the table and read; reading, he found strength to make the great decision that changed his whole life. It is a story which must not be told, however, except in Augustine's own moving words.[64]

[63] " Confessiones," viii. 8. 19.
[64] " Confessiones," viii. 8. 19; 11. 25; 12. 28–30.

There was a little garden to our lodging of which we had the use. . . . Thither the tumult of my heart drove me, where no one could interrupt the fierce quarrel which I was waging with myself, until it should reach the issue known to Thee but not to me. . . . Thus was I sick and tormented, reproaching myself more bitterly than ever, twisting and writhing in my chain, until it should be entirely broken, since now it held me but slightly — though it held me yet. . . . And I kept saying in my heart, " O let it be now! let it be now! " and as I spoke I almost resolved — I almost did it, but I did it not. . . . So when searching reflection had drawn out from the hidden depths all my misery and piled it up in the sight of my heart, a great tempest broke over me, bearing with it a great flood of tears. . . . And I went further off . . . and flung myself at random under a fig tree there and gave free vent to tears; and the flood of my eyes broke forth, an acceptable sacrifice to Thee. And not indeed in these words, but to this purport, I cried to Thee incessantly, " But Thou, O Lord, how long? How long, O Lord? Wilt Thou be angry forever? O remember not against us our iniquities of old! " I felt myself held by them: I raised sorrowful cries: " How long, How long? To-morrow, and to-morrow? Why not now, why not this instant, end my wickedness? "

I was speaking thus and weeping in the bitterest contrition of heart, when lo, I heard a voice, I know not whether of boy or girl, saying in a chant and repeating over and over: Take and read, Take and read. At once with changed countenance I began most intently to think whether there was any kind of game in which children chanted such a thing, but I could not recall ever hearing it. I choked back the rush of tears and rose, interpreting it no otherwise than as a divine command to me to open the book and read whatever passage I first lighted upon. For I had heard of Anthony, that he had received the admonition from the Gospel lesson which he chanced to come in upon, as if what was read was spoken to himself: " Go, sell all that thou hast and give to the poor, and thou shalt have treasure in heaven: and come, follow me "; and was at once converted by this oracle to Thee. So I returned quickly to the place where Alypius was sitting, for I had laid down the volume of the apostle there when I left him. I seized it, opened it, and read in silence the passage on which my eyes first fell: " Not in rioting and drunkenness, not in chambering and wantonness, not in strife and envying; but put ye on the Lord Jesus Christ, and make not provision for the flesh, to fulfil the lusts thereof." No further did I wish to read: nor was there need. Instantly, as I reached the end of this sentence, it was as if the light of peace was poured into my heart and all the shades of doubt faded away. . . . For Thou didst convert me to Thyself in such a manner that I sought neither a wife nor any hope of this world — taking my stand on that Rule of Faith on which Thou didst reveal me to my mother so many years before.

Thus there was given to the Church, as Harnack says,[65] incomparably the greatest man whom " between St. Paul the Apostle and Luther the Reformer the Christian Church has possessed "; and the thankful Church has accordingly made a festival of the day on which the great event occurred — according this honor of an annual commemoration of their conversions only to Paul and Augustine among all her saints, " thus seeming to say," as Boissier remarks,[66] " that she owes almost an equal debt of gratitude to each." But it would be more in accordance with Augustine's own heart to say, Thus a soul was brought to its God, and made so firmly His that throughout a long life of service to Him it never knew the slightest wavering of its allegiance. It is easy to make merry over the impure elements that entered into the process of his conversion. It is easy to point scornfully to the superstition which made out of the voice of a child at play a message from heaven; and which resorted to the sacred volume as to a kind of book of divination. It is easy to exclaim that after all Augustine's " conversion " was not to Christianity but to Monachism [67] — with its entire ascetic ideal, including its depreciation of woman and its perversion of the whole sexual relation. It is easy to raise doubts whether the conversion was as sudden or as complete as Augustine represents it: to trace out the steps that led up to it with curious care and to lay stress on every hint of incompleteness of Christian knowledge or sentiment which may plausibly be brought forward from his writings of the immediately suc-

[65] " Monasticism and the Confessions of Augustine," E. T. p. 123.

[66] " La Fin du Paganisme," i. p. 291.

[67] Loofs says Augustine " was converted, because he permitted himself to be shamed — by Monachism " (*op. cit.*, p. 267, 1. 31).

ceeding months.[68] But surely all this is to confuse the kernel with the husk. Of course, the conversion was led up to by a gradual approach, and Augustine himself analyzes for us with incomparable skill the progress of this preparation through all the preceding years. And, equally of course, there was left a great deal for him to learn after the crisis was past: and he does not conceal from us how much of a babe in Christ he was and felt himself to be as he emerged new-born from the stress of the conflict. And of course, in the preparation for it and in the gradual realization of its effects in his thought and life alike, and even in the very act itself by which he gave himself to God, there were mingled elements derived from his stage of Christian knowledge and feeling, from the common sentiments of the time, which powerfully affected him, and from his own personality and ingrained tendencies. But these things, which could not by any possibility have been absent, not only do not in any respect derogate from the reality or the profundity of the revolution then accomplished — the reality and profundity of which are attested by his whole subsequent life [69] — but do not even detract from the humanity or attractiveness of the narrative or of the personality presented to us in it. He must be sadly lacking not only in dramatic imagination, but in human sympathy as well, who can find it strange that in the stress of his great crisis, when his sensibilities were strained to the breaking point, Augustine could see the voice of heaven in the

[68] So especially Harnack and Boissier: they are sufficiently though briefly answered by Wörter, " Die Geistesentwickelung des hl. Aurelius Augustinus bis zu seiner Taufe," Paderborn, 1892, pp. 63 sq.

[69] Even Loofs, who is quite ready to correct the " Confessions " by what he deems the testimony of the treatises emanating from the period just after the conversion, is free to admit that a revolutionary crisis did take place in Augustine's life at this time, and that, therefore, the " Confessions," in describing such a crisis, give us a necessary complement to what we could derive from these treatises. He says (Herzog, " Realencyclopädie für protestantische Theologie und Kirche ³," p. 267) that there must have happened *something* between Augustine's adoption of Neo-Platonism at a time when he still lived in concubinage and his decisive revulsion from all sexual life, witnessed in the " Soliloquies " (i. 17), which will account for the great change: and this *something* the " Confessions " alone give us. This is a testimony to the historicity of the " Confessions " of the first value.

vagrant voice of a child; or should have followed out the hint thus received into his heated imagination and committed his life, as it were, to the throw of a die. Surely this is as psychologically true to life as it is touching to the sensibilities: and in no way, in the circumstances, can it be thought derogatory to either the seriousness of his mind or the greatness of his character. And how could he, in the revulsion from what he felt his special sin, fail to be carried in the swing of the pendulum far beyond the point of rest, in his estimate of the relation that could safely obtain between the sexes? The appearance of such touches of human weakness in the story contributes not only to the narrative the transparent traits of absolute truth and to the scene depicted a reality which deeply affects the heart of the reader, but to the man himself just that touch of nature which "makes the whole world kin." In such traits as these we perceive indeed one of the chief elements of the charm of the "Confessions." The person we meet in them is a person, we perceive, who towers in greatness of mind and heart, in the loftiness of his thought and in his soaring aspirations, far above ordinary mortals: and yet he is felt to be compacted of the same clay from which we have ourselves been molded. If it were not so obviously merely the art of artless truth, we should say that herein lies, more than in anything else, the art of the "Confessions." For it is the very purpose of this book to give the impression that Augustine himself was a weak and erring sinner, and that all of good that came into his life was of God.

It is especially important for us precisely at this point to recall our minds to the fact that to give such an impression is the supreme purpose of the "Confessions." This whole account of his life-history which we have tried to follow up to its crisis in his conversion is written, let us remind ourselves, not that we may know Augustine, but that we may know God: and it shows us Augustine only that we may see God. The seeking and saving grace of God is the fundamental theme throughout. The events of Augustine's life are not, then, set forth in it *simpliciter*. Only such events of his life are set down as manifest how much he needed the salvation of God and how God gradually brought him to that salvation: and they are so set down and so dealt with as to make them take their places, rightly marshaled, in this great argument. This is the account to give of that coloring of self-accusation that is thrown over the narrative which is so offensive to some of its readers; as if Augustine were set upon painting his life in the blackest tints imaginable, and wished us to believe that his " quiet and honest youth " and strenuous and laborious manhood, marked as they really were by noble aspiration and adequate performance, were rather " all sin ": nay, that the half-instinctive acts of his infancy itself and the very vitality of his boyish spirits were but the vents which a peculiarly sinful nature formed for itself. In these traits of the narrative, however, Augustine is not passing judgment on himself alone, but in himself on humanity at large in its state of sin and misery. By an analysis of his own life-history he realizes for himself, and wishes to make us realize with him, what man is in his sinful development on the earth, that our eyes may be raised from man to see what God is in His loving dealing with the children of men. We err, if from the strong, dark lines in which he paints his picture we should infer that he would have us believe that in his infancy, youth, or manhood he was a sinner far beyond the sinfulness of other men. Rather would he say to us in his Savior's words: " Nay, but except ye repent ye shall all likewise perish." But we should err still more deeply, should we fancy that he meant us to suppose that it was due to any superiority to other men on his part that God had sought him out and granted to him His saving grace. He knew his own sinfulness as he knew the sinfulness of no other man, and it was his one burning desire that he should in his recovery to God recognize and celebrate the ineffableness of the grace of God. The pure grace of God is thus his theme throughout, and nowhere is it more completely so than in this culminating scene of his conversion. The human elements that enter into the process, or even into the act itself by which he came to God, only heightened the clearness of his own perception that it was to the grace of God alone that he owed his recovery, and he would have them similarly heighten the clearness with which his readers perceive it with him.[70]

With his conversion, therefore, the narrative of the " Confessions " culminates and practically ends. There follows, indeed, another book of narration in which he tells us briefly of his preparation for baptism and of the baptism itself and its meaning to him; but chiefly of his mother and of that remarkable conversation he held with her at Ostia in which they fairly scaled heaven together in their ardent aspirations; and then of how he laid her away with a heart full of appreciation of her goodness and of his loss. And then, in yet another book, he undertakes to tell us not what he was, but what he had become, but quickly passes into such searching psychological and ethical analyses that the note of autobiography is lost. Not in this book, then, is the revelation of what Augustine had become to be found; it is rather given us by means of the narrative which fills the first nine books, in the judgment he passes there on his former self and in the cries of gratitude he raises there to God for the great deliverance he had wrought in his soul. We see without difficulty that this new Augustine who is writing is a different Augustine from him whom he depicts in the narrative: we see that it is even a different Augustine from him whom he leaves with us at the end of the narrative — after his conversion, and his emergence from his country retreat for baptism, and his return to his native Africa. And yet we see also that the making of this new Augustine was in essence completed at the point where the narrative leaves him. Whatever development came after this came in the processes of natural growth, and argues no essential change.

IV. The Development of Augustine

It is convenient to draw a distinction between what we may call, by a somewhat artificial application of the terms, the

---

[70] Augustine's testimony that it was to the grace of God that he owed his conversion is drawn out at some length by T. Bret, " La Conv. d. St. Augustine," pp. 60–66. See also Wörter, *op. cit.*, especially the summary, pp. 62 ff.

making and the development of Augustine. Under the former term we may sum up the factors that coöperated to make the man who emerged from the crisis of his conversion just the man he was; and by the latter we may designate the gradual ripening of his thought and life after he had become a Christian to their final completeness. The factors that enter into his " making," in this sense, are exhibited to us in his own marvelous analysis in the vital narrative of the " Confessions." It is in the mirror of the works which he composed through the course of his busy life that we must seek the manner of man he was when he entered upon his Christian race and the man he became as he pressed forward steadily to his goal. Soundly converted though he was, it was yet the man who had been formed by the influences which had worked upon him through those thirty eager years who was converted: and his Christianity took form and color from the elements he brought with him to it.

An interesting indication of the continued significance to him of those old phases of his experience is discoverable in his setting about, at once upon his conversion, to refute precisely those systems of error in the toils of which he had himself been holden, and that in the reverse order in which he had passed through them. And that is as much as to say that he attacked them in the order in which they may be supposed to have been still living memories to him. It was during the very first months after his conversion, and even before his baptism, that his treatise " Against the Academics " was written. And before the year was out his first work against the Manichæans was published, inaugurating a controversy which was to engage much of his time and powers for the next ten years.[71] This very polemic reveals the completeness with which he had outgrown these phases of belief, or rather of unbelief: there is no trace in it of remaining sympathy with them, and his entanglement in them is obviously purely a matter of memory.

[71] On the place in his works of a polemic against Polytheism — which would be going back to the very beginning — see Naville, " Saint-Augustin," etc., pp. 70–71, note.

He entered at this time into no such refutation of Neo- ✓
platonism: this was reserved for the teeming pages of the
"City of God." Rather it was as a Neo-platonic thinker that
Augustine became a Christian; and he carried his Neo-platonic
conceptions over into Christianity with him. This is not to say,
however, as has been said, that his thinking "was still essentially Neo-platonic," and "his Christianity during this period
was merely Neo-platonism with a Christian stain and a Christian veneering." [72] Much less is it to say, as also has been said,
that what we call his "conversion" was a conversion not to
Christianity but merely to Neo-platonic spiritualism, while
actual Christianity was embraced by him only some years later
on [73] — if indeed it was ever fully assimilated, for still others
insist that his thinking remained "essentially Neo-platonic"
throughout his life, or at least a complete Neo-platonic system
lay always in his mind alongside his superinduced Christianity,
unassimilated and unassimilable by it.[74] All this is the gravest
kind of exaggeration. An analysis of Augustine's writings composed during his retreat at Cassiciacum while he was awaiting
baptism, presents to our observation already a deeply devout
and truly Christian thinker, although it reveals the persistence
in his thought and in his modes of expression alike, of conceptions and terms derived from his engrossment with Neo-
platonic forms of thought and speech, which in his later writings no longer appear.[75]

The reality of a gradual development of Augustine's thought
is already indicated by this circumstance, and it remains only
to fix its course with such precision as may be attainable and to
determine its stages and its rate of progress. It has become
quite common to mark off in it quite a series of definite changes.

[72] Loofs, Herzog, "Realencyclopädie für protestantische Theologie und
Kirche 3," p. 270, l. 31.

[73] L. Gourdon, op. cit., pp. 45–50, 83.

[74] Harnack, "History of Dogma" (E. T.), V. chap. iv.

[75] Such an analysis, brief but admirably done (except that justice is not
done to the *Christianity* of this period of Augustine's life), may be found in
Loofs' article, Herzog, "Realencyclopädie für protestantische Theologie und
Kirche 3," pp. 270, line 11; 274, line 8. See also Wörter, op. cit.

Thus we read [76] that it was only "on his entrance upon a clerical career," that is, only on his ordination as presbyter in 391, that Augustine entered upon a new phase of thought, marked by increasing knowledge of the Scriptures and deepening Church feeling; and only on his consecration as bishop, late in 395, that he at length attained in principle that complete system of thought which we know as "Augustinianism." Even greater detail is sometimes attempted with respect to the development of the preëpiscopal period. The presbyterial period (391–395) is appropriately called "the last section of his apprenticeship," and the preceding four or five years are subdivided into the period between conversion and baptism in which the first place is given to reason and the effort is to conciliate religion with philosophy; and the period from baptism to ordination in which the first place is given to Scripture and the effort has come to be to conciliate philosophy with religion.[77] Four successive epochs in Augustine's thought are thus distinguished, marked by the progressive retirement of philosophy — Neo-platonism in this case — and the progressive advancement of Scripture to its rightful place as primary source of divine knowledge: and these four epochs are sharply divided from one another by external occurrences in Augustine's life — his baptism, ordination as presbyter, and consecration as bishop.

It is scarcely possible to avoid the impression that the scheme of development thus outlined suffers from overprecision and undue elaboration. We are struck at once by the rapidity of the movement which is supposed to have taken place. Augustine's conversion occurred in the late summer of 386: the treatise "On Divers Questions to Simplicianus," in which it is allowed on all hands that "Augustinianism" appears, in principle, in its completeness, was written before the end of 396. Only ten years are available, then, for a development which is supposed to run through four well-marked

[76] Loofs, Herzog, "Realencyclopädie für protestanische Theologie und Kirche [3]," loc. cit., pp. 270, 279.

[77] Nourisson, "La philos. de St. Augustine," i. pp. 33–34.

stages. The exact synchronism of the periods of development with changes of importance in the external conditions of Augustine's life raises further suspicion: there seems to be nothing either in the external changes fitted to produce the internal ones, or in the internal changes to produce the external ones. We begin to wonder whether the assumed internal " development " may not be largely an illusion produced merely by the gradual shifting of interest, accompanied by the natural adjustments of emphasis, which was inevitable in the passage of a layman to official positions in the Church of increasing responsibility. Color is given to this suggestion by the actual series of treatises proceeding from each of these periods of Augustine's life. When Augustine connected himself with the Church in 386, and entered the arena of discussion, he entered it not as an accredited teacher clothed with ecclesiastical authority, but in the rôle of Christian philosopher. His earliest writings bear entirely this character; and it does not appear that writings on the same themes and with the same end in view, if proceeding from him later in life, would not have assimilated themselves closely to these in tone and character. The shifting of the emphasis to more positive Christian elements in the later treatises belonging to his lay period, follows closely the change in the subjects which he treated. His polemic against the Manichæans, already begun in Rome, continued during his residence in Thagaste to absorb his attention. This controversy still largely occupied him through his presbyterial period: but already not only was the Donatist conflict commenced, but his positive expositions of Scripture began to take a large place in his literary product. Speaking now from the point of view of an official teacher of the Church, it is not strange that a stronger infusion of positive elements found their way into his works. In his episcopal period purely thetical treatises enter into the product in important proportions, and the anti-Manichæan polemic gave way first to the anti-Donatist, and after 412 to the anti-Pelagian, both of which were favorable to the fuller expression of the positive elements of his Christian doctrine — the one in its ecclesiastical and the other in its individualistic aspects. On a survey of the succession of treatises we acquire a conviction that such a series of treatises could not fail to give the impression of a developing doctrinal position such as is outlined by the expositors, whether such a development was actual or not. In other words, the doctrinal development of Augustine as drawn out by the expositors may very well be and probably is largely illusory. Its main elements may be fully accounted for by the different occasions and differing purposes on and for which the successive treatises were written.

We must, then, look deeper than this gradual change from treatises of thoroughly philosophical tenor to treatises of thoroughly Christian contents before we can venture to affirm a marked doctrinal growth in Augustine from 386 to 396 and beyond. On seeking to take this deeper view we are at once struck by two things. The first of these is that the essence of " Augustinianism " as expounded in the treatises of the episcopal period is already present in principle in the earliest of Augustine's writings and, indeed, from the first constitutes the heart of his teaching. The second is that the working of this " Augustinianism " outwards, so as to bring all the details of teaching into harmony with itself, was, nevertheless, a matter of growth — and a growth, we may add, which had not reached absolute completeness, we do not say merely, until Augustine had obtained his episcopacy in 396, but when he laid down his pen and died in 430. Augustine's great idea was the guiding star of his life from the very beginning of his Christian career. It more and more took hold of his being and extruded more and more perfectly the remainders of inconsistent thinking. But up to the end it had not, with absolute completeness, adjusted to itself his whole circle of ideas. An attempt must now be made at least to illustrate this suggestion.

What is the essence of " Augustinianism " ? Is it not that sense of absolute dependence on God which, conditioning all the life and echoing through all the thought, produces the type of religion we call " evangelical " and the type of theology we call " Augustinian " ? This is the keynote of the " Confessions," and gives it at once its evangelical character and its

appeal to the heart of the sinner. It is summed up in the famous prayer: " Command what Thou wilt, and give what Thou
commandest " — hearing which, Pelagius, representative of
anti-Augustinianism at its height, recognized in it the very
heart of Augustinianism and was so incensed as to come nearly
to blows with him who had rashly repeated it to him. Now it
is notable that this note is already struck in the earliest class
of Augustine's writings. " Command, I beg," he prays in the
" Soliloquies " (i. 5) — " Command and ordain, I beg, whatsoever Thou wilt; but heal and open my ears. . . . If it is by
faith that those who take refuge in Thee find Thee, give faith."
When exhorted to believe — if, indeed, that is in our power —
his pious response is: " Our power He Himself is." These great
words, " Da fidem," " Potestas nostra Ipse est," sum up in
themselves implicitly the whole of " Augustinianism "; and
they need only consistent explication and conscious exposition
so as to cover the entirety of life and thought, to give us all
that " Augustinianism " ever gave us.

It may still, indeed, be asked whether the note they strike is
the fundamental note of these earlier writings and whether
such expressions constitute as large an element in them as
might be expected from Augustine. On the whole, we think,
both questions must be answered in the affirmative. But
this answer must be returned with some discrimination. It is
not meant, of course, that the substance of these books is made
up of such sentences, even in the sense in which this is true,
say, of the " Confessions." What is meant is that these books,
being of an entirely different character from, say, the " Confessions," and written to subserve an entirely different purpose,
yet betray this fundamental note throbbing behind the even
flow of their own proper discourse, and thus manifest themselves as the product of a soul which was resting wholly upon
its God. We must profess our inability fully to understand the
standpoint of those who read these earliest books as the lucu-
brations of a Neo-platonic philosopher throwing over the mere
expression of his thoughts a thin veil of Christian forms.
Plainly it is not the philosopher, only slightly touched by

Christianity, that is speaking in them, but the Christian theologian, who finds all his joy in the treasures he has discovered in his newly gained faith. Through the Socratic severity of their philosophical discourse — which is, after all, but the stillness after the storm — there continually breaks the undercurrent of suppressed emotion. The man who is writing has obviously passed through severe conflicts and has only with difficulty attained his present peace. He has escaped from the bonds of superfluous desires, and, the burden of dead cares being laid aside, now breathes again, has recovered his senses, returned to himself.[78] There is no direct reference made to the conversion that had so lately transformed him into a new man, but the consciousness of it lies ever in the background and it is out of its attainment that he now speaks.[79]

We may be sure that when this man gives himself up after passing through such a crisis to philosophical discourses, it is not because there lies nothing more than these abstract reasonings deep in his heart, but because he has a conscious end of importance to serve by them. The end he has set before him in them certainly is not, as Harnack supposes, merely to " find himself " after the turmoil of the revolution he has experienced, to clarify to his own thinking his new religio-philosophical position. There is indication enough that he does not speak his whole heart out. He is rather seeking, as Boissier hints, to serve the religion to which he has at last yielded his heart and his life. In breaking with the world had he taken an irrational step? Had he sacrificed his intellect in bowing to authority? No, he would have all men know he is rather just entering now upon the riches of his inheritance — in which, moreover, all that he has really gained from the best thought of the world has its proper place and its highest part to play. He is, in a word, not expounding here the Neo-platonic philosophy in Christian terms: he is developing the philosophy of Christianity in terms of the best philosophic thought of the day — serving himself as a Christian heir to the heritage of the ages.

[78] " Cont. Acad.," ii. 2. 4, ad init.
[79] Cf. " Cont. Acad.," ii. 2. 5.

The task he had set himself [80] was to construct a Christian philosophy-out of Platonic materials. Nor will the notion that he was at the outset so keen an advocate of the hegemony of reason that he was unprepared to submit his thought to the authority of Christ and of the Scriptures which He has given us, bear investigation: it shatters itself not only against the whole tone of the discussion, but also against repeated express declarations. In the very earliest of his books he tells us, for example, that to him the authority of Him who says " Seek and ye shall find " is greater than that of all philosophy; [81] and he sets the authority of Christ over against that of reason with the declaration that it is certain that he shall never fall away from it, because he cannot find a stronger.[82]

Although, however, he had thus firmly from the beginning laid hold of what we may call both the formal and the material principles of his theology — the authority of the divine revelation in and through Christ, embodied in the Scriptures, and the utter dependence of man on God for all good; it does not in the least follow that he had already drawn out from Scripture all that was to be believed on its authority or worked out all the implications of his profound sense of absolute dependence on God. The explication of the teaching of Scripture and the realization of the implications of his fundamental principle of dependence on God constituted, on the contrary, precisely his life-work, on which he was just entering. As we read on from book to book we do not fail to feel, even within the limits of his lay life, a gradual deepening and widening of his knowledge of Scripture, and under the influence of this growing knowledge, a gradual modification of his opinions philosophical and theological alike, and even a gradual change in his very style.[83]

[80] Cf. Naville, *op. cit.,* p. 69.

[81] " Cont. Acad.," ii. 3. 9.

[82] *Ibid.,* iii. 20. 43. For this point of view see especially R. Schmid's paper in the *Zeitschrift für Theologie und Kirche,* 1897, vii. p. 94.

[83] Cf. Naville, *op. cit.,* p. 70: " Beyond doubt, when we study in their chronological succession the works of these five years, we perceive the rôle of Scripture gradually to increase. The author, we feel, has immersed himself in the study of Scripture. He has acquired a knowledge of it, of ever-increasing

His earliest writings certainly contain indications enough of crudities of thought which were subsequently transcended. We do not need to advert here to such peripheral matters as his confession that he cannot understand why infants are baptized.[84] Despite the passion of his dependence on God and the vigor of his reference to God alone of all that is good, he had not throughout this whole period learned to exclude the human initiative from the process of salvation itself. "God does not have mercy," he says,[85] "unless the will has preceded." "It belongs to us to believe and to will, but to Him to give to those that believe and will the power to do well, through the Holy Spirit, through whom love is shed abroad in our hearts." [86] "God has not predestinated any one except whom He foreknew would believe and answer His call." [87] Thus his zeal for free will which burned warmly throughout this whole period of his life, did not expend itself merely in its strong assertion over against the notion of involuntary sin,[88] but was carried over also into the matter of salvation. No doubt this zeal was in large measure due to the stress of his conflict with Manicheism, which colored the thought of the whole period: but what it concerns us here to note especially is that it was possible for him to hold and proclaim these views of human initiative in salvation although the center of his thought and feeling alike lay in the great confession: "Our power He Himself is." It is quite clear that throughout this period his most central ideas had not yet succeeded in coming fully to their rights. He had not yet attained to a thorough understanding of himself as a Christian teacher.

---

depth. His very style becomes modified under its influence. No doubt, also, the idea of the Church is more and more emphasized up to the book on the True Religion, in which Augustine expressly undertakes to expound the faith of the Catholic Church. Finally the philosophical thought itself undergoes on some points alterations, which we shall point out." This is all very justly said.

[84] "De quantitate animae," 36. 80.

[85] "De diversis quaestionibus lxxxiii." 68. 5.

[86] "Exposito quarumdam propositionum ex Epistola ad Romanos," 61.

[87] *Ibid.*, 55.

[88] E.g., "De vera religione," 14. 27.

It is well to focus our attention on the particular instance of as yet unformed views which we have adduced. For it happens that with reference to it we have the means of tracing the whole process of his change of view; and it is most instructive. It was indeed just at the opening of his episcopal period that the change took place; but it stood in no direct connection with this alteration in his external status. Nor was it the result of any controversial sharpening of his sight: it is characteristic of Augustine's life that his views were not formed through or even in controversy, but were ready always to be utilized in controversies which arose after their complete formation. It was the result purely and simply of deeper and more vital study of Scripture.

The corrected views find their first expression in the first book of the work " On Divers Questions to Simplicianus," which was written in 396, the same year in which he was made bishop. The " questions " discussed in this book were Rom. vii. 7–25 and Rom. ix. 10–29. In the " Retractations " [89] he says relatively to the latter " question ": " Later in this book the question is taken from that passage where it says, ' But not only so, but Rebecca also having conceived of one, even our father Isaac ' — down to where it says, ' Except the God of Sabaoth had left us a seed we had been made a Sodom and had been like unto Gomorrah.' In the solution of this question, we struggled indeed for the free choice of the human will; [90] but the grace of God conquered: otherwise the apostle could not have been understood to speak with obvious truth when he says, ' For who maketh thee to differ? and what has thou that thou didst not receive? But if thou didst receive it why dost thou glory, as if thou hadst not received it? ' It was because he wished to make this clear that the martyr Cyprian set forth the whole meaning of this passage by saying: ' We are to glory in nothing because nothing is ours ' " (*Cypr.*, lib. 3, testim. 4). Driven thus by purely exegetical considerations — working, no doubt, on a heart profoundly sensible of its utter dependence

[89] ii. 1. 1.

[90] " Laboratum est quidem pro libero arbitrio voluntatis humanæ."

on God — Augustine was led somewhat against his will to recognize that the " will to believe " is itself from God. Accordingly, in this " question " he teaches at length that whether man despises or does not despise the call does not lie in his own power.[91] For, he reasons, " if it lies in the power of him that is called not to obey, it is possible to say, ' Therefore it is not of God that showeth mercy, but of man that willeth and runneth,' because the mercy of him that calls is in that case not enough unless it is followed by the obedience of him that is called." [92] No, he argues, " God has mercy on no one in vain: but so calls him on whom He has mercy — after a fashion He knows will be congruous to him — that he does not repulse Him that calls." [93]

At a much later time, Augustine details to us the entire history of this change of view.[94] The whole passage is well worth reading, but we can adduce only the salient points here. His earlier view he speaks of as merely an unformed view. He " had not yet very carefully inquired into or sought out the nature of the election of grace of which the apostle speaks " in Rom. x. 1–5. He had not yet thought of inquiring whether faith itself is not God's gift. He did not sufficiently carefully search into the meaning of the calling that is according to God's purpose. It was chiefly I Cor. iv. 7 that opened his eyes. But here we will listen to his own words: " It was especially by this passage that I myself also was convinced, when I erred in a similar manner " — with the Semi-Pelagians, that is — " thinking that the faith by which we believe in God is not the gift of God, but that it is in us of ourselves, and that by it we obtain the gifts of God whereby we may live temperately and righteously and piously in this world. For I did not think that faith was preceded by God's grace — so that by its means might be given us what we might profitably ask — except in the sense that we could not believe unless the proclamation of the truth preceded; but to consent after the Gospel had been

---

[91] " De diversis quaestionibus ad Simplicianum," i. 2. 12.
[92] *Ibid.*
[93] *Ibid.*, 13.   [94] " De praedest. sanctt.," iii. 7.

preached to us, I thought belonged to ourselves, and came to us from ourselves."

That it was precisely at the beginning of his episcopate that he attained to his better and more consistent doctrine on this cardinal point, thus giving its completed validity for the first time to his fundamental principle of utter dependence on God, was obviously a pure accident. And there is a single clause in the expression he gives to his new doctrine on this the first occasion of its enunciation which exhibits to us that even yet he had not worked it out in its completeness. " But him on whom He has mercy," we read, " He calls, *in the manner that He knows will be congruous to him,* so that he will not repulse the Caller." [95] About this clause there was much disputation a thousand years later between the Jansenists and the Congruists. As it stands in the text it is only a chance clause, in no way expressive of Augustine's developed thought, in which undoubtedly the grace of God is conceived as creative. Indeed, immediately before it occurs the declaration that " the effect of the Divine mercy can by no means be abandoned to the powers of man, as if, unless man willed it, God would vainly have exercised His mercy," the doctrine suggested by which is scarcely wholly congruous with the notion of " congruous grace." What the clause indicates to us is not, therefore, a determinate teaching of Augustine's, but rather the fact that he had not even yet very carefully inquired into the nature of the operation of God which he called grace, and was liable to suggest inconsistent views of its mode of operation in immediately contiguous sentences. Was it the *quâ* or merely a *sine quâ non* of salvation? To this question his fundamental principle of absolute dependence on God, that God alone is " our power," had a very decisive reply to give: and he was destined to find that reply and to announce it with great decision. But as yet he had not been led to think it out with precision. In important respects his view remained still unformed.

This instance of the gradual elaboration even of Augustine's most fundamental conceptions is only one of many that

[95] " De diversis quaestionibus ad Simplicianum," i. 2. 13.

could be adduced. Another striking illustration is offered by the slow clarification of his doctrine of predestination — purely again under the influence of deeper study of Scripture.[96] The totality of Augustine's development consists, in a word, of ever fuller and clearer evolution of the contents of his primary principle of complete dependence on God, in the light of ever richer and more profound study of Scripture: and we can follow out this development quite independently of external influences, which in his case never conditioned his thought, but only gave occasion to its fuller expression. It might fairly be said that his entire growth is simply a logical development of his fundamental material principle of dependence on God under the guidance of his formal principle of the authority of Scripture. One of the most striking results of this was that he learned little or nothing of primary moment from the controversies in which he was constantly engaged: but rather met them with already formed convictions. No doubt his conceptions were brought out in more varied and even in part clearer and stronger expression during the course of these controversies: but in point of mere fact they were in each case already formed and had been formally announced before the controversies arose. If Loofs says of Athanasius, for example, that he did not make the Nicænum, but the Nicænum made him; he is compelled to say, on the contrary, of Augustine, that he was not formed in the Pelagian controversy, but his preformation was the occasion of it. " Pelagianism," he remarks,[97] perhaps with some slight exaggeration, " was first of all nothing but a reaction of the old moralistic rationalism against the monergism of grace that was exalted by Augustine's type of piety." Of course, we are not to imagine that on this showing Augustine had from the first nothing to learn: or even that he ultimately worked out his fundamental principle perfectly into all the details of his teaching. We have already intimated that a

96 " Expositio quarumdam propositionum, etc.," 60. The matter is sufficiently expounded by Loofs, Herzog, " Realencyclopädie für protestantische Theologie und Kirche 3," p. 276, line 21.

97 Leitfaden zum Studium der Dogmengeschichte 2," § 53, p. 210.

process of growth is traceable in him and that the process of his growth to a perfect elaboration of his principle was never completed. Had it been, Harnack could not say of him that he bequeathed to posterity only "problems."

In very fact, there remained to the end, as the same writer puts it, " two Augustines," which is as much as to say, that he embraced in his public teaching inconsistent elements of doctrine.[98] It is indeed quite possible by attending alternately to one element of his teaching alone to draw out from his writings two contradictory systems: and this is just what has been done in the vital processes of historical development. To him as to their founder both Romanist and Protestant make their appeal.[99] The specific estimate which the Catholic places on the *unitas ecclesiæ* goes back to him, who it was that gave that compactness and far-reaching elaboration to the doctrine of the Church and its Sacraments which rendered the immense structure of Catholicism possible. It was equally he who by his doctrine of grace contributed the factor of positive doctrine by which the Reformation was rendered possible; for the Reformation on its theological and religious side was just an Augustinian revival. Two children were thus struggling in the womb of his mind. There can be no doubt which was the child of his heart. His doctrine of the Church he had received whole from his predecessors and himself gave it only the sharpness and depth which insured its vitality. His doctrine of grace was all his own, his greatest contribution to Christian thought. He was pleased to point out how this element of it and that had found broken expression in the pages of his great predecessors. He was successful in showing that all the true religious life of the Church from the beginning had flowed in the channels determined by it. But after all it was his, or rather it was he

[98] Harnack, " Dogmengeschichte," iii. p. 90 (E. T. " History of Dogma," v. p. 102); cf. Schaff, " Saint Chrysostom and Saint Augustin," p. 154.

[99] And not Romanist and Protestant alone: in a finely conceived passage Loofs, Herzog, " Realencyclopädie für protestantische Theologie und Kirche [3]," ii. p. 277 outlines Augustine's position as the spring out of which many different waters flow. Cf. also his " Leitfaden zum Studium der Dogmengeschichte," § 46 (p. 176).

himself translated into forms of doctrine. It represented the very core of his Christian being: by it he lived; and his whole progress in Christian thinking is only the increasing perfection with which its fundamental principle applied itself in his mind to every department of Christian thought and life. Everything else gave way gradually before it, and it was thus that his thought advanced steadily toward a more and more consistent system.

But his doctrine of the Church and Sacraments had not yet given way before his doctrine of grace when he was called away from this world of partial attainment to the realms of perfect thought and life above. It still maintained a place by its side, fundamentally inconsistent with it, limited, modified by it, but retaining its own inner integrity. It is the spectacle of collectivism and individualism striving to create a *modus vivendi;* of dependence on God alone, and the intermediation of a human institution endeavoring to come to good understanding. It was not and is not possible for them to do so. Augustine had glimpses of the distinction between the invisible and the visible Church afterward elaborated by his spiritual children: he touched on the problem raised by the notions of baptismal regeneration and the necessity of the intermediation of the Church for salvation in the face of his passionately held doctrine of the free grace of God, and worked out a sort of compromise between them. In one way or another he found a measure of contentment for his double mind. But this could not last. We may say with decision that it was due only to the shortness of human life; to the distraction of his mind with multifarious cares; to the slowness of his solid advance in doctrinal development — that the two elements of his thought did not come to their fatal conflict before his death. Had they done so, there can be no question what the issue would have been. The real Augustine was the Augustine of the doctrine of grace.[100] The whole history of his inner life is a history of the

[100] Cf. Reuter, "Augustinische Studien," Studies First and Second; e.g., p. 102: "It was not the idea of the Church as the institute of grace that was dominant in his later years, but that of predestinating grace"; "the doctrine

progressive extension of the sway of this doctrine into all the chambers of his thought; of the gradual subjection to it of every element of his inherited teaching. In the course of time — had time been allowed — it was inevitable that his inherited doctrine of the Church also would have gone down before it, and he would have bequeathed to the Church not " problems " but a thoroughly worked-out system of purely evangelical religion.

No doubt it was the weakness of Augustine that this was not accomplished during the span of his six and seventy years. But it was a weakness in which there abode an element of strength. No facile theorizer he. Only as the clearly ascertained teaching of the Word slowly and painfully acquired moved him, did he move at all. Steadily and surely his thought worked its way through the problems presented to it; solidly but slowly. He left behind him, therefore, a structure which was not complete: but what he built he built to last. Had he been granted, perhaps, ten years longer of vigorous life, he might have thought his way through this problem also. He bequeathed it to the Church for solution, and the Church required a thousand years for the task. But even so, it is Augustine who gave us the Reformation. For what was the Reformation, inwardly considered, but the triumph of Augustine's doctrine of grace over Augustine's doctrine of the Church?

---

of predestinating grace was the fundamental principle of his religious consciousness. *It* must be unconditionally maintained, while all else must give way to it."

V

AUGUSTINE AND THE PELAGIAN
CONTROVERSY

AUGUSTINE AND THE PELAGIAN CONTROVERSY [1]

I. THE ORIGIN AND NATURE OF PELAGIANISM

IT was inevitable that the energy of the Church in intellectually realizing and defining its doctrines in relation to one another, should first be directed towards the objective side of Christian truth. The chief controversies of the first four centuries and the resulting definitions of doctrine concerned the nature of God and the person of Christ; and it was not until these theological and Christological questions were well upon their way to final settlement, that the Church could turn its attention to the more subjective side of truth. Meanwhile she bore in her bosom a full recognition, side by side, of the freedom of the will, the evil consequences of the fall, and the necessity of divine grace for salvation. Individual writers, or even the several sections of the Church, might exhibit a tendency to throw emphasis on one or another of the elements that made up this deposit of faith that was the common inheritance of all. The East, for instance, laid especial stress on free will: and the West dwelt more pointedly on the ruin of the human race and the absolute need of God's grace for salvation. But neither did the Eastern theologians forget the universal sinfulness and need of redemption, or the necessity, for the realization of that redemption, of God's gracious influences; nor did those of the West deny the self-determination or accountability of men. All the elements of the composite doctrine of man were everywhere confessed; but they were variously emphasized, according to the temper of the writers or the controversial demands of the times. Such a state of affairs, however, was an invita-

[1] From " A Select Library of the Nicene and Post-Nicene Fathers of the Christian Church," First Series, v. pp. xiii.–lxxi. Used by permission of the publishers, Charles Scribner's Sons.

tion to heresy, and a prophecy of controversy; just as the simultaneous confession of the unity of God and the deity of Christ, or of the deity and the humanity of Christ, inevitably carried in its train a series of heresies and controversies, until the definitions of the doctrines of the Trinity and of the person of Christ were complete. In like manner, it was inevitable that sooner or later someone should arise who would do so one-sidedly emphasize one element or the other of the Church's teaching as to salvation, as to throw himself into heresy, and drive the Church, through controversy with him, into a precise definition of the doctrines of free will and grace in their mutual relations.

This new heresiarch came, at the opening of the fifth century, in the person of the British monk, Pelagius. The novelty of the doctrine which he taught is repeatedly asserted by Augustine,[2] and is evident to the historian; but it consisted not in the emphasis that he laid on free will, but rather in the fact that, in emphasizing free will, he denied the ruin of the race and the necessity of grace. This was not only new in Christianity; it was even anti-Christian. Jerome, as well as Augustine, saw this at the time, and speaks of Pelagianism as the " heresy of Pythagoras and Zeno ";[3] and modern writers of the various schools have more or less fully recognized it. Thus Dean Milman thinks that " the greater part " of Pelagius' letter to Demetrias " might have been written by an ancient academic ";[4] and Bishop Hefele openly declares that their fundamental doctrine, that " man is virtuous entirely of his own merit, not of the gift of grace," seems to him " to be a rehabilitation of the general heathen view of the world," and compares with it Cicero's words:[5] " For all the blessings of life, we have to re-

[2] " On the Merits and Remission of Sins," iii. 6, 11, 12; " Against Two Letters of the Pelagians," iv. 32; " The Unfinished Work Against Julian," i. 2; " On Heresies," 88; and often elsewhere. Jerome found *roots* for the theory in Origen and Rufinus (*Letter* 133. 3), but this is a different matter. Compare " On Original Sin," 25.

[3] Preface to Book iv. of his work on Jeremiah.

[4] " History of Latin Christianity," 1899, i. p. 166, note [2].

[5] " De Natura Deorum," iii. 36.

turn thanks to the Gods; but no one ever returned thanks to God for virtue." [The struggle with Pelagianism was thus in reality a struggle for the very foundations of Christianity; and even more dangerously than in the previous theological and Christological controversies, here the practical substance of Christianity was in jeopardy. The real question at issue was whether there was any need for Christianity at all; whether by his own power man might not attain eternal felicity; whether the function of Christianity was to save, or only to render an eternity of happiness more easily attainable by man.[7]

Genetically speaking, Pelagianism was the daughter of legalism; but when it itself conceived, it brought forth an essential deism. It is not without significance that its originators were " a certain sort of monks "; that is, laymen of ascetic life. From this point of view the Divine law is looked upon as a collection of separate commandments, moral perfection as a simple complex of separate virtues, and a distinct value as a meritorious demand on Divine approbation is ascribed to each good work or attainment in the exercises of piety. It was because this was essentially his point of view that Pelagius could regard man's powers as sufficient to the attainment of sanctity — nay, that he could even assert it to be possible for a man to do more than was required of him. But this involved an essentially deistic conception of man's relations to his Maker. God had endowed His creature with a capacity (*possibilitas*) or ability (*posse*) for action, and it was for him to use it. Man was thus a machine, which, just because it was well made, needed no Divine interference for its right working; and the Creator, having once framed him, and endowed him with the *posse*, henceforth leaves the *velle* and the *esse* to him.

At this point we have touched the central and formative principle of Pelagianism. It lies in the assumption of the plenary ability of man; his ability to do all that righteousness

---

[6] " A History of the Councils of the Church," (E. T.) ii. p. 446, note [3].

[7] Compare the excellent statement in Thomasius' " Die Christliche Dogmengeschichte," i. p. 483.

can demand — to work out not only his own salvation, but also his own perfection. This is the core of the whole theory; and all the other postulates not only depend upon it, but arise out of it. Both chronologically and logically this is the root of the system.

When we first hear of Pelagius, he is already advanced in years, living in Rome in the odour of sanctity,[8] and enjoying a well-deserved reputation for zeal in exhorting others to a good life, which grew especially warm against those who endeavoured to shelter themselves, when charged with their sins, behind the weakness of nature.[9] He was outraged by the universal excuses on such occasions — "It is hard!" "it is difficult!" "we are not able!" "we are men!" — "Oh, blind madness!" he cried: "we accuse God of a twofold ignorance — that He does not seem to know what He has made, nor what He has commanded — as if forgetting the human weakness of which He is Himself the Author, He has imposed laws on man which He cannot endure."[10] He himself tells us[11] that it was his custom, therefore, whenever he had to speak on moral improvement and the conduct of a holy life, to begin by pointing out the power and quality of human nature, and by showing what it was capable of doing. For (he says) he esteemed it of small use to exhort men to what they deemed impossible: hope must rather be our companion, and all longing and effort die when we despair of attaining. So exceedingly ardent an advocate was he of man's unaided ability to do all that God commanded, that when Augustine's noble and entirely scriptural prayer — "Give what Thou commandest, and command what Thou wilt" — was repeated in his hearing, he was unable to endure it; and somewhat inconsistently contradicted it with such violence as almost to become involved in a strife.[12] The powers of man, he held, were gifts of God; and it was, there-

---

[8] "On the Proceedings of Pelagius," 46; "On the Merits and Remission of Sins," iii. 1; "Epist." 186, etc.

[9] "On Nature and Grace," 1.

[10] Pelagius' "Epistle to Demetrias," 16.

[11] *Ibid.*, 2.

[12] "On the Gift of Perseverance," 53.

fore, a reproach against Him as if He had made man ill or evil,
to believe that they were insufficient for the keeping of His
law. Nay, do what we will, we cannot rid ourselves of their
sufficiency: "whether we will, or whether we will not, we
have the capacity of not sinning." [13] "I say," he says, "that
man is able to be without sin, and that he is able to keep
the commandments of God;" and this sufficiently direct statement of human ability is in reality the hinge of his whole
system.

There were three specially important corollaries which
flowed from this assertion of human ability, and Augustine
himself recognized these as the chief elements of the system. [14]
It would be inexplicable on such an assumption, if no man had
ever used his ability in keeping God's law; and Pelagius consistently asserted not only that all might be sinless if they
chose, but also that many saints, even before Christ, had actually lived free from sin. Again, it follows from man's inalien-
able ability to be free from sin, that each man comes into the
world without entailment of sin or moral weakness from the
past acts of men; and Pelagius consistently denied the whole
doctrine of original sin. And still again, it follows from the
same assumption of ability that man has no need of supernatural assistance in his striving to obey righteousness; and
Pelagius consistently denied both the need and reality of divine
grace in the sense of an inward help (and especially of a prevenient help) to man's weakness.

It was upon this last point that the greatest stress was
laid in the controversy, and Augustine was most of all disturbed that thus God's grace was denied and opposed. No
doubt the Pelagians spoke constantly of "grace," but they
meant by this the primal endowment of man with free will,
and the subsequent aid given him in order to its proper use by
the revelation of the law and the teaching of the gospel, and,
above all, by the forgiveness of past sins in Christ and by

[13] "On Nature and Grace," 57.
[14] "On the Gift of Perseverance," 4; "Against Two Letters of the Pelagians," iii. 24; iv. 2 sq.

Christ's holy example.] Anything further than this external help they utterly denied; and they denied that this external help itself was absolutely necessary, affirming that it only rendered it easier for man to do what otherwise he had plenary ability for doing. Chronologically, this contention seems to have preceded the assertion which must logically lie at its base, of the freedom of man from any taint, corruption, or weakness due to sin. It was in order that they might deny that man needed help, that they denied that Adam's sin had any further effect on his posterity than might arise from his bad example. "Before the action of his own proper will," said Pelagius plainly, "that only is in man which God made." [16] "As we are procreated without virtue," he said, "so also without vice." [17] In a word, "Nothing that is good and evil, on account of which we are either praiseworthy or blameworthy, is born with us — it is rather done by us; for we are born with capacity for either, but provided with neither." [18] So his later follower, Julian, plainly asserts his "faith that God creates men obnoxious to no sin, but full of natural innocence, and with capacity for voluntary virtues." [19] So intrenched is free will in nature, that, according to Julian, it is "just as complete after sins as it was before sins;" [20] and what this means may be gathered from Pelagius' definition in the "Confession of Faith," that he sent to Innocent: "We say that man is always able both to sin and not to sin, so as that we may confess that we have free will." That sin in such circumstances was so common as to be well-nigh universal, was accounted for by the bad example of Adam and the power of habit, the latter being simply the result of imitation of the former. "Nothing makes well-doing so hard," writes Pelagius to Demetrias, "as the

---

[15] "On the Spirit and Letter," 4; "On Nature and Grace," 53; "On the Proceedings of Pelagius," 20, 22, 38; "On the Grace of Christ," 2, 3, 8, 31, 42, 45; "Against Two Letters of the Pelagians," iv. 11; "On Grace and Free Will," 23–26, and often.   [17] *Ibid.*

[16] "On Original Sin," 14.   [18] *Ibid.*

[19] "The Unfinished Work Against Julian," iii. 82.

[20] Do. i. 91; compare do. i. 48, 60; ii. 20. "There is nothing of sin in man, if there is nothing of his own will." "There is no original sin in infants at all."

long custom of sins which begins from childhood and gradually brings us more and more under its power until it seems to
have in some degree the force of nature (*vim naturæ*)." He is
even ready to allow for the force of habit in a broad way, on
the world at large; and so divides all history into progressive
periods, marked by God's (external) grace. At first the light of
nature was so strong that men by it alone could live in holiness. And it was only when men's manners became corrupt
and tarnished nature began to be insufficient for holy living,
that by God's grace the Law was given as an addition to mere
nature; and by it " the original lustre was restored to nature
after its blush had been impaired." And so again, after the
habit of sinning once more prevailed among men, and "the
law became unequal to the task of curing it," [21] Christ was
given, furnishing men with forgiveness of sins, exhortations to
imitation of the example and the holy example itself.[22] But
though thus a progressive deterioration was confessed, and
such a deterioration as rendered desirable at least two supernatural interpositions (in the giving of the law and the coming
of Christ), yet no corruption of nature, even by growing habit,
is really allowed. It was only an ever-increasing facility in imi-
tating vice which arose from so long a schooling in evil; and all
that was needed to rescue men from it was a new explanation
of what was right (in the law), or, at the most, the encouragement of forgiveness for what was already done, and a holy example (in Christ) for imitation. Pelagius still asserted our continuous possession of "a free will which is unimpaired for
sinning and for not sinning;" and Julian, that "our free will is
just as full after sins as it was before sins;" although Augustine does not fail to twit him with a charge of inconsistency.[23]

The peculiar individualism of the Pelagian view of the
world comes out strongly in their failure to perceive the effect
of habit on nature itself. Just as they conceived of virtue as a
complex of virtuous acts, so they conceived of sin exclusively

[21] " On Original Sin," 30.
[22] " On the Grace of Christ," 43.
[23] " The Unfinished Work," i. 91; compare 69.

as an act, or series of disconnected acts. They appear not to
have risen above the essentially heathen view which had no
notion of holiness apart from a series of acts of holiness, or of
sin apart from a like series of sinful acts.[24] Thus the will was
isolated from its acts, and the acts from each other, and all or-
ganic connection or continuity of life was not only overlooked
but denied.[25] After each act of the will, man stood exactly where
he did before: indeed, this conception scarcely allows for the
existence of a " man " — only a willing machine is left, at each
click of the action of which the spring regains its original position, and is equally ready as before to reperform its function.
In such a conception there was no place for character: freedom of will was all. Thus it was not an unnatural mistake
which they made, when they forgot the man altogether, and
attributed to the faculty of free will, under the name of " *possibilitas* " or " *posse*," the ability that belonged rather to the
man whose faculty it is, and who is properly responsible for the
use he makes of it. Here lies the essential error of their doctrine
of free will: they looked upon freedom in its *form* only, and not
in its *matter;* and, keeping man in perpetual and hopeless
equilibrium between good and evil, they permitted no growth
of character and no advantage to himself to be gained by man
in his successive choices of good. It need not surprise us that
the type of thought which thus dissolved the organism of the
man into a congeries of disconnected voluntary acts, failed to
comprehend the solidarity of the race. To the Pelagian, Adam
was a man, nothing more; and it was simply unthinkable that
any act of his that left his own subsequent acts uncommitted,
could entail sin and guilt upon other men. The same alembic
that dissolved the individual into a succession of voluntary
acts, could not fail to separate the race into a heap of uncon-

[24] Dr. Matheson finely says (*Expositor*, i. ix. 21, 1879), " There is the same
difference between the Christian and the Pagan idea of Prayer as there is between the Christian and Pagan idea of sin. Paganism knows nothing of sin,
it knows only of sins: it has no conception of the principle of evil; it com-
prehends only a collection of evil acts." This is Pelagianism too.

[25] Compare Schaff, " History of the Christian Church," iii. 804; and
Thomasius' " Die Christliche Dogmengeschichte," i. 487–488.

nected units. If sin, as Julian declared, is nothing but will, and the will itself remained intact after each act, how could the individual act of an individual will condition the acts of men as yet unborn? By "imitation" of his act alone could (under such a conception) other men be affected. And this carried with it the corresponding view of man's relation to Christ. He could forgive us the sins we had committed; He could teach us the true way; He could set us a holy example; and He could exhort us to its imitation. But He could not touch us to enable us to will the good, without destroying the absolute equilibrium of the will between good and evil; and to destroy this was to destroy its freedom, which was the crowning good of our divinely created nature. Surely the Pelagians forgot that man was not made for will, but will for man.

In defending their theory, as we are told by Augustine, there were five claims that they especially made for it.[26] It allowed them to praise as was their due, the creature that God had made, the marriage that He had instituted, the law that He had given, the free will which was His greatest endowment to man, and the saints who had followed His counsels. By this they meant that they proclaimed the sinless perfection of human nature in every man as he was brought into the world, and opposed this to the doctrine of original sin; the purity and holiness of marriage and the sexual appetites, and opposed this to the doctrine of the transmission of sin; the ability of the law, as well as and apart from the gospel, to bring men into eternal life, and opposed this to the necessity of inner grace; the integrity of free will to choose the good, and opposed this to the necessity of divine aid; and the perfection of the lives of the saints, and opposed this to the doctrine of universal sinfulness. Other questions, concerning the origin of souls, the necessity of baptism for infants, the original immortality of Adam, lay more on the skirts of the controversy, and were rather consequences of their teaching than parts of it. As it was an obvious fact that all men died, they could not admit that Adam's death was a consequence of sin lest they should

[26] " Against Two Letters of the Pelagians," iii. 25, and iv. at the beginning.

be forced to confess that his sin had injured all men; they therefore asserted that physical death belonged to the very nature of man, and that Adam would have died even had he not sinned.[27] So, as it was impossible to deny that the Church everywhere baptized infants, they could not refuse them baptism without confessing themselves innovators in doctrine; and therefore they contended that infants were not baptized for forgiveness of sins, but in order to attain a higher state of salvation. Finally, they conceived that if it was admitted that souls were directly created by God for each birth, it could not be asserted that they came into the world soiled by sin and under condemnation; and therefore they loudly championed this theory of the origin of souls.

The teachings of the Pelagians, it will be readily seen, easily welded themselves into a system, the essential and formative elements of which were entirely new in the Christian Church; and this startlingly new reading of man's condition, powers, and dependence for salvation, it was, that broke like a thunderbolt upon the Western Church at the opening of the fifth century, and forced her to reconsider, from the foundations, her whole teaching as to man and his salvation.

II. The External History of the Pelagian Controversy

Pelagius seems to have been already somewhat softened by increasing age when he came to Rome about the opening of the fifth century. He was also constitutionally averse to controversy; and although in his zeal for Christian morals, and in his conviction that no man would attempt to do what he was not persuaded he had natural power to perform, he diligently propagated his doctrines privately, he was careful to rouse no opposition, and was content to make what progress he could quietly and without open discussion. His methods of work sufficiently appear in the pages of his "Commentary on the Epistles of Saint Paul," which was written and published during

---

[27] This belongs to the earlier Pelagianism; Julian was ready to admit that death came from Adam, but not sin.

these years, and which exhibits learning and a sober and correct but somewhat shallow exegetical skill. In this work, he manages to give expression to all the main elements of his system, but always introduces them indirectly, not as the true exegesis, but by way of objections to the ordinary teaching, which were in need of discussion. The most important fruit of his residence in Rome was the conversion to his views of the Advocate Cœlestius, who brought the courage of youth and the argumentative training of a lawyer to the propagation of the new teaching. It was through him that it first broke out into public controversy, and received its first ecclesiastical examination and rejection. Fleeing from Alaric's second raid on Rome, the two friends landed together in Africa (A.D. 411), whence Pelagius soon afterwards departed for Palestine, leaving the bolder and more contentious [28] Cœlestius behind at Carthage. Here Cœlestius sought ordination as a presbyter. But the Milanese deacon Paulinus stood forward in accusation of him as a heretic, and the matter was brought before a synod under the presidency of Bishop Aurelius.[29]

Paulinus' charge consisted of seven items,[30] which asserted that Cœlestius taught the following heresies: that Adam was made mortal, and would have died, whether he sinned or did not sin; that the sin of Adam injured himself alone, not the human race; that new-born children are in that state in which Adam was before his sin; that the whole human race does not, on the one hand, die on account of the death or the fall of Adam, nor, on the other, rise again on account of the resurrection of Christ; that infants, even though not baptized, have eternal life; that the law leads to the kingdom of heaven in the same way as the gospel; and that, even before the Lord's coming, there had been men without sin. Only two fragments of

---

[28] "On Original Sin," 13.

[29] Early in 412, or, less probably, according to the Ballerini and Hefele 411.

[30] See "On Original Sin," 2, 3, 13; "On the Proceedings of Pelagius," 23. They are also given by Marius Mercator (Migne, "Patrologia Latina," xlviii. 69, 70), and the fifth item (on the salvation of unbaptized infants) omitted — though apparently by an error.

the proceedings of the synod in investigating this charge have come down to us; [31] but it is easy to see that Cœlestius was contumacious, and refused to reject any of the propositions charged against him, except the one which had reference to the salvation of infants that die unbaptized — the sole one that admitted of sound defence. As touching the transmission of sin, he would only say that it was an open question in the Church, and that he had heard both opinions from Church dignitaries; so that the subject needed investigation, and should not be made the ground for a charge of heresy. The natural result was that, on refusing to condemn the propositions charged against him, he was himself condemned and excommunicated by the synod. Soon afterwards he sailed to Ephesus, where he obtained the ordination which he sought.

Meanwhile Pelagius was living quietly in Palestine, whither in the summer of 415 a young Spanish presbyter, Paulus Orosius by name, came with letters from Augustine to Jerome, and was invited, near the end of July in that year, to a diocesan synod, presided over by John of Jerusalem. There he was asked about Pelagius and Cœlestius, and proceeded to give an account of the condemnation of the latter at the synod of Carthage, and of Augustine's literary refutation of the former. Pelagius was sent for, and the proceedings became an examination into his teachings. The chief matter brought up was his assertion of the possibility of men living sinlessly in this world; but the favor of the bishop towards him, the intemperance of Orosius, and the difficulty of communication between the parties arising from difference of language, combined so to clog proceedings that nothing was done; and the whole matter, as Western in its origin, was referred to the Bishop of Rome for examination and decision.[32]

Soon afterwards two Gallic bishops — Heros of Arles, and Lazarus of Aix — who were then in Palestine, lodged a formal accusation against Pelagius with the metropolitan, Eulogius

[31] Preserved by Augustine, "On Original Sin," 3, 4.

[32] An account of this synod is given by Orosius himself in his " Apology for the Freedom of the Will."

of Cæsarea; and he convened a synod of fourteen bishops which met at Lydda (Diospolis), in December of the same year (415), for the trial of the case. Perhaps no greater ecclesiastical farce was ever enacted than this synod exhibited.[33] When the time arrived, the accusers were prevented from being present by illness, and Pelagius was confronted only by the written accusation. This was both unskilfully drawn, and was written in Latin which the synod did not understand. It was, therefore, not even consecutively read, and was only head by head rendered into Greek by an interpreter. Pelagius began by reading aloud several letters to himself from various men of reputation in the Episcopate — among them a friendly note from Augustine. Thoroughly acquainted with both Latin and Greek, he was enabled skilfully to thread every difficulty, and pass safely through the ordeal. Jerome called this a "miserable synod," and not unjustly: at the same time it is sufficient to vindicate the honesty and earnestness of the bishops' intentions, that even in such circumstances, and despite the more undeveloped opinions of the East on the questions involved, Pelagius escaped condemnation only by a course of most ingenious disingenuousness, and only at the cost both of disowning Cœlestius and his teachings, of which he had been the real father, and of leading the synod to believe that he was anathematizing the very doctrines which he was himself proclaiming. There is really no possibility of doubting, as any one will see who reads the proceedings of the synod, that Pelagius obtained his acquittal here either by a "lying condemnation or a tricky interpretation"[34] of his own teachings; and Augustine is perfectly justified in asserting that the heresy was not acquitted, but the man who denied the heresy,[35] and who would himself have been anathematized had he not anathematized the heresy.

However obtained, the acquittal of Pelagius was yet an accomplished fact. Neither he nor his friends delayed to make

[33] A full account and criticism of the proceedings are given by Augustine in his "On the Proceedings of Pelagius."

[34] "On Original Sin," 13, at the end.

[35] "On the Proceedings of Pelagius," 59, 60, *sq.*

the most widely extended use of their good fortune. Pelagius himself was jubilant. Accounts of the synodal proceedings were sent to the West, not altogether free from uncandid alterations; and Pelagius soon put forth a work " In Defence of Free Will," in which he triumphed in his acquittal and " explained his explanations " at the synod. Nor were the champions of the opposite opinion idle. As soon as the news arrived in North Africa, and before the authentic records of the synod had reached that region, the condemnation of Pelagius and Cœlestius was re-affirmed in two provincial synods — one, consisting of sixty-eight bishops, met at Carthage about midsummer of 416; and the other, consisting of about sixty bishops, met soon afterwards at Mileve (Mila). Thus Palestine and North Africa were arrayed against one another, and it became of great importance to obtain the support of the Patriarchal See of Rome. Both sides made the attempt, but fortune favored the Africans. Each of the North-African synods sent a synodal letter to Innocent I, then Bishop of Rome, engaging his assent to their action: to these, five bishops, Aurelius of Carthage and Augustine among them, added a third " familiar " letter of their own, in which they urged upon Innocent to examine into Pelagius' teaching, and provided him with the material on which he might base a decision. The letters reached Innocent in time for him to take advice of his clergy, and send favorable replies on Jan. 27, 417. In these he expressed his agreement with the African decisions, asserted the necessity of inward grace, rejected the Pelagian theory of infant baptism, and declared Pelagius and Cœlestius excommunicated until they should return to orthodoxy. In about six weeks more he was dead: but Zosimus, his successor, was scarcely installed in his place before Cœlestius appeared at Rome in person to plead his cause; while shortly afterwards letters arrived from Pelagius addressed to Innocent, and by an artful statement of his belief and a recommendation from Praylus, lately become bishop of Jerusalem in John's stead, he attempted to enlist Rome in his favor. Zosimus, who appears to have been a Greek and therefore inclined to make little of the merits of this Western controversy, went over to Cœlestius at once, upon his profession of willingness to anathematize all doctrines which the pontifical see had condemned or should condemn; and wrote a sharp and arrogant letter to Africa, proclaiming Cœlestius "catholic," and requiring the Africans to appear within two months at Rome to prosecute their charges, or else to abandon them. On the arrival of Pelagius' papers, this letter was followed by another (September, 417), in which Zosimus, with the approbation of the clergy, declared both Pelagius and Cœlestius to be orthodox, and severely rebuked the Africans for their hasty judgment. It is difficult to understand Zosimus' action in this matter: neither of the confessions presented by the accused teachers ought to have deceived him, and if he was seizing the occasion to magnify the Roman see, his mistake was dreadful. Late in 417, or early in 418, the African bishops assembled at Carthage, in number more than two hundred, and replied to Zosimus that they had decided that the sentence pronounced against Pelagius and Cœlestius should remain in force until they should unequivocally acknowledge that "we are aided by the grace of God, through Christ, not only to know, but to do what is right, in each single act, so that without grace we are unable to have, think, speak, or do anything pertaining to piety." This firmness made Zosimus waver. He answered swellingly but timidly, declaring that he had maturely examined the matter, but it had not been his intention finally to acquit Cœlestius; and now he had left all things in the condition in which they were before, but he claimed the right of final judgment to himself. Matters were hastening to a conclusion, however, that would leave him no opportunity to escape from the mortification of an entire change of front. This letter was written on the 21st of March, 418; it was received in Africa on the 29th of April; and on the very next day an imperial decree was issued from Ravenna ordering Pelagius and Cœlestius to be banished from Rome, with all who held their opinions; while on the next day, May 1, a plenary council of about two hundred bishops met at Carthage, and in nine canons condemned all the essential features of Pelagianism. Whether this simultaneous action was the result of skilful arrangement, can only be conjectured: its effect was in any case necessarily crushing. There could be no appeal from the civil decision, and it played directly into the hands of the African definition of the faith. The synod's nine canons part naturally into three triads.[36] The first of these deals with the relation of mankind to original sin, and anathematizes in turn those who assert that physical death is a necessity of nature, and not a result of Adam's sin; those who assert that new-born children derive nothing of original sin from Adam to be expiated by the laver of regeneration; and those who assert a distinction between the kingdom of heaven and eternal life, for entrance into the former of which alone baptism is necessary. The second triad deals with the nature of grace, and anathematizes those who assert that grace brings only remission of past sins, not aid in avoiding future ones; those who assert that grace aids us not to sin, only by teaching us what is sinful, not by enabling us to will and do what we know to be right; and those who assert that grace only enables us to do more easily what we should without it still be able to do. The third triad deals with the universal sinfulness of the race, and anathematizes those who assert that the apostles' (1 John i. 8) confession of sin is due only to their humility; those who say that " Forgive us our trespasses " in the Lord's Prayer, is pronounced by the saints, not for themselves, but for the sinners in their company; and those who say that the saints use these words of themselves only out of humility and not truly. Here we see a careful traversing of the whole ground of the controversy, with a conscious reference to the three chief contentions of the Pelagian teachers.[37]

The appeal to the civil power, by whomsoever made, was, of course, indefensible, although it accorded with the opinions of the day, and was entirely approved by Augustine. But it was the ruin of the Pelagian cause. Zosimus found himself forced either to go into banishment with his wards, or to desert their

---

[36] Compare Canon Bright's *Introduction* in his " Select Anti-Pelagian Treatises of St. Augustine," p. xli.

[37] See above, pp. 293–294, and the passages in Augustine cited in note 16.

cause. He appears never to have had any personal convictions on the dogmatic points involved in the controversy, and so, all the more readily, yielded to the necessity of the moment. He cited Cœlestius to appear before a council for a new examination; but that heresiarch consulted prudence, and withdrew from the city. Zosimus, possibly in the effort to appear a leader in the cause he had opposed, not only condemned and excommunicated the men whom less than six months before he had pronounced " orthodox " after a " mature consideration of the matters involved," but, in obedience to the imperial decree, issued a stringent paper which condemned Pelagius and the Pelagians, and affirmed the African doctrines as to corruption of nature, true grace, and the necessity of baptism. To this he required subscription from all bishops as a test of orthodoxy. Eighteen Italian bishops refused their signature, with Julian of Eclanum, henceforth to be the champion of the Pelagian party, at their head, and were therefore deposed, although several of them afterwards recanted, and were restored. In Julian, the heresy obtained an advocate, who, if aught could have been done for its re-instatement, would surely have proved successful. He was the boldest, the strongest, at once the most acute and the most weighty, of all the disputants of his party. But the ecclesiastical standing of this heresy was already determined. The policy of Zosimus' test act was imposed by imperial authority on North Africa in 419. The exiled bishops were driven from Constantinople by Atticus in 424; and they are said to have been condemned at a Cilician synod in 423, and at an Antiochian one in 424. Thus the East itself was preparing for the final act in the drama. The exiled bishops were with Nestorius at Constantinople in 429; and that patriarch unsuccessfully interceded for them with Cœlestine, then Bishop of Rome. The conjunction was ominous. And at the ecumenical synod at Ephesus in 431, we again find the " Cœlestians " side by side with Nestorius, sharers in his condemnation.

But Pelagianism did not so die as not to leave a legacy behind it. " Remainders of Pelagianism " [38] soon showed them-

---

[38] Prosper's phrase.

selves in Southern Gaul, where a body of monastic leaders attempted to find a middle ground on which they could stand, by allowing the Augustinian doctrine of assisting grace, but retaining the Pelagian conception of our self-determination to good. We first hear of them in 428, through letters from two laymen, Prosper and Hilary, to Augustine, as men who accepted original sin and the necessity of grace, but asserted that men began their turning to God, and God helped their beginning. They taught [39] that all men are sinners, and that they derive their sin from Adam; that they can by no means save themselves, but need God's assisting grace; and that this grace is gratuitous in the sense that men cannot really deserve it, and yet that it is not irresistible, nor given always without the occasion of its gift having been determined by men's attitude towards God; so that, though not given on account of the merits of men, it is given according to those merits, actual or foreseen. The leader of this new movement was John Cassian, a pupil of Chrysostom (to whom he attributed all that was good in his life and will), and the fountain-head of Gallic monasticism; and its chief champion at a somewhat later day was Faustus of Rhegium (Riez).

The Augustinian opposition was at first led by the vigorous controversialist, Prosper of Aquitaine, and, in the next century, by the wise, moderate, and good Cæsarius of Arles, who brought the contest to a conclusion in the victory of a softened Augustinianism. Already in 431 a letter was obtained from Pope Cœlestine, designed to close the controversy in favor of Augustinianism, and in 496 Pope Gelasius condemned the writings of Faustus in the first index of forbidden books; while, near the end of the first quarter of the sixth century, Pope Hormisdas was appealed to for a renewed condemnation. The end was now in sight. The famous second Synod of Orange met under the presidency of Cæsarius at that ancient town on the 3d of July, 529, and drew up a series of moderate articles which received the ratification of Boniface II in the following year.

---

[39] Augustine gives their teaching carefully in his " On the Predestination of the Saints," 2.

In these articles there is affirmed an anxiously guarded Augustinianism, a somewhat weakened Augustinianism, but yet a distinctive Augustinianism; and, so far as a formal condemnation could reach, semi-Pelagianism was suppressed by them in the whole Western Church. But councils and popes can only decree; and Cassian and Vincent and Faustus, despite Cæsarius and Boniface and Gregory, retained an influence among their countrymen which never died away.

III. Augustine's Part in the Controversy

Both by nature and by grace, Augustine was formed to be the champion of truth in this controversy. Of a naturally philosophical temperament, he saw into the springs of life with a vividness of mental perception to which most men are strangers; and his own experiences in his long life of resistance to, and then of yielding to, the drawings of God's grace, gave him a clear apprehension of the great evangelic principle that God seeks men, not men God, such as no sophistry could cloud. However much his philosophy or theology might undergo change in other particulars, there was one conviction too deeply imprinted upon his heart ever to fade or alter — the conviction of the ineffableness of God's grace. Grace — man's absolute dependence on God as the source of all good — this was the common, nay, the *formative* element, in all stages of his doctrinal development, which was marked only by the ever growing consistency with which he built his theology around this central principle. Already in 397 — the year after he became bishop — we find him enunciating with admirable clearness all the essential elements of his teaching, as he afterwards opposed them to Pelagius.[40] It was inevitable, therefore, that although he was rejoiced when he heard, some years later, of the zealous labors of this pious monk in Rome towards stemming the tide of luxury and sin, and esteemed him for his devout life, and

[40] Compare his work written this year, " On Several Questions to Simplicianus." For the development of Augustine's theology, see the admirable statement in Neander's " General History of the Christian Religion and Church," E. T. ii. 625 *sq.*

loved him for his Christian activity, he yet was deeply troubled when subsequent rumors reached him that he was "disputing against the grace of God." He tells us over and over
again, that this was a thing no pious heart could endure; and
we perceive that, from this moment, Augustine was only biding
his time, and awaiting a fitting opportunity to join issue with
the denier of the Holy of holies of his whole, I will not say
theology merely, but life. "Although I was grieved by this,"
he says, "and it was told me by men whom I believed, I yet
desired to have something of such sort from his own lips or in
some book of his, so that, if I began to refute it, he would not
be able to deny it." [41] Thus he actually excuses himself for not
entering into the controversy earlier. When Pelagius came to
Africa, then, it was almost as if he had deliberately sought his
fate. But circumstances secured a lull before the storm. He
visited Hippo; but Augustine was absent, although he did not
fail to inform himself on his return that Pelagius while there
had not been heard to say "anything at all of this kind." The
controversy against the Donatists was now occupying all the
energies of the African Church, and Augustine himself was a
ruling spirit in the great conference now holding at Carthage
with them. While there, he was so immersed in this business,
that, although he once or twice saw the face of Pelagius, he
had no conversation with him; and although his ears were
wounded by a casual remark which he heard, to the effect "that
infants were not baptized for remission of sins, but for consecration to Christ," he allowed himself to pass over the matter,
"because there was no opportunity to contradict it, and those
who said it were not such men as could cause him solicitude
for their influence." [42]

It appears from these facts, given us by himself, that Augustine was not only ready for, but was looking for, the coming
controversy. It can scarcely have been a surprise to him when
Paulinus accused Cœlestius (412); and, although he was not a
member of the council which condemned him, it was inevitable

[41] "On the Proceedings of Pelagius," 46.
[42] "On the Merits and Remission of Sins," iii. 12.

that he should at once take the leading part in the consequent controversy. Cœlestius and his friends did not silently submit to the judgment that had been passed upon their teaching: they could not openly propagate their heresy, but they were diligent in spreading their plaints privately and by subterraneous whispers among the people.[43] This was met by the Catholics in public sermons and familiar colloquies held everywhere. But this wise rule was observed — to contend against the erroneous teachings, but to keep silence as to the teachers, that so (as Augustine explains [44]) "the men might rather be brought to see and acknowledge their error through fear of ecclesiastical judgment than be punished by the actual judgment." Augustine was abundant in these oral labors; and many of his sermons directed against Pelagian error have come down to us, although it is often impossible to be sure as to their date. For one of them (170) he took his text from Phil. iii. 6–16, "as touching the righteousness which is by the law blameless; howbeit what things were gain to me, those have I counted loss for Christ. . . ." He begins by asking how the apostle could count his blameless conversation according to the righteousness which is from the law as dung and loss, and then proceeds to explain the purpose for which the law was given, our state by nature and under law, and the kind of blamelessness that the law could produce, ending by showing that man can have no righteousness except from God, and no perfect righteousness except in heaven. Three others (174, 175, 176) had as their text 1 Tim. i. 15, 16, and developed its teaching, that the universal sin of the world and its helplessness in sin constituted the necessity of the incarnation; and especially that the necessity of Christ's grace for salvation was just as great for infants as for adults. Much is very forcibly said in these sermons which was afterwards incorporated in his treatises. "There was no reason," he insists, "for the coming of Christ the Lord except to save sinners. Take away diseases, take away wounds, and there is no reason for medicine. If the great Physician came from heaven,

---

[43] "Epist." 157. 22.
[44] "On the Proceedings of Pelagius," 46.

a great sick man was lying ill through the whole world. That sick man is the human race" (175, 1). "He who says, 'I am not a sinner,' or 'I was not,' is ungrateful to the Saviour. No one of men in that mass of mortals which flows down from Adam, no one at all of men is not sick: no one is healed without the grace of Christ. Why do you ask whether infants are sick from Adam? For they, too, are brought to the church; and, if they cannot run thither on their own feet, they run on the feet of others that they may be healed. Mother Church accommodates others' feet to them so that they may come, others' heart so that they may believe, others' tongue so that they may confess; and, since they are sick by another's sin, so when they are healed they are saved by another's confession in their behalf. Let, then, no one buzz strange doctrines to you. *This* the Church has always had, has always held; this she has received from the faith of the elders; this she will perseveringly guard until the end. Since the whole have no need of a physician, but only the sick, what need, then, has the infant of Christ, if he is not sick? If he is well, why does he seek the physician through those who love him? If, when infants are brought, they are said to have no sin of inheritance (*peccatum propaginis*) at all, and yet come to Christ, why is it not said in the church to those that bring them, 'Take these innocents hence; the physician is not needed by the well, but by the sick; Christ came not to call the just, but sinners'? It never has been said, and it never will be said. Let each one therefore, brethren, speak for him who cannot speak for himself. It is much the custom to intrust the inheritance of orphans to the bishops; how much more the grace of infants! The bishop protects the orphan lest he should be oppressed by strangers, his parents being dead. Let him cry out more for the infant who, he fears, will be slain by his parents. Who comes to Christ has something in him to be healed; and he who has not, has no reason for seeking the physician. Let parents choose one of two things: let them either confess that there is sin to be healed in their infants, or let them cease bringing them to the physician. This is something else than to wish to bring a well person to the physician. Why do you bring him? To be baptized. Whom? The infant. To whom do you bring him? To Christ. To Him, of course, who came into the world? Certainly, he says. Why did He come into the world? To save sinners. Then he whom you bring has in him that which needs saving? " [45] So again: " He who says that the age of infancy does not need Jesus' salvation, says nothing else than that the Lord Christ is not *Jesus* to faithful infants; i.e., to infants baptized in Christ. For what is *Jesus? Jesus* means saviour. He is not Jesus to those whom He does not save, who do not need to be saved. Now, if your hearts can bear that Christ is not *Jesus* to any of the baptized, I do not know how you can be acknowledged to have sound faith. They are infants, but they are made members of Him. They are infants, but they receive His sacraments. They are infants, but they become partakers of His table, so that they may have life." [46] The preveniency of grace is explicitly asserted in these sermons. In one he says, " Zacchaeus was seen, and saw; but unless he had been seen, he would not have seen. For ' whom He predestinated, them also He called.' . . . In order that we may see, we are seen; that we may love, we are loved. 'My God, may His pity prevent me!' " [47] And in another, at more length: " His calling has preceded you, so that you may have a good will. Cry out, 'My God, let Thy mercy prevent me ' (Ps. lix. 10). That you may be, that you may feel, that you may hear, that you may consent, His mercy prevents you. It prevents you in all things; and do you too prevent His judgment in something. In what, do you say? In what? In confessing that you have all these things from God, whatever you have of good; and from yourself whatever you have of evil " (176. 5). " We owe therefore to Him that we are, that we are alive, that we understand: that we are men, that we live well, that we understand aright, we owe to Him. Nothing is ours except the sin that we have. For what have we that we did not receive? " (1 Cor. iv. 7) (176. 6).

It was not long, however, before the controversy was driven

---

[45] " Sermon " 176. 2.   [46] " Sermon " 174. 7.   [47] Do.

out of the region of sermons into that of regular treatises. The occasion for Augustine's first appearance in a written document bearing on the controversy, was given by certain questions which were sent to him for answer by "the tribune and notary" Marcellinus, with whom he had cemented his intimacy at Carthage, the previous year, when this notable official was presiding, by the emperor's orders, over the great conference of the Catholics and Donatists. The mere fact that Marcellinus, still at Carthage, where Cœlestius had been brought to trial, wrote to Augustine at Hippo for written answers to important questions connected with the Pelagian heresy, speaks volumes for the prominent position he had already assumed in the controversy. The questions that were sent, concerned the connection of death with sin, the transmission of sin, the possibility of a sinless life, and especially infants' need of baptism.[48] Augustine was immersed in abundant labors when they reached him: [49] but he could not resist this appeal, and that the less as the Pelagian controversy had already grown to a place of the first importance in his eyes. The result was his treatise, " On the Merits and Remission of Sins and on the Baptism of Infants," consisting of two books, and written in 412. The first book of this work is an argument for original sin, drawn from the universal reign of death in the world (2–8), from the teaching of Rom. v. 12–21 (9–20), and chiefly from the baptism of infants (21–70).[50] It opens by exploding the Pelagian contention that death is of nature, and Adam would have died even had he not sinned, by showing that the penalty threatened to Adam included physical death (Gen. iii. 19), and that it is due to him that we all die (Rom. viii. 10, 11; 1 Cor. xv. 21) (2–8). Then the Pelagian assertion that we are

[48] " On the Merits and Remission of Sins," iii. 1.

[49] Do., i. 1. Compare " Epist." 139.

[50] On the prominence of infant baptism in the controversy, and why it was so, see " Sermon " 165. 7 *sq.* " What do you say? ' Just this,' he says, ' that God creates every man immortal.' Why, then, do infant children die? For if I say, ' Why do adult men die? ' you would say to me, ' They have sinned.' Therefore I do not argue about the adults: I cite infancy as a witness against you," and so on, eloquently developing the argument.

injured in Adam's sin only by its bad example, which we imitate, not by any propagation from it, is tested by an exposition of Rom. v. 12 *sq.* (9–20). And then the main subject of the book is reached, and the writer sharply presses the Pelagians with the universal and primeval fact of the baptism of infants, as a proof of original sin (21–70). He tracks out all their subterfuges — showing the absurdity of the assertions that infants are baptized for the remission of sins that they have themselves committed since birth (22), or in order to obtain a higher stage of salvation (23–28), or because of sin committed in some previous state of existence (31–33). Then turning to the positive side, he shows at length that the Scriptures teach that Christ came to save sinners, that baptism is for the remission of sins, and that all that partake of it are confessedly sinners (34 *sq.*); then he points out that John iii. 3, 5, on which the Pelagians relied, cannot be held to distinguish between ordinary salvation and a higher form, under the name of " the kingdom of God " (58 *sq.*); and he closes by showing that the very manner in which baptism was administered, with its exorcism and exsufflation, implied the infant to be a sinner (63), and by suggesting that the peculiar helplessness of infancy, so different not only from the earliest age of Adam, but also from that of many young animals, may possibly be itself penal (64–69). The second book treats, with similar fulness, the question of the perfection of human righteousness in this life. After an exordium which speaks of the will and its limitations, and of the need of God's assisting grace (1–6), the writer raises four questions. First, whether it may be said to be possible, by God's grace, for a man to attain a condition of entire sinlessness in this life (7). This he answers in the affirmative. Secondly, he asks, whether any one has ever done this, or may ever be expected to do it, and answers in the negative on the testimony of Scripture (8–25). Thirdly, he asks why not, and replies briefly because men are unwilling, explaining at length what he means by this (26–33). Finally, he inquires whether any man has ever existed, exists now, or will ever exist, entirely without sin — this question differing from the second inasmuch as that asked after the attainment in this life of a state in which sinning should cease, while this seeks a man who has never been guilty of sin, implying the absence of original as well as of actual sin. After answering this in the negative (34), Augustine discusses anew the question of original sin. Here after expounding from the positive side (35–38) the condition of man in paradise, the nature of his probation, and of the fall and its effects both on him and his posterity, and the kind of redemption that has been provided in the incarnation, he proceeds to answer certain cavils (39 *sq.*), such as, " Why should children of baptized people need baptism? " — " How can a sin be remitted to the father and held against the child? " — " If physical death comes from Adam, ought we not to be released from it on believing in Christ? " — and concludes with an exhortation to hold fast to the exact truth, turning neither to the right nor left — neither saying that we have no sin, nor surrendering ourselves to our sin (57 *sq.*).

After these books were completed, Augustine came into possession of Pelagius' " Commentary on Paul's Epistles," which was written while he was living in Rome (before 410), and found it to contain some arguments that he had not treated — such arguments, he tells us, as he had not imagined could be held by any one.[51] Unwilling to re-open his finished argument, he now began a long supplementary letter to Marcellinus, which he intended to serve as a third and concluding book to his work. He was some time in completing this letter. He had asked to have the former two books returned to him; and it is a curious indication of his overworked state of mind, that he forgot what he wanted with them:[52] he visited Carthage while the letter was in hand, and saw Marcellinus personally; and even after his return to Hippo, it dragged along, amid many distractions, slowly towards completion. Meanwhile, a long letter was written to Honoratus, in which a section on the grace of the New Testament was incorporated.[53] At

[51] " On the Merits and Remission of Sins," iii. 1.
[52] " Epist." 139. 3.   [53] " Epist." 140.

length the promised supplement was completed. It was professedly a criticism of Pelagius' "Commentary," and therefore naturally mentioned his name; but Augustine even goes
out of his way to speak as highly of his opponent as he can [54] —
although it is apparent that his esteem is not very high for his
strength of mind, and is even less high for the moral quality
that led to his odd, oblique way of expressing his opinions.
There is even a half sarcasm in the way he speaks of Pelagius'
care and circumspection, which was certainly justified by the
event. The letter opens by stating and criticising in a very
acute and telling dialectic, the new arguments of Pelagius,
which were such as the following: "If Adam's sin injured
even those who do not sin, Christ's righteousness ought likewise to profit even those who do not believe" (2–4); "No
man can transmit what he has not; and hence, if baptism
cleanses from sin, the children of two baptized parents ought
to be free from sin"; "God remits one's own sins, and can
scarcely, therefore, impute another's to us"; and "if the soul
is created, it would certainly be unjust to impute Adam's alien
sin to it" (5). The stress of the letter, however, is laid upon
two contentions — 1. That whatever else may be ambiguous
in the Scriptures, they are perfectly clear that no man can
have eternal life except in Christ, who came to call sinners to
repentance (7); and 2. That original sin in infants has always
been, in the Church, one of the fixed facts, to be used as a basis
of argument, in order to reach the truth in other matters, and
has never itself been called in question before (10–14). At this
point, the writer returns to the second and third of the new
arguments of Pelagius mentioned above, and discusses them
more fully (15–20), closing with a recapitulation of the three
great points that had been raised; viz., that both death and
sin are derived from Adam's sin by all his posterity; that infants need salvation, and hence baptism; and that no man
ever attains in this life such a state of holiness that he cannot
truly pray, "Forgive us our trespasses."

Augustine was now to learn that one service often entails

[54] "On the Merits and Remission of Sins," iii. 1, 5.

another. Marcellinus wrote to say that he was puzzled by what had been said in the second book of this work, as to the possibility of man's attaining to sinlessness in this life, while yet it was asserted that no man ever had attained, or ever would attain, it. How, he asked, can that be said to be possible which is, and which will remain, unexampled? In reply, Augustine wrote, during this same year (412), and sent to his noble friend, another work, which he calls " On the Spirit and the Letter," from the prominence which he gives in it to the words of 2 Cor. iii. 6.[55] He did not content himself with a simple, direct answer to Marcellinus' question, but goes at length into a profound disquisition into the roots of the doctrine, and thus gives us, not a mere explanation of a former contention, but a new treatise on a new subject — the absolute necessity of the grace of God for any good living. He begins by explaining to Marcellinus that he has affirmed the possibility while denying the actuality of a sinless life, on the ground that all things are possible to God — even the passage of a camel through the eye of a needle, which nevertheless has never occurred (1, 2). For, in speaking of man's perfection, we are speaking really of a work of God — and one which is none the less His work because it is wrought through the instrumentality of man, and in the use of his free will. The Scriptures, indeed, teach that no man lives without sin, but this is only the proclamation of a matter of fact; and although it is thus contrary to fact and Scripture to assert that men may be found that live sinlessly, yet such an assertion would not be fatal heresy. What is unbearable, is that men should assert it to be possible for man, unaided by God, to attain this perfection. This is to speak against the grace of God: it is to put in man's power what is only possible to the almighty grace of God (3, 4). No doubt, even these men do not, in so many words, exclude the aid of grace in perfecting human life — they affirm God's help; but they make it consist in His gift to man of a perfectly free will, and in His addition to this of commandments and teachings which make known to him what he is to

[55] " Sermon " 163 treats the text similarly.

seek and what to avoid, and so enable him to direct his free will to what is good. What, however, does such a "grace" amount to? (5). Man needs something more than to know the right way: he needs to love it, or he will not walk in it; and all mere teaching, which can do nothing more than bring us knowledge of what we ought to do, is but the letter that killeth. What we need is some inward, Spirit-given aid to the keeping of what by the law we know ought to be kept. Mere knowledge slays; while to lead a holy life is the gift of God — not only because He has given us will, nor only because He has taught us the right way, but because by the Holy Spirit He sheds love abroad in the hearts of all those whom He has predestinated, and will call and justify and glorify (Rom. viii. 29, 30). To prove this, he states to be the object of the present treatise; and after investigating the meaning of 2 Cor. iii. 6, and showing that "the letter" there means the law as a system of precepts, which reveals sin rather than takes it away, points out the way rather than gives strength to walk in it, and therefore slays the soul by shutting it up under sin — while "the Spirit" is God's Holy Ghost who is shed abroad in our hearts to give us strength to walk aright — he undertakes to prove this position from the teachings of the Epistle to the Romans at large. This contention, it will be seen, cut at the very roots of Pelagianism: if all mere teaching slays the soul, as Paul asserts, then all that what they called "grace" could, when alone, do, was to destroy; and the upshot of "helping" man by simply giving him free will, and pointing out the way to him, would be the loss of the whole race. Not that the law is sin: Augustine teaches that it is holy and good, and God's instrument in salvation. Not that free will is done away: it is by free will that men are led into holiness. But the purpose of the law (he teaches) is to make men so feel their lost estate as to seek the help by which alone they may be saved; and will is only then liberated to do good when grace has made it free. "What the law of works enjoins by menace, that the law of faith secures by faith. What the law of works does is to say, 'Do what I command thee'; but

by the law of faith we say to God, ' Give me what thou commandest.' " (22).[56] In the midst of this argument, Augustine
is led to discuss the differentiating characteristics of the Old
and New Testaments; and he expounds at length (33–42) the
passage in Jer. xxxi. 31–34, showing that, in the prophet's
view, the difference between the two covenants is that in the
Old, the law is an external thing written on stones; while in
the New, it is written internally on the heart, so that men
now wish to do what the law prescribes. This writing on the
heart is nothing else, he explains, than the shedding abroad by
the Holy Spirit of love in our hearts, so that we love God's
will, and therefore freely do it. Towards the end of the treatise
(50–61), he treats in an absorbingly interesting way of the
mutual relations of free will, faith, and grace, contending that
all co-exist without the voiding of any. It is by free will that
we believe; but it is only as grace moves us, that we are able
to use our free will for believing; and it is only after we are
thus led by grace to believe, that we obtain all other goods. In
prosecuting this analysis, Augustine is led to distinguish very
sharply between the faculty and use of free will (58), as well
as between ability and volition (53). Faith is an act of the man
himself; but only as he is given the power from on high to
will to believe, will he believe (57, 60).

By this work, Augustine completed, in his treatment of
Pelagianism, the circle of that triad of doctrines which he
himself looked upon as most endangered by this heresy [57] —
original sin, that imperfection of human righteousness, the
necessity of grace. In his mind, the last was the kernel of the
whole controversy; and this was a subject which he could never
approach without some heightened fervor. This accounts for
the great attractiveness of the present work — through the
whole fabric of which runs the golden thread of the praise of
God's ineffable grace. In Canon Bright's opinion, it " perhaps,
next to the ' Confessions,' tells us most of the thoughts of that

[56] See this prayer beautifully illustrated from Scripture in *On the Merits
and Remission of Sins*, ii. 5.

[57] See above, p. 293.

' rich, profound, and affectionate mind ' on the soul's relations to its God." [58]

After the publication of these treatises, the controversy certainly did not lull; but it relapsed for nearly three years again, into less public courses. Meanwhile, Augustine was busy, among other most distracting cares ("Epist." 145. 1), still defending the grace of God, by letters and sermons. A fair illustration of his state of mind at this time may be obtained from his letter to Anastasius (145), which assuredly must have been written soon after the treatise " On the Spirit and the Letter." Throughout this letter, there are adumbrations of the same train of thought that filled this treatise; and there is one passage which may almost be taken as a summary of it. Augustine is so weary of the vexatious cares that filled his life, that he is ready to long for the everlasting rest, and yet bewails the weakness which allowed the sweetness of external things still to insinuate itself into his heart. Victory over, and emancipation from, this, he asserts, " cannot, without God's grace, be achieved by the human will, which is by no means to be called free so long as it is subject to enslaving lusts." Then he proceeds: " The law, therefore, by teaching and commanding what cannot be fulfilled without grace, demonstrates to man his weakness, in order that the weakness, thus proved, may resort to the Saviour, by whose healing the will may be able to do what it found impossible in its weakness. So, then, the law brings us to faith, faith obtains the Spirit in fuller measure, the Spirit sheds love abroad in us, and love fulfils the law. For this reason the law is called a schoolmaster under whose threatening and severity ' whosoever shall call on the name of the Lord shall be delivered.' But ' how shall they call on Him in whom they have not believed? ' Wherefore, that the letter without the Spirit may not kill, the life-giving Spirit is given to those that believe and call upon Him; but the love of God is poured out into our hearts by the Holy Spirit who is given to us, so that the words of the same apostle, ' Love is the fulfilling of the law,' may be realized. Thus the law

[58] As referred to above, note 36.

is good to him that uses it lawfully; and he uses it lawfully,
who, understanding wherefore it was given, betakes himself,
under the pressure of its threatening, to liberating grace.
Whoever ungratefully despises this grace by which the ungodly is justified, and trusts in his own strength for fulfilling
the law, being ignorant of God's righteousness, and going
about to establish his own righteousness, is not submitting
himself to the righteousness of God; and therefore the law is
made to him not a help to pardon, but the bond of guilt; not
because the law is evil, but because 'sin,' as it is written,
'works death to such persons by that which is good.' For by
the commandment, he sins more grievously, who, by the commandment, knows how evil are the sins which he commits."
Although Augustine states clearly that this letter is written
against those "who arrogate too much to the human will, im-
agining that, the law being given, the will is, of its own
strength, sufficient to fulfill the law, though not assisted by any
grace imparted by the Holy Ghost, in addition to instruction
in the law" — he refrains still from mentioning the names of
the authors of this teaching, evidently out of a lingering tenderness in his treatment of them. This will help us to explain
the courtesy of a note which he sent to Pelagius himself at
about this time, in reply to a letter he had received some time
before from him; of which Pelagius afterwards (at the Synod
of Diospolis) made, to say the least of it, an ungenerous use.
This note,[59] Augustine tells us, was written with "tempered
praises" (wherefrom we see his lessening respect for the
man), and so as to admonish Pelagius to think rightly concerning grace — so far as could be done without raising the
dregs of the controversy in a formal note. This he accomplished by praying from the Lord for him, those good things
by which he might be good forever, and might live eternally
with Him who is eternal; and by asking his prayers in return,
that he, too, might be made by the Lord such as he seemed to
suppose he already was. How Augustine could really intend
these prayers to be understood as an admonition to Pelagius

[59] "Epist." 146. See "On the Proceedings of Pelagius," 50, 51, 52.

to look to God for what he was seeking to work out for himself, is fully illustrated by the closing words of this almost contemporary letter to Anastasius: " Pray, therefore, for us," he writes, " that we may be righteous — an attainment wholly beyond a man's reach, unless he know righteousness, and be willing to practise it, but one which is immediately realized when he is perfectly willing; but this cannot be in him unless he is healed by the grace of the Spirit, and aided to be able." The point had already been made in the controversy, that, by the Pelagian doctrine, so much power was attributed to the human will, that no one ought to pray, " Lead us not into temptation, but deliver us from evil."

If he was anxious to avoid personal controversy with Pelagius himself in the hope that he might even yet be reclaimed, Augustine was equally anxious to teach the truth on all possible occasions. Pelagius had been intimate, when at Rome, with the pious Paulinus, bishop of Nola; and it was understood that there was some tendency at Nola to follow the new teachings. It was, perhaps, as late as 414, when Augustine made reply in a long letter,[60] to a request of Paulinus' for an exposition of certain difficult Scriptures, which had been sent him about 410.[61] Among them was Rom. xi. 28; and, in explaining it, Augustine did not withhold a tolerably complete account of his doctrine of predestination, involving the essence of his whole teaching as to grace: " For when he had said, ' according to the election they are beloved for their father's sake,' he added, ' for the gifts and calling of God are without repentance.' You see that those are certainly meant who belong to the number of the predestinated. . . . ' Many indeed are called,⁺ but few chosen '; but those who are elect, these are called ' according to His purpose '; and it is beyond doubt that in them God's foreknowledge cannot be deceived. These He foreknew and predestinated to be conformed to the image of His Son, in order that He might be the first born among many brethren. But ' whom He predestinated, them He also called.' This calling is ' according to His purpose,' this calling is ' without repent-

⁶⁰ " Epist." 149. See especially 18 sq.   ⁶¹ " Epist." 121.

ance,'" etc., quoting Rom. viii. 30–31. Then continuing, he
says, "Those are not in this vocation, who do not persevere
unto the end in the faith that worketh by love, although they
walk in it a little while. . . . But the reason why some belong to it, and some do not, can easily be hidden, but cannot
be unjust. For is there injustice with God? God forbid! For
this belongs to those high judgments which, so to say, terrified
the wondering apostle to look upon."

Among the most remarkable of the controversial sermons
that were preached about this time, especial mention is due to
two that were delivered at Carthage, midsummer of 413. The
former of these [62] was preached on the festival of John the
Baptist's birth (June 24), and naturally took the forerunner
for its subject. The nativity of John suggesting the nativity
of Christ, the preacher spoke of the marvel of the incarnation.
He who was in the beginning, and was the Word of God, and
was Himself God, and who made all things, and in whom was
life, even this one "came to us. To whom? To the worthy?
Nay, but to the unworthy! For Christ died for the ungodly,
and for the unworthy, though He was worthy. We indeed were
unworthy whom He pitied; but He was worthy who pitied us,
to whom we say, For Thy pity's sake, Lord, free us! Not for
the sake of our preceding merits, but for Thy pity's sake, Lord,
free us; and for Thy name's sake be propitious to our sins,'
not for our merit's sake. . . . For the merit of sins is, of
course, not reward, but punishment." He then dwelt upon the
necessity of the incarnation, and the necessity of a mediator
between God and "the whole mass of the human race alien-
ated from Him by Adam." Then quoting 1 Cor. iv. 7, he asserts that it is not our varying merits, but God's grace alone,
that makes us differ, and that we are all alike, great and small,
old and young, saved by one and the same Saviour. "What
then, some one says," he continues, "even the infant needs
a liberator? Certainly he needs one. And the witness to it is
the mother that faithfully runs to church with the child to be
baptized. The witness is Mother Church herself, who receives

[62] "Sermon" 293.

the child for washing, and either for dismissing him [from this life] freed, or nurturing him in piety. . . . Last of all, the tears of his own misery are witness in the child himself. . . . Recognize the misery, extend the help. Let all put on bowels of mercy. By as much as they cannot speak for themselves, by so much more pityingly let us speak for the little ones " — and then follows a passage calling on the Church to take the grace of infants in their charge as orphans committed to their care, which is in substance repeated from a former sermon.[63] The speaker proceeded to quote Matt. i. 21, and apply it. If Jesus came to save from sins, and infants are brought to Him, it is to confess that they, too, are sinners. Then, shall they be withheld from baptism? " Certainly, if the child could speak for himself, he would repel the voice of opposition, and cry out, ' Give me Christ's life! In Adam I died: give me Christ's life; in whose sight I am not clean, even if I am an infant whose life has been but one day in the earth.' " " No way can be found," adds the preacher, " of coming into the life of this world except by Adam; no way can be found of escaping punishment in the next world except by Christ. Why do you shut up the one door? " Even John the Baptist himself was born in sin; and absolutely no one can be found who was born apart from sin, until you find one who was born apart from Adam. " ' By one man sin entered into the world, and by sin, death; and so it passed through upon all men.' If these were my words, could this sentiment be expressed more expressly, more clearly, more fully? "

Three days afterwards,[64] on the invitation of the Bishop of Carthage, Augustine preached a sermon professedly directed against the Pelagians,[65] which takes up the threads hinted at in the former discourse, and develops a full polemic

---

[63] " Sermon " 176. 2.

[64] The inscription says, " V Calendas Julii," i.e., June 27; but it also says, " *In natalis martyris Guddentis*," whose day appears to have been July 18. Some of the martyrologies assign 28th of June to Gaudentius (which some copies read here), but possibly none to Guddene.

[65] " Sermon " 294.

with reference to the baptism of infants. He began, formally enough, with the determination of the question in dispute. The Pelagians concede that infants should be baptized. The only question is, for what are they baptized? We say that they would not otherwise have salvation and eternal life; but they say it is not for salvation, not for eternal life, but for the kingdom of God. " The child, they say, although not baptized, by the desert of his innocence, in that he has no sin at all, either actual or original, either from himself or contracted from Adam, necessarily has salvation and eternal life even if not baptized; but is to be baptized for this reason — that he may enter into the kingdom of God, i.e., into the kingdom of heaven." He then shows that there is no eternal life outside the kingdom of heaven, no middle place between the right and left hand of the judge at the last day, and that, therefore, to exclude one from the kingdom of God is to consign him to the pains of eternal fire; while, on the other side, no one ascends into heaven unless he has been made a member of Christ, and this can only be by faith — which, in an infant's case, is professed by another in his stead. He then treats, at length, some of the puzzling questions with which the Pelagians were wont to try the catholics; and then breaking off suddenly, he took a volume in his hands. " I ask you," he said, " to bear with me a little: I will read somewhat. It is St. Cyprian whom I hold in my hand, the ancient bishop of this see. What he thought of the baptism of infants — nay, what he has shown that the Church always thought — learn in brief. For it is not enough for them to dispute and argue, I know not what impious novelties: they even try to charge us with asserting something novel. It is on this account that I read here St. Cyprian, in order that you may perceive that the orthodox understanding and catholic sense reside in the words which I have been just now speaking to you. He was asked whether an infant ought to be baptized before he was eight days old, seeing that by the ancient law no infant was allowed to be circumcised unless he was eight days old. A question arose from this as to the day of baptism — for concerning the origin of sin there was no question; and therefore from this thing of which there was no question, that question that had arisen was settled." And then he read to them the passage out of Cyprian's letter to Fidus, which declared that he, and all the council with him, unanimously thought that infants should be baptized at the earliest possible age, lest they should die in their inherited sin, and so pass into eternal punishment.[66] The sermon closed with a tender warning to the teachers of these strange doctrines: he might call them heretics with truth, but he will not; let the Church seek still their salvation, and not mourn them as dead; let them be exhorted as friends, not striven with as enemies. " They disparage us," he says, " we will bear it; let them not disparage the rule [of faith], let them not disparage the truth; let them not contradict the Church, which labours every day for the remission of infants' original sin. This thing is settled. The errant disputer may be borne with in other questions that have not been thoroughly canvassed, that are not yet settled by the full authority of the Church — their error should be borne with: it ought not to extend so far, that they endeavour to shake even the very foundation of the Church! " He hints that although the patience hitherto exhibited towards them is " perhaps not blame-worthy," yet patience may cease to be a virtue, and become culpable negligence: in the mean time, however, he begs that the catholics should continue amicable, fraternal, placid, loving, long suffering.

Augustine himself gives us a view of the progress of the controversy at this time in a letter written in 414.[67] The Pelagians had everywhere scattered the seeds of their new error; and although some, by his ministry and that of his brother workers, had, " by God's mercy," been cured of their pest, yet they still existed in Africa, especially about Carthage, and were everywhere propagating their opinions in subterraneous whispers, for fear of the judgment of the Church. Whenever

[66] The passage is quoted at length in " On the Merits and Remission of Sins," iii. 10. Compare " Against Two Letters of the Pelagians," iv. 23.

[67] " Epist." 157. 22.

they were not refuted, they were seducing others to their following; and they were so spread abroad that he did not know where they would break out next. Nevertheless, he was still unwilling to brand them as heretics, and was more desirous of healing them as sick members of the Church than of cutting them off finally as too diseased for cure. Jerome also tells us that the poison was spreading in both the East and the West, and mentions particularly as seats where it showed itself the islands of Rhodes and Sicily. Of Rhodes we know nothing further; but from Sicily an appeal came to Augustine in 414 from one Hilary,[68] setting forth that there were certain Christians about Syracuse who taught strange doctrines, and beseeching Augustine to help him in dealing with them. The doctrines were enumerated as follows: " They say (1) that man can be without sin, (2) and can easily keep the commandments of God if he will; (3) that an unbaptized infant, if he is cut off by death, cannot justly perish, since he is born without sin; (4) that a rich man that remains in his riches cannot enter the kingdom of God, except he sell all that he has; . . . (5) that we ought not to swear at all; " (6) and, apparently, that the Church is to be in this world without spot or blemish. Augustine suspected that these Sicilian disturbances were in some way the work of Cœlestius, and therefore in his answer [69] informs his correspondent of what had been done at the Synod of Carthage (412) against him. The long letter that he sent back follows the inquiries in the order they were put by Hilary. To the first he replies, in substance, as he had treated the same matter in the second book of the treatise, " On the Merits and Remission of Sins," that it was opposed to Scripture, but was less a heresy than the wholly unbearable opinion that this state of sinlessness could be attained without God's help. " But when they say that free will suffices to man for fulfilling the precepts of the Lord, even though unaided to good works by God's grace and the gift of the Holy Spirit, it is to be altogether anathematized and detested with all execrations. For those who assert this are inwardly alien from God's grace,

[68] " Epist." 156.   [69] " Epist." 157. 22.

because being ignorant of God's righteousness, like the Jews of whom the apostle speaks, and wishing to establish their own, they are not subject to God's righteousness, since there is no fulfilment of the law except love; and of course the love of God is shed abroad in our hearts, not by ourselves, nor by the force of our own will, but by the Holy Ghost who is given to us." Dealing next with the second point, he drifts into the matter he had more fully developed in his work " On the Spirit and the Letter." " Free will avails for good works," he says, " if it be divinely aided, and this comes by humble seeking and doing; but when deserted by divine aid, no matter how excellent may be its knowledge of the law, it will by no means possess solidity of righteousness, but only the inflation of ungodly pride and deadly arrogance. This is taught us by that same Lord's Prayer; for it would be an empty thing for us to ask God ' Lead us not into temptation,' if the matter was so placed in our power that we would avail for fulfilling it without any aid from Him. . . . For this free will is free in proportion as it is sound, but it is sound in proportion as it is subject to divine pity and grace. For it faithfully prays, saying, ' Direct my ways according to Thy word, and let no iniquity reign over me.' For how is that free over which iniquity reigns? But see who it is that is invoked by it, in order that it may not reign over it. For it says not, ' Direct my ways according to free will because no iniquity shall rule over me,' but ' Direct my ways according to Thy *word, and let no iniquity rule over me.*' It is a prayer, not a promise; it is a confession, not a profession; it is a wish for full freedom, not a boast of personal power. For it is not every one ' who confides in his own power,' but ' every one who calls on the name of God, that shall be saved.' ' But how shall they call upon Him,' he says, ' in whom they have not believed? ' Accordingly, then, they who rightly believe, believe in order to call on Him in whom they have believed, and to avail for doing what they receive in the precepts of the law; since what the law commands, faith prays for."
" God, therefore, commands continence, and gives continence; He commands by the law, He gives by grace; He commands

by the letter, He gives by the spirit; for the law without grace makes the transgression to abound, and the letter without the spirit kills. He commands for this reason — that we who have endeavoured to do what He commands, and are worn out in our weakness under the law, may know how to ask for the aid of grace; and if we have been able to do any good work, that we may not be ungrateful to Him who aids us." The answer to the third point traverses the ground that was fully covered in the first book of the treatise " On the Merits and Remission of Sins," beginning by opposing the Pelagians to Paul in Rom. v. 12–19: " But when they say that an infant, cut off by death, unbaptized, cannot perish since he is born without sin — it is not this that the apostle says; and I think that it is better to believe the apostle than them." The fourth and fifth questions were new in this controversy; and it is not certain that they belong properly to it, though the legalistic asceticism of the Pelagian leaders may well have given rise to a demand on all Christians to sell what they had, and give to the poor. This one of the points, Augustine treats at length, pointing out that many of the saints of old were rich, and that the Lord and His apostles always so speak that their counsels avail to the right use, not the destruction, of wealth. Christians ought so to hold their wealth that they are not held by it, and by no means prefer it to Christ. Equal good sense and mildness are shown in his treatment of the question concerning oaths, which he points out were used by the Lord and His apostles, but advises to be used as little as possible lest by the custom of frequent oaths we learn to swear lightly. The question as to the Church, he passes over as having been sufficiently treated in the course of his previous remarks.

To the number of those who had been rescued from Pelagianism by his efforts, Augustine was now to have the pleasure of adding two others, in whom he seems to have taken much delight. Timasius and James were two young men of honorable birth and liberal education, who had, by the exhortation of Pelagius, been moved to give up the hope that they had in this world, and enter upon the service of God in an ascetic life.[70] Naturally, they had turned to him for instruction, and had received a book to which they had given their study. They met somewhere with some of Augustine's writings, however, and were deeply affected by what he said as to grace, and now began to see that the teaching of Pelagius opposed the grace of God by which man becomes a Christian. They gave their book, therefore, to Augustine, saying that it was Pelagius', and asking him for Pelagius' sake, and for the sake of the truth, to answer it. This was done, and the resulting book, " On Nature and Grace," sent to the young men, who returned a letter of thanks[71] in which they professed their conversion from their error. In this book, too, which was written in 415, Augustine refrained from mentioning Pelagius by name,[72] feeling it better to spare the man while not sparing his writings. But he tells us, that, on reading the book of Pelagius to which it was an answer, it became clear to him beyond any doubt that his teaching was distinctly anti-Christian;[73] and when speaking of his own book privately to a friend, he allows himself to call it " a considerable book against *the heresy* of Pelagius, which he had been constrained to write by some brethren whom he had persuaded to adopt his fatal error, denying the grace of Christ."[74] Thus his attitude towards the persons of the new teachers was becoming ever more and more strained, in despite of his full recognition of the excellent motives that might lie behind their " zeal not according to knowledge." This treatise opens with a recognition of the zeal of Pelagius, which, as it burns most ardently against those who, when reproved for sin, take refuge in censuring their nature, Augustine compares with the heathen view as expressed in Sallust's saying, " The human race falsely complains of its own nature,"[75] and which he charges with not being according to knowledge, and proposes to oppose by an

---

[70] " Epist." 177.; and 179. 2.

[71] " Epist." 168. " On the Proceedings of Pelagius," 48.

[72] " On the Proceedings of Pelagius," 47; and " Epist." 186. 1.

[73] Compare " On Nature and Grace," 7; and " Epist." 186. 1.

[74] " Epist." 169. 13.

[75] " On Nature and Grace," 1. Sallust's " Jugurthine War," 1, *ad init.*

equal zeal against all attempts to render the cross of Christ of none effect. He then gives a brief but excellent summary of the more important features of the catholic doctrine concerning nature and grace (2–7). Opening the work of Pelagius, which had been placed in his hands, he examines his doctrine of sin, its nature and effects. Pelagius, he points out, draws a distinction, sound enough in itself, between what is "possible" and what is "actual," but applies it unsoundly to sin, when he says that every man has the *possibility* of being without sin (8–9), and therefore without condemnation. Not so, says Augustine; an infant who dies unbaptized has no possibility of salvation open to him; and the man who has lived and died in a land where it was impossible for him to hear the name of Christ, has had no possibility open to him of becoming righteous by nature and free will. If this be not so, Christ is dead in vain, since all men then might have accomplished their salvation, even if Christ had never died (10). Pelagius, moreover, he shows, exhibits a tendency to deny the sinful character of all sins that are impossible to avoid, and so treats of sins of ignorance as to show that he excuses them (13–19). When he argues that no sin, because it is not a substance, can change nature, which is a substance, Augustine replies that this destroys the Saviour's work — for how can He save from sins if sins do not corrupt? And, again, if an act cannot injure a substance, how can abstention from food, which is a mere act, kill the body? In the same way sin is not a substance; but God is a substance — yea, the height of substance, and only true sustenance of the reasonable creature; and the consequence of departure from Him is to the soul what refusal of food is to the body (22). To Pelagius' assertion that sin cannot be punished by more sin, Augustine replies that the apostle thinks differently (Rom. i. 21–31). Then putting his finger on the main point in controversy, he quotes the Scriptures as declaring the present condition of man to be that of spiritual death. "The truth then designates as *dead* those whom this man declares to be unable to be damaged or corrupted by sin,

— because, forsooth, he has discovered sin to be no substance!" (25). It was by free will that man passed into this state of death; but a dead man needs something else to revive him — he needs nothing less than a Vivifier. But of vivifying grace, Pelagius knew nothing; and by knowing nothing of a Vivifier, he knows nothing of a Saviour; but rather by making nature of itself able to be sinless, he glorifies the Creator at the expense of the Saviour (39). Next is examined Pelagius' contention that many saints are enumerated in the Scriptures as having lived sinlessly in this world. While declining to discuss the question of fact as to the Virgin Mary (42), Augustine opposes to the rest the declaration of John in 1 John i. 8, as final, but still pauses to explain why the Scriptures do not mention the sins of all, and to contend that all who ever were saved under the Old Testament or the New, were saved by the sacrificial death of Christ, and by faith in Him (40–50). Thus we are brought, as Augustine says, to the core of the question, which concerns, not the fact of sinlessness in any man, but man's ability to be sinless. This ability Pelagius affirms of all men, and Augustine denies of all " unless they are justified by the grace of God through our Lord Jesus Christ and Him crucified " (51). Thus, the whole discussion is about grâce, which Pelagius does not admit in any true sense, but places only in the nature that God has made (52). We are next invited to attend to another distinction of Pelagius', in which he discriminates sharply between the nature that God has made, the crown of which is free will, and the use that man makes of this free will. The endowment of free will is a " capacity " ; it is, because given by God in our making, a necessity of nature, and not in man's power to have or not have. It is the right use of it only, which man has in his power. This analysis, Pelagius illustrates at length, by appealing to the difference between the possession and use of the various bodily senses. The ability to see, for instance, he says, is a necessity of our nature; we do not make it, we cannot help having it; it is ours only to use it. Augustine criticises this presentation of the matter with great sharpness (although he is not averse to the analysis itself) — showing the inapplicability of the illustrations used — for, he asks, is it not possible for us to blind ourselves, and so no longer have the ability to see? and would not many a man like to control the " use " of his " capacity " to hear when a screechy saw is in the neighborhood? (55); and as well the falsity of the contention illustrated, since Pelagius has ignored the fall, and, even, were that not so, has so ignored the need of God's aid for all good, in any state of being, as to deny it (56). Moreover, it is altogether a fallacy, Augustine argues, to contend that men have the " ability " to make every use we can conceive of our faculties. We *cannot* wish for unhappiness; God *cannot* deny Himself (57); and just so, in a corrupt nature, the mere possession of a *faculty of choice* does not imply the ability to use that faculty for not sinning. " Of a man, indeed, who has his legs strong and sound, it may be said admissibly enough, ' whether he will or not, he has the capacity of walking ' ; but if his legs be broken, however much he may wish, he has not the ' capacity.' The nature of which our author speaks is corrupted " (57). What, then, can he mean by saying that, whether we will or not, we have the capacity of not sinning — a statement so opposite to Paul's in Rom. vii. 15? Some space is next given to an attempted rebuttal by Pelagius of the testimony of Gal. v. 17, on the ground that the " flesh " there does not refer to the baptized (60–70); and then the passages are examined which Pelagius had quoted against Augustine out of earlier writers — Lactantius (71), Hilary (72), Ambrose (75), John of Constantinople (76), Xystus — a blunder of Pelagius, who quoted from a Pythagorean philosopher, mistaking him for the Roman bishop Sixtus (77), Jerome (78), and Augustine himself (80). All these writers, Augustine shows, admitted the universal sinfulness of man — and especially he himself had confessed the necessity of grace in the immediate context of the passage quoted by Pelagius. The treatise closes (82 *sq.*) with a noble panegyric on that love which God sheds abroad in the heart, by the Holy Ghost, and by which alone we can be made keepers of the law.

The treatise " On Nature and Grace " was as yet unfinished, when the over-busy [76] scriptorium at Hippo was invaded by another young man seeking instruction. This time it was a zealous young presbyter from the remotest part of Spain, " from the shore of the ocean " — Paulus Orosius by name, whose pious soul had been afflicted with grievous wounds by the Priscillianist and Origenist heresies that had broken out in his country, and who had come with eager haste to Augustine, on hearing that he could get from him the instruction which he needed for confuting them. Augustine seems to have given him his heart at once; and, feeling too little informed as to the special heresies which he wished to be prepared to controvert, persuaded him to go on to Palestine to be taught by Jerome, and gave him introductions which described him as one " who is in the bond of catholic peace a brother, in point of age a son, and in honour a fellow-presbyter — a man of quick understanding, ready speech, and burning zeal." His departure to Palestine gave Augustine an opportunity to consult with Jerome on the one point that had been raised in the Pelagian controversy on which he had not been able to see light. The Pelagians had early argued,[77] that, if souls are created anew for men at their birth, it would be unjust in God to impute Adam's sin to them. And Augustine found himself unable either to prove that souls are transmitted (*traduced,* as the phrase is), or to show that it would not involve God in injustice to make a soul only to make it subject to a sin committed by another. Jerome had already put himself on record as a believer in both original sin and the creation of souls at the time of birth. Augustine feared the logical consequences of this assertion, and yet was unable to refute it. He therefore seized this occasion to send a long treatise on the origin of the soul to his friend, with the request that he would consider the subject anew, and answer his doubts.[78] In this treatise he

---

[76] For Augustine's press of work just now, see " Epist." 169. 1, 13.

[77] The argument occurs in Pelagius' " Commentary on Paul," written before 410, and is already before Augustine in " On the Merits and Remission of Sins," iii. 5.   [78] " Epist." 166.

stated that he was fully persuaded that the soul had fallen
into sin, but by no fault of God or of nature, but of its own free
will; and asked when could the soul of an infant have contracted the guilt, which, unless the grace of Christ should come
to its rescue by baptism, would involve it in condemnation, if
God (as Jerome held, and as he was willing to hold with him,
if this difficulty could be cleared up) makes each soul for each
individual at the time of birth? He professed himself embarrassed on such a supposition by the penal sufferings of infants,
the pains they endured in this life, and much more the danger
they are in of eternal damnation, into which they actually go
unless saved by baptism. God is good, just, omnipotent: how,
then, can we account for the fact that " in Adam all die," if
souls are created afresh for each birth? " If new souls are made
for men," he affirms, " individually at their birth, I do not see,
on the one hand, that they could have any sin while yet in infancy; nor do I believe, on the other hand, that God condemns
any soul which He sees to have no sin; " " and yet, whoever
says that those children who depart out of this life without
parting of the sacrament of baptism, shall be made alive in
Christ, certainly contradicts the apostolic declaration," and
" he that is not made alive in Christ must necessarily remain
under the condemnation of which the apostle says that by
the offence of one, judgment came upon all men to condemnation." " Wherefore," he adds to his correspondent, " if that
opinion of yours does not contradict this firmly grounded article of faith, let it be mine also; but if it does, let it no longer
be yours." [79] So far as obtaining light was concerned, Augustine might have spared himself the pain of this composition:
Jerome simply answered [80] that he had no leisure to reply to
the questions submitted to him. But Orosius' mission to Palestine was big with consequences. Once there, he became the
accuser of Pelagius before John of Jerusalem, and the occa-

---

[79] An almost contemporary letter to Oceanus (" Epist." 180, written in
416) adverts to the same subject and in the same spirit, showing how much
it was in Augustine's thoughts. Compare " Epist." 180. 2, 5.

[80] " Epist." 172.

sion, at least, of the trials of Pelagius in Palestine during the summer and winter of 415 which issued so disastrously, and ushered in a new phase of the conflict.

Meanwhile, however, Augustine was ignorant of what was going on in the East, and had his mind directed again to Sicily. About a year had passed since he had sent thither his long letter to Hilary. Now his conjecture that Cœlestius was in some way at the bottom of the Sicilian outbreak, received confirmation from a paper which certain catholic brethren brought out of Sicily, and which was handed to Augustine by two exiled Spanish bishops, Eutropius and Paul. This paper bore the title, " Definitions Ascribed to Cœlestius," and presented internal evidence, in style and thought, of being correctly so ascribed.[81] It consisted of three parts, in the first of which were collected a series of brief and compressed " definitions," or " ratiocinations " as Augustine calls them, in which the author tries to place the catholics in a logical dilemma, and to force them to admit that man can live in this world without sin. In the second part, he adduced certain passages of Scripture in defence of his doctrine. In the third part, he undertook to deal with the texts that had been quoted against his contention, not, however, by examining into their meaning, or seeking to explain them in the sense of his theory, but simply by matching them with others which he thought made for him. Augustine at once (about the end of 415) wrote a treatise in answer to this, which bears the title of " On the Perfection of Man's Righteousness." The distribution of the matter in this work follows that of the treatise to which it is an answer. First of all (1–16), the " ratiocinations " are taken up one by one and briefly answered. As they all concern sin, and have for their object to prove that man cannot be accounted a sinner unless he is able, in his own power, wholly to avoid sin — that is, to prove that a plenary natural ability is the necessary basis of responsibility — Augustine argues *per contra* that man can entail a sinfulness on himself for which and for the deeds of which he remains responsible, though he is no longer able to avoid sin; thus ad-

[81] See " On the Perfection of Man's Righteousness," 1.

mitting that for the race, plenary ability must stand at the root
of sinfulness. Next (17–22) he discusses the passages which
Cœlestius had advanced in defence of his teachings, viz., (1)
passages in which God commands men to be without sin, which
Augustine meets by saying that the point is, whether these
commands are to be fulfilled *without God's aid,* in the body of
this death, while absent from the Lord (17–20); and (2) passages in which God declares that His commandments are not
grievous, which Augustine meets by explaining that all God's
commandments are fulfilled only by *Love,* which finds nothing
grievous; and that this love is shed abroad in our hearts by the
Holy Ghost, without whom we have only fear, to which the
commandments are not only grievous, but impossible. Lastly,
Augustine patiently follows Cœlestius through his odd "op-
positions of texts," explaining carefully all that he had adduced, in an orthodox sense (23–42). In closing, he takes up
Cœlestius' statement, that " it is quite possible for man not to
sin even in word, if God so will," pointing out how he avoids
saying " if God give him His help," and then proceeds to distinguish carefully between the differing assertions of sinlessness that may be made. To say that any man ever lived, or will
live, without needing forgiveness, is to contradict Rom. v. 12,
and must imply that he does not need a Saviour, against Mt.
ix. 12, 13. To say that after his sins have been forgiven, any
one has ever remained without sin, contradicts 1 Jno. i. 8 and
Mt. vi. 12. Yet, if God's help be allowed, this contention is
not so wicked as the other; and the great heresy is to deny the
necessity of God's constant grace, for which we pray when we
say, " Lead us not into temptation."

Tidings were now (416) beginning to reach Africa of what
was doing in the East. There was diligently circulated everywhere, and came into Augustine's hands, an epistle of Pelagius'
own " filled with vanity," in which he boasted that fourteen
bishops had approved his assertion that " man can live without sin, and easily keep the commandments if he wishes," and
had thus " shut the mouth of opposition in confusion," and
" broken up the whole band of wicked conspirators against

him." Soon afterwards a copy of an "apologetical paper," in which Pelagius used the authority of the Palestinian bishops against his adversaries, not altogether without disingenuousness, was sent by him to Augustine through the hands of a common acquaintance, Charus by name. It was not accompanied, however, by any letter from Pelagius; and Augustine wisely refrained from making public use of it. Towards midsummer Orosius came with more authentic, information, and bearing letters from Jerome and Heros and Lazarus. It was apparently before his coming that a controversial sermon was preached, only a fragment of which has come down to us.[82] So far as we can learn from the extant part, its subject seems to have been the relation of prayer to Pelagianism; and what we have, opens with a striking anecdote: "When these two petitions — 'Forgive us our debts as we also forgive our debtors,' and 'Lead us not into temptation' — are objected to the Pelagians, what do you think they reply? I was horrified, my brethren, when I heard it. I did not, indeed, hear it with my own ears; but my holy brother and fellow-bishop Urbanus, who used to be presbyter here, and now is bishop of Sicca," when he was in Rome, and was arguing with one who held these opinions, pressed him with the weight of the Lord's Prayer, and "what do you think he replied to him? 'We ask God,' he said, 'not to lead us into temptation, lest we should suffer something that is not in our power — lest I should be thrown from my horse; lest I should break my leg; lest a robber should slay me, and the like. For these things,' he said, 'are not in my power; but for overcoming the temptations of my sins, I both have ability if I wish to use it, and am not able to receive God's help.'[83] You see, brethren," the good bishop adds, "how malignant this heresy is: you see how it horrifies all of you. Have a care that you be not taken by it." He then presses the general doctrine of prayer as proving that all good things come from God, whose aid is always necessary to us, and is always attainable by prayer; and closes as follows: "Consider, then, these things, my brethren,

[82] Migne's Edition of Augustine's Works, vol. v. Coll. 1719–1723.
[83] Compare the words of Cicero quoted above, p. 290.

when any one comes to you and says to you, ' What, then, are we to do if we have nothing in our power, unless God gives all things? God will not then crown us, but He will crown Himself.' You already see that this comes from that vein: it is a vein, but it has poison in it; it is stricken by the serpent; it is not sound. For what Satan is doing today is seeking to cast out from the Church by the poison of heretics, just as he once cast out from Paradise by the poison of the serpent. Let no one tell you that this one was acquitted by the bishops: there was an acquittal, but it was his confession, so to speak, his amendment, that was acquitted. For what he said before the bishops seemed catholic; but what he wrote in his books, the bishops who pronounced the acquittal were ignorant of. And perchance he was really convinced and amended. For we ought not to despair of the man who perchance preferred to be united to the catholic faith, and fled to its grace and aid. Perchance this was what happened. But, in any event, it was not the heresy that was acquitted, but the man who denied the heresy." [84]

The coming of Orosius must have dispelled any lingering hope that the meaning of the council's finding was that Pelagius had really recanted. Councils were immediately assembled at Carthage and Mileve, and the documents which Orosius had brought were read before them. We know nothing of their proceedings except what we can gather from the letters which they sent [85] to Innocent at Rome, seeking his aid in their condemnation of the heresy now so nearly approved in Palestine. To these two official letters, Augustine, in company with four other bishops, added a third private letter,[86] in which they took care that Innocent should be informed on all the points necessary to his decision. This important letter begins almost abruptly with a characterization of Pelagianism as inimical to the grace of God, and has grace for its subject throughout. It

[84] Compare the similar words in " Epist." 177. 3, which was written, not only after what had occurred in Palestine was known, but also after the condemnatory decisions of the African synods.

[85] " Epist." 175 and 176.

[86] " Epist." 177. The other bishops were Aurelius, Alypius, Evodius, and Possidius.

accounts for the action of the Palestinian synod, as growing out of a misunderstanding of Pelagius' words, in which he seemed to acknowledge grace, which these catholic bishops understood naturally to mean that grace of which they read in the Scriptures, and which they were accustomed to preach to their people — the grace by which we are justified from iniquity, and saved from weakness; while he meant nothing more than that by which we are given free will at our creation. " For if these bishops had understood that he meant only that grace which we have in common with the ungodly and with all, along with whom we are men, while he denied that by which we are Christians and the sons of God, what Catholic priest could have patiently listened to him — or even have borne him before his eyes? " The letter then proceeds to point out the difference between grace and natural gifts, and between grace and the law, and to trace out Pelagius' meaning when he speaks of grace, and when he contends that man can be sinless without any really inward aid. It suggests that Pelagius be sent for, and thoroughly examined by Innocent, or that he should be examined by letter or in his writings; and that he be not cleared until he unequivocally confessed the grace of God in the catholic sense, and anathematized the false teachings in the books attributed to him. The book of Pelagius which was answered in the treatise " On Nature and Grace " was enclosed, with this letter, with the most important passages marked: and it was suggested that more was involved in the matter than the fate of one single man, Pelagius, who, perhaps, was already brought to a better mind; the fate of multitudes already led astray, or yet to be deceived by these false views, was in danger.

At about this same time (417), the tireless bishop sent a short letter [87] to a Hilary, who seems to be Hilary of Norbonne, which is interesting from its undertaking to convey a characterization of Pelagianism to one who was as yet ignorant of it. It thus brings out what Augustine conceived to be its essential features. " An effort has been made," we read, " to raise a certain new heresy, inimical to the grace of Christ, against the

[87] " Epist." 178.

Church of Christ. It is not yet openly separated from the Church. It is the heresy of men who dare to attribute so much power to human weakness that they contend that this only belongs to God's grace — that we are created with free will and the possibility of not sinning, and that we receive God's commandments which are to be fulfilled by us; but, for keeping and fulfilling these commandments, we do not need any divine aid. No doubt, the remission of sins is necessary for us; for we have no power to right what we have done wrong in the past. But for avoiding and overcoming sins in the future, for conquering all temptations with virtue, the human will is sufficient by its natural capacity without any aid of God's grace. And neither do infants need the grace of the Saviour, so as to be liberated by it through His baptism from perdition, seeing that they have contracted no contagion of damnation from Adam." [88] He engages Hilary in the destruction of this heresy, which ought to be "concordantly condemned and anathematized by all who have hope in Christ," as a "pestiferous impiety," and excuses himself for not undertaking its full refutation in a brief letter. A much more important letter was sent off, at about the same time, to John of Jerusalem, who had conducted the first Palestinian examination of Pelagius, and had borne a prominent part in the synod at Diospolis. He sent with it a copy of Pelagius' book which he had examined in his treatise "On Nature and Grace," as well as a copy of that reply itself, and asked John to send him an authentic copy of the proceedings at Diospolis. He took this occasion seriously to warn his brother bishop against the wiles of Pelagius, and begged him, if he loved Pelagius, to let men see that he did not so love him as to be deceived by him. He pointed out that in the book sent with the letter, Pelagius called nothing the grace of God except nature; and that he affirmed, and even vehemently contended, that by free will alone, human nature was able to suffice for itself for working righteousness and keeping all God's commandments; whence any one could see that he opposed the grace of God of which the apostle spoke in Rom. vii. 24, 25,

[88] "Epist." 178.

and contradicted, as well, all the prayers and benedictions of the Church by which blessings were sought for men from God's grace. " If you love Pelagius, then," he continued, " let him, too, love you as himself — nay, more than himself; and let him not deceive you. For when you hear him confess the grace of God and the aid of God, you think he means what you mean by it. . . . But let him be openly asked whether he desires that we should pray God that we sin not; . . . whether he proclaims the assisting grace of God, without which we would do much evil; . . . whether he believes that even children who have not yet been able to do good or evil are nevertheless, on account of one man by whom sin entered into the world, . . . in need of being delivered by the grace of Christ." If he openly denies such things, Augustine would be pleased to hear of it.

Thus we see the great bishop sitting in his library at Hippo, placing his hands on the two ends of the world. That nothing may be lacking to the picture of his universal activity, we have another letter from him, coming from about this same time, that exhibits his care for the individuals who had placed themselves in some sort under his tutelage. Among the refugees from Rome in the terrible times when Alaric was a second time threatening the city, was a family of noble women — Proba, Juliana, and Demetrias [89] — grandmother, mother, and daughter — who, finding an asylum in Africa, gave themselves to God's service, and sought the friendship and counsel of Augustine. In 413 the granddaughter " took the veil " under circumstances that thrilled the Christian world, and brought out letters of congratulation and advice from Augustine and Jerome, and also from Pelagius. This letter of Pelagius seems not to have fallen into Augustine's way until now (416): he was so disturbed by it that he wrote to Juliana a long letter warning her against its evil counsels.[90] It was so shrewdly phrased, that, at first sight, Augustine was himself almost persuaded that it

[89] See " A Select Library of the Nicene and Post-Nicene Fathers of the Christian Church," First Series, i. p. 459, and the references there given. Compare Canon Robertson's vivid account of them in his " History of the Christian Church," 1904, ii. pp. 18, 145.   [90] " Epist." 188.

did somehow acknowledge the grace of God; but when he compared it with others of Pelagius' writings, he saw that here, too, he was using ambiguous phrases in a non-natural sense. The object of his letter (in which Alypius is conjoined, as joint author) to Juliana is to warn her and her holy daughter against all opinions that opposed the grace of God, and especially against the covert teaching of the letter of Pelagius to Demetrias.[91] "In this book," he says, "were it lawful for such an one to read it, a virgin of Christ would read that her holiness and all her spiritual riches are to spring from no other source than herself; and thus before she attains to the perfection of blessedness, she would learn — which may God forbid! — to be ungrateful to God." Then, after quoting the words of Pelagius, in which he declares that "earthly riches came from others, but your spiritual riches no one can have conferred on you but yourself; for these, then, you are justly praised, for these you are deservedly to be preferred to others — for they can exist only from yourself and in yourself," he continues: "Far be it from any virgin of Christ to listen willingly to statements like these, who understands the innate poverty of the human heart, and therefore declines to be adorned otherwise than by the gifts of her spouse. . . . Let her not listen to him who says, 'No one can confer them on you but yourself, and they cannot exist except from you and in you:' but to him who says, 'We have this treasure in earthen vessels, that the excellency of the power may be of God, and not of us.' . . . And be not surprised that we speak of these things as yours, and not from you; for we speak of daily bread as 'ours,' but yet add 'give it to us,' lest it should be thought it was from ourselves." Again, he warns her that grace is not mere knowledge any more than mere nature; and that Pelagius, even when using the word "grace," means no inward or efficient aid, but mere nature or knowledge or forgiveness of past sins; and beseeches her not to forget the God of all grace from whom (Wisdom viii. 21) Demetrias had that very virgin continence which was so justly her boast.

[91] Compare "On the Grace of Christ," 40. In the succeeding sections, some of its statements are examined.

With the opening of 417, came the answers from Innocent to the African letters.[92] And although they were marred by much boastful language concerning the dignity of his see, which could not but be distasteful to the Africans, they admirably served their purpose in the satisfactory manner in which they, on the one hand, asserted the necessity of the " daily grace, and help of God," for our good living, and, on the other, determined that the Pelagians had denied this grace, and declared their leaders Pelagius and Cœlestius deprived of the communion of the Church until they should " recover their senses from the wiles of the Devil by whom they are held captive according to his will." Augustine may be pardoned for supposing that a condemnation pronounced by two provincial synods in Africa, and heartily concurred in by the Roman bishop, who had already at Jerusalem been recognized as in some sort the fit arbiter of this Western dispute, should settle the matter. If Pelagius had been before jubilant, Augustine found this a suitable time for his rejoicing.

About the same time with Innocent's letters, the official proceedings of the synod of Diospolis at last reached Africa, and Augustine lost no time (early in 417) in publishing a full account and examination of them (" On the Proceedings of Pelagius "), thus providing us with that inestimable boon, a full contemporary history of the chief events connected with the controversy up to this time. This treatise, which is addressed to Aurelius, bishop of Carthage, opens with a brief explanation of Augustine's delay heretofore, in discussing Pelagius' defence of himself in Palestine, as due to his not having received the official copy of the Proceedings of the Council at Diospolis (1–2a). Then Augustine proceeds at once to discuss at length the doings of the synod, point by point, following the official record step by step (2b–45). He treats at large here eleven items in the indictment, with Pelagius' answers and the synod's decision, showing that in all of them Pelagius either explained away his heresy, taking advantage of the ignorance of the judges of his books, or else openly repudiated or anathematized

[92] " Epist." 181, 182, 183, among Augustine's letters.

it. When the twelfth item of the indictment was reached (41b–43), Augustine shows that the synod was so indignant at its character (it charged Pelagius with teaching that men cannot be sons of God unless they are sinless, and with condoning sins of ignorance, and with asserting that choice is not free if it depends on God's help, and that pardon is given according to merit), that, without waiting for Pelagius' answer, it condemned the statement, and Pelagius at once repudiated and anathematized it (43). How could the synod act in such circumstances, he asks, except by acquitting the man who condemned the heresy? After quoting the final judgment of the synod (44), Augustine briefly characterizes it and its effect (45) as being indeed all that could be asked of the judges, but of no moral weight to those better acquainted than they were with Pelagius' character and writings. In a word, they approved his answers to them, as indeed they ought to have done; but they by no means approved, but both they and he condemned, his heresies as expressed in his writings. To this statement, Augustine appends an account of the origin of Pelagianism, and of his relations to it from the beginning, which has the very highest value as history (46–49); and then speaks of the character and doubtful practices of Pelagius (50–58), returning at the end (59–65) to a thorough canvass of the value of the acquittal which he obtained by such doubtful practices at the synod. He closes with an indignant account of the outrages which the Pelagians had perpetrated on Jerome (66).

This valuable treatise is not, however, the only account of the historical origin of Pelagianism that we have, from Augustine's hands. Soon after the death of Innocent (March 12, 417), he found occasion to write a very long letter [93] to the venerable Paulinus of Nola, in which he summarized both the history of, and the arguments against, this " worldly philosophy." He begins by saying that he knows Paulinus has loved Pelagius as a servant of God, but is ignorant in what way he

[93] " Epist." 186, written conjointly with Alypius.

now loves him. For he himself not only has loved him, but loves him still, but in different ways. Once he loved him as apparently a brother in the true faith: now he loves him in the longing that God will by His mercy free him from his noxious opinions against God's grace. He is not merely following report in so speaking of him: no doubt report did for a long time represent this of him, but he gave the less heed to it because report is accustomed to lie. But a book of his [94] at last came into his hands, which left no room for doubt, since in it he asserted repeatedly that God's grace consisted of the gift to man of the capacity to will and act, and thus reduced it to what is common to pagans and Christians, to the ungodly and godly, to the faithful and infidels. He then gives a brief account of the measures that had been taken against Pelagius, and passes on to a treatment of the main matters involved in the controversy — all of which gather around the one magic word of " the grace of God." He argues first that we are all lost — in one mass and concretion of perdition — and that God's grace alone makes us to differ. It is therefore folly to talk of deserving the beginnings of grace. Nor can a faithful man say that he merits justification by his faith, although it is given to faith; for at once he hears the words, " What hast thou that thou didst not receive? " and learns that even the deserving faith is the gift of God. But if, peering into God's inscrutable judgments, we go farther, and ask why, from the mass of Adam, all of which undoubtedly has fallen from one into condemnation, this vessel is made for honor, that for dishonor — we can only say that we do not know more than the fact; and God's reasons are hidden, but His acts are just. Certain it is that Paul teaches that all die in Adam; and that God freely chooses, by a sovereign election, some out of that sinful mass, to eternal life; and that He knew from the beginning to whom He would give this grace, and so the number of the saints has always been fixed, to whom he gives in due time the Holy Ghost. Others, no doubt, are called; but no others are elect, or " called according

[94] The book given him by Timasius and James, to which " On Nature and Grace " is a reply.

to his purpose." On no other body of doctrines, can it be possibly explained that some infants die unbaptized, and are lost. Is God unjust to punish innocent children with eternal pains? And are they not innocent if they are not partakers of Adam's sin? And can they be saved from that, save by the undeserved, and that is the gratuitous, grace of God? The account of the Proceedings at the Palestinian synod is then taken up, and Pelagius' position in his latest writings is quoted and examined. "But why say more?" he adds. . . . "Ought they not, since they call themselves Christians, to be more careful than the Jews that they do not stumble at the stone of offence, while they subtly defend nature and free will just like philosophers of this world who vehemently strive to be thought, or to think themselves, to attain for themselves a happy life by the force of their own will? Let them take care, then, that they do not make the cross of Christ of none effect by the wisdom of words (1 Cor. i. 17), and thus stumble at the rock of offense. For human nature, even if it had remained in that integrity in which it was created, could by no means have served its own Creator without His aid. Since then, without God's grace it could not keep the safety it had received, how can it without God's grace repair what it has lost?" With this profound view of the Divine immanence, and of the necessity of His moving grace in all the acts of all his creatures, as over against the heathen-deistic view of Pelagius, Augustine touched in reality the deepest point in the whole controversy, and illustrated the essential harmony of all truth.[95]

The sharpest period of the whole conflict was now drawing on.[96] Innocent's death brought Zosimus to the chair of the Roman See, and the efforts which he made to re-instate Pelagius and Cœlestius now began (September, 417). How little the

[95] Compare also Innocent's letter ("Epist." 181) to the Carthaginian Council, chap. 4, which also Neander, "History of the Christian Religion and Church," E. T. ii. 646, quotes in this connection, as showing that Innocent "perceived that this dispute was connected with a different way of regarding the relation of God's providence to creation." As if Augustine did not see this too!

[96] The book addressed to Dardanus, in which the Pelagians are confuted, but not named, belongs about at this time. Compare "Retractations," ii. 49.

Africans were likely to yield to his remarkable demands, may be seen from a sermon [97] which Augustine preached on the 23d of September, while Zosimus' letter (written on the 21st of September) was on its way to Africa. The preacher took his text from John vi. 54-66. " We hear here," he said, " the true Master, the Divine Redeemer, the human Saviour, commending to us our ransom, His blood. . . . He calls His body food, and His blood drink; and, in commending such food and drink, He says, ' Unless you eat My flesh, and drink My blood, ye shall have no life in you.' . . . What, then, is this eating and drinking, but to live? Eat life, drink life; you shall have life, and life is whole. This will come — that is, the body and blood of Christ will be life to every one — if what is taken visibly in the sacrament is in real truth spiritually eaten and spiritually drunk. . . . But that He might teach us that even to believe in Him is of gift, not of merit, He said, . . . ' No one comes to Me, except the Father who sent Me draw him.' *Draw* him, not *lead* him. This violence is done to the *heart,* not the flesh. Why do you marvel? Believe, and you come; love, and you are drawn. Think not that this is harsh and injurious violence; it is soft, it is sweet; it is sweetness itself that draws you. Is not the sheep drawn when the succulent herbage is shown to him? And I think that there is no compulsion of the body, but an assembling of the desire. So, too, do you come to Christ; wish not to plan a long journey — when you believe, then you come. For to Him who is everywhere, one comes by loving, not by taking a voyage. . . . And even after you have come, and are walking in the right way, become not proud, lest you perish from it: . . . ' happy are those that confide in Him,' not in *themselves,* but in *Him.* We are saved by grace, not of ourselves: it is the gift of God. . . . Why do I continually say this to you? . . . It is because there are men who are ungrateful to grace, and attribute much to unaided and wounded nature. It is true that man received great powers of free will at his creation; but he lost them by sinning. He has fallen into death; he has been made weak; he has been left half dead in the way, by

[97] " Sermon " 131, preached at Carthage.

robbers; the good Samaritan passing by . . . has lifted him
up upon his ass, and borne him to the inn. Why should we
boast? . . . But I am told that it is enough that sins are remitted in baptism. But does the removal of sin take away weakness too? . . . What! will you not see that after pouring the
oil and the wine into the wounds of the man left half dead by
the robbers, . . . he must still go to the inn where his weakness may be healed? . . . Nay, so long as we are in this life we
bear a fragile body; . . . it is only after we are redeemed from
all corruption that we shall find no sin, and receive the crown of
righteousness. Grace, that was hidden in the Old Testament,
is revealed in the New. Even though the Jew may be ignorant
of it, why should Christians be enemies of grace? why pre-
sumptuous of themselves? why ungrateful to grace? For, why
did Christ come? Was not nature already here — that very nature by the praise of which you are beguiled? Was not the law
here? But the apostle says, ' If righteousness is of the law, then
is Christ dead in vain.' What the apostle says of the law, that
we say to these men about nature: if righteousness is by nature, then Christ is dead in vain. What then was said of the
Jews, this we see repeated in these men. They have a zeal for
God: I bear them witness that they have a zeal of God, but not
according to knowledge. For, being ignorant of God's righteousness, and wishing to establish their own, they are not subject to the righteousness of God. My brethren, share my com-
passion. Where you find such men, wish no concealment; let
there be no perverse pity in you: where you find them, wish
no concealment at all. Contradict and refute, resist, or persuade them to us. For already two councils have, in this cause,
sent letters to the Apostolic See, whence also rescripts have
come back. The cause is ended: would that the error might
some day end! Therefore we admonish so that they may take
notice, we teach so that they may be instructed, we pray so
that their way be changed." Here is certainly tenderness to the
persons of the teachers of error; readiness to forgive, and readiness to go all proper lengths in recovering them to the truth.
But here is also absolute firmness as to the truth itself, and a

manifesto as to policy. Certainly, on the lines of the policy here indicated, the Africans fought out the coming campaign. They met in council at the end of this year, or early in the next (418); and formally replied to Zosimus, that the cause had been tried, and was finished, and that the sentence that had been already pronounced against Pelagius and Cœlestius should remain in force until they should unequivocally acknowledge that "we are aided by the grace of God through Christ, not only to know, but to do, what is right, and that in each single act; so that without grace we are unable to have, think, speak, or do anything belonging to piety (Migne, " Patrologia Latina," x. col. 1723)." As we may see Augustine's hand in this, so, doubtless, we may recognize it in that remarkable piece of engineering which crushed Zosimus' plans within the next few months. There is, indeed, no direct proof that it was due to Augustine, or to the Africans under his leading, or to the Africans at all, that the State interfered in the matter; it is even in doubt whether the action of the Empire was put forth as a rescript, or as a self-moved decree: but surely it is difficult to believe that such a *coup de théâtre* could have been prepared for Zosimus by chance; and as it is well known, both that Augustine believed in the righteousness of civil penalty for heresy, and invoked it on other occasions, and defended and used it on this, and that he had influential friends at court with whom he was in correspondence, it seems, on internal grounds, altogether probable that he was the *Deus ex machinâ* who let loose the thunders of ecclesiastical and civil enactment simultaneously on the poor Pope's devoted head.

The "great African Council" met at Carthage, on the 1st of May, 418; and, after its decrees were issued, Augustine remained at Carthage, and watched the effect of the combination of which he was probably one of the moving causes. He had now an opportunity to betake himself once more to his pen. While still at Carthage, at short notice, and in the midst of much distraction, he wrote a large work, in two books which have come down to us under the separate titles of " On the Grace of Christ," and " On Original Sin," at the instance of another of those ascetic families which formed so marked a feature in those troubled times. Pinianus and Melania, the daughter of Albina, were husband and wife, who, leaving Rome amid the wars with Alaric, had lived in continence in Africa for some time, but now in Palestine had separated, he to become head of a monastery, and she an inmate of a convent. While in Africa, they had lived at Sagaste under the tutelage of Alypius, and in the enjoyment of the friendship and instruction of Augustine. After retiring to Bethlehem, like the other holy ascetics whom he had known in Africa, they kept up their relations with him. Like the others, also, they became acquainted with Pelagius in Palestine, and were well-nigh deceived by him. They wrote to Augustine that they had begged Pelagius to condemn in writing all that had been alleged against him, and that he had replied in the presence of them all, that " he anathematized the man who either thinks or says that the grace of God whereby Christ Jesus came into the world to save sinners is not necessary, not only for every hour and for every moment, but also for every act of our lives," and asserted that " those who endeavor to disannul it are worthy of everlasting punishment." [98] Moreover, they wrote that Pelagius had read to them, out of his book that he had sent to Rome,[99] his assertion " that infants ought to be baptized with the same formula of sacramental words as adults." [100] They wrote that they were delighted to hear these words from Pelagius, as they seemed exactly what they had been desirous of hearing; and yet they preferred consulting Augustine about them, before they were fully committed regarding them.[101] It was in answer to this appeal, that the present work was written; the two books of which take up the two points in Pelagius' asseveration — the theme of the first being " the assistance of the Divine grace towards our justification, by which God co-operates in all things for good to those who love Him, and whom He first

---

[98] " On the Grace of Christ," 2.

[99] The so-called " Confession of Faith " sent to Innocent after the Synod of Diospolis, but which arrived after Innocent's death.

[100] " On Original Sin," 1.

[101] Do., 5.

loved, giving to them that He may receive from them " — while the subject of the second is " the sin which by one man has entered the world along with death, and so has passed upon all men." [102]

The first book, " On the Grace of Christ," begins by quoting and examining Pelagius' anathema of all those who deny that grace is necessary for every action (2 *sq.*). Augustine confesses that this would deceive all who were not fortified by knowledge of Pelagius' writings; but asserts that in the light of them it is clear that he means that grace is always necessary, because we need continually to remember the forgiveness of our sins, the example of Christ, the teaching of the law, and the like. Then he enters (4 *sq.*) upon an examination of Pelagius' scheme of human faculties, and quotes at length his account of them given in his book, " In Defence of Free Will," wherein he distinguishes between the *possibilitas* (*posse*), *voluntas* (*velle*), and *actio* (*esse*), and declares that the first only is from God and receives aid from God, while the others are entirely ours, and in our own power. Augustine opposes to this the passage in Phil. ii. 12, 13 (6), and then criticises (7 *sq.*) Pelagius' ambiguous acknowledgment that God is to be praised for man's good works, because the capacity for any action on man's part is from God, by which he reduces all grace to the primeval endowment of nature with " capacity " (*possibilitas, posse*), and the help afforded it by the law and teaching. Augustine points out the difference between law and grace, and the purpose of the former as a pedagogue to the latter (9 *sq.*), and then refutes Pelagius' further definition of grace as consisting in the promise of future glory and the revelation of wisdom, by an appeal to Paul's thorn in the flesh, and his experience under its discipline (11 *sq.*). Pelagius' illustrations from our senses, of his theory of natural faculty, are then sharply tested (16); and the criticism on the whole doctrine is then made and pressed (17 *sq.*), that it makes God equally sharer in our blame for evil acts as in our praise for good ones, since if God does help, and His help is only His gift to us of

[102] " On the Grace of Christ," 55.

ability to act in either part, then He has equally helped to the evil deeds as to the good. The assertion that this " capacity of either part " is the fecund root of both good and evil is then criticised (19 *sq.*), and opposed to Mt. vii. 18, with the result of establishing that we must seek two roots in our dispositions for so diverse results — covetousness for evil, and love for good — not a single root for both in nature. Man's " capacity," it is argued, is the root of nothing; but it is capable of both good and evil according to the moving cause, which, in the case of evil, is man-originated, while, in the case of good, it is from God (21). Next, Pelagius' assertion that grace is given according to our merits (23 *sq.*) is taken up and examined. It is shown, that, despite his anathema, Pelagius holds to this doctrine, and in so extreme a form as explicitly to declare that man comes and cleaves to God by his freedom of will alone, and without God's aid. He shows that the Scriptures teach just the opposite (24–26); and then points out how Pelagius has confounded the functions of knowledge and love (27 *sq.*), and how he forgets that we cannot have merits until we love God, while John certainly asserts that *God loved us first* (1 Jno. iv. 10). The representation that what grace does is to render obedience *easier* (28–30), and the twin view that prayer is only relatively necessary, are next criticised (32). That Pelagius never acknowledges real grace, is then demonstrated by a detailed examination of all that he had written on the subject (31–45). The book closes (46–55) with a full refutation of Pelagius' appeal to Ambrose, as if he supported him; and exhibition of Ambrose's contrary testimony as to grace and its necessity.

The object of the second book — " On Original Sin " — is to show, that, in spite of Pelagius' admissions as to the baptism of infants, he yet denies that they inherit original sin and contends that they are born free from corruption. The book opens by pointing out that there is no question as to Cœlestius' teaching in this matter (2–8), as he at Carthage refused to condemn those who say that Adam's sin injured no one but himself, and that infants are born in the same state that Adam was in before the fall, and openly asserted at Rome that there is no sin *ex traduce*. As for Pelagius, he is simply more cautious and mendacious than Cœlestius: he deceived the Council at Diospolis, but failed to deceive the Romans (5–13), and, as a matter of fact (14–18), teaches exactly what Cœlestius does. In support of this assertion, Pelagius' " Defence of Free Will " is quoted, wherein he asserts that we are born neither good nor bad, " but with a capacity for either," and " as without virtue, so without vice; and previous to the action of our own proper will, that that alone is in man which God has formed " (14). Augustine also quotes Pelagius' explanation of his anathema against those who say Adam's sin injured only himself, as meaning that he has injured man by setting a bad " example," and his even more sinuous explanation of his anathema against those who assert that infants are born in the same condition that Adam was in before he fell, as meaning that they are *infants* and he was a *man!* (16–18). With this introduction to them, Augustine next treats of Pelagius' subterfuges (19–25), and then animadverts on the importance of the issue (26–37), pointing out that Pelagianism is not a mere error, but a deadly heresy, and strikes at the very center of Christianity. A counter argument of the Pelagians is then answered (38–45), " Does not the doctrine of original sin make marriage an evil thing? " No, says Augustine, marriage is ordained by God, and is good; but it is a diseased good, and hence what is born of it is a good nature made by God, but this good nature in a diseased condition — the result of the Devil's work. Hence, if it be asked why God's gift produces any thing for the Devil to take possession of, it is to be answered that God gives his gifts liberally (Mt. v. 45), and makes men; but the Devil makes these men sinners (46). Finally, as Ambrose had been appealed to in the former book, so at the end of this it is shown that he openly proclaimed the doctrine of original sin, and here too, before Pelagius, condemned Pelagius (47 *sq.*).

What Augustine means by writing to Pinianus and his family that he was more oppressed by work at Carthage than anywhere else, may perhaps be illustrated from his diligence in preaching while in that capital. He seems to have been almost constantly in the pulpit, during this period " of the sharpest conflict with them," [103] preaching against the Pelagians. There is one series of his sermons, of the exact dates of which we can be pretty sure, which may be adverted to here — Sermons 151 and 152, preached early in October, 418; Sermon 155 on October 14, 156 on October 17, and 26 on October 18; thus following one another almost with the regularity of the days. The first of these was based on Rom. vii. 15–25, which he declares to contain dangerous words if not properly understood; for men are prone to sin, and when they hear the apostle so speaking they do evil, and think they are like him. They are meant to teach us, however, that the life of the just in this body is a war, not yet a triumph: the triumph will come only when death is swallowed up in victory. It would, no doubt, be better not to have an enemy than even to conquer. It would be better not to have evil desires: but we have them; therefore, let us not go after them. If they rebel against us, let us rebel against them; if they fight, let us fight; if they besiege, let us besiege: let us look only to this, that they do not conquer. With some evil desires we are born: others we make, by bad habit. It is on account of those with which we are born, that infants are baptized; that they may be freed from the guilt of inheritance, not from any evil of custom, which, of course, they have not. And it is on account of these, too, that our war must be endless: the concupiscence with which we are born cannot be done away as long as we live; it may be diminished, but not done away. Neither can the law free us, for it only reveals the sin to our greater apprehension. Where, then, is hope, save in the superabundance of grace? The next sermon (152) takes up the words in Rom. viii. 1–4, and points out that the inward aid of the Spirit brings all the help we need. " We, like farmers in the field, work from without: but, if there were no one who worked from within, the seed would not take root in the ground, nor would the sprout arise in the field, nor would the shoot grow strong and become a tree, nor would branches and fruit and leaves be

[103] " On the Gift of Perseverance," 55.

produced. Therefore the apostle himself distinguishes between the work of the workmen and of the Creator (1 Cor. iii. 6, 7). . . . If God give not the increase, empty is this sound within your ears; but if he gives, it avails somewhat that we plant and water, and our labor is not in vain." He then applies this to the individual, striving against his lusts; warns against Manichean error; and distinguishes between the three laws — the law of sin, the law of faith, and the law of deeds — defending the latter, the law of Moses, against the Manicheans; and then he comes to the words of the text, and explains its chief phrases, closing thus: "What other do we read here than that Christ is a sacrifice for sin? . . . Behold by what 'sin' he condemned sin: by the sacrifice which he made for sins, he condemned sin. This is the law of the Spirit of life which has freed you from the law of sin and death. For that other law, the law of the letter, the law that commands, is indeed good; 'the commandment is holy and just and good:' but 'it was weak by the flesh,' and what it commanded it could not bring about in us. Therefore there is one law, as I began by saying, that reveals sin to you, and another that takes it away: the law of the letter reveals sin, the law of grace takes it away." Sermon 155 covers the same ground, and more, taking the broader text, Rom. viii. 1–11, and fully developing its teaching, especially as discriminating between the law of sin and the law of Moses and the law of faith; the law of Moses being the holy law of God written with His finger on the tables of stone, while the law of the Spirit of life is nothing other than the same law written in the heart, as the prophet (Jer. xxxi. 33) clearly declares. So written, it does not terrify from without, but soothes from within. Great care is also taken, lest by such phrases as, "walk in the Spirit, not in the flesh," "who shall deliver me from the body of this death?" a hatred of the body should be begotten. "Thus you shall be freed from the body of this death, not by having no body, but by having another one and dying no more. If, indeed, he had not added, 'of this death,' . . . perchance an error might have been suggested to the human mind, and it might have been said, 'You see that God does not wish us

to have a body.' But He says, ' the body of this death.' Take
away death, and the body is good. Let our last enemy, death,
be taken away, and my dear flesh will be mine for eternity. For
no one can ever ' hate his own flesh.' Although the ' spirit lusts
against the flesh, and the flesh against the spirit,' although
there is now a battle in this house, yet the husband is seeking
by his strife not the ruin of, but concord with, his wife. Far be
it, far be it, my brethren, that the spirit should hate the flesh
in lusting against it! It hates the vices of the flesh; it hates the
wisdom of the flesh; it hates the contention of death. This corruption shall put on incorruption — this mortal shall put on
immortality; it is sown a natural body; it shall rise a spiritual
body; and you shall see full and perfect concord — you shall
see the creature praise the Creator." One of the special interests of such passages is to show, that, even at this early date,
Augustine was careful to guard his hearers from Manichean
error while proclaiming original sin. One of the sermons which,
probably, was preached about this time (153), is even entitled,
" Against the Manicheans openly, but tacitly against the Pelagians," and bears witness to the early development of the
method that he was somewhat later to use effectively against
Julian's charges of Manicheanism against the catholics.[104]
Three days afterwards, Augustine preached on the next few
verses, Rom. viii. 12–17 (156), but can scarcely be said to have
risen to the height of its great argument. The greater part of
the sermon is occupied with a discussion of the law, why it
was given, how it is legitimately used, and its usefulness as a
pedagogue to bring us to Christ; then of the need of a mediator; and then, of what it is to live according to the flesh, which
includes living according to merely human nature; and the
need of mortifying the flesh in this world. All this, of course,
gave full opportunity for opposing the leading Pelagian errors;
and the sermon is brought to a close by a direct polemic against
their assertion that the function of grace is only to make it

[104] Compare, below, pp. 376–384. Neander, in the second volume (E. T.)
of his " History of the Christian Religion and Church," p. 659, discusses the
matter in a very fair spirit.

more easy to do what is right. " With the sail more easily, with
the oar with more difficulty: nevertheless even with the oar
we can go. On a beast more easily, on foot with more difficulty:
nevertheless progress can be made on foot. It is not true! For
the true Master who flatters no one, who deceives no one —
the truthful Teacher and very Saviour to whom the most grievous pedagogue has led us — when he was speaking about good
works, i.e., about the fruits of the twigs and branches, did not
say, ' Without me, indeed, you can do something, but you will
do it more easily with me; ' He did not say, ' You can make
your fruit without me, but more richly with me.' He did not
say this! Read what He said: it is the holy gospel — bow the
proud necks! Augustine does not say this: the Lord says it.
What says the Lord? ' Without me you can do *nothing* ! ' " On
the very next day, he was again in the pulpit, and taking for his
text chiefly the ninety-fourth Psalm.[105] The preacher began[106]
by quoting the sixth verse, and laying stress on the words " our
Maker." " No Christian," he said, " doubted that God had
made him, and that in such a sense that God created not only
the first man, from whom all have descended, but that God to-
day creates every man — as He said to one of His saints, ' Before that I formed thee in the womb, I knew thee.' At first He
created man apart from man; now He creates man from man:
nevertheless, whether man apart from man, or man from man,
' it is He that made us, and not we ourselves.'. . . Nor has He
made us and then deserted us; He has not cared to make us, and
not cared to keep us. . . . Will He who ' made us without being
asked, desert us when He is besought? ' But is it not just as
foolish to say, as some say or are ready to say, that God made
them men, but they make themselves righteous? . . . Why,
then, do we pray to God to make us righteous? . . . The first
man was created in a nature that was without fault or flaw. He
was made righteous: he did not make himself righteous; what
he did for himself was to fall and break his righteousness. God
permitted it, as if He had said, ' Let him desert Me; let him find

105 English version, xcv.; see verse 6.
106 " Sermon " 26.

himself; and let his misery prove that he has no ability without Me.' In this way God wished to show man what free will was worth without God. O evil free will without God! . . . Behold, man was made good; and by free will man was made evil! When will the evil man make himself good by free will deserting God? When good, he was not able to keep himself good; and now that he is evil, is he to make himself good? . . . Nay, behold, He that made us has also made us 'His people' (Ps. xciv. 7, Eng. Vers. xcv. 7). Nature is common to all, but grace is not. It is not to be confounded with nature; but if it were, it would still be gratuitous. For certainly no man, before he existed, deserved to come into existence. And yet God has made him, and that not like the beasts or a stock or a stone, but in His own image. Who has given this benefit? . . . He gave it who was in existence: he received it who was not. And only He could do this, who calls the things that are not as though they were: of whom the apostle says that 'He chose us before the foundation of the world.' We have been made in this world, and yet the world was not when we were chosen. Ineffable! wonderful! They are chosen who are not: neither does He err in choosing, nor choose in vain. He chooses, and has elect whom He is to create to be chosen: He has them in Himself, not indeed in His nature, but in His prescience. Let us not, then, glory. If we are men, He made us. If we are believers, He made us this too. . . . He who sent the Lamb to be slain has, out of wolves, made us sheep. This is grace. And it is an even greater grace than that grace of nature by which we were all made men." " I am continually endeavouring to discuss such things as these," said the preacher, " against a new heresy which is attempting to rise; because I wish you to be fixed in the good, untouched by the evil. . . . For, disputing against grace in favor of free will, they became an offence to pious and catholic ears. They began to create horror; they began to be avoided as a fixed pest; it began to be said of them, that they argued against grace. And they found such a device as this: . . . ' Because I defend man's free will, and say that free will is sufficient in order that I may be righteous,' says one, ' I do not

say that it is without the grace of God.' The ears of the pious
are pricked up, and he who hears this, already begins to rejoice:
'Thanks be to God! He does not defend free will without the
grace of God! There is free will, but it avails nothing without the grace of God.' If, then, they do not defend free will
without the grace of God, what evil do they say? Expound
to us, O teacher, what grace you mean? 'When I say,' he says,
'the free will of man, you observe that I say "of man"?'
What then? 'Who created man?' God. 'Who gave him free
will?' God. 'If, then, God created man, and God gave man
free will, whatever man is able to do by free will, to whose
grace does he owe it, except to His who made him with free
will?' And this is what they think they say so acutely! You
see, nevertheless, my brethren, how they preach that general
grace by which we were created and by which we are men;
and, of course, we are men in common with the ungodly, and
are Christians apart from them. It is this grace by which we
are Christians, that we wish them to preach, this that we wish
them to acknowledge, this that we wish — of which the apostle says, 'I do not make void the grace of God, for if righteousness is by the law, Christ is dead in vain.'" Then the
true function of the law is explained, as a revealer of our sinfulness, and a pedagogue to lead us to Christ: the Manichean
view of the Old Testament law is attacked, but its insufficiency
for salvation is pointed out; and so we are brought back to
the necessity of grace, which is illustrated from the story of
the raising of the dead child in 2 Kings iv. 18–37 — the dead
child being Adam; the ineffective staff (by which we ought
to walk), the law; but the living prophet, Christ with his
grace, which we must preach. "The prophetic staff was not
enough for the dead boy: would dead nature itself have been
enough? Even this, by which we are made, although we nowhere read of it under this name, we nevertheless, because it
is given gratuitously, confess to be grace. But we show to you
a greater grace than this, by which we are Christians. . . .
This is the grace by Jesus Christ our Lord: it was He that
made us, — both before we were at all, it was He that made us,

and now, after we are made and fallen, it is He that has made us righteous, — and not we ourselves." There was but one mass of perdition from Adam, to which nothing was due but punishment; and from that mass vessels have been made unto honor. " Rejoice because you have escaped; you have escaped the death that was due, — you have received the life that was not due. 'But,' you ask, 'why did He make me unto honor, and another unto dishonor?' . . . Will you who will not hear the apostle saying, ' O man, who art thou that repliest against God? ' hear Augustine? . . . Do you wish to dispute with me? Nay, wonder with me, and cry out with me, ' Oh the depth of the riches! ' Let us both be afraid, — let us both cry out, ' Oh the depth of the riches! ' Let us both agree in fear, lest we perish in error."

Augustine was not less busy with his pen, during these months, than with his voice. Quite a series of letters belong to the last half of 418, in which he argues to his distant correspondents on the same themes which he was so iterantly trying to make clear to his Carthaginian auditors. One of the most interesting of these was written to a fellow-bishop, Optatus, on the origin of the soul.[107] Optatus, like Jerome, had expressed himself as favoring the theory of a special creation of each at birth; and Augustine, in this letter as in the paper sent to Jerome, lays great stress on so holding our theories on so obscure a matter as to conform to the indubitable fact of the transmission of sin. This fact, such passages as 1 Cor. xv. 21 *sq.*, Rom. v. 12 *sq.*, make certain; and in stating this, Augustine takes the opportunity to outline the chief contents of the catholic faith over against the Pelagian denial of original sin and grace: that all are born under the contagion of death and in the bond of guilt; that there is no deliverance except in the one Mediator, Christ Jesus; that before His coming men received him as promised, now as already come, but with the same faith; that the law was not intended to save, but to shut up under sin and so force us back upon the one Saviour; and that the distribution of grace is sovereign. Au-

[107] " Epist." 190.

gustine pries into God's sovereign counsels somewhat more freely here than is usual with him. " But why those also are created who, the Creator foreknew, would belong to damnation, not to grace, the blessed apostle mentions with as much succinct brevity as great authority. For he says that God, ' wishing to show His wrath and demonstrate His power, endured with much longsuffering vessels of wrath fitted unto destruction ' (Rom. ix. 22). . . . Justly, however, would he seem unjust in forming vessels of wrath for perdition, if the whole mass from Adam were not condemned. That, therefore, they are made on birth vessels of anger, belongs to the punishment due to them; but that they are made by re-birth vessels of mercy, belongs to the grace that is not due to them. God, therefore, shows his wrath — not, of course, perturbation of mind, such as is called wrath among men, but a just and fixed vengeance. . . . He shows also his power, by which he makes a good use of evil men, and endows them with many natural and temporal goods, and bends their evil to admonition and instruction of the good by comparison with it, so that these may learn from them to give thanks to God that they have been made to differ from them, not by their own deserts which were of like kind in the same mass, but by His pity. . . . But by creating so many to be born who, He foreknew, would not belong to his grace, so that they are more by an incomparable multitude than those whom he deigned to predestinate as children of the promise into the glory of His Kingdom — He wished to show by this very multitude of the rejected how entirely of no moment it is to the just God what is the multitude of those most justly condemned. And that hence also those who are redeemed from this condemnation may understand, that what they see rendered to so great a part of the mass was the due of the whole of it — not only of those who add many others to original sin, by the choice of an evil will, but as well of so many children who are snatched from this life without the grace of the Mediator, bound by no bond except that of original sin alone." With respect to the question more immediately concerning which the letter was written, Augustine explains that he is willing to accept the opinion that souls are created for men as they are born, if only it can be made plain that it is consistent with the original sin that the Scriptures so clearly teach. In the paper sent to Jerome, the difficulties of creationism are sufficiently urged; this letter is interesting on account of its statement of some of the difficulties of traducianism also — thus evidencing Augustine's clear view of the peculiar complexity of the problem, and justifying his attitude of balance and uncertainty between the two theories. "The human understanding," he says, "can scarcely comprehend how a soul arises from a parent's soul in the offspring; or is transmitted to the offspring as a candle is lighted from a candle and thence another fire comes into existence without loss to the former one. Is there an incorporeal seed for the soul, which passes, by some hidden and invisible channel of its own, from the father to the mother, when it is conceived in the woman? Or, even more incredible, does it lie enfolded and hidden within the corporeal seed?" He is lost in wonder over the question whether, when conception does not take place, the immortal seed of an immortal soul perishes; or, does the immortality attach itself to it only when it lives? He even expresses the doubt whether traducianism will explain what it is called in to explain, much better than creationism; in any case, who denies that God is the maker of every soul? Isaiah (lvii. 16) says, "I have made every breath"; and the only question that can arise is as to method — whether He "makes every breath from the one first breath, just as he makes every body of man from the one first body; or whether he makes new bodies indeed, from the one body, but new souls out of nothing." Certainly nothing but Scripture can determine such a question; but where do the Scriptures speak unambiguously upon it? The passages to which the creationists point only affirm the admitted fact that God makes the soul; and the traducianists forget that the word "soul" in the Scriptures is ambiguous, and can mean "man," and even a "dead man." What more can be done, then, than to assert what is certain, viz., that sin is propagated, and leave what is uncertain in the doubt in which God has chosen to place it?

This letter was written not long after the issue of Zosimus' "Tractoria," demanding the signature of all to African orthodoxy; and Augustine sends Optatus "copies of the recent letters which have been sent forth from the Roman see, whether specially to the African bishops or generally to all bishops," on the Pelagian controversy, "lest perchance they had not yet reached" his correspondent, who, it is very evi-dent, he was anxious should thoroughly realize "that the authors, or certainly the most energetic and noted teachers," of these new heresies, "had been condemned in the whole Christian world by the vigilance of episcopal councils aided by the Saviour who keeps His Church, as well as by two venerable overseers of the Apostolical see, Pope Innocent and Pope Zosimus, unless they should show repentance by being convinced and reformed." To this zeal we owe it that the letter contains an extract from Zosimus' "Tractoria," one of the two brief fragments of that document that have reached our day.

There was another ecclesiastic in Rome, besides Zosimus, who was strongly suspected of favoring the Pelagians — the presbyter Sixtus, who afterwards became Pope Sixtus III. But when Zosimus sent forth his condemnation of Pelagianism, Sixtus sent also a short letter to Africa addressed to Aurelius of Carthage, which, though brief, indicated a considerable vigor against the heresy which he was commonly believed to have before defended,[108] and which claimed him as its own.[109] Some months afterwards, he sent another similar, but longer, letter to Augustine and Alypius, more fully expounding his rejection of "the fatal dogma" of Pelagius, and his acceptance of "that grace of God freely given by Him to small and great, to which Pelagius' dogma was diametrically opposed." Augustine was overjoyed with these developments. He quickly replied in a short letter [110] in which he expresses the delight

---

[108] See "Epist." 194. 1.
[109] See "Epist." 191. 1.
[110] "Epist." 191.

he has in learning from Sixtus' own hand that he is not a defender of Pelagius, but a preacher of grace. And close upon the heels of this he sent another much longer letter,[111] in which he discusses the subtler arguments of the Pelagians with an anxious care that seems to bear witness to his desire to confirm and support his correspondent in his new opinions. Both letters testify to Augustine's approval of the persecuting measures which had been instituted by the Roman see in obedience to the emperor; and urge on Sixtus his duty not only to bring the open heretics to deserved punishment, but to track out those who spread their poison secretly, and even to remember those whom he had formerly heard announcing the error before it had been condemned, and who were now silent through fear, and to bring them either to open recantation of their former beliefs, or to punishment. It is pleasanter to recall our thoughts to the dialectic of these letters. The greater part of the second is given to a discussion of the gratuitousness of grace, which, just because grace, is given to no preceding merits. Many subtle objections to this doctrine were brought forward by the Pelagians. They said that "free will was taken away if we asserted that man did not have even a good will without the aid of God"; that we made "God an accepter of persons, if we believed that without any preceding merits He had mercy on whom He would, and whom He would He called, and whom He would He made religious"; that " it was unjust, in one and the same case, to deliver one and punish another"; that, if such a doctrine is preached, " men who do not wish to live rightly and faithfully, will excuse themselves by saying that they have done nothing evil by living ill, since they have not received the grace by which they might live well"; that it is a puzzle " how sin can pass over to the children of the faithful, when it has been remitted to the parents in baptism"; that " children respond truly by the mouth of their sponsors that they believe in remission of sins, but not because sins are remitted to *them*, but because they believe that sins are remitted in the church or in baptism to

---

[111] " Epist." 194.

those in whom they are found, not to those in whom they do not exist," and consequently they said that "they were unwilling that infants should be so baptized unto remission of sins as if this remission took place in them," for (they contend) "they have no sin; but they are to be baptized, although without sin, with the same rite of baptism through which remission of sins takes place in any that are sinners." This last objection is especially interesting,[112] because it furnishes us with the reply which the Pelagians made to the argument that Augustine so strongly pressed against them from the very act and ritual of baptism, as implying remission of sins.[113] His rejoinder to it here is to point to the other parts of the same ritual, and to ask why, then, infants are exorcised and exsufflated in baptism. "For, it cannot be doubted that this is done fictitiously, if the Devil does not rule over them; but if he rules over them, and they are therefore not falsely exorcised and exsufflated, why does that prince of sinners rule over them except because of sin?" On the fundamental matter of the gratuitousness of grace, this letter is very explicit. "If we seek for the deserving of hardening, we shall find it. . . . But if we seek for the deserving of pity, we shall not find it; for there is none, lest grace be made a vanity if it is not given gratis, but rendered to merits. But, should we say that faith preceded and in it there is desert of grace, what desert did man have before faith that he should receive faith? For, what did he have that he did not receive? and if he received it, why does he glory as if he received it not? For as man would not have wisdom, understanding, prudence, fortitude, knowledge, piety, fear of God, unless he had received (according to the prophet) the spirit of wisdom and understanding, of prudence and fortitude, of knowledge and piety and the fear of God; as he would not have justice, love, continence, except the spirit was received of whom the apostle says, 'For you did not receive the spirit of fear, but of virtue, and love, and

---

[112] It appears to have been first reported to Augustine, by Marius Mercator, in a letter received at Carthage. See "Epist." 193. 3.

[113] As, for example, in "On the Merits and Remission of Sins," etc., i.

continence: ' so he would not have faith unless he received the spirit of faith of whom the same apostle says, ' Having then the same spirit of faith, according to what is written, " I believed and therefore spoke," we too believe and therefore speak.' But that He is not received by desert, but by His mercy who has mercy on whom He will, is manifestly shown where he says of himself, ' I have obtained mercy to be faithful.' "
" If we should say that the merit of prayer precedes, that the gift of grace may follow, . . . even prayer itself is found among the gifts of grace " (Rom. viii. 26). " It remains, then, that faith itself, whence all righteousness takes beginning; . . . it remains, I say, that even faith itself is not to be attributed to the human will which they extol, nor to any preceding merits, since from it begin whatever good things are merits: but it is to be confessed to be the gratuitous gift of God, since we consider it true grace, that is, without merits, inasmuch as we read in the same epistle, ' God divides out the measure of faith to each ' (Rom. xii. 3). Now, good works are done by man, but faith is wrought in man, and without it these are not done by any man. For all that is not of faith is sin " (Rom. xiv. 23).

By the same messenger who carried this important letter to Sixtus, Augustine sent also a letter to Mercator,[114] an African layman who was then apparently at Rome, but who was afterwards (in 429) to render service by instructing the Emperor Theodosius as to the nature and history of Pelagianism, and so preventing the appeal of the Pelagians to him from being granted. Now he appears as an inquirer: Augustine, while at Carthage, had received a letter from him in which he had consulted him on certain questions that the Pelagians had raised, but in such a manner as to indicate his opposition to them. Press of business had compelled the postponement of the reply until this later date. One of the questions that Mercator had put concerned the Pelagian account of infants sharing in the one baptism unto remission of sins, which we have seen Augustine answering when writing to Sixtus. In this

---

[114] " Epist." 193.

letter he replies: " Let them, then, hear the Lord (Jno. iii. 36). Infants, therefore, who are made believers by others, by whom they are brought to baptism, are, of course, unbelievers by others, if they are in the hands of such as do not believe that they should be brought, inasmuch as they believe they are nothing profited; and accordingly, if they believe by believers, and have eternal life, they are unbelievers by unbelievers, and shall not see life, but the wrath of God abideth on them. For it is not said, ' it *comes* on them,' but ' it *abideth* on them,' because it was on them from the beginning, and will not be taken from them except by the grace of God through Jesus Christ, our Lord. . . . Therefore, when children are baptized, the confession is made that they are believers, and it is not to be doubted that those who are not believers are condemned: let them, then, dare to say now, if they can, that they contract no evil from their origin to be condemned by the just God, and have no contagion of sin." The other matter on which Mercator sought light concerned the statement that universal death proved universal sin: [115] he reported that the Pelagians replied that not even death was universal — that Enoch, for instance, and Elijah, had not died. Augustine adds those who are to be found living at the second advent, who are not to die, but be " changed"; and replies that Rom. v. 12 is perfectly explicit that there is no death in the world except that which comes from sin, and that God is a Saviour, and we cannot at all " deny that He is able to do that, now, in any that he wishes, without death, which we undoubtingly believe is to be done in so many after death." He adds that the difficult question is not why Enoch and Elijah did not die, if death is the punishment of sin; but why, such being the case, the justified ever die; and he refers his correspondent to his book " On the Baptism of Infants " [116] for a resolution of this greater difficulty.

It was probably at the very end of 418 that Augustine wrote a letter of some length [117] to Asellicus, in reply to one

---

[115] Compare " On Dulcitius' Eight Questions," question 3.

[116] That is, " On the Merits and Remission of Sins," etc., ii. 49 *sq.*

[117] " Epist." 196.

which he had written on "avoiding the deception of Judaism," to the primate of the Bizacene province, and which that ecclesiastic had sent to Augustine for answering. He discusses in this the law of the Old Testament. He opens by pointing out that the apostle forbids Christians to Judaize (Gal. ii. 14–16), and explains that it is not merely the ceremonial law that we may not depend upon, "but also what is said in the law, 'Thou shalt not covet' (which no one, of course, doubts is to be said to Christians too), does not justify man, except by faith in Jesus Christ and the grace of God through Jesus Christ our Lord." He then expounds the use of the law: "This, then, is the usefulness of the law: that it shows man to himself, so that he may know his weakness, and see how, by the prohibition, carnal concupiscence is rather increased than healed. . . . The use of the law is, thus, to convince man of his weakness, and force him to implore the medicine of grace that is in Christ." " Since these things are so," he adds, " those who rejoice that they are Israelites after the flesh, and glory in the law apart from the grace of Christ, these are those concerning whom the apostle said that 'being ignorant of God's righteousness, and wishing to establish their own, they are not subject to God's righteousness;' since he calls 'God's righteousness' that which is from God to man; and 'their own,' what they think that the commandments suffice for them to do without the help and gift of Him who gave the law. But they are like those who, while they profess to be Christians, so oppose the grace of Christ, that they suppose that they fulfil the divine commands by human powers, . . . and, 'wishing to establish their own,' are 'not subject to the righteousness of God,' and so, not indeed in name, but yet in error, Judaize. This sort of men found heads for themselves in Pelagius and Cœlestius, the most acute asserters of this impiety, who by God's recent judgment, through his diligent and faithful servants, have been deprived even of catholic communion, and, on account of an impenitent heart, persist still in their condemnation."

At the beginning of 419, a considerable work was published by Augustine on one of the more remote corollaries which the Pelagians drew from his teachings. It had come to his ears, that they asserted that his doctrine condemned marriage: " If only sinful offspring come from marriage," they asked, " is not marriage itself made a sinful thing? " The book which Augustine composed in answer to this query, he dedicated to, and sent along with an explanatory letter to, the Comes Valerius, a trusted servant of the Emperor Honorius, and one of the most steady opponents at court of the Pelagian heresy. Augustine explains [118] why he has desired to address the book to him: first, because Valerius was a striking example of those continent husbands of which that age furnishes us with many instances, and, therefore, the discussion would have especial interest for him; secondly, because of his eminence as an opponent of Pelagianism; and, thirdly, because Augustine had learned that he had read a Pelagian document in which Augustine was charged with condemning marriage by defending original sin.[119] The book in question is the first book of the treatise " On Marriage and Concupiscence." It is, naturally, tinged, or rather stained, with the prevalent ascetic notions of the day. Its doctrine is that marriage is good, and God is the maker of the offspring that comes from it, although now there can be no begetting and hence no birth without sin. Sin made concupiscence, and now concupiscence perpetuates sinners. The specific object of the work, as it states it itself, is " to distinguish between the evil of carnal concupiscence, from which man, who is born therefrom, contracts original sin, and the good of marriage " (i. 1). After a brief introduction, in which he explains why he writes, and why he addresses his book to Valerius (1–2), Augustine points out that conjugal chastity, like its higher sister-grace of continence, is God's gift. Thus copulation, but only for the propagation of children, has divine allowance (3–5). Lust, or " shameful concupiscence," however, he teaches, is not of the essence, but only an accident, of marriage. It did not

[118] " On Marriage and Concupiscence," i. 2.
[119] Compare the Benedictine Preface to " The Unfinished Work."

exist in Eden, although true marriage existed there; but arose from, and therefore only after, sin (6–7). Its addition to marriage does not destroy the good of marriage: it only conditions the character of the offspring (8). Hence it is that the apostle allows marriage, but forbids the " disease of desire " (1 Thess. iv. 3–5); and hence the Old Testament saints were even permitted more than one wife, because, by multiplying wives, it was not lust, but offspring, that was increased (9–10). Nevertheless, fecundity is not to be thought the only good of marriage: true marriage can exist without offspring, and even without cohabitation (11–13), and cohabitation is now, under the New Testament, no longer a duty as it was under the Old Testament (14–15), but the apostle praises continence above it. We must, then, distinguish between the goods of marriage, and seek the best (16–19). But thus it follows that it is not due to any inherent and necessary evil in marriage, but only to the presence, now, of concupiscence in all cohabitation, that children are born under sin, even the children of the regenerate, just as from the seed of olives only oleasters grow (20–24). And yet again, concupiscence is not itself sin in the regenerate; it is remitted as guilt in baptism: but it is the daughter of sin, and it is the mother of sin, and in the unregenerate it is itself sin, as to yield to it is even to the regenerate (25–39). Finally, as so often, the testimony of Ambrose is appealed to, and it is shown that he too teaches that all born from cohabitation are born guilty (40). In this book, Augustine certainly seems to teach that the bond of connection by which Adam's sin is conveyed to his offspring is not mere descent, or heredity, or mere inclusion in him, in a realistic sense, as partakers of the same numerical nature, but concupiscence. Without concupiscence in the act of generation, the offspring would not be a partaker of Adam's sin. This he had taught also previously, as, e.g., in the treatise " On Original Sin," from which a few words may be profitably quoted as succinctly summing up the teaching of this book on the subject: " It is, then, manifest, that that must not be laid to the account of marriage, in the absence of which even marriage would still have existed. . . .

Such, however, is the present condition of mortal men, that the connubial intercourse and lust are at the same time in action. . . . Hence it follows that infants, although incapable of sinning, are yet not born without the contagion of sin, . . . not, indeed, because of what is lawful, but on account of that which is unseemly: for, from what is lawful, nature is born; from what is unseemly, sin " (42).

Towards the end of the same year (419), Augustine was led to take up again the vexed question of the origin of the soul — both in a new letter to Optatus,[120] and by the zeal of the same monk, Renatus, who had formerly brought Optatus' inquiries to his notice — in an elaborate treatise entitled " On the Soul and its Origin," by way of reply to a rash adventure of a young man named Vincentius Victor, who blamed him for his uncertainty on such a subject, and attempted to determine all the puzzles of the question, though, as Augustine insists, on assumptions that were partly Pelagian and partly worse. Optatus had written in the hope that Augustine had heard by this time from Jerome, in reply to the treatise he had sent him on this subject. Augustine, in answering his letter, expresses his sorrow that he has not yet been worthy of an answer from Jerome, although five years had passed away since he wrote, but his continued hope that such an answer will in due time come. For himself, he confesses that he has not yet been able to see how the soul can contract sin from Adam and yet not itself be contracted from Adam; and he regrets that Optatus, although holding that God creates each soul for its birth, has not sent him the proofs on which he depends for that opinion, nor met its obvious difficulties. He rebukes Optatus for confounding the question of whether God makes the soul, with the entirely different one of how he makes it, whether *ex propagine* or *sine propagine*. No one doubts that God makes the soul, as no one doubts that He makes the body. But when we consider how he makes it, sobriety and vigilance become necessary lest we should unguardedly fall into the Pelagian heresy. Augustine defends his attitude of uncertainty, and enumerates the

[120] " Epist." **202**, *bis.* Compare " Epist." **190**.

points as to which he has no doubt: viz., that the soul is spirit, not body; that it is rational or intellectual; that it is not of the nature of God, but is so far a mortal creature that it is capable of deterioration and of alienation from the life of God, and so far immortal that after this life it lives on in bliss or punishment for ever; that it was not incarnated because of, or according to, preceding deserts acquired in a previous existence, yet that it is under the curse of sin which it derives from Adam, and therefore in all cases alike needs redemption in Christ.

The whole subject of the nature and origin of the soul, however, is most fully discussed in the four books which are gathered together under the common title of " On the Soul and its Origin." Vincentius Victor was a young layman who had recently been converted from the Rogatian heresy; on being shown by his friend Peter, a presbyter, a small work of Augustine's on the origin of the soul, he expressed surprise that so great a man could profess ignorance on a matter so intimate to his very being, and, receiving encouragement, wrote a book for Peter in which he attacked and tried to solve all the difficulties of the subject. Peter received the work with transports of delighted admiration; but Renatus, happening that way, looked upon it with distrust, and, finding that Augustine was spoken of in it with scant courtesy, felt it his duty to send him a copy of it, which he did in the summer of 419. It was probably not until late in the following autumn that Augustine found time to take up the matter; but then he wrote to Renatus, to Peter, and two books to Victor himself, and it is these four books together which constitute the treatise that has come down to us. The first book is a letter to Renatus, and is introduced by an expression of thanks to him for sending Victor's book, and of kindly feeling towards and appreciation for the high qualities of Victor himself (1–3). Then Victor's errors are pointed out — as to the nature of the soul (4–9), including certain far-reaching corollaries that flow from these (10–15), as well as, as to the origin of the soul (16–30); and the letter closes with some remarks on the danger of arguing from the silence of Scripture (30), on the self-contradictions of Victor (34), and on the errors that must be avoided in any theory of the origin of the soul that hopes to be acceptable — to wit, that souls become sinful by an alien original sin, that unbaptized infants need no salvation, that souls sinned in a previous state, and that they are condemned for sins which they have not committed but would have committed had they lived longer. The second book is a letter to Peter, warning him of the responsibility that rests on him as Victor's trusted friend and a clergyman, to correct Victor's errors, and reproving him for the uninstructed delight he had taken in Victor's crudities. It opens by asking Peter what was the occasion of the great joy which Victor's book brought him? could it be that he learned from it, for the first time, the old and primary truths it contained? (2–3); or was it due to the new errors that it proclaimed — seven of which he enumerates? (4–16). Then, after animadverting on the dilemma in which Victor stood, either of being forced to withdraw his violent assertion of creationism, or else of making God unjust in His dealings with new souls (18), he speaks of Victor's unjustifiable dogmatism in the matter (19–21), and closes with severely solemn words to Peter on his responsibility in the premises (22–23). In the third and fourth books, which are addressed to Victor, the polemic, of course, reaches its height. The third book is entirely taken up with pointing out to Victor, as a father to a son, the errors into which he has fallen, and which, in accordance with his professions of readiness for amendment, he ought to correct. Eleven are enumerated: 1. That the soul was made by God out of Himself (3–7); 2. That God will continuously create souls forever (8); 3. That the soul has desert of good before birth (9); 4. (contradictingly) That the soul has desert of evil before birth (10); 5. That the soul deserved to be sinful before any sin (11); 6. That unbaptized infants are saved (12); 7. That what God predestinates may not occur (13); 8. That Wisd. iv. 11 is spoken of infants (14); 9. That some of the mansions with the Father are outside of God's kingdom (15–17); 10. That the sacrifice of Christ's blood may be offered for the unbaptized (18); 11. That the unbaptized may attain at the resurrection even to the kingdom of heaven (19). The book closes by reminding Victor of his professions of readiness to correct his errors, and warning him against the obstinacy that makes the heretic (20–23). The fourth book deals with the more personal elements of the controversy, and discusses the points in which Victor had expressed dissent from Augustine. It opens with a statement of the two grounds of complaint that Victor had urged against Augustine; viz., that he refused to express a confident opinion as to the origin of the soul, and that he affirmed that the soul was not corporeal, but spirit (1–2). These two complaints are then taken up at length (2–16 and 17–37). To the first, Augustine replies that man's knowledge is at best limited, and often most limited about the things nearest to him; we do not know the constitution of our bodies; and, above most others, this subject of the origin of the soul is one on which no one but God is a competent witness. Who remembers his birth? Who remembers what was before birth? But this is just one of the subjects on which God has not spoken unambiguously in the Scriptures. Would it not be better, then, for Victor to imitate Augustine's cautious ignorance, than that Augustine should imitate Victor's rash assertion of errors? That the soul is not corporeal, Augustine argues (18–35) from the Scriptures and from the phenomena of dreams; and then shows, in opposition to Victor's trichotomy, that the Scriptures teach the identity of " soul " and " spirit " (36–37). The book closes with a renewed enumeration of Victor's eleven errors (38), and a final admonition to his rashness (39). It is pleasant to know that Augustine found in this case, also, that righteousness is the fruit of the faithful wounds of a friend. Victor accepted the rebuke, and professed his better instruction at the hands of his modest but resistless antagonist.

The controversy now entered upon a new stage. Among the evicted bishops of Italy who refused to sign Zosimus' " Epistola Tractoria," Julian of Eclanum was easily the first, and at this point he appears as the champion of Pelagianism. It was a sad fate that arrayed this beloved son of his old friend against

Augustine, just when there seemed to be reason to hope that the controversy was at an end, and the victory won, and the plaudits of the world were greeting him as the saviour of the Church.[121] But the now fast-aging bishop was to find, that, in this "very confident young man," he had yet to meet the most persistent and most dangerous advocate of the new doctrines that had arisen. Julian had sent, at an earlier period, two letters to Zosimus, one of which has come down to us as a "Confession of Faith," and the other of which attempted to approach Augustinian forms of speech as much as possible; the object of both being to gain standing ground in the Church for the Italian Pelagians. Now he appears as a Pelagian controversialist; and in opposition to the book "On Marriage and Concupiscence," which Augustine had sent Valerius, he published an extended work in four thick books addressed to Turbantius. Extracts from the first of these books were sent by some one to Valerius, and were placed by him in the hands of Alypius, who was then in Italy, for transmission to Augustine. Meanwhile, a letter had been sent to Rome by Julian,[122] designed to strengthen the cause of Pelagianism there; and a similar one, in the names of the eighteen Pelagianizing Italian bishops, was addressed to Rufus, bishop of Thessalonica, and representative of the Roman see in that portion of the Eastern Empire which was regarded as ecclesiastically a part of the West, the design of which was to obtain the powerful support of this important magnate, perhaps, also, a refuge from persecution within his jurisdiction. These two letters came into the hands of the new Pope, Boniface, who gave them also to Alypius for transmission to Augustine. Thus provided, Alypius returned to Africa. The tactics of all these writings of Julian were essentially the same; he attempted not so much to defend Pelagianism, as to attack Augustinianism, and thus literally to carry the war into Africa. He insisted that the corruption of nature which Augustine

---

[121] Compare "Epist." 195.

[122] Julian afterwards repudiated this letter, perhaps because of some falsifications it had suffered; it seems to have been certainly his.

taught was nothing else than Manichæism; that the sovereignty of grace, as taught by him, was only the attribution of " acceptance of persons," and partiality, to God; and that his doctrine of predestination was mere fatalism. He accused the anti-Pelagians of denying the goodness of the nature that God had created, of the marriage that He had ordained, of the law that He had given, of the free will that He had implanted in man, as well as the perfection of His saints.[123] He insisted that this teaching also did dishonor to baptism itself which it professed so to honor, inasmuch as it asserted the continuance of concupiscence after baptism — and thus taught that baptism does not take away sins, but only shaves them off as one shaves his beard, and leaves the roots whence the sins may grow anew, and need cutting down again. He complained bitterly of the way in which Pelagianism had been condemned — that bishops had been compelled to sign a definition of dogma, not in council assembled, but sitting at home; and he demanded a rehearing of the whole case before a lawful council, lest the doctrine of the Manichæans should be forced upon the acceptance of the world.

Augustine felt a strong desire to see the whole work of Julian against his book " On Marriage and Concupiscence " before he undertook a reply to the excerpts sent him by Valerius; but he did not feel justified in delaying obedience to that officer's request, and so wrote at once two treatises, one an answer to these excerpts, for the benefit of Valerius, constituting the second book of his " On Marriage and Concupiscence "; and the other, a far more elaborate examination of the letters sent by Boniface, which bears the title, " Against Two Letters of the Pelagians." The purpose of the second book of " On Marriage and Concupiscence," Augustine himself states, in its introductory sentences, to be " to reply to the taunts of his adversaries with all the truthfulness and scriptural authority he could command." He begins (2) by identifying the source of the extracts forwarded to him by Valerius, with Julian's work against his

---

[123] Compare " Against Two Letters of the Pelagians," iii. 24; and see above, p. 293.

first book, and then remarks upon the garbled form in which he is quoted in them (3–6), and passes on to state and refute Julian's charge that the Catholics had turned Manichæans (7–9). At this point, the refutation of Julian begins in good earnest, and the method that he proposes to use is stated; viz., to adduce the adverse statements, and refute them one by one (10). Beginning at the beginning, he quotes first the title of the paper sent him, which declares that it is directed against "those who condemn matrimony, and ascribe its fruit to the Devil" (11), which certainly, says Augustine, does not describe him or the Catholics. The next twenty chapters (10–30), accordingly, following Julian's order, labor to prove that marriage is good, and ordained by God, but that its good includes *fecundity* indeed, but not *concupiscence,* which arose from sin, and contracts sin. It is next argued, that the doctrine of original sin does not imply an evil origin for man (31–51); and in the course of this argument, the following propositions are especially defended: that God makes offspring for good and bad alike, just as He sends the rain and sunshine on just and unjust (31–34); that God makes everything to be found in marriage except its *flaw,* concupiscence (35–40); that marriage is not the cause of original sin, but only the channel through which it is transmitted (41–47); and that to assert that evil cannot arise from what is good leaves us in the clutches of that very Manichæism which is so unjustly charged against the Catholics — for, if evil be not eternal, what else was there from which it could arise but something good? (48–51). In concluding, Augustine recapitulates, and argues especially, that shameful concupiscence is of sin, and the author of sin, and was not in paradise (52–54); that children are made by God, and only marred by the Devil (55); that Julian, in admitting that Christ died for infants, admits that they need salvation (56); that what the Devil makes in children is not a substance, but an injury to a substance (57–58); and that to suppose that concupiscence existed in any form in paradise introduces incongruities in our conception of life in that abode of primeval bliss (59–60).

The long and important treatise, " Against Two Letters of the Pelagians," consists of four books, the first of which replies to the letter sent to Rome, and the other three to that sent to Thessalonica. After a short introduction, in which he thanks Boniface for his kindness, and gives reasons why heretical writings should be answered (1-3), Augustine begins at once to rebut the calumnies which the letter before him brings against the Catholics (4-28). These are seven in number: 1. That the Catholics destroy free will; to which Augustine replies that none are " forced into sin by the necessity of their flesh," but all sin by free will, though no man can have a righteous will save by God's grace, and that it is really the Pelagians that destroy free will by exaggerating it (4-8); 2. That Augustine declares that such marriage as now exists is not of God (9); 3. That sexual desire and intercourse are made a device of the Devil, which is sheer Manichæism (10-11); 4. That the Old Testament saints are said to have died in sin (12); 5. That Paul and the other apostles are asserted to have been polluted by lust all their days; Augustine's answer to which includes a running commentary on Rom. vii. 7 *sq.*, in which (correcting his older exegesis) he shows that Paul is giving here a transcript of his own experience as a typical Christian (13-24); 6. That Christ is said not to have been free from sin (25); 7. That baptism does not give complete remission of sins, but leaves roots from which they may again grow; to which Augustine replies that baptism does remit all sins, but leaves concupiscence, which, although not sin, is the source of sin (26-28). Next, the positive part of Julian's letter is taken up, and his profession of faith against the Catholics examined (29-41). The seven affirmations that Julian makes here are designed as the obverse of the seven charges against the Catholics. He believed: 1. That free will is in all by nature, and could not perish by Adam's sin (29); 2. That marriage, as now existent, was ordained by God (30); 3. That sexual impulse and virility are from God (31-35); 4. That men are God's work, and no one is forced to do good or evil unwillingly, but is assisted by grace to good, and incited by the Devil to evil (36-

38); 5. That the saints of the Old Testament were perfected in righteousness here, and so passed into eternal life (39); 6. That the grace of Christ (ambiguously meant) is necessary for all, and all children — even those of baptized parents — are to be baptized (40); 7. And that baptism gives full cleansing from all sins; to which Augustine pointedly asks, " What does it do for infants, then? " (41). The book concludes with an answer to Julian's conclusion, in which he demands a general council, and charges the Catholics with Manichæism.

The second, third, and fourth books deal with the letter to Rufus in a somewhat similar way, the second and third books being occupied with the calumnies brought against the Catholics, and the fourth with the claims made by the Pelagians. The second begins by repelling the charge of Manichæism brought against the Catholics (1–4), to which the pointed remark is added, that the Pelagians cannot hope to escape condemnation because they are willing to condemn another heresy; and then defends (with less success) the Roman clergy against the charge of prevarication in their dealing with the Pelagians (5–8), in the course of which all that can be said in defense of Zosimus' wavering policy is said well and strongly. Next the charges against Catholic teaching are taken up and answered (9–16), especially the two important accusations that they maintain fate under the name of grace (9–12), and that they make God an " accepter of persons " (13–16). Augustine's replies to these charges are in every way admirable. The charge of " fate " rests solely on the Catholic denial that grace is given according to preceding merits; but the Pelagians do not escape the same charge when they acknowledge that the " fates " of baptized and unbaptized infants do differ. It is, in truth, not a question of " fate," but of *gratuitous bounty;* and " it is not the Catholics that assert fate under the name of grace, but the Pelagians that choose to call divine grace by the name of ' fate ' " (12). As to " acceptance of persons," we must define what we mean by that. God certainly does not accept one's " person " above another's; He does not give to one rather than to another because He sees something to please Him in one rather than an another: quite the opposite. He gives of His bounty to one while giving all their due to all, as in the parable (Mt. xx. 9 *sq.*). To ask why He does this, is to ask in vain: the apostle answers by not answering (Rom. ix.); and before the dumb infants, who are yet made to differ, all objection to God is dumb. From this point, the book becomes an examination of the Pelagian doctrine of prevenient merit (17–23), concluding that God gives all by grace from the beginning to the end of every process of doing good. 1. He commands the good; 2. He gives the desire to do it; and, 3. He gives the power to do it: and all, of His gratuitous mercy. The third book continues the discussion of the calumnies of the Pelagians against the Catholics, and enumerates and answers six of them: viz., that the Catholics teach, 1. That the Old Testament law was given, not to justify the obedient, but to serve as cause of greater sin (2–3); 2. That baptism does not give entire remission of sins, but the baptized are partly God's and partly the Devil's (4–5); 3. That the Holy Ghost did not assist virtue in the Old Testament (6–13); 4. That the Bible saints were not holy, but only less wicked than others (14–15); 5. That Christ was a sinner by necessity of His flesh (doubtless, Julian's inference from the doctrine of race-sin) (16); 6. That men will begin to fulfill God's commandments only after the resurrection (17–23). Augustine shows that at the basis of all these calumnies lies either misapprehension or misrepresentation; and, in concluding the book, enumerates the three chief points in the Pelagian heresy, with the five claims growing out of them, of which they most boasted, and then elucidates the mutual relations of the three parties, catholics, Pelagians, and Manicheans, with reference to these points, showing that the catholics stand asunder from both the others, and condemn both (24–26). This conclusion is really a preparation for the fourth book, which takes up these five Pelagian claims, and, after showing the catholic position on them all in brief (1–3), discusses them in turn (4–19): viz., the praise of the creature (4–8), the praise of marriage (9), the praise of the law (10–11), the praise of free will (12–16), and the praise of the saints (17–18). At the end, Augustine calls on the Pelagians to cease to oppose the Manichæans, only to fall into as bad heresy as theirs (19); and then, in reply to their accusation that the Catholics were proclaiming novel doctrine, he adduces the testimony of Cyprian and Ambrose, both of whom had received Pelagius' praise, on each of the three main points of Pelagianism (20–32),[124] and then closes with the declaration that the " impious and foolish doctrine," as they called it, of the Catholics, is immemorial truth (33), and with a denial of the right of the Pelagians to ask for a general council to condemn them (34). All heresies do not need an ecumenical synod for their condemnation; usually it is best to stamp them out locally, and not allow what may be confined to a corner to disturb the whole world.

These books were written late in 420, or early in 421, and Alypius appears to have conveyed them to Italy during the latter year. Before its close, Augustine, having obtained and read the whole of Julian's attack on the first book of his work " On Marriage and Concupiscence," wrote out a complete answer to it [125] — a task that he was all the more anxious to complete, on perceiving that the extracts sent by Valerius were not only all from the first book of Julian's treatise, but were somewhat altered in the extracting. The resulting work, " Against Julian," one of the longest that he wrote in the whole course of the Pelagian controversy, shows its author at his best: according to Cardinal Noris's judgment, he appears in it " almost divine," and Augustine himself clearly set great store by it. In the first book of this noble treatise, after professing his continued love for Julian, " whom he was unable not to love, whatever he [Julian] should say against him " (35), he undertakes to show that in affixing the opprobrious name of Manichæans on those who assert original sin, Julian is incriminating many of the most famous fathers, of both the Latin and Greek Churches.

[124] To wit: Cyprian's testimony on original sin (20–24), on gratuitous grace (25–26), on the imperfection of human righteousness (27–28), and Ambrose's testimony on original sin (29), on gratuitous grace (30), and on the imperfection of human righteousness (31).

[125] Compare " Epist." 207, written probably in the latter half of 421.

In proof of this, he makes appropriate quotations from Irenæus, Cyprian, Reticius, Olympius, Hilary, Ambrose, Gregory Nazianzenus, Basil, John of Constantinople.[126] Then he argues, that, so far from the Catholics falling into Manichæan heresy, Julian plays, himself, into the hands of the Manichæans in their strife against the Catholics, by many unguarded statements, such as, e.g., when he says that an evil thing cannot arise from what is good, that the work of the Devil cannot be suffered to be diffused by means of a work of God, that a root of evil cannot be placed within a gift of God, and the like. The second book advances to greater detail, and adduces the five great arguments which the Pelagians urged against the Catholics, in order to test them by the voice of antiquity. These arguments are stated as follows (2): "For you say, 'That we, by asserting original sin, affirm that the Devil is the maker of infants, condemn marriage, deny that all sins are remitted in baptism, accuse God of the guilt of sin, and produce despair of perfection.' You contend that all these are consequences, if we believe that infants are born bound by the sin of the first man, and are therefore under the Devil unless they are born again in Christ. For, 'It is the Devil that creates,' you say, 'if they are created from that wound which the Devil inflicted on the human nature that was made at first.' 'And marriage is condemned,' you say, 'if it is to be believed to have something about it whence it produces those worthy of condemnation.' 'And all sins are not remitted in baptism,' you say, 'if there remains any evil in baptized couples whence evil offspring are produced.' 'And how is God,' you ask, 'not unjust, if He, while remitting their own sins to baptized persons, yet condemns their offspring, inasmuch as, although it is created by Him, it yet ignorantly and involuntarily contracts the sins of others from those very parents to whom they are remitted?' 'Nor can men believe,' you add, 'that virtue — to which corruption is to be understood to be contrary — can be perfected, if they cannot believe that it can destroy the inbred vices, although, no doubt, these can scarcely be considered vices, since he does

[126] That is, Chrysostom.

not sin, who is unable to be other than he was created.' " These arguments are then tested, one by one, by the authority of the earlier teachers who were appealed to in the first book, and shown to be condemned by them. The remaining four books follow Julian's four books, argument by argument, refuting him in detail. In the third book it is urged that although God is good, and made man good, and instituted marriage which is, therefore, good, nevertheless concupiscence is evil, and in it the flesh lusts against the spirit. Although chaste spouses use this evil well, continent believers do better in not using it at all. It is pointed out, how far all this is from the madness of the Manichæans, who dream of matter as essentially evil and co-eternal with God; and shown that evil concupiscence sprang from Adam's disobedience and, being transmitted to us, can be removed only by Christ. It is shown, also, that Julian himself confesses lust to be evil, inasmuch as he speaks of remedies against it, wishes it to be bridled, and speaks of the continent waging a glorious warfare. The fourth book follows the second book of Julian's work, and makes two chief contentions: that unbelievers have no true virtues, and that even the heathen recognize concupiscence as evil. It also argues that grace is not given according to merit, and yet is not to be confounded with fate; and explains the text that asserts that " God wishes all men to be saved," in the sense that " all men " means " all that are to be saved, since none are saved except by His will." [127] The fifth book, in like manner, follows Julian's third book, and treats of such subjects as these: that it is due to sin that any infants are lost; that shame arose in our first parents through sin; that sin can well be the punishment of preceding sin; that concupiscence is always evil, even in those who do not assent to it; that true marriage may exist without intercourse; that the "flesh" of Christ differs from the "sinful flesh" of other men; and the like. In the sixth book, Julian's fourth book is followed, and original sin is proved from the baptism of infants, the teaching of the apostles, and the rites of exorcism and exsufflation incorporated in the form of baptism.

[127] Compare " On Rebuke and Grace," 44.

Then, by the help of the illustration drawn from the olive and the oleaster, it is explained how Christian parents can produce unregenerate offspring; and the originally voluntary character of sin is asserted, even though it now comes by inheritance.

After the completion of this important work, there succeeded a lull in the controversy, of some years duration; and the calm refutation of Pelagianism and exposition of Christian grace, which Augustine gave in his "Enchiridion,"[128] might well have seemed to him his closing word on this all-absorbing subject. But he had not yet given the world all he had in treasure for it, and we can rejoice in the chance that five or six years afterwards drew from him a renewed discussion of some of the more important aspects of the doctrine of grace. The circumstances which brought this about are sufficiently interesting in themselves, and open up to us an unwonted view into the monastic life of the times. There was an important monastery at Adrumetum, the metropolitan city of the province of Byzacium,[129] from which a monk named Florus went out on a journey of charity to his native country of Uzalis about 426. On the journey he met with Augustine's letter to Sixtus[130] in which the doctrines of gratuitous and prevenient grace were expounded. He was much delighted with it, and, procuring a copy, sent it back to his monastery for the edification of his brethren, while he himself went on to Carthage. At the monastery, the letter created great disturbance: without the knowledge of the abbot, Valentinus, it was read aloud to the monks, many of whom were unskilled in theological questions; and some five or more were greatly offended, and declared that free will was destroyed by it. A secret strife arose among the brethren, some taking extreme grounds on both sides. Of all this, Valentinus remained ignorant until the return of Florus, who was attacked as the author of all the trouble, and who felt it

---

[128] See "A Select Library of the Nicene and Post-Nicene Fathers of the Christian Church," Series I. iii. pp. 237 sq.

[129] Now a portion of Tunis.

[130] "Epist." 194.

his duty to inform the abbot of the state of affairs. Valentinus applied first to the bishop, Evodius, for such instruction as would make Augustine's letter clear to the most simple. Evodius replied, praising their zeal and deprecating their contentiousness, and explaining that Adam had full free will, but that it is now wounded and weak, and Christ's mission was as a physician to cure and recuperate it. " Let them read," is his prescription, " the words of God's elders. . . . And when they do not understand, let them not quickly reprehend, but pray to understand." This did not, however, cure the malcontents, and the holy presbyter Sabrinus was appealed to, and sent a book with clear interpretations. But neither was this satisfactory; and Valentinus, at last, reluctantly consented that Augustine himself should be consulted — fearing, he says, lest by making inquiries he should seem to waver about the truth. Two members of the community were consequently permitted to journey to Hippo, but they took with them no introduction and no commendation from their abbot. Augustine, nevertheless, received them without hesitation, as they bore themselves with too great simplicity to allow him to suspect them of deception. Now we get a glimpse of life in the great bishop's monastic home. The monks told their story, and were listened to with courtesy and instructed with patience; and, as they were anxious to get home before Easter, they received a letter for Valentinus [131] in which Augustine briefly explains the nature of the misapprehension that had arisen, and points out that both grace and free will must be defended, and neither so exaggerated as to deny the other. The letter of Sixtus, he explains, was written against the Pelagians, who assert that grace is given according to merit, and briefly expounds the true doctrine of grace as necessarily gratuitous and therefore prevenient. When the monks were on the point of starting home, they were joined by a third companion from Adrumetum, and were led to prolong their visit. This gave him the opportunity he craved for their fuller instruction: he read with them and explained to them not only his letter to Sixtus,

[131] " Epist." 214.

from which the strife had risen, but much of the chief literature of the Pelagian controversy,[132] copies of which also were
made for them to take home with them; and when they were
ready to go, he sent by them another and longer letter to
Valentinus, and placed in their hands a treatise composed for
their especial use, which, moreover, he explained to them. This
longer letter is essentially an exhortation " to turn aside
neither to the right hand nor to the left " — neither to the left
hand of the Pelagian error of upholding free will in such a
manner as to deny grace, nor to the right hand of the equal
error of so upholding grace as if we might yield ourselves to
evil with impunity. Both grace and free will are to be proclaimed; and it is true both that grace is not given to merits,
and that we are to be judged at the last day according to our
works. The treatise which Augustine composed for a fuller
exposition of these doctrines is the important work " On Grace
and Free Will." After a brief introduction, explaining the occasion of his writing, and exhorting the monks to humility and
teachableness before God's revelations (1), Augustine begins
by asserting and proving the two propositions that the Scriptures clearly teach that man has free will (2–5), and, as
clearly, the necessity of grace for doing any good (6–9). He
then examines the passages which the Pelagians claim as teaching that we must first turn to God, before He visits us with His
grace (10–11), and then undertakes to show that grace is not
given to merit (12 sq.), appealing especially to Paul's teaching and example, and replying to the assertion that forgiveness is the only grace that is not given according to our merits
(15–18), and to the query, " How can eternal life be both of
grace and of reward? " (19–21). The nature of grace, what it
is, is next explained (22 sq.). It is not the law, which gives only
knowledge of sin (22–24), nor nature, which would render
Christ's death needless (25), nor mere forgiveness of sins, as
the Lord's Prayer (which should be read with Cyprian's comments on it) is enough to show (26). Nor will it do to say that
it is given to the merit of a good will, thus distinguishing the

[132] " Epist." 215. 2 sq.

good work which is of grace from the good will which precedes grace (27–30); for the Scriptures oppose this, and our prayers for others prove that we expect God to be the *first mover,* as indeed both Scripture and experience prove that He is. It is next shown that both free will and grace are concerned in the heart's conversion (31–32), and that love is the spring of all good in man (33–40), which, however, we have only because God first loved us (38), and which is certainly greater than knowledge, although the Pelagians admit only the latter to be from God (40). God's sovereign government of men's wills is then proved from Scripture (41–43), and the wholly gratuitous character of grace is illustrated (44), while the only possible theodicy is found in the certainty that the Lord of all the earth will do right. For, though no one knows why He takes one and leaves another, we all know that He hardens judicially and saves graciously — that He hardens none who do not deserve hardening, but none that He saves deserve to be saved (45). The treatise closes with an exhortation to its prayerful and repeated study (46).

The one request that Augustine made, on sending this work to Valentinus, was that Florus, through whom the controversy had arisen, should be sent to him, that he might converse with him and learn whether he had been misunderstood, or himself had misunderstood Augustine. In due time Florus arrived at Hippo, bringing a letter [133] from Valentinus which addresses Augustine as " Lord Pope " (*domine papa*), thanks him for his " sweet " and " healing " instruction, and introduces Florus as one whose true faith could be confided in. It is very clear, both from Valentinus' letter and from the hints that Augustine gives, that his loving dealing with the monks had borne admirable fruit: " none were cast down for the worse, some were built up for the better." [134] But it was reported to him that some one at the monastery had objected to the doctrine he had taught them, that " no man ought, then, to be rebuked for not keeping God's commandments; but only

[133] " Epist." 216.
[134] " On Rebuke and Grace," 1.

God should be besought that he might keep them." [135] In other words, it was said that if all good was, in the last resort, from God's grace, man ought not to be blamed for not doing what he could not do, but God ought to be besought to do for man what He alone could do: we ought, in a word, to apply to the source of power. This occasioned the composition of yet another treatise " On Rebuke and Grace," [136] the object of which was to explain the relations of grace to human conduct, and especially to make it plain that the sovereignty of God's grace does not supersede our duty to ourselves or our fellow-men. It begins by thanking Valentinus for his letter and for sending Florus (whom Augustine finds well instructed in the truth), thanking God for the good effect of the previous book, and recommending its continued study, and then by briefly expounding the Catholic faith concerning grace, free will, and the law (1–2). The general proposition that is defended is that the gratuitous sovereignty of God's grace does not supersede human means for obtaining and continuing it (3 sq.) This is shown by the apostle's example, who used all human means for the prosecution of his work, and yet confessed that it was " God that gave the increase " (3). Objections are then answered (4 sq.) — especially the great one that " it is not my fault if I do not do what I have not received grace for doing " (6); to which Augustine replies (7–10), that we deserve rebuke for our very unwillingness to be rebuked, that on the same reasoning the prescription of the law and the preaching of the gospel would be useless, that the apostle's example opposes such a position, and that our consciousness witnesses that we deserve rebuke for not persevering in the right way. From this point an important discussion arises, in this interest, of the gift of perseverance (11–19), and of God's election (20–24); the teaching being that no one is saved who does not persevere, and all that are predestinated or " called according to the pur-

---

[135] " Retractations," ii. 67. Compare " On Rebuke and Grace," 5 sq.

[136] On the importance of this treatise for Augustine's doctrine of predestination, see Wiggers' " Augustinianism and Pelagianism," E. T. p. 236, where a sketch of the history of this doctrine in Augustine's writings may be found.

pose " (Augustine's phrase for what we should call " effectual calling ") will persevere, and yet that we coöperate by our will in all good deeds, and deserve rebuke if we do not. Whether Adam received the gift of perseverance, and, in general, the difference between the grace given to him, (which was that grace by which he could stand) and that now given to God's children (which is that grace by which we are actually made to stand), are next discussed (26–38), with the result of showing the superior greatness of the gifts of grace now to those given before the fall. The necessity of God's mercy at all times, and our constant dependence on it, are next vigorously asserted (39–42); even in the day of judgment, if we are not judged " with mercy " we cannot be saved (41). The treatise is brought to an end by a concluding application of the whole discussion to the special matter in hand, *rebuke* (43–49). Seeing that rebuke is one of God's means of working out his gracious purposes, it cannot be inconsistent with the sovereignty of that grace; for, of course, God predestinates the means with the end (43). Nor can we know, in our ignorance, whether our rebuke is, in any particular case, to be the means of amendment or the ground of greater condemnation. How dare we, then, withhold it? Let it be, however, graduated to the fault, and let us always remember its purpose (46–48). Above all, let us not dare hold it back, lest we hold back from our brother the means of his recovery, and, as well, disobey the command of God (49).

It was not long afterwards (about 427) when Augustine was called upon to attempt to reclaim a Carthaginian brother, Vitalis by name, who had been brought to trial on the charge of teaching that the beginning of faith was not the gift of God, but the act of man's own free will (*ex propria voluntatis*). This was essentially the semi-Pelagian position which was subsequently to make so large a figure in history; and Augustine treats it now as necessarily implying the basal idea of Pelagianism. In the important letter which he sent to Vitalis,[137] he first argues that his position is inconsistent with the prayers of the Church. He, Augustine, prays that Vitalis may

[137] " Epist." 217.

come to the true faith; but does not this prayer ascribe the
origination of right faith to God? The Church so prays for all
men: the priest at the altar exhorts the people to pray God
for unbelievers, that He may convert them to the faith; for
catechumens, that He may breathe into them a desire for regeneration; for the faithful, that by His aid they may persevere in what they have begun: will Vitalis refuse to obey these
exhortations, because, forsooth, faith is of free will and not of
God's gift? Nay, will a Carthaginian scholar array himself
against Cyprian's exposition of the Lord's Prayer? for he certainly teaches that we are to ask of God what Vitalis says is to
be had of ourselves. We may go farther: it is not Cyprian, but
Paul, who says, "Let us pray to God that we do no evil" (2
Cor. xiii. 7); it is the Psalmist who says, "The steps of man
are directed by God" (Ps. xxxvii. 23). "If we wish to defend
free will, let us not strive against that by which it is made free.
For he who strives against grace, by which the will is made
free for refusing evil and doing good, wishes his will to remain
captive. Tell us, I beg you, how the apostle can say, 'We give
thanks to the Father who made us fit to have our lot with the
saints in light, who delivered us from the power of darkness,
and translated us into the kingdom of the Son of His love'
(Col. i. 12, 13), if not He, but itself, frees our choice? It is,
then, a false rendering of thanks to God, as if He does what He
does not do; and he has erred who has said that 'He makes us
fit, etc.' . . . The grace of God, therefore, does not consist
in the nature of free-will, and in law and teaching, as the Pelagian perversity dreams; but it is given for each single act by
His will, concerning whom it is written," — quoting Ps. lxviii.
9. About the middle of the letter, Augustine lays down twelve
propositions against the Pelagians, which are important as
communicating to us what he thought, at the end of the controversy, were the chief points in dispute. "Since, therefore
. . . ," he writes, " we are Catholic Christians: 1. We know that
new-born children have not yet done anything in their own
lives, good or evil, neither have they come into the miseries of
this life according to the deserts of some previous life, which

none of them can have had in their own persons; and yet, because they are born carnally after Adam, they contract the
contagion of ancient death, by the first birth, and are not freed
from the punishment of eternal death (which is contracted by
a just condemnation, passing over from one to all), except they
are by grace born again in Christ. 2. We know that the grace of
God is given neither to children nor to adults according to our
deserts. 3. We know that it is given to adults for each several
act. 4. We know that it is not given to all men; and to those
to whom it is given, it is not only not given according to the
merits of works, but it is not even given to them according to
the merits of their will; and this is especially apparent in
children. 5. We know that to those to whom it is given, it is
given by the gratuitous mercy of God. 6. We know that to
those to whom it is not given, it is not given by the just judgment of God. 7. We know that we shall all stand before the
tribunal of Christ, and each shall receive according to what
he has done through the body, — not according to what he
would have done, had he lived longer, — whether good or evil.
8. We know that even children are to receive according to what
they have done through the body, whether good or evil. But
according to what 'they have done' not by their own act, but
by the act of those by whose responses for them they are said
both to renounce the Devil and to believe in God, wherefore
they are counted among the number of the faithful, and have
part in the statement of the Lord when He says, 'Whosoever shall believe and be baptized, shall be saved.' Therefore also, to those who do not receive this sacrament, belongs
what follows, 'But whosoever shall not have believed, shall
be damned' (Mk. xvi. 16). Whence these too, as I have said,
if they die in that early age, are judged, of course, according to what they have done through the body, i.e., in the time
in which they were in the body, when they believe or do not
believe by the heart and mouth of their sponsors, when they
are baptized or not baptized, when they eat or do not eat the
flesh of Christ, when they drink or do not drink His blood, —
according to those things, then, which they have done through

the body, not according to those which, had they lived longer, they would have done. 9. We know that blessed are the dead that die in the Lord; and that what they would have done had they lived longer, is not imputed to them. 10. We know that those that believe, with their own heart, in the Lord, do so by their own free will and choice. 11. We know that we who already believe act with right faith towards those who do not wish to believe, when we pray to God that they may wish it. 12. We know that for those who have believed out of this number, we both ought and are rightly and truly accustomed to return thanks to God, as for his benefits." Certainly such a body of propositions commends their author to us as Christian both in head and heart: they are admirable in every respect; and even in the matter of the salvation of infants, where he had not yet seen the light of truth, he expresses himself in a way as engaging in its hearty faith in God's goodness as it is honorable in its loyalty to what he believed to be truth and justice. Here his doctrine of the Church ran athwart and clouded his view of the reach of grace; but we seem to see between the lines the promise of the brighter dawn of truth that was yet to come. The rest of the epistle is occupied with an exposition and commendation of these propositions, which ranks with the richest passages of the anti-Pelagian writings, and which breathes everywhere a yearning for his correspondent which we cannot help hoping proved salutary to his faith.

It is not without significance, that the error of Vitalis took a semi-Pelagian form. Pure Pelagianism was by this time no longer a living issue. Augustine was himself, no doubt, not yet done with it. The second book of his treatise " On Marriage and Concupiscence," which seems to have been taken to Italy by Alypius, in 421, received at once the attention of Julian, and was elaborately answered by him, during that same year, in eight books addressed to Florus. But Julian was now in Cilicia, and his book was slow in working its way westward. It was found at Rome by Alypius, apparently in 427 or 428, and he at once set about transcribing it for his friend's use. An opportunity arising to send it to Africa before it was finished, he forwarded to Augustine the five books that were ready, with an urgent request that they should receive his immediate attention, and a promise to send the other three as soon as possible. Augustine gives an account of his progress in his reply to them in a letter written to Quodvultdeus, apparently in 428.[138] This deacon was urging Augustine to give the Church a succinct account of all heresies; and Augustine excuses himself from immediately undertaking that task by the press of work on his hands. He was writing his " Retractations," and had already finished two books of them, in which he had dealt with two hundred and thirty-two works. His letters and homilies remained, and he had given the necessary reading to many of the letters. Also, he tells his correspondent, he was engaged on a reply to the eight books of Julian's new work. Working night and day, he had already completed his response to the first three of Julian's books, and had begun on the fourth while still expecting the arrival of the last three which Alypius had promised to send. If he had completed the answer to the five books of Julian which he already had in hand, before the other three reached him, he might begin the work which Quodvultdeus so earnestly desired him to undertake. In due time, whatever may have been the trials and labors that needed first to be met, the desired treatise " On Heresies " was written (about 428), and the eighty-eighth chapter of it gives us a welcome compressed account of the Pelagian heresy, which may be accepted as the obverse of the account of catholic truth given in the letter (217) to Vitalis.[139] But the composition of this

[138] " Epist." 224.

[139] The account given of Pelagianism is as follows: " They are in such degree enemies of the grace of God, by which we have been predestinated into the adoption of sons by Jesus Christ unto Himself (Eph. i. 5), and by which we are delivered from the power of darkness so as to believe in Him, and be translated into His kingdom (Col. i. 13) — wherefore He says, ' No man comes to Me, except it be given him of my Father ' (Jno. vi. 65) — and by which love is shed abroad in our hearts (Rom. v. 5), so that faith may work by love: that they believe that man is able, without it, to keep all the Divine commandments, — whereas, if this were true, it would clearly be an empty thing that the Lord said, ' Without Me ye can do nothing ' (Jno. xv. 5).

work was not the only interruption which postponed the completion of the second elaborate work against Julian. It was in

When Pelagius was at length accused by the brethren, because he attributed nothing to the assistance of God's grace towards the keeping of His commandments, he yielded to their rebuke, so far as not to place this grace above free will, but with faithless cunning to subordinate it, saying that it was given to men for this purpose; viz., that they might be able more easily to fulfil by grace, what they were commanded to do by free will. By saying, 'that they might be able more easily,' he, of course, wished it to be believed that, although with more difficulty; nevertheless men were able without divine grace to perform the divine commands. But that grace of God, without which we can do nothing good, they say does not exist except in free will, which without any preceding merits our nature received from Him; and that He adds His aid only in that by His law and teaching we may learn what we ought to do, . . . but not in that by the gift of His Spirit we may do what we have learned ought to be done. Accordingly, they confess that knowledge by which ignorance is banished is divinely given to us, but deny that love by which we may live a pious life is given; so that, forsooth, while knowledge, which, without love, puffeth up, is the gift of God, love itself, which edifieth so that knowledge may not puff up, is not the gift of God (1 Cor. viii. 11). They also destroy the prayers which the Church offers, whether for those that are unbelieving and resisting God's teaching, that they may be converted to God; or for the faithful, that faith may be increased in them, and they may persevere in it. For they contend that men do not receive these things from Him, but have them from ourselves, saying that the grace of God, by which we are freed from impiety, is given according to our merits. Pelagius was compelled, no doubt, to condemn this by his fear of being condemned by the episcopal judgment in Palestine; but he is found to teach it still in his later writings. They also advanced so far as to say that the life of the righteous in this world is without sin, and the Church of Christ is perfected by them in this mortality, to the point of being entirely without spot or wrinkle (Eph. v. 27); as if it were not the Church of Christ, that, in the whole world, cries to God, 'Forgive us our debts.' (Mt. vi. 12.) They also deny that children, who are carnally born after Adam, contract the contagion of ancient death from their first birth. For they assert that they are born so without any bond of original sin, that there is absolutely nothing that ought to be remitted to them in the second birth, yet they are to be baptized; but for this reason, that, adopted in regeneration, they may be admitted to the kingdom of God, and thus be translated from good into better, — not that they may be washed by that renovation from any evil of the old bond. For although they be not baptized, they promise to them, outside the kingdom of God indeed, but nevertheless, a certain eternal and blessed life of their own. They also say that Adam himself, even had he not sinned, would have died in the body, and that this death would not have come as a desert to a fault, but as a condition of nature. Certain other things also are objected to them, but these are the chief, and also either all, or nearly all, the others may be understood to depend on these." (" On Heresies," 88.)

the providence of God that the life of this great leader in the battle for grace should be prolonged until he could deal with semi-Pelagianism also. Information as to the rise of this new form of the heresy at Marseilles and elsewhere in Southern Gaul was conveyed to Augustine along with entreaties, that, as " faith's great patron," he would give his aid towards meeting it, by two laymen with whom he had already had correspondence — Prosper and Hilary.[140] They pointed out [141] the difference between the new party and thoroughgoing Pelagianism; but, at the same time, the essentially Pelagianizing character of its formative elements. Its representatives were ready, as a rule, to admit that all men were lost in Adam, and no one could recover himself by his own free will, but all needed God's grace for salvation. But they objected to the doctrines of prevenient and of irresistible grace; and asserted that man could initiate the process of salvation by turning first to God, that all men could resist God's grace, and no grace could be given which they could not reject, and especially they denied that the gifts of grace came irrespective of merits, actual or foreseen. They said that what Augustine taught as to the calling of God's elect according to His own purpose was tantamount to fatalism, was contrary to the teaching of the fathers and the true Church doctrine, and, even if true, should not be preached, because of its tendency to drive men into indifference or despair. Hence, Prosper especially desired Augustine to point out the dangerous nature of these views, and to show that prevenient and coöperating grace is not inconsistent with free will, that God's predestination is not founded on foresight of receptivity in its objects, and that the doctrines of grace may be preached without danger to souls.

Augustine's answer to these appeals was a work in two books, " On the Predestination of the Saints," the second book of which is usually known under the separate title of " The Gift of Perseverance." The former book begins with a careful dis-

---

[140] Compare " Epist." 225. 1, and 156. It is, of course, not certain that this is the same Hilary that wrote to Augustine from Sicily, but it seems probable.
[141] In " Epist." 225 and 226.

crimination of the position of his new opponents: they have made a right beginning in that they believe in original sin, and acknowledge that none are saved from it save by Christ, and that God's grace leads men's wills, and without grace no one can suffice for good deeds. These things will furnish a good starting-point for their progress to an acceptance of predestination also (1–2). The first question that needs discussion in such circumstances is, whether God gives the very beginnings of faith (3 *sq.*); since they admit that what Augustine had previously urged sufficed to prove that faith was the gift of God so far as that the increase of faith was given by Him, but not so far but that the beginning of faith may be understood to be man's, to which, then, God adds all other gifts (compare 43). Augustine insists that this is no other than the Pelagian assertion of grace according to merit (3), is opposed to Scripture (4–5), and begets arrogant boasting in ourselves (6). He replies to the objection that he had himself once held this view, by confessing it, and explaining that he was converted from it by 1 Cor. iv. 7, as applied by Cyprian (7–8), and expounds that verse as containing in its narrow compass a sufficient answer to the present theories (9–11). He answers, further, the objection that the apostle distinguishes faith from works, and works alone are meant in such passages, by pointing to Jno. vi. 28, and similar statements in Paul (12–16). Then he answers the objection that he himself had previously taught that God acted on foresight of faith, by showing that he was misunderstood (17–18). He next shows that no objection lies against predestination that does not lie with equal force against grace (19–22) — since predestination is nothing but God's foreknowledge of and preparation for grace, and all questions of sovereignty and the like belong to grace. Did God not know to whom he was going to give faith (19)? or did he promise the results of faith, works, without promising the faith without which, as going before, the works were impossible? Would not this place God's fulfilment of his promise out of His power, and make it depend on man (20)? Why are men more willing to trust in their weakness than in God's strength? do they count God's promises more uncertain than their own performance (22)? He next proves the sovereignty of grace, and of predestination, which is but the preparation for grace, by the striking examples of infants, and, above all, of the human nature of Christ (23–31), and then speaks of the twofold calling, one external and one " according to purpose " — the latter of which is efficacious and sovereign (32–37). In closing, the semi-Pelagian position is carefully defined and re- futed as opposed, alike with the grosser Pelagianism, to the Scriptures of both Testaments (38–42).

The purpose of the second book, which has come down to us under the separate title of " On the Gift of Perseverance," is to show that that perseverance which endures to the end is as much of God as the beginning of faith, and that no man who has been " called according to God's purpose," and has received this gift, can fall from grace and be lost. The first half of the treatise is devoted to this theme (1–33). It begins by dis- tinguishing between temporary perseverance, which endures for a time, and that which continues to the end (1), and affirms that the latter is certainly a gift of God's grace, and is, there- fore, asked from God: which would otherwise be but a mock- ing petition (2–3). This, the Lord's Prayer itself might teach us, as under Cyprian's exposition it does teach us — each peti- tion being capable of being read as a prayer for perseverance (4–9). Of course, moreover, it cannot be lost, otherwise it would not be " to the end." If man forsakes God, of course it is he that does it, and he is doubtless under continual tempta- tion to do so; but if he abides with God, it is God who secures that, and God is equally able to *keep* one when drawn to Him, as He is to *draw* him to Him (10–15). He argues anew at this point, that grace is not according to merit, but always in mercy; and explains and illustrates the unsearchable ways of God in His sovereign but merciful dealing with men (16–25), and closes this part of the treatise by a defense of himself against adverse quotations from his early work " On Free Will," which he has already corrected in his " Retractations." The sec- ond half of the book discusses the objections that were being urged against the preaching of predestination (34-62), as if it opposed and enervated the preaching of the Gospel. He replies that Paul and the apostles, and Cyprian and the fathers, preached both together; that the same objections will lie against the preaching of God's foreknowledge and grace itself, and, indeed, against preaching any of the virtues, as, e.g., obedience, while declaring them God's gifts. He meets the objections in detail, and shows that such preaching is food to the soul, and must not be withheld from men; but explains that it must be given gently, wisely, and prayerfully. The whole treatise ends with an appeal to the prayers of the Church as testifying that all good is from God (63-65), and to the great example of unmerited grace and sovereign predestination in the choice of one human nature without preceding merit, to be united in one person with the Eternal Word — an illustration of his theme of the gratuitous grace of God which he is never tired of adducing (66-67).

These books were written in 428-429, and after their completion the unfinished work against Julian was resumed. Alypius had sent the remaining three books, and Augustine slowly toiled on to the end of his reply to the sixth book. But he was to be interrupted once more, and this time by the most serious of all interruptions. On the 28th of August, 430, with the Vandals thundering at the gates of Hippo, full of good works and of faith, he turned his face away from the strifes — whether theological or secular — of earth, and entered into rest with the Lord whom he loved. The last work against Julian was already one of the most considerable in size of all his books; but it was never finished, and retains until today the significant title of " The Unfinished Work." Augustine had hesitated to undertake this work, because he found Julian's arguments too silly either to deserve refutation, or to afford occasion for really edifying discourse. And certainly the result falls below Augustine's usual level, though this is not due, as is so often said, to failing powers and great age; for nothing that he wrote surpasses in mellow beauty and chastened strength the two books, " On the Predestination of the Saints," which were written after four books of this work were completed. The plan of the work is to state Julian's arguments in his own words, and follow it with his remarks; thus giving it something of the form of a dialogue. It follows Julian's work, book by book. The first book states and answers certain calumnies which Julian had brought against Augustine and the Catholic faith on the ground of their confession of original sin. Julian had argued, that, since God is just, He cannot impute another's sins to innocent infants; since sin is nothing but evil will, there can be no sin in infants who are not yet in the use of their will; and, since the freedom of will that is given to man consists in the capacity of both sinning and not sinning, free will is denied to those who attribute sin to nature. Augustine replies to these arguments, and answers certain objections that are made to his work " On Marriage and Concupiscence," and then corrects Julian's false explanations of certain Scriptures from Jno. viii., Rom. vi., vii., and 2 Tim. The second book is a discussion of Rom. v. 12, which Julian had tried, like the other Pelagians, to explain by the " imitation " of Adam's bad example. The third book examines the abuse by Julian of certain Old Testament passages — in Deut. xxiv., 2 Kings xiv., Ezek. xviii. — in his effort to show that God does not impute the father's sins to the children; as well as his similar abuse of Heb. xi. The charge of Manichæism, which was so repetitiously brought by Julian against the Catholics, is then examined and refuted. The fourth book treats of Julian's strictures on Augustine's " On Marriage and Concupiscence " ii. 4–11, and proves from 1 Jno. ii. 16 that concupiscence is evil, and not the work of God, but of the Devil. He argues that the shame that accompanies it is due to its sinfulness, and that there was none of it in Christ; also, that infants are born obnoxious to the first sin, and proves the corruption of their origin from Wisd. x. 10, 11. The fifth book defends " On Marriage and Concupiscence " ii. 12 *sq.*, and argues that a sound nature could not have shame on account of its members, and the need of regeneration for what is generated by means of shameful concupiscence. Then Julian's abuse of 1 Cor. xv., Rom. v., Mt.

vii. 17 and 33, with reference to " On Marriage and Concupiscence " ii. 14, 20, 26, is discussed; and then the origin of evil, and God's treatment of evil in the world. The sixth book traverses Julian's strictures on " On Marriage and Concupiscence " ii. 34 *sq.*, and argues that human nature was changed for the worse by the sin of Adam, and thus was made not only sinful, but the source of sinners; and that the forces of free will by which man could at first do rightly if he wished, and refrain from sin if he chose, were lost by Adam's sin. He attacks Julian's definition of free will as " the capacity for sinning and not sinning " (*possibilitas peccandi et non peccandi*); and proves that the evils of this life are the punishment of sin — including, first of all, physical death. At the end, he treats of 1 Cor. xv. 22.

Although the great preacher of grace was taken away by death before the completion of this book, yet his work was not left incomplete. In the course of the next year (431) the Ecumenical Council of Ephesus condemned Pelagianism for the whole world; and an elaborate treatise against the pure Pelagianism of Julian was already in 430 an anachronism. Semi-Pelagianism was yet to run its course, and to work its way so into the heart of a corrupt church as not to be easily displaced; but Pelagianism was to die with the first generation of its advocates. As we look back now through the almost millennium and a half of years that has intervened since Augustine lived and wrote, it is to his " Predestination of the Saints " — a completed, and well-completed, treatise — and not to " The Unfinished Work," that we look as the crown and completion of his labors for grace.

IV. THE THEOLOGY OF GRACE

The theology which Augustine opposed, in his anti-Pelagian writings, to the errors of Pelagianism, is, shortly, the theology of grace. Its roots were planted deeply in his own experience, and in the teachings of Scripture, especially of that apostle whom he delights to call " the great preacher of grace," and to follow whom, in his measure, was his greatest desire. The grace of God in Jesus Christ, conveyed to us by the Holy Spirit and evidenced by the love that He sheds abroad in our hearts, is the center around which this whole side [142] of His system revolves, and the germ out of which it grows. He was the more able to make it thus central because of the harmony of this view of salvation with the general principle of his whole theology, which was theocentric and revolved around his conception of God as the immanent and vital spirit in whom all things live and move and have their being.[143] In like manner, God is the absolute good, and all good is either Himself or from Him; and only as God makes us good, are we able to do anything good.

The *necessity of grace* to man, Augustine argued from the condition of the race as partakers of Adam's sin. God created man upright, and endowed him with human faculties, including free will;[144] and gave to him freely that grace by which he was able to retain his uprightness.[145] Being thus put on probation,

[142] This is a necessary limitation, for there is another side — a churchly side — of Augustine's theology, which was only laid alongside of, and artificially combined with, his theology of grace. This was the *traditional* element in his teaching, but was far from the determining or formative element. As Thomasius truly points out (" Die Christliche Dogmengeschichte," i. p. 495), both his experience and the Scriptures stood with him above tradition.

[143] It is only one of the strange assertions in Professor Allen's " Continuity of Christian Thought," that he states that " the Augustinian theology rests upon the transcendence of Deity as its controlling principle " (p. 3), which is identified with a tacit assumption of deism (p. 171), and explained to include a localization of God " as a physical essence in the infinite remoteness," " separated from the world by infinite reaches of space " (p. 1). As a matter of mere fact, Augustine's conception of God was that of an immanent Spirit, and his tendency was consequently distinctly towards a pantheistic rather than a deistic view of His relation to His creatures. Nor is this true only " at a certain stage of his career " (p. 6), which is but Professor Allen's attempt to reconcile fact with his theory, but of his whole life and all his teaching. He, no doubt, did not so teach the Divine immanence as to make God the author of the *form* as well as the *matter* of all acts of His creatures, or to render it impossible for His creatures to turn from Him; this would be to pass the limits that separate the conception of Christian immanence from pure pantheism, and to make God the author of sin, and all His creatures but manifestations of Himself.   [144] " On Rebuke and Grace," 27, 28.

[145] " On Rebuke and Grace," 29, 31 *sq.*

with divine aid to enable him to stand if he chose, Adam used his free choice for sinning, and involved his whole race in his fall.[146] It was on account of this sin that he died physically and spiritually, and this double death passes over from him to us.[147] That all his descendants by ordinary generation are partakers in Adam's guilt and condemnation, Augustine is sure from the teachings of Scripture; and this is the fact of original sin, from which no one generated from Adam is free, and from which no one is freed save as regenerated in Christ.[148] But how we are made partakers of it, he is less certain: sometimes he speaks as if it came by some mysterious unity of the race, so that we were all personally present in the individual Adam, and thus the whole race was the one man that sinned; [149] sometimes he speaks more in the sense of modern realists, as if Adam's sin corrupted the nature, and the nature now corrupts those to whom it is communicated; [150] sometimes he speaks as if it were due to simple heredity; [151] sometimes, again, as if it depended on the presence of shameful concupiscence in the act of procreation, so that the propagation of guilt depends on the propagation of offspring by means of concupiscence.[152] However transmitted, it is yet a fact that sin is propagated, and all mankind became sinners in Adam. The result of this is that we have lost the divine image, though not in such a sense that no lineaments of it remain to us; [153] and, the sinning soul making the flesh corruptible, our whole nature is corrupted, and we are unable to do anything of ourselves truly good.[154] This includes, of course, an injury to our will.

[146] "On Rebuke and Grace," 28.

[147] "On the City of God," xiii. 2, 12, 14; "On the Trinity," iv. 13.

[148] "On the Merits and Remission of Sins," i. 15, and often.

[149] "Against Two Letters of the Pelagians," iv. 7; "On the Merits and Remission of Sins," iii. 14, 15.

[150] "On Marriage and Concupiscence," ii. 57; "On the City of God," xiv. 1.

[151] "Against Two Letters of the Pelagians," iv. 7.

[152] "On Original Sin," 42.

[153] "Retractationes," ii. 24.

[154] "Against Julian," iv. 25, 26. Compare Thomasius' "Die Christliche Dogmengeschichte," i. pp. 501 and 507.

Augustine, writing for the popular eye, treats this subject in popular language. But it is clear that he distinguished, in his thinking, between will as a faculty and will in a broader sense. As a mere faculty, will is and always remains an indifferent thing [155] — after the fall, as before it, continuing poised in indifferency, and ready, like a weathercock, to be turned whithersoever the breeze that blows from the heart ("will," in the broader sense) may direct.[156] It is not the faculty of willing, but the man who makes use of that faculty, that has suffered change from the fall. In paradise man stood in full ability: he had the *posse non peccare,* but not yet the *non posse peccare;* [157] that is, he was endowed with a capacity for either part, and possessed the grace of God by which he was able to stand if he would, but also the power of free will by which he might fall if he would. By his fall he has suffered a change, is corrupt, and under the power of Satan; his will (in the broader sense) is now injured, wounded, diseased, enslaved — although the faculty of will (in the narrow sense) remains indifferent.[155] Augustine's criticism of Pelagius' discrimination [158] of "capacity" (*possibilitas, posse*), "will" (*voluntas, velle*), and "act" (*actio, esse*), does not turn on the discrimination itself, but on the incongruity of placing the *power, ability* in the mere capacity or possibility, rather than in the living agent who "wills" and "acts." He himself adopts an essentially similar distribution, with only this correction;[159] and thus keeps the faculty of will indifferent, but places the power of using it in the active agent, man. According, then, to the character of this *man,* will the use of the free will be. If the man be holy he will make a holy use of it, and if he be corrupt he will make a sinful use of it: if he be essentially holy, he cannot (like God Himself) make a sinful use of his will; and if he be enslaved to sin, he cannot make a good use of it. The last is the present con-

---

[155] "On the Spirit and Letter," 58.
[156] "On the Merits and Remission of Sins," ii. 30.
[157] Cf. "On Rebuke and Grace," 29–32.
[158] "On the Grace of Christ," 4 *sq.*
[159] "On the Predestination of the Saints," 10.

dition of men by nature. They have free will; [160] the faculty by which they act remains in indifferency, and they are allowed to use it just as they choose: but such as they cannot desire and therefore cannot choose anything but evil; [161] and therefore they, and therefore their choice, and therefore their willing, is always evil and never good. They are thus the slaves of sin, which they obey; and while their free will avails for sinning, it does not avail for doing any good unless they be first freed by the grace of God. It is undeniable that this view is in consonance with modern psychology: let us once conceive of "the will" as simply the whole man in the attitude of willing, and it is immediately evident, that, however abstractly free the "will" is, it is conditioned and enslaved in all its action by the character of the willing agent: a bad man does not cease to be bad in the act of willing, and a good man remains good even in his acts of choice.

In its nature, grace is assistance, help from God; and all divine aid may be included under the term — as well what may be called natural, as what may be called spiritual, aid. [162] Spiritual grace includes, no doubt, all external help that God gives man for working out his salvation, such as the law, the preaching of the gospel, the example of Christ, by which we may learn the right way; it includes also forgiveness of sins, by which we are freed from the guilt already incurred; but above all it includes that help which God gives by His Holy Spirit, working within, not without, by which man is enabled to choose and to do what he sees, by the teachings of the law, or by the gospel, or by the natural conscience, to be right. [163] Within this aid are included all those spiritual exercises which we call regeneration, justification, perseverance to the end — in a word, all the divine assistance by which, in being made Christians, we are made to differ from other men. Augustine

---

[160] " Against Two Letters of the Pelagians," i. 5. " Epist." 215. 4, and often.
[161] " Against Two Letters of the Pelagians," i. 7. Compare i. 5, 6.
[162] " Sermon " 26.
[163] " On Nature and Grace," 62. " On the Grace of Christ," 13. " On Rebuke and Grace," 2 *sq.*

is fond of representing this grace as in essence the writing of
God's law (or of God's will) on our hearts, so that it appears
hereafter as our own desire and wish; and even more preva-
lently as the shedding abroad of love in our hearts by the
Holy Ghost, given to us in Christ Jesus; therefore, as a change
of disposition, by which we come to love and freely choose,
in coöperation with God's aid, just the things which hitherto
we have been unable to choose because in bondage to sin.
Grace, thus, does not make void free will: [164] it acts through
free will, and acts upon it only by liberating it from its bondage to sin, i.e., by liberating the agent that uses the free will,
so that he is no longer enslaved by his fleshly lusts, and is enabled to make use of his free will in choosing the good; and
thus it is only by grace that free will is enabled to act in good
part. But just because grace changes the disposition, and so
enables man, hitherto enslaved to sin, for the first time to desire and use his free will for good, it lies in the very nature of
the case that it is *prevenient*.[165] Also, as the very name imports, it is necessarily *gratuitous;* [166] since man is enslaved to
sin until it is given, all the merits that he can have prior to it
are bad merits, and deserve punishment, not gifts of favor.
When, then, it is asked, *on the ground of what,* grace is given,
it can only be answered, "on the ground of God's infinite
mercy and undeserved favor." [167] There is nothing in man to
merit it, and it first gives merit of good to man. All men alike
deserve death, and all that comes to them in the way of
blessing is necessarily of God's free and unmerited favor. This
is equally true of all grace. It is preëminently clear of that
grace which gives faith, the root of all other graces, which is
given of God, not to merits of good will or incipient turning
to Him, but of His sovereign good pleasure.[168] But equally
with faith, it is true of all other divine gifts: we may, indeed,

---

[164] " On the Spirit and Letter," 52; " On Grace and Free Will," 1 *sq.*
[165] " On the Spirit and Letter," 60, and often.
[166] " On Nature and Grace," 4, and often.
[167] " On the Grace of Christ," 27, and often.
[168] " On the Grace of Christ," 34, and often.

speak of "merits of good" as succeeding faith; but as all these merits find their root in faith, they are but "grace on grace," and men need God's mercy always, throughout this life, and even on the judgment day itself, when, if they are judged without mercy, they must be condemned.[169] If we ask, then, why God gives grace, we can only answer that it is of His unspeakable mercy; and if we ask why He gives it to one rather than to another, what can we answer but that it is of His will? The *sovereignty* of grace results from its very gratuitousness: [170] where none deserve it, it can be given only of the sovereign good pleasure of the great Giver — and this is necessarily inscrutable, but cannot be unjust. We can faintly perceive, indeed, some reasons why God may be supposed not to have chosen to give His saving grace to all,[171] or even to the most; [172] but we cannot understand why He has chosen to give it to just the individuals to whom He has given it, and to withhold it from just those from whom He has withheld it. Here we are driven to the apostle's cry, "Oh the depth of the riches both of the mercy and the justice of God! " [173]

The *effects of grace* are according to its nature. Taken as a whole, it is the re-creative principle sent forth from God for the recovery of man from his slavery to sin, and for his reformation in the divine image. Considered as to the time of its giving, it is either *operating* or *coöperating* grace, i.e., either the grace that first enables the will to choose the good, or the grace that coöperates with the already enabled will to do the good; and it is, therefore, also called either *prevenient* or *subsequent* grace.[174] It is not to be conceived of as a series of disconnected divine gifts, but as a constant efflux from God; but

[169] "On Rebuke and Grace," 41.

[170] "On Grace and Free Will," 30, and often.

[171] "On the Gift of Perseverance," 16; "Against Two Letters of the Pelagians," ii. 15.

[172] "Epist." 190 (to Optatus) 12.

[173] "On the Predestination of the Saints," 17, 18.

[174] "On Grace and Free Will," 17; "On the Proceedings of Pelagius," 34, and often.

we may look upon it in the various steps of its operation in
men, as bringing forgiveness of sins, faith, which is the beginning of all good, love to God, progressive power of good
working, and perseverance to the end.[175] In any case, and in all
its operations alike, just because it is power from on high and
the living spring of a new and re-created life, it is *irresistible*
and *indefectible*.[176] Those on whom the Lord bestows the gift
of faith working from within, not from without, of course,
have faith, and cannot help believing. Those to whom perseverance to the end is given must persevere to the end. It is
not to be objected to this, that many seem to begin well who
do not persevere: this also is of God, who has in such cases
given great blessings indeed, but not *this* blessing, of perseverance to the end. Whatever of good men have, that God has
given; and what they have not, why, of course, God has not
given it. Nor can it be objected, that this leaves all uncertain:
it is only unknown to us, but this is not uncertainty; we cannot know that we are to have any gift which God sovereignly
gives, of course, until it is given, and we therefore cannot
know that we have perseverance unto the end until we actually persevere to the end; [177] but who would call what God
does, and knows He is to do, uncertain, and what man is to
do certain? Nor will it do to say that thus nothing is left for
us to do: no doubt, all things are in God's hands, and we
should praise God that this is so, but we must coöperate with
Him; and it is just because it is He that is working in us the
willing and the doing, that it is worth our while to work out
our salvation with fear and trembling. God has not determined the end without determining the appointed means.[178]

Now, Augustine argues, since grace certainly is gratuitous,
and given to no preceding merits — prevenient and antecedent to all good — and, therefore, sovereign, and bestowed

---

[175] Compare Thomasius' "Die Christliche Dogmengeschichte," i. p. 510.
[176] "On Rebuke and Grace," 40, 45; "On the Predestination of the Saints,"
13.
[177] "On Rebuke and Grace," 40.
[178] "On the Gift of Perseverance," 56.

only on those whom God selects for its reception; we must, of course, believe that the eternal God has foreknown all this from the beginning. He would be something less than God, had He not foreknown that He intended to bestow this prevenient, gratuitous, and sovereign grace on some men, and had He not foreknown equally the precise individuals on whom He intended to bestow it. To foreknow is to prepare beforehand. And this is *predestination*.[179] He argues that there can be no objection to predestination, in itself considered, in the mind of any man who believes in a God: what men object to is the gratuitous and sovereign grace to which no additional difficulty is added by the necessary assumption that it was foreknown and prepared for from eternity. That predestination does not proceed on the foreknowledge of good or of faith,[180] follows from its being nothing more than the foresight and preparation of grace, which, in its very idea, is gratuitous and not according to any merits, sovereign and according only to God's purpose, prevenient and in order to faith and good works. It is the sovereignty of grace, not its foresight or the preparation for it, which places men in God's hands, and suspends salvation absolutely on his unmerited mercy. But just because God is God, of course, no one receives grace who has not been foreknown and afore-selected for the gift; and, as much of course, no one who has been foreknown and afore-selected for it, fails to receive it. Therefore the number of the predestinated is fixed, and fixed by God.[181] Is this fate? Men may call God's grace fate if they choose; but it is not fate, but undeserved love and tender mercy, without which none would be saved.[182] Does it paralyze effort? Only to those who will not strive to obey God because obedience is His gift. Is it unjust? Far from it: shall not God do what He will with His own undeserved favor? It is nothing

[179] "On the Predestination of the Saints," 36 *sq.*
[180] "On the Gift of Perseverance," 41 *sq.*, 47.
[181] "On Rebuke and Grace," 39. Compare 14.
[182] "On the Gift of Perseverance," 29; "Against Two Letters of the Pelagians," ii. 9 *sq.*

but gratuitous mercy, sovereignly distributed, and foreseen and provided for from all eternity by Him who has selected us in His Son.

When Augustine comes to speak of *the means of grace,* i.e., of the channels and circumstances of its conference to men, he approaches the meeting point of two very dissimilar streams of his theology — his doctrine of grace and his doctrine of the Church — and he is sadly deflected from the natural course of his theology by the alien influence. He does not, indeed, bind the conference of grace to the means in such a sense that the grace must be given at the exact time of the application of the means. He does not deny that " God is able, even when no man rebukes, to correct whom He will, and to lead him on to the wholesome mortification of repentance by the most hidden and most mighty power of His medicine." [183] Though the Gospel must be known in order that man may be saved [184] (for how shall they believe without a preacher?), yet the preacher is nothing, and the preachment is nothing, but God only that gives the increase. [185] He even has something like a distant glimpse of what has since been called the distinction between the visible and invisible Church — speaking of men not yet born as among those who are " called according to God's purpose," and, therefore, of the saved who constitute the Church [186] — asserting that those who are so called, even before they believe, are " already children of God, enrolled in the memorial of their Father with unchangeable surety," [187] and, at the same time, allowing that there are many already in the visible Church who are not of it, and who can therefore depart from it. But he teaches that those who are thus lost out of the visible Church are lost because of some fatal flaw in their baptism, or on account of post-baptismal sins; and that those who are of the " called

[183] " On Rebuke and Grace," 8.

[184] " On the Predestination of the Saints," 17, 18; if the Gospel is not preached at any given place, it is proof that God has no elect there.

[185] " On the Merits and Remission of Sins," etc., i. 37.

[186] " On Rebuke and Grace," 23.

[187] Do., 20.

according to the purpose " are predestinated not only to salvation, but to salvation by baptism. Grace is not tied to the means in the sense that it is not conferred save in the means; but it is tied to the means in the sense that it is not conferred without the means. Baptism, for instance, is absolutely necessary for salvation: no exception is allowed except such as save the principle — baptism of blood (martyrdom),[188] and, somewhat grudgingly, baptism of intention. And baptism, when worthily received, is absolutely efficacious: " if a man were to die immediately after baptism, he would have nothing at all left to hold him liable to punishment." [189] In a word, while there are many baptized who will not be saved, there are none saved who have not been baptized; it is the grace of God that saves, but baptism is a channel of grace without which none receive it.[190]

The saddest corollary that flowed from this doctrine was that by which Augustine was forced to assert that all those who died unbaptized, including infants, are finally lost and depart into eternal punishment. He did not shrink from the inference, although he assigned the place of lightest punishment in hell to those who were guilty of no sin but original sin, but who had departed this life without having washed this away in the " laver of regeneration." This is the dark side of his soteriology; but it should be remembered that it was not his theology of grace, but the universal and traditional belief in the necessity of baptism for remission of sins, which he inherited in common with all of his time, that forced it upon him. The theology of grace was destined in the hands of his successors, who have rejoiced to confess that they were taught by him, to remove this stumbling-block also from Christian teaching; and if not to Augustine, it is to Augustine's theology that the Christian world owes its liberation from so terrible and incredible a tenet. Along with the doc-

---

[188] " On the Soul and its Origin," i. 11; ii. 17.

[189] " On the Merits and Remission of Sins," etc., ii. 46.

[190] On Augustine's teaching as to baptism, see the Rev. James Field Spalding's " The Teaching and Influence of Augustine," pp. 39 *sq.*

trine of infant damnation, another stumbling-block also, not so much of Augustinian, but of Church theology, has gone. It was not because of his theology of grace, or of his doctrine of predestination, that Augustine taught that comparatively few of the human race are saved. It was, again, because he believed that baptism and incorporation into the visible Church were necessary for salvation. And it is only because of Augustine's theology of grace, which places man in the hands of an all-merciful Saviour and not in the grasp of a human institution, that men can see that in the salvation of all who die in infancy, the invisible Church of God embraces the vast majority of the human race — saved not by the washing of water administered by the Church, but by the blood of Christ administered by God's own hand outside of the ordinary channels of his grace. We are indeed born in sin, and those that die in infancy are, in Adam, children of wrath even as others; but God's hand is not shortened by the limits of His Church on earth, that it cannot save. In Christ Jesus, all souls are the Lord's, and only the soul that itself sinneth shall die (Ezek. xviii. 1–4); and the only judgment wherewith men shall be judged proceeds on the principle that as many as have sinned without law shall also perish without law, and as many as have sinned under law shall be judged by the law (Rom. ii. 12).

Thus, although Augustine's theology had a very strong churchly element within it, it was, on the side that is presented in the controversy against Pelagianism, distinctly anti-ecclesiastical. Its central thought was the absolute dependence of the individual on the grace of God in Jesus Christ. It made everything that concerned salvation to be of God, and traced the source of all good to Him. "Without me ye can do nothing," is the inscription on one side of it; on the other stands written, "All things are yours." Augustine held that he who builds on a human foundation builds on sand, and founded all his hope on the Rock itself. And there also he founded his teaching; as he distrusted man in the matter of salvation, so he distrusted him in the form of theology. No other of the fathers so conscientiously wrought out his theology from the revealed Word; no other of them so sternly excluded human additions. The subjects of which theology treats, he declares, are such as " we could by no means find out unless we believed them on the testimony of the inspired Scriptures." [191] "Where Holy Scripture gives no certain testimony," he says, " human presumption must beware how it decides in favor of either side." [192] " We must first bend our necks to the authority of the Holy Scriptures," he insists, " in order that we may each arrive at understanding through faith." [193] And this was not merely his theory, but his practice.[194] No theology was ever, it may be more broadly asserted, more conscientiously wrought out from the Scriptures. Is it without error? No; but its errors are on the surface, not of the essence. It leads to God, and it came from God; and in the midst of the controversies of so many ages it has shown itself an edifice whose solid core is built out of material " which cannot be shaken." [195]

[191] " On the Soul and its Origin," iv. 14.
[192] " On the Merits and Remission of Sins," etc., ii. 59.
[193] " On the Merits and Remission of Sins," i. 29.
[194] Compare " On the Spirit and the Letter," 63.
[195] On the subject of this whole section, compare Reuter's " Augustinische Studien," which has come to hand only after the whole was already in type, but which in all essential matters — such as the formative principle, the sources, and the main outlines of Augustine's theology — is in substantial agreement with what is here said.